MAN AND WORLD IN THE LIGHT OF ANTHROPOSOPHY

by

STEWART C. EASTON

THE ANTHROPOSOPHIC PRESS

SPRING VALLEY   NEW YORK

CONTENTS

PART II. Anthroposophy in Practical Life

ACKNOWLEDGMENT

I wish to thank Paul Marshall Allen, author of *The Writings and Lectures of Rudolf Steiner,* and editor of several of Rudolf Steiner's more important works, for his aid and encouragement. He read each chapter of the manuscript promptly and with great care as it was written; he contributed invaluable criticism and many useful suggestions that have been incorporated into the text, and he has as well put his wide bibliographical knowledge at my disposal.

Stewart C. Easton

Longeville, Vendée, France
December, 1974

PART I

ANTHROPOSOPHY AS A BODY
OF KNOWLEDGE

CHAPTER I

Introductory

In the last decades of the eighteenth century when France, in the throes of her Revolution, was disseminating the idea of freedom and a desire for it throughout the rest of Europe, two of the greatest German writers of the time were engaged in the effort to discover the nature of freedom and how man could hope to attain it in view of the limitations of his own nature. Friedrich Schiller concerned himself particularly with the question of how the ordinary everyday man could live in harmony with the "ideal" human being living within him. The compulsions arising from his life of feeling and his passions were an obvious hindrance to achieving such a harmony; but so also was a one-sided rationality. Man is not free if (like Robespierre) he uses his reason and will to suppress his feelings; nor is he free if (like Danton) he merely allows his passions to express themselves unhindered. Schiller held that the only truly free being is one whose feeling life is permeated by spirituality, and whose thinking life was permeated by strong feeling. For, he was convinced that only in this way could the two apparent opposites in the human soul be reconciled, and free personalities come into being. These free personalities could then work

3

toward establishing a harmonious social life in human communities.

Schiller's older friend, Johann Wolfgang von Goethe, though greatly interested in, and appreciative of Schiller's ideas, especially as he expressed them in his *Letters on the Aesthetic Education of Man*,* did not feel able to discuss them in the abstract terms used by his friend. But the *Letters*, combined with his own thoughts on human freedom and the development of the human spirit, seem to have stimulated his imagination in an extraordinary manner. As a result he composed an entirely original "fairy tale," or legend, whose hidden meanings commentators have been trying to fathom ever since. Rudolf Steiner gave several lectures on the so-called *Fairy Tale of the Green Snake and the Beautiful Lily*, each time revealing more of its profound secrets, making us realize why certain truths (as Plato understood) cannot really be expressed in ordinary descriptions or explanations, but can be grasped, and then but fleetingly, only by our imagination as it develops throughout our life; and it is certain that even Goethe himself did not fully *comprehend* all that, in the freedom of his imagination, he had created.

The central theme concerns the building of a bridge across a river separating the earthly from the supersensible or spiritual world. In this latter world lives the Beautiful Lily, whose touch means death to anyone who tries to reach her without first having been purified—though she herself longs for the companionship of the living and sorrows because of her deadly power that cuts her off from it. Every noontime the Green Snake, who lives in the clefts of the rocks on the other side of the river, creates a bridge across it with her own body, until one day a

---

* The material in this part of the chapter is largely drawn from Steiner's essay, "The Character of Goethe's Spirit," published in the *Magazin für Litteratur* in 1899, of which he was the editor. The essay is reprinted in Rudolf Steiner, *The Portal of Initiation* (Englewood, New Jersey: Rudolf Steiner Publications, Inc., 1961), pp. 243–261. *The Legend of the Green Snake and the Beautiful Lily*, by Goethe, appears also in this volume in the translation by Thomas Carlyle. Another translation and Steiner's lectures on the Fairy Story itself are given in the Reading List at the end of the chapter.

4

headstrong prince crosses over her, determined at all costs to reach the Lily, and, like all his predecessors, is killed. In this instance, however, the Green Snake rescues him by sacrificing herself and out of her own body building a permanent bridge, strong enough and wide enough for all mankind to pass over. The prince, who has been magically revived, is then granted developed powers of thinking, feeling and willing by the three kings of gold, silver, and bronze, who have custody of them; then the prince can be united with the Lily.

Many other characters play a part in this story; there are also other sub-themes, all of deep interest and significance. The crucial question underlying the whole imaginative tale, however, is how man can attain within himself to what Schiller thought of as the ideal element, and what Goethe thought of as the supersensible or spiritual world inhabited by the Lily. The supersensible, Goethe is telling us, cannot simply be grasped by all who desire it; it cannot be taken by force without bringing death upon the man who attempts it. But when earthly knowledge (the Green Snake) has purified itself and reached the stage of total selflessness, offering itself up in love, then and then alone can the bridge be built.

Such an imagination goes much further and deeper than Schiller's thinking, which, after the manner of most eighteenth century thinking, took for granted the perfectibility of man and his ability, especially by enlightened reasoning, to transform his character. Goethe, however, is saying in his fairy story that the ideal element in man, as perceived by Schiller, is rooted in the supersensible world, and if man is to move toward the perfecting of his being, he must find his way to this world. Man's earthly knowledge and his thinking are valuable and necessary on the path, but they must be *transformed*. It is this same message that Rudolf Steiner also gave to mankind, almost a century after Goethe had written his *Fairy Tale of the Green Snake and the Beautiful Lily*. Few people then or since have understood this tale as Steiner understood it, and now Steiner himself has been dead for fifty years. But in our modern world there exists a thirst

5

for spiritual knowledge and spiritual experience that did not exist in such intensity in Steiner's own time, still less in Goethe's.

As will become clear in the course of this book there are various spiritual reasons for the appearance of this phenomenon at this particular moment in history. This should not be regarded solely as a natural swing of the pendulum, a reaction against the excessive materialism of the nineteenth and early twentieth centuries. Nor should the thirst for spiritual knowledge and spiritual experience be regarded as simply the expression of a natural human longing for deeper experiences than are to be found in our ordinary everyday life of the senses, a longing that has always in some measure existed. It is, as a matter of actual fact, easier today, in the sense of Goethe's picture, to cross over the bridge between the sensible and supersensible worlds than it was, for example, a century ago; it is also easier for young people today than for the old. Indeed, this longing exists because there is the possibility of satisfying it. The river has become narrower, and various bridges are being built across it. Nevertheless, the Beautiful Lily does not make herself accessible to all travelers, by whatever path they come to her.

There is no doubt that by the use of certain drugs and chemical preparations it is possible to "enlarge" the consciousness, that is, to become aware of what appears to be another world by the side of the everyday one. By similar means the acuity of the senses can be heightened, so that the ordinary external world appears far more interesting and exciting and more filled with color and life than usual, and all this can be experienced far more intensely. Moreover the ordinary inhibitions of everyday life are greatly relaxed, making for more varied, more intense, and less conventional human relationships. Thus it is easy to appreciate why so many people in this technological age experiment with drugs, even though the outsider may regard as pure hallucination the belief that they are really experiencing a different world to which these drugs give them the key. The existence of this world, however, has always been asserted by Oriental teachers and philosophers and holy men, and over the millennia they claim to have perfected the means by which it can be experienced. Such means, which include adopting certain traditional postures and conscious control of the breathing, usually in conjunction with various forms of concentration and meditation, are undoubtedly effective in enlarging the consciousness and usually in convincing their devotees of the relative unimportance of the earthly world by comparison with the spiritual. Indeed, a general criticism that can be leveled against both the drug-takers and the students of yoga and zen is that their practices to a greater or lesser degree unfit them for the life of the ordinary world. Some will indignantly deny this, while others will regard it not as a criticism at all but as a recommendation, our modern world being what it is!

Anthroposophy, which is the subject of this book, is squarely based—as must be stated at the outset—on the actual *knowledge* of the spiritual world that Rudolf Steiner, its founder, acquired and perfected through the conscious development of those higher faculties that, as he told us, "slumber within every human being."* He insisted that such knowledge must be acquired through conscious effort, or it will be subject to illusion and error. In referring to his own experience he reports that even as a child the spiritual world was fully open to him, and from an early age he knew that it would be his task in his present incarnation to give out such elements of spiritual knowledge as higher powers wished him to reveal in the first quarter of the twentieth century. But knowing that even the very *possibility* of such knowledge would be denied by all but a handful of his contemporaries, he made it his business to become fully acquainted with the physical science of his day, and to show his competence in philosophy by taking his doctorate in that discipline. He thus did his best to avoid being dismissed as a mere dreamer, and it is surely true that none of those who have

---

* Part of the opening sentence of *Knowledge of the Higher Worlds and its Attainment.*

laid claim in the past century to direct knowledge of the spiritual worlds has also been as rigorous and well-disciplined a thinker and investigator in other fields as was Rudolf Steiner.

Even so, neither in his own time nor since his death has he achieved recognition from the world in any way commensurate with the magnitude of his achievement. Few men have as yet been willing to recognize that it is possible for anyone to acquire a true knowledge of the spiritual world, that there can be a real science of spirit, comparable to the knowledge of the physical world that we call simply "science," as if there were nothing else entitled to the name. Although he wrote more than a score of books that have been in print both in the original German and in many European languages, including English, almost from the time they were written, and although he delivered over six thousand lectures, a substantial number of which are likewise in print, most encyclopaedias devote little space to him, and much of the information given is often erroneous as well as hopelessly inadequate as a description of his work.* An important international school movement was founded by him that now includes more than ninety flourishing schools, all of which follow the educational principles laid down by him, and their number increases every year. Yet this growing movement receives far less attention than other types of so-called experimental education that become fashionable, often enough, solely because of the gift of their founders for public relations. Few of them are based on new educational principles in any way comparable with those rooted in the nature of man that were enunciated by Rudolf Steiner.

Why, then, has Steiner's work been so neglected, even when it has had such visible fruits as this educational movement, the many hundreds of farms that use the "biodynamic" methods he was the first to give to mankind, the large number of homes for the care of maladjusted or retarded children established throughout the world in accordance with his indications, and the

---

* There are some honorable exceptions, notably the French Larousse.

certainly very visible building called the Goetheanum that he designed in Dornach, Switzerland? If Steiner had been nothing but a philosopher, or theologian, or educator, or authority on Goethe, or agricultural expert, or architect, or knowledgeable in medicinal plants, or dramatist, or gifted artistic innovator, inventor of eurythmy, an age that respects specialization would have reserved a respected niche for him. But Steiner was *all* these things at the same time, and he owed his preeminence in them to the fact that he was able to perceive the spiritual world behind the physical one, and he learned to speak and write about the spiritual world in words and concepts that can be grasped by healthy human understanding. He did not have to proceed by trial and error, as the physical scientist must usually do (though the mathematician may work in a way similar to Steiner's without quite knowing how he does it); he could use his developed intuition to discover in a moment the spiritual reality behind the earthly phenomena, and thus grasp the totality. When he lectured he always seemed to be drawing his ideas directly from the spiritual worlds as he spoke—although, of course, his previous work and the thorough disciplining of his faculties had alone made this possible.

Men who do not possess such faculties tend, not unnaturally, to deny that they exist; they are thus likely to dismiss Steiner's teachings as "mysticism," in a wholly pejorative sense, or as the fruits of an over-fertile imagination. There are various ways of refuting these charges. One obvious method is to point out how some of these so-called "mystical" ideas can be put to work fruitfully in the external world—as, for example, in biodynamic agriculture whose achievements are capable of being tested by "scientifically" acceptable means. It could also be pointed out how Steiner in the early part of the twentieth century remarked on the relation between fluorine and the teeth—a relationship not discovered by scientists until much later.

But Steiner's work should not be judged by such criteria as these, which might be lucky guesses and in any event prove nothing about his other teachings, nor the genuineness of his

9

spiritual gifts. Indeed, David Hume's well-known observation about the miracles attributed to Jesus Christ apply equally to Steiner's "predictions." The miracles at most, said Hume, prove that Christ could perform them and was thus a wonder-worker. They say nothing about his sanctity, still less his messiahship.

In my opinion, what might be called a "pragmatic" test—does this knowledge "make sense," does it help us to understand better the world we live in?—is one that Steiner passes with flying colors. For many of his students, the world does indeed suddenly begin to make sense. It takes on a meaning and significance it did not have before; man's place in it, his tasks now and in the future can be glimpsed. So many of our questions are answered in a way that satisfies both our intellect and our feelings. This would not be true if there were not an extraordinarily impressive consistency in all that Steiner taught, and it is precisely in face of this consistency that any truly serious student should find it scarcely possible to continue to harbor the suspicion—a suspicion natural enough in our age—that Steiner was simply a charlatan, nor even that he was a gifted but mistaken man. The most sceptical of students, as they persist in their studies, eventually come to recognize that he really knew what he was talking about, that his spiritual gifts were genuine. This experience, common to almost all anthroposophists, suggests the possibility that Steiner's own explanation for it is the correct one—that man possesses a faculty for recognizing truth that can be developed in a way somewhat analogous to the recognition of the correctness of a mathematical equation before it has been tested against the facts of the natural world.

Steiner spoke of anthroposophical knowledge as a "seed" that must be brought to fruition within each human being. For this reason it cannot be simplified into a philosophical or religious "system," and it cannot be digested in philosophical manuals, as can to some extent the philosophies of even such seminal thinkers as Kant or Hegel. Although I have in this book attempted to set forth anthroposophy, insofar as it consists of

10

knowledge, under various topics, somewhat in the manner of a text book, *it is in no sense intended to be used as a substitute for direct personal study of Steiner's own writings and lectures, still less to take the place of the inner work that must be done by the student himself and can be done only by him.* It is written primarily as a stimulus to such work by outlining the teachings in the many areas in which Steiner made his contributions, and by giving the reader a glimpse of the enormous wealth and richness of what Steiner gave to mankind.

The student's attitude toward the body of anthroposophical knowledge contained in this book should undoubtedly be that recommended by Steiner—an attitude neither of acceptance nor rejection, but of simply *receiving* it, with all belief and disbelief suspended. He warned strongly against accepting his teachings on "blind faith"; at the same time he also characterized unconsidered rejection of them as "negative superstition," intellectually as serious a fault as the positive superstition of the past, which is rightly rejected today. Pondering these revelations from the spiritual world with an open mind and heart is also an important step in personal development, and provides a good preparation for possible later direct knowledge and experience of the spiritual worlds. By dwelling in his thoughts and feelings on what has been imparted by others a student becomes more capable of awakening faculties within himself that can eventually lead to individual perception of the spiritual world. Nevertheless, it should be emphasized that, contrary to the teachings of most modern cults and to the wishes of most of their adherents, it is not man's task simply to develop his own personal self and to enlarge his own consciousness. Indeed, if a man does succeed in coming to a direct knowledge of the spiritual worlds, this very achievement only increases his responsibilities toward his fellowmen. The very width and scope of anthroposophy make it truly impossible for any serious student to content himself with his little concerns and his own personal spiritual development, which indeed will always be used and directed wrongly so long as it remains only personal. Chapter 3

11

of this book, in particular, concerned as it is with the true nature of human freedom, will discuss how man can come by his own efforts to the realization of his true tasks in the world, the performance of which can alone fulfill the needs of his inner being.

As Steiner grew older and the movement he founded became gradually more mature, and its members became more capable of practical work based on anthroposophical indications, he gave ever more lectures on the practical tasks facing mankind. This is especially true of the period following World War I, which had demonstrated so clearly the directions in which mankind was moving and the new dangers that would come from increasing materialism and improved technology. It was also in this period that he gave almost all his fundamental lectures on the various arts, and that he founded the first Steiner School, the so-called Waldorf School for boys and girls in Stuttgart. It is also true that at this period he often gave a series of lectures covering material similar to what he had given out earlier, but now from a different viewpoint. It is therefore essential for serious students to take into account the year in which a lecture was given or a book written, and not simply to assume that an early lecture contained the last word he had to give on a particular subject.

All Steiner's writings and lectures were originally given, of course, in German, and his German was itself so idiomatic, and in a sense uniquely creative, as was necessitated by his subject, that it does not go easily into any other language—though it goes better into a partly Teutonic language such as English than it does into any of the Latin tongues. Aside from the difficulties of translation it must be admitted that many of his works do not at first attract the reader, and many of them may repel or intimidate students by their apparent difficulty. This applies, in particular, perhaps, to some of his fundamental works such as *Theosophy, An Outline of Occult Science,* and *The Philosophy of Freedom* (or *Philosophy of Spiritual Activity*), all of which are quite indispensable for the serious student. But if a reader dips into some other work, too often questions will arise in his mind that could have been answered if he had read the fundamental works. It has, therefore, been a main purpose in writing this book to give Steiner's teachings as a whole, together with such comments and explanations as have seemed to me to be helpful, in the belief that humanity should not be deprived of the opportunity of becoming acquainted with a thinker of such surpassing importance simply because his work is so difficult of access.

The book, insofar as I have been able to plan it, is intended to be an introduction to Steiner's work, and it will fail of its purpose completely if it is ever used as a substitute for it. Each chapter will deal with a particular aspect of his teaching, and at the end of each appears a selection of those works of Rudolf Steiner that have a special relevance to the subject discussed. If, therefore, a particular topic is found by the reader to be of interest, it is suggested that he then proceed on to the works of Steiner himself that deal with the subject, always remembering that anthroposophy is not only *knowledge*, but also a seed for knowledge and a path of development. Indeed, a mere acquaintance with any topic such as can alone be gained from a reading of any chapter in this book is of scarcely any value unless it is enriched by a study of what Steiner himself said on the subject in his own inimitable way. The reading list will also include certain outstanding works by students of anthroposophy, who have in some cases tested and added to what Steiner himself may have given only in embryonic form. Throughout his life Steiner answered questions put to him in such a way that he indicated directions for research that could be carried out by the questioner for himself, and research is still being continued by other students who were not old enough to have known Steiner personally.

There will be little biographical material on Rudolf Steiner himself. This lack has at least partly been filled by my book *Rudolf Steiner: Herald of a New Epoch* (1980). In the last year of his life Steiner began an autobiography which he was unable to

13

complete beyond the year 1909. It did not therefore include the years of his most productive anthroposophical activity. Guenther Wachsmuth, one of his most faithful co-workers, provided some further biographical as well as valuable bibliographical information in his *Life and Work of Rudolf Steiner,* carrying the story down to his death. These two books are most important for a year by year account of his life and activity. In order to help the reader to orient himself in time whenever a book or lecture is mentioned in the text its year of writing or delivery will also be given. The place of delivery of lectures is likewise included, because Steiner spoke differently on similar themes in different places. Certain information that he wished to give, say, to Norwegians or English, he may not necessarily have wished to impart in that particular form to Germans; or in certain countries he may have been, and in some cases he certainly was, stimulated by the natural conditions that were especially favorable to new insights. In particular, the lectures he gave in Penmaenmawr in Wales in 1923 and those he gave in London and Torquay in 1924 were influenced by his spiritual impressions gained during visits to Druid remains in Wales and King Arthur's Castle in Tintagel, Cornwall. The latter moved him to speak further on the Holy Grail, about which he had spoken in a different manner at Leipzig ten years earlier. The serious student will thus learn, as almost second nature, to take into account the place and time of Steiner's lectures he is studying, the period of Steiner's life at which they were given, and especially the context, including the other lectures he was giving at the time.

But it is also good for students to know something of what Rudolf Steiner was like personally, how he appeared to his fellow workers and pupils. For this study there are available only scattered memoirs from different hands, some of which were used in my own book, which supplements the information given in the present work, which is exclusively devoted to the world and man in the light of anthroposophy. But these personal impressions are invaluable nevertheless because above all Rudolf Steiner was a warm and kindly human being, as well as a spiritual leader. From these memoirs a rounded picture can be gleaned of impressive consistency, of a man of unfailing goodness and helpfulness and utterly without arrogance or pride. In short, a true initiate and a true twentieth century servant of the Christ, who left enough material behind him at his death to occupy the attention of all of us for at least a century. This book constitutes an inadequate attempt to show to those who have never occupied themselves with it, something of the dimensions of his work.

SUGGESTIONS FOR FURTHER READING
FOR CHAPTER 1.

N.B. The reading lists that appear at the end of each Chapter will not necessarily include all the works that may have been mentioned in footnotes in this chapter. When the work to which reference is made in a footnote is not included in the reading list, the bibliographical information will be included in the footnote. If this information does not appear in the footnote, the reader will know that it can be found at the end of the chapter.

There are two major publishing houses for anthroposophical works, one of them in New York, and known from the beginning as the Anthroposophic Press; the other, located in London, has been known under different names, including its present name of Rudolf Steiner Press. This latter house, and its predecessors will appear in the reading lists simply as London; the Anthroposophic Press, now at Spring Valley, New York and formerly in New York City will appear simply as New York. All other publishing houses, anthroposophical or not, will be given their full name, as well as the city where their books are published. Two important periodicals are now published by Rudolf Steiner Press in London, *The Golden Blade,* an annual, and *Anthroposophic Quarterly.* The Anthroposophical Society in America publishes twice yearly *The Journal for Anthroposophy.* When any of these publications is quoted, no publisher or place of publication will be included.

Further works on Goethe's The Green Snake and the Beautiful Lily:
Rudolf Steiner, *Goethe's Standard of the Soul* (1902) London, n.d. This work contains also a translation of the fairy story itself.
Goethe's Secret Revelation. Two lectures given in Berlin October 22 and 24, 1908. (London, 1933.)

Biographical material on Rudolf Steiner.

Rudolf Steiner: An Autobiography, translated by Rita Stebbing, Blauvelt, New York, 1977. This edition, which is accompanied by more than 600 notes by Paul M. Allen, supersedes the older translation by Olin D.Wannamaker, published under the title *The Course of My Life (Mein Lebensgang).*
This work, begun by Rudolf Steiner a year before his death, was originally written in the form of a series of essays, which were published every week in the official publication of the General Anthroposophical Society. The book is indispensable for all students of Steiner's work, supplying as it does a first hand account of his early years written from his own point of view. Unfortunately the book ends in 1909, since Steiner did not live to complete it.
Guenther Wachsmuth, *The Life and Work of Rudolf Steiner from the Turn of the Century to his Death.* Trans. Olin D. Wannamaker and Reginald E. Raab. New York: Whittier Books, Inc. 1955.
The first part of this book, which was published in German in 1941, was naturally based on Steiner's autobiography. The remainder was based on personal recollections and careful research by the author, who was a close friend and frequent companion of Steiner on his lecture tours, and a member of the first Executive Council of the Society as founded in 1923.

16

Invaluable as a work of reference, and by no means difficult to read consecutively in this good translation. There is little attempt to evaluate Steiner's whole work in this book, but this year by year account of his working life provides the strongest possible impression of the sheer bulk, quality and variety of his work.

Albert Steffen, *Meetings with Rudolf Steiner.* Dornach: Philosophic-Anthroposophic Press, 1961. A recollection, often very moving, of Steiner by his friend and first successor as president of the Anthroposophical Society.

A.P. Shepherd, *A Scientist of the Invisible,* London: Hodder and Stoughton Ltd., 1954.

This relatively short book by a canon of the Anglican Church has been found by many, especially in England, to be an extremely helpful introduction to Steiner's life and work. Approximately a third of the book is devoted to his life, and the remainder consists of a series of chapters on different aspects of his work. It attempts to do, on a somewhat smaller scale, what the present book is also trying to do, but from a quite different point of view.

Friedrich W. Rittelmayer, *Rudolf Steiner Enters my Life,* London, Christian Community Press, 1963. This is certainly one of the best books available for a description of what Steiner was like as a man. Rittelmayer, founder of the Christian Community, was originally a Protestant pastor in Germany, and the book describes how his friendship with Rudolf Steiner led him from an initial skepticism about anthroposophy to a certainty that in it was to be found the only true Christian impulse for the future.

"Rudolf Steiner: Recollections by Some of his Pupils" *The Golden Blade,* 1958. This is by far the most comprehensive account in English of Rudolf Steiner as he appeared to those who worked with him. All fourteen of the articles are interesting, but the first, entitled, "Rudolf Steiner in England," by one of his closest young associates, George Adams, is especially recommended.

Margarita Woloschin, "Life Memories," *Journal for Anthro-*

posophy Autumn, 1972 and Spring, 1973. These two articles consist of extracts from the author's autobiography which describe her meetings with Rudolf Steiner. They are exceptionally valuable as throwing light on the delicate and understanding way in which Steiner dealt with a student whose potentialities he recognized but whose failure to realize them in anthroposophical work in spite of all his encouragement must have been a deep disappointment to him.

D. N. Dunlop, "Rudolf Steiner and the Fulfillment of a Quest," *Anthroposophical Quarterly,* Autumn, 1973.

This short article, originally published in 1935 and now reprinted, is of great value as a picture of a lifelong seeker after truth who had for a long time been a student of theosophy and the overwhelming impression the meeting with Rudolf Steiner had upon him, an impression that never changed when he came to know him so much better and, as leader of the Anthroposophical Society in Great Britain, accompanied Steiner on his lecture tours in England. As Dunlop puts it, Steiner left his pupils completely free: "He made one feel, here in the service of his mission, there is, in very truth, perfect freedom. The soul began to breathe in his presence and to have wings—to have feet as well, planted on free and independent soil for action."

Frans Carlgren, *Rudolf Steiner, 1861–1925* (Dornach: School of Spiritual Science, 2nd edit., 1964). A useful, more or less official account of Steiner's life directed toward the general public interested in knowing more about his life and work.

Johannes Hemleben, *Rudolf Steiner: a Documentary Biography*, translated by Leo Twyman, East Grinstead, Henry Goulden Ltd. 1975. A well-illustrated biography by a Christian Community priest, stronger on the earlier part of his life, published originally by a leading German publisher as part of a series. The book was a considerable success in Germany, but the English translation is marred by several important mistakes in translation.

Stewart C. Easton. *Rudolf Steiner: Herald of a New Epoch*, New York, 1980. The only fullscale biography originally written

18

in the English language.

Bibliographical aid.

Paul Marshall Allen, *The Writings and Lectures of Rudolf Steiner: A Bibliography.* New York: Whittier Press, Inc., 1956. An indispensable work of reference for all English speaking students of Rudolf Steiner, it provides details of all the books and lectures of Steiner that had been translated into English by 1956. There is usually a brief description of the content of the lectures, and even when the lecture has never appeared in book or brochure form, the periodical in which it appeared is mentioned. Since the leading Anthroposophical Societies in the English speaking world have as a rule excellent reference libraries, this information can be of great help in serious studies. This particular edition's usefulness is limited by its publication date, since many lectures have been published since 1956.

Ulrich Babbel and Craig Giddens, eds. *Bibliographical Reference List,* London, 1977. This helpful compilation does not altogether supersede the last mentioned title, since its usefulness is limited by the fact that the books and cycles are listed in alphabetical order, followed by the relevant information regarding the latest published edition. Paul Allen's work, which presents Steiner's writings and lectures in chronological order, enables the student to follow the development of his work and see at a glance what subjects he was covering in a particular year. There remains a need to bring Allen's book up to date by including all Steiner's works published in English translation since 1956, though this in no way detracts from the value of this reference list for the information it was designed to give.

CHAPTER II

*History and the Evolution
of Human Consciousness*

The major purpose of this chapter is to show how human consciousness has evolved from prehistoric times to the present —an idea that may not be too difficult for the layman to accept, even though historians tend to shy away from the concept because it cannot be demonstrated as true by the methods available to them. Historians tend to believe that man's consciousness, his psychic faculties, have always been much as they are now. Even if they were to admit that in far distant epochs man's soul life was different, it never occurs to them to claim that such relatively recent personages as Plato and Aristotle could have had capacities different from ours. It was, they say, their *cultural environment* that was different. When, for example, Hero of Alexandria, who probably lived in the second century of the Christian era, invented a real steam engine of a primitive kind, nothing momentous followed as a result of this invention because his cultural environment was unfavorable. If it had been different, then it might have been possible to produce his steam engine in large numbers, with the result that something comparable to the Industrial Revolution of the eighteenth century

20

could well have followed. In short, Hero's invention was premature in relation to the environment in which he lived.

An anthroposophical historian would never make such an observation, not because he would deny the importance of man's cultural environment, but because he holds that the environment itself results from the soul configuration of a particular epoch, and not vice versa. By the second century of the Christian era, even the most advanced men on earth had reached only that stage of consciousness known as the intellectual or mind soul; it was not until more than a millennium later that mankind entered the era characterized by that soul configuration known as the consciousness soul. Modern science is the creation of the consciousness soul, as, of course, is the modern industrial economy. Neither could have been produced, as we shall hope to show, in the age of the intellectual soul.

In studying history backward from our own time we soon arrive at an epoch that represents a watershed between history and "pre-history." We can no longer adduce any convincing evidence from the historical record to confirm, or indeed throw any light upon, the changing consciousness of man. The soul configuration of the age preceding that of the intellectual soul is called in anthroposophy the sentient soul, and its character was such that it was possible for this soul for the first time to invent writing. All earlier development is shrouded, for lack of a written record, in the mists of prehistory. History, properly so-called, is replaced by archeology, with its mute remains, its artifacts, which we have to interpret as best we can in the light of our imaginative insights. It is therefore not surprising that archeology is one of the most controversial of all fields of study, and that historians, almost to a man, fight shy of it.

Nevertheless, we are not necessarily required to believe that beyond the realms of the historian, the archeologist, and possibly the geologist, we are faced with the absolute impossibility of penetrating any further back into the past. We now in fact reach the realm that can be penetrated only by the true occultist, by such a man as Rudolf Steiner, who was able to develop his spiritual faculties so that he could read what is usually called the "Akasha Chronicle," an occult "script," in which is inscribed, so to speak, all that has ever happened in the history of the universe. The spiritual scientist, in effect, frees himself from the limits of space and time, so that he perceives what took place in the remote past "in its eternal character," as if it were happening now.* It may be difficult for most people to believe that such a possibility exists, and that Steiner could indeed read the script. But it is essential for the understanding of his work to recognize that he did have this capacity, and all that will be said here about the remote past, even before the earth itself had come into being, is based upon it.

The statement that anything can be known about the period before the earth came into being must appear to most readers, to say the least, startling. Steiner, however, goes into considerable detail about the three former "embodiments" of the earth, which he calls Old Saturn, Old Sun, and Old Moon.** During these earlier embodiments of the earth, he tells us, higher beings than man were working together to make it possible for man at last to

---

* The best description of the nature of this Akasha Chronicle was given by Steiner himself as a preface to a series of articles on the prehistory of earth and man, published in *Cosmic Memory,* pp. 38–41, to which book the reader is referred if he desires further information on the subject. Occultists of past ages have, of course, in many cases had access to this Chronicle, which they have described with more or less accuracy according to the degree of their spiritual development.

** He gives them these names because of a certain connection between them and the present planetary bodies that bear their names, a connection that need not concern us here. The reader is referred to Chapter 4 of *An Outline of Occult Science* for the most clear and systematic account of Old Saturn, Old Sun, and Old Moon, and for the work performed on them by the various spiritual hierarchies above man. The teachings about the spiritual hierarchies themselves form one of the most fundamental elements in anthroposophy, and hundreds, even thousands, of references to them are to be found scattered throughout Steiner's lectures. But a detailed knowledge of these beings does not fall within the scope of this book, and the reader is therefore especially directed, in addition to the chapter mentioned above, to a cycle called *The Spiritual Hierarchies and their Reflection in the Physical World,* ten lectures given in Dusseldorf in April, 1909 (2nd edit., New York, 1970).

live in a physical body on our earth. The existence of these higher beings has always been known to initiates, and until fairly recent times at least some of them could be perceived with the eye of clairvoyance. St. Paul alludes to them and names some of them in his Epistle to the Ephesians (6:12),* an early Christian writer known as Dionysius the Areopagite devoted an extensive treatise to them, naming each of the nine; Thomas Aquinas commented on this work in the thirteenth century, though himself disclaiming any personal knowledge of them; and Dante peoples his Paradise with them. All medieval churchmen accepted their existence, and they were commonly known as "intelligences." They were thus in no sense a new "revelation" of Rudolf Steiner, but he did distinguish between them and the work done by each rank of these beings in a more detailed manner than any of his predecessors. Since he always calls them "hierarchies," we shall refer to them in this book by this name, on the rare occasions when it will be necessary to speak of them. The fundamental fact that should be recognized about these spiritual hierarchies at a higher stage of development than man, and about the other invisible beings of a lower rank than they, is that they are always ceaselessly active, working not only upon the development of man but of the earth.

Whereas it is not essential in this introductory book to have a detailed knowledge of the beings other than man, it is essential that the constitution of man, as it is understood by the science of spirit, should be grasped because this knowledge will have to be taken for granted throughout the book. But it is hoped that what will necessarily appear to be abstract in this first description will gradually take on life as it is seen in different contexts in later chapters. In ancient times when clairvoyant knowledge was widespread among men, the true nature of the human being was glimpsed by ordinary men, while later it came to be known only to some highly developed men, and preserved in mystery centers

---

* The "principalities" and "powers" referred to in this verse are names given in Christian esotericism to the third and fourth hierarchies above man.

23

as knowledge that must never be divulged to the uninitiated. It is to some degree even today known to some so-called "primitive" peoples; Malays, for example, have words to denote the different "bodies." The oldest "body" of man is the physical body, which is, in a sense, the most perfectly developed of his bodies. Its beginning dates back to Old Saturn. The physical body of man is not, however, in itself *alive*. Its life is bestowed on it by the "etheric" body, the germ of which was laid down on Old Sun. The physical body we share with all nature, animate or inanimate, the etheric body with everything that lives on earth. Thus the rocks have their physical body, but, during their earth existence, no etheric body; the plants have physical and etheric bodies. When the etheric body separates from the physical body at death (as happens with plants, animals, and men) the physical body returns to its original elements through the process of decay. On Old Moon appeared the germ of the next body of man, usually known as the "astral" body. This body man shares with the animal world. It is the sentient or feeling body through which men and animals experience pleasure and pain and all desires. Only man has the fourth "body," which was given to him only on earth. This is the ego or self, which enables man to think and plan and direct his own activity from within. Every night in sleep the astral body and ego withdraw from man into the spiritual world, returning to him when he wakes. At death the astral body and ego withdraw altogether into the spiritual world, while the etheric body, though withdrawn from man, continues in existence for about three days, and then is dissolved into that part of the spiritual atmosphere surrounding the earth from which its substance was originally drawn. This atmosphere may be thought of as the "etheric world," which at all times interpenetrates the visible physical world open to our ordinary senses. When the etheric body withdraws, the physical body can no longer retain its form and is dissolved in time into its physical and chemical components.

Now when it is said that the "germ" of the physical body was laid down on Old Saturn, it should not be thought that an actual physical body such as we now know it, even in an extremely primitive form, could have been perceived by anyone who had our present physical senses, if such a being had existed then. Steiner speaks of this physical germ as consisting of nothing but "warmth," difficult and almost impossible as it is for us even to imagine such a condition of being. If a being with our senses had been around at that time, he would suddenly have perceived a kind of warmth in the desolation of "space," and this would have indicated the presence of what was in the fullness of time to become the physical body of man. When the etheric body of man was added to the physical on Old Sun by the activity of the Spirits of Wisdom (Kyriotetes), and when on the Old Moon the Spirits of Motion (Dynameis) endowed him with an astral body, man even as he had thus far evolved would still not have been visible. Indeed, on the earth itself for a long time man was not visible in the sense in which we use the word today.

The creation in succession of these four "bodies" of man was therefore not the work of one single supreme being whom we for reasons of simplicity and because of the Hebraic tradition are accustomed to call "God," but of four of the higher hierarchies. Man, who may be thought of as the tenth hierarchy, could not have been created in a moment in the twinkling of an eye; a long period of gestation was necessary for the evolution of such a complex being, who was destined to be totally different from all others in the universe because in the fullness of time he was to be granted *freedom*. No other hierarchy possesses this freedom. The supremely exalted beings of the higher hierarchies, however great their power and glory, can only serve and obey. It is of the essence of their being that they should do this, always furthering the purposes of the Godhead, and it is their joy and delight thus to serve. Nevertheless, as can readily be understood, man could not be free unless a choice between good and evil was possible for him. For this reason certain higher beings were given the task of acting as hindering forces in man's evolution.

It is extremely difficult for us to understand in human terms just what was involved in this deed, and it is no wonder that theologians throughout the ages have struggled with the question of the existence of evil in the world, and why "God" permits it. Even at the risk of excessive simplification the attempt must be made to provide an answer from Steiner's teachings.

The world in itself is perfect, created as it was by higher beings acting in accordance with the Divine Will. Man himself could have been as perfect as the beings of the hierarchies above him, but he could not *also* have been free, since freedom must involve the possibility of disobeying the Divine Will. To make possible man's disobedience other beings higher than man were first given the possibility of disobeying, or rebelling against the Divine Will before the earth had yet come into existence. By rebelling in this way they renounced for themselves for the time being the possibility of progressing upward in their own evolution, for even higher beings evolve. This renunciation was, in a sense, a sacrifice, but the sacrifice had to be made if man, who as yet existed only in potentiality, was in the fullness of time to be endowed with free will, and the possibility of choice. These beings (known to Christian traditional thought as "fallen angels," though they did not in fact all belong to the hierarchy of the angels, the next above man) rebelled against the Divine Will, and as a consequence became, during earth evolution, what we can only think of as evil beings, no longer living in the spiritual world, their former home, but within the spiritual atmosphere of the earth itself, and thus able to influence man directly, especially in his feelings and will, which are not fully conscious during his earthly life.

Evil is therefore now a reality in earthly evolution, not an unreality (as, for instance, Christian Scientists hold it to be). Evil is a force opposed to the Divine Will, and is "embodied" in actual beings of two different categories, known to anthroposophy as Luciferic and Ahrimanic. These beings, who will be discussed more fully later, have it as their task to divert men from their true goal, or, as the Bible speaks of it, to tempt them and thus win power over them for their own ends, which are now opposed to those of the divine world. This rebellion of beings higher than man has had the consequence, for man, that he does have a real moral choice. He may follow the Good or the Evil. No higher being may coerce him into doing the Good; the choice is strictly his.

The beneficent higher beings care so greatly about man that they give him all the help they can, short of actually *compelling* him to choose the good, which would destroy his freedom. Man is the creation of higher beings, but once he was created he was gradually in the course of his history left ever more and more on his own, so that he had the possibility of fulfilling his task through his own freely chosen deeds. The world and man's physical and etheric bodies were created perfect; the greatest possible divine wisdom was embedded in them. No human wisdom can ever equal the wisdom we find in the world of nature or in the human organism. What man can do is *discover* (and reverence) this wisdom, but he cannot possibly add to it or improve upon the perfection of the world or of the human organism. It was the evil that entered into his astral body that was and is responsible for human ills and death.

What man can do, however, is to develop love out of his own inner being, a human quality that cannot be compelled from him, nor instilled into him from outside. A truly free action of man, as will be discussed further in the next chapter, can only be a deed of love. Hence freedom and love go together, and it is the cosmic task of man to transform his world through the action of love. From this stems the truly awe-inspiring statement of Steiner that "man is the religion of the divine beings." As man's own religion consists in loving and worshipping these beings, so they themselves in turn honor and cherish man and his task, and their delight is in aiding, when they can, and rejoicing whenever a free and loving deed is performed by man in accordance with the task he has been set by them that cannot be performed by them but only by man.

The early history of our earth may be passed over briefly since man had not yet descended into physical existence. In the earliest times the earth, sun, and moon were united in one body.

27

What later was to become our sun and shine on earth from the outside split off first, leaving earth and moon together. Gradually, in what anthroposophy calls the third great epoch of earth evolution, and gives the name, Lemurian, human beings acquired something like a human earthly form, and earthly conditions became such that men could live on it. But the moon forces, which when within the earth had the tendency to condense and harden all material substance, had the same effect on man's physical body, so that it became increasingly difficult for his spiritual being to incarnate in it, and the population decreased so seriously that there were scarcely any men left on earth. To make further evolution possible the moon was then withdrawn from the earth, later to become the satellite we now know, which encircles it. The excessive condensation process was thus halted, and it again became possible for human beings to incarnate. In due course the Lemurian age came to an end in a series of great catastrophes resulting from volcanic activity, and of those human beings who survived most migrated to a continent known as Atlantis in the Atlantic Ocean, memories of which remained in human culture as late as the Grecian epoch. Although Steiner has given us much information about Atlantis, this need not concern us here. Atlantis, in turn, disappeared into the Atlantic Ocean, though not all at one time. Its inhabitants were gradually led over a long period eastward into Asia and thence to North Africa, while smaller migrations went westward to America. It is with the eastward migrations that we shall here be concerned. Although the remnants of the Atlantean peoples in America succeeded in maintaining themselves and creating civilizations not unlike those of Atlantis, their consciousness did not evolve as did that of the peoples who traveled eastward under the leadership of great initiates. Since it is with the evolution of human consciousness that we are concerned in this chapter, we shall follow here the history of these latter peoples.

Before entering on the history of this evolution, however, some attention should be given to the great question that has exercised much human ingenuity since the middle of the nineteenth century, the question of human physical evolution. It should be clear from what has been said above that man did not evolve from animals, but that the creation of man was planned and directed from the beginning by the higher hierarchies directed by the Divine Will. The facts uncovered by the proponents of the modern theory of evolution are not contested, but they may be interpreted differently, and thus lead to opposite conclusions. According to anthroposophy, the animals in fact evolved from man, and not vice versa, but from man before he had become a physical, still less a visible being. It would take us too far afield to go into the detail necessary to explain this evolution (see the books by Poppelbaum and Wachsmuth in the reading list at the end of the chapter), and it need only be said that the animals were beings that incarnated prematurely, becoming hardened and fixed in form before the human organism had developed to the stage where it could contain an individual spirit and soul. The animals therefore are beings who could, so to speak, have become men if they had waited, but they did not. Thus they took on bodies that were the physical counterparts of their astral bodies of that time. Lacking individual egos, they could not evolve further. They became static in form, then slowly degenerated. Only later, with man's aid, were some species developed further. By contrast the beings that later became the bird world waited too long and never did incarnate fully. Thus the bird does not have a complete body; it is virtually all head. The great primates, as the evolutionary record shows, incarnated last before man, having evolved up to the stage where they had bodies not so dissimilar to those of men. But this incarnation was still premature, and took place too early to enable them to incorporate a human ego.

The first post-Atlantean civilization lies far back in prehistory. All our information concerning it therefore comes from the Akasha Chronicle, but much later echoes of this ancient civilization are also to be found in the earliest written works of the Indians, the Vedas. In the period when these works were first written down, the third post-Atlantean epoch, when direct clairvoyance, or perception of the spiritual worlds was dying out, many of the sublime teachings of the first epoch, which had been based on a living clairvoyance, were still preserved as a kind of folk memory, and after the invention of writing could be written down under the direction of the priests. Even such a late poem as the Bhagavad Gita still preserves some of the teachings of the sages, known as the Seven Holy Rishis, who were pupils of the Atlantean initiate Manu, founder of the civilization. Steiner tells us that these seven Rishis would have been regarded by their contemporaries as ordinary unassuming human beings except at the moments when they were inspired by higher beings who spoke through them, giving guidance for the earthly life of the people. Yet even to say that higher beings "spoke" through them would not be quite correct, for there was as yet no human language, and the initiates did not speak in words. Their "auditors'" attention was directed to them by supersensible means, and a message then passed from etheric body to etheric body without the medium of speech. This was possible because during this Indian epoch the etheric body came to maturity, as the astral body came to maturity in the next epoch, the ancient Persian.

At this time all the people were clairvoyant in that they perceived the spiritual worlds and spiritual beings more clearly than they could perceive the earth and its beings, but only a few initiates and their pupils could understand messages received from the spiritual world. This world was simply experienced, but not with any kind of clarity. In a real sense the ancient Indian civilization was directed from the spiritual world by higher beings, and men were simply the instruments of the Divine Will, without any ego consciousness comparable with ours and without any possibility of free action. The influence of the hindering forces was minimal. Since the astral and not the etheric body is the seat of passions and desires, and the astral bodies of the ancient Indians were still not fully developed, man as yet could not and did not turn to evil as a possible line of conduct as against the good—that is, the path laid out for him by the beneficent higher beings.

At the end of the Atlantean age man's physical body had come to maturity, and would have therefore been visible even to our eyes, and, as we have seen, his etheric body came to maturity during the first post-Atlantean epoch. Not until the following epoch did his astral body come to maturity, and with it the possibility of doing evil. When in this second epoch we first find in the records references to Ahriman, the lord of evil and illusion, this was due to the fact that he had indeed now begun to be active in the individual astral bodies of men.

At this point it becomes necessary to explain the nature of what we have just called epochs, or, as they will more often be called in this book "cultural epochs." The ages of Atlantis and Lemuria lasted much longer than the length of time assigned to the post-Atlantean age, which is divided into seven "cultural epochs" each of approximately the same length, and each marked by a change in human consciousness. A post-Atlantean cultural epoch lasts for approximately 2,160 years, or one twelfth of the period during which the sun moves through the whole zodiac, a period lasting 25,920 years, usually known as the "Platonic Year." The very approximate date of the beginning of the first post-Atlantean age already described may be given as 7227 B.C.; the second, or old Persian age began in 5067 B.C. and ended in 2907 B.C. The third age itself ended in 747 B.C., the approximate date of the founding of Rome.*

---

* For those interested in astronomical matters it may be noted that the zodiacal constellations are of unequal size. The cultural epochs do not therefore correspond exactly, or even approximately, to the period of time the sun spends in a particular constellation. Nor does the sun move into a new constellation at the time of the opening of a new cultural epoch. On the contrary, it moves into a new constellation about half way through the cultural epoch. But, perhaps more significant than the opening of the new cultural epoch, the great leader who is to give the impulse for that epoch does usually appear at approximately the time when the sun moves into a new constellation. As we shall shortly suggest, the original Zarathustra who gave the impulse for the founding of the second post-Atlantean epoch, was born about 6400 B.C., a date that corresponds exactly with the date when the sun moved from Cancer into Gemini, while Hermes or

31

The second post-Atlantean epoch is, for the most part, prehistoric as far as historians are concerned. There were still no written records, but we do not have to rely entirely upon spiritual science for information about it as long as we are willing to make the assumption that the first great prophet to be named Zarathustra (or Zoroaster) lived in the seventh millennium B.C., as tradition held during the early Christian era. Both the Greek Plutarch and the Roman Pliny give such a date, the former giving his birth as some 5000 years before the Trojan War, and the latter 6000 years before the death of Plato, which occurred in 347 B.C. Van Bemmelen, in the book referred to in the last footnote, offers much evidence to show that the oldest part of the Avesta, known as the Gathas, can be reasonably traced back to this first Zarathustra.

The Gathas, however, being primarily religious documents, do not in themselves give us much information about the outstanding achievement assigned to Zarathustra by Steiner—the beginnings of agriculture. This innovation was attributed to kings who long antedated the great prophet. The discoveries of archeologists give more support to the theory that agriculture originated in the seventh millennium B.C. in the general area occupied by the peoples described in the Gathas, although this does not preclude the possibility that agriculture originated at a still earlier epoch in and around the city of Jericho, Palestine, as most archaeological evidence now available would seem to support. Almost certainly agriculture in the New World originated independently of any contact with Europe, and the same thing could easily have happened in Asia.

The gradual substitution of agriculture, with its settled life, for nomadic food gathering is usually called by historians the

---

Thoth (usually regarded by historians as a mythical figure, but a real person, according to Rudolf Steiner) appeared in ancient Egypt about 4200 B.C. when the sun moved into Taurus, while Moses appeared about 1400 B.C. when the sun moved into Aries. For this material see the book by Van Bemmelen on Zarathustra given in the reading list at the end of the chapter, as also for material on the prophet himself, on which the present author is largely relying.

Neolithic Revolution, and its significance for the future has always been recognized. It is, indeed, such a revolutionary change in the life of mankind that we might assume, even if Rudolf Steiner had not specifically told us, that an actual change in consciousness was being brought to realization in that far distant epoch. This was in fact nothing less than a new orientation toward the earth, and a new relationship with it. Whereas in the first post-Atlantean epoch men felt (Indian philosophy of later times reflects this feeling) that the earth was a Maya, an illusion, and that their real life was as spiritual beings in a world of spirit, in the second epoch they were taught to regard the earth as their true home. The clairvoyance, which had enabled even the ordinary man to see directly into the spiritual world, began to die out.

As a result of this new orientation Ahrimanic beings could enter more deeply into man's astral body. The task of these evil spirits, who possess a superhuman cleverness and power, is to "tempt" men to believe that they are solely earthly beings, and to forget their divine origin and the mission set them by the gods. The spiritual mission of Zarathustra was therefore to reveal to his people the truths that he received directly from the great Lord of the Sun, Ahura Mazda, and to instruct them on the manifold dangers to which they were exposed by the lord of lies, the evil god Aingra Mainu or Ahriman. From this time onward man's soul is the battleground between the good and evil powers, and the ethical teachings of the historical Zoroastrianism of later times still consist essentially of instructions as to how they can help Ahura Mazda to overcome the evil powers that remain within their souls and within the earth. Steiner therefore characterizes this epoch as the period during which man's astral body came to a certain level of maturity. As a result of the activity of Ahriman man was no longer able to perceive the spiritual worlds for himself and know himself as a spiritual being, and because his own self, his ego, was not yet fully incarnated in him, he was also as yet incapable of purifying his astral body through his own efforts. His task was therefore to

33

heed the teachings of Zarathustra and his successor priests, obeying them implicitly and not deviating from them until in later ages, with the full incorporation of his ego within his physical, etheric and astral bodies, it became possible for him at last to be free.

The old Persian epoch came to an end more or less at the same time as the close of one of the great 5000 year cosmic epochs of which there is no need to speak further here. About 3100 B.C. the world entered into an age called by the Indians Kali Yuga or the Dark Age, which lasted until the turn of the twentieth century A.D. It was dark because direct perception of the spiritual worlds became by its end almost wholly extinct, surviving only in an infinitesimally small number of initiates. The teachings of older times were, however, preserved in mystery centers in which instruction was given, and rites of initiation were administered to those who had passed certain tests. Almost all peoples have preserved some mystery knowledge dating from ancient times when there was a direct perception of the spiritual worlds, but it was difficult to add to this knowledge in later times, and all the mysteries sooner or later became decadent. This decadence is especially visible in the historical evidence from ancient Egypt. In the early Pyramid Age it is clear that both kings and priests had a profound spiritual knowledge, whereas during the much later so-called New Kingdom some mystery knowledge was presumably preserved in the initiation centers, but popular religion guided by the priests became ever more superstitious and filled with magical practices. It should, however, be recognized that little accurate information about the mystery teachings has come down to us from antiquity since all initiates were pledged to a strict secrecy. It was not until Rudolf Steiner, and a few of his older contemporaries such as H.P. Blavatsky and G.R.S. Mead, who had a far less exact knowledge than he, began to reveal some of their teachings just before and after the end of Kali Yuga that any reliable knowledge of these mysteries became available to men.

34

With the beginning of Kali Yuga we reach the first historical records, and pass out of prehistory. From time to time we shall now be able to adduce some evidence for what has perhaps thus far appeared to be nothing but pontifical statements enunciated by Rudolf Steiner that cannot be substantiated in any way known to historians or scientists. The very heart of Steiner's teachings on the development of man in both historic and prehistoric times is his description of the evolution of human consciousness, and the development of new soul faculties at definite periods of time. When the historical records are studied with a view to tracing this evolution, I personally as a historian believe that the evidence is to be found, and it will be offered in the course of this chapter. According to Steiner, in the two post-Atlantean periods we have hitherto been considering, man was not as yet truly an ego being, an "I." His fourth "body" or principle, which we have thus far called his "ego," was not yet incorporated within him.* For this reason his consciousness differed from ours, being more pictorial and imaginative than our ordinary consciousness and without our clear perception of external reality. Even in the third post-Atlantean epoch, called Egypto-Chaldean by Steiner, it was still not possible for men to engage in intellectual thinking as the Greeks did; they could not speculate, nor did they look for explanations of earthly phenomena. Only toward the end of this epoch, as we shall see, did the Hebrews begin to approach self-consciousness, and prepare the way for the incorporation of the "I" within the other three bodies, which became possible for the majority of mankind only in the following epoch.

---

* In view of the current technical and popular use of the word "ego," we shall try to avoid its use as far as possible in this book, replacing it with "the self" or the "I," when feasible. In German there is no difficulty, since the word "Ich" is in current use and the Greco-Latin word "ego" is not needed. In German when Steiner uses the word "Ich" it will always be understood as referring to that fourth "body" or principle of man with which he was endowed for the first time in earth evolution as a gift of higher beings. When the word "ego" is used in this book as cannot sometimes be avoided it should *never* be equated with any of the meanings given to it either by psychologists or in popular parlance. Steiner himself described the ego as "that which says 'I' to itself."

The three historical epochs that we shall be discussing in the rest of this chapter are, as might be supposed, characterized by the ever greater influence of man's "I" on his other bodies. These three epochs are called by Steiner the ages of the sentient, intellectual, and consciousness souls. The sentient soul age lasted until about 747 B.C. with the founding of Rome; the intellectual soul age until 1413 A.D., and we are now a third way through the consciousness soul age, which is destined to end about 3513 A.D.* The use of the word "soul," which we have not needed to use up to this point requires a definition, since it is far from being identical with the meaning attached to it in popular thought or even by the Churches.

The human being may be described not only as a fourfold being (physical, etheric and astral bodies and the ego) as we have done, but also as a threefold being—possessing body, soul, and spirit.** He can, however, *never* be correctly described as a twofold being, consisting simply of body and soul, as most Churches regard him. Man's true self (ego) belongs wholly to the spiritual world, while his physical body belongs wholly to the material world to which it returns after death. Between the body and the spirit is the soul, which may be regarded as a mediator or bridge between them, and Steiner speaks of how it gathers treasures from the earthly experience to bestow on the spirit. The soul is not immortal, as the spirit is; after death it is gradually dissolved into the "soul world." Every newly incarnating human being creates for itself a new soul with the qualities needed for the fulfillment of its new destiny. All this will be explained more fully in Chapter 4.

In an individual human life the soul passes through successive

---

* Throughout this chapter the reader unfamiliar with historical chronology should find the brief chronological chart of antiquity useful (page 37).
** Steiner's fundamental book *Theosophy* (1904) describes man from this threefold point of view, and any serious student should attempt to view man also in this way by studying intensively the first chapter of this book, which also describes the three soul configurations (sentient, intellectual and consciousness) and the three higher spiritual faculties, which we possess as yet only in germ, but are to be developed through the course of earth evolution.

36

CHRONOLOGICAL CHART
of cultural epochs and important dates in antiquity, mentioned in text

	Historical data	Soul development
Before 7227 B.C.	Gradual sinking of Atlantis.	Physical body
c. 7227–5007	Ancient Indian Epoch	Etheric Body
6400 B.C.	Zarathustra the Prophet	
5067–2907	Ancient Persian Epoch	Astral Body
3500 B.C.	Sumerian temple communities and invention of writing	
3100 B.C.	Beginning of Kali Yuga	
3000–2200 B.C.	Old Kingdom in Egypt	
2907–747 B.C.	Egypto–Chaldean epoch	Sentient Soul
2000 B.C.	End of specific Sumerian civilization in Mesopotamia	
1760 B.C.	Hammurabi Code (Babylon)	
1450	Abraham	
1370	Religious revolution of Akhenaton in Egypt	
1250	Exodus of Hebrews from Egypt	
747 B.C.–1413 A.D.	Greco–Roman cultural epoch	Intellectual soul
747 B.C.	Founding of Rome	
538	Conquest of Mesopotamia by Cyrus the Persian	
332–330	Conquest of Egypt and Persia by Alexander the Great	
31 B.C.–14 A.D.	Caesar Augustus, first Roman emperor	
1413 onward	Fifth post-Atlantean cultural epoch	Consciousness soul
1899	End of Kali Yuga.	

All dates prior to intellectual soul are approximate, sometimes mere conjecture.

stages of development, and it ought to become ever more mature as the spirit or true self lays its impress on it and helps transform it. These stages are the same for individual men as they have been in history and will be in the future. We pass through in our own lives the age of the sentient soul, the intellectual soul, and the consciousness soul, but it was not possible before our present age for individual men to develop more than a germ of what was later to become the consciousness soul, nor could men develop for themselves the intellectual soul in the Egypto-Chaldean epoch, the age of the sentient soul.

In this latter age, as we have noted earlier, man could not as yet act independently as a fully self-conscious being because he had not yet incorporated his "I" within him. Even by the end of the epoch the more advanced human beings, for example the great leaders and prophets among the ancient Hebrews, cannot be regarded as fully autonomous. When they took action that we should think of as independent, it was under the inspiration of higher beings, especially Yahweh or Jehovah.* An apparently highly individualized Pharaoh such as the great "heretic" Akhenaton, who singlehandedly attempted to introduce a new religion into Egypt, himself claimed to be inspired by the god Aton. Nevertheless toward the end of this epoch we can glimpse the arrival on the world stage of recognizable human beings with marked personalities of their own, such as Saul and David among the Hebrews, and perhaps the Pharaoh Rameses II. With the Greeks and especially the Romans all this changes, and fully incarnated personages appear, self-reliant and autonomous, who think and act much as we do (or at least appear to do so). This change reflects the coming of the intellectual soul. By contrast, not only could the peoples of ancient Egypt and Mesopotamia not, properly speaking, think at all, nor speculate upon either themselves or the world, but even in their folk tales there are no clearly differentiated *characters*. The personages who appear in

---

* No satisfactory word exists in English for the Hebrew God, and all are compromises. Yahweh is used here following most historians in the English language.

these tales are all types, virtually interchangeable from story to story. They did not lack ethics and morality, but ethical and moral behavior was prescribed in accordance with instructions handed down from ancient times.

In the age before autonomous (or apparently autonomous) thinking, men perceived and *interpreted*, if the word may be used, the world through their feeling. Thus to the ancient Egyptian there was no contradiction when his literature provided him with many different stories of creation and assigned the deed to various gods. When Hathor, the cow-goddess, was said to have created the world, no doubt the Egyptians recognized what we should call the fruitfulness of the world and reverenced it accordingly; when another god made fast the boundaries of the earth and divided it from the heavens, we might say that its stability and permanence were accorded their due. When the god Ptah had a thought in his heart, and the thought was then spoken as a word and the world was created, the wisdom, order and intelligence behind the world were recognized. All these qualities, as we say, may indeed be predicated of the world, but all the creation stories cannot be equally true unless these gods cooperated with each other, of which there is no mention in the Egyptian records. Similarly, the Pharaoh after his death cannot be thought without contradiction to have ascended to heaven on a ladder, a beam of light, and in a boat. But no contradiction was presented to the Egyptians because contradiction belongs to thinking, not to the feelings. To the feelings each separate concept (as we call them) enriched the whole, and may increase our awe and reverence.

Indeed, it may be that polytheism is a necessary aspect of all religions prior to the development of abstract thinking; at all events monotheism appeared for the first time in history only toward the end of the sentient soul age. Monotheism, as introduced by the Hebrews, is essentially an abstract notion— one reason, no doubt, why so many of the Hebrews resisted it for so long. It has the effect of dissolving all those contradictions that are so important to *thinking* men. With one supreme god, all other minor "gods" must be subordinated to him, acting, like the angels in the Old Testament, as his servitors. Gods believed in by other peoples must be simply idols, as the later Hebrew prophets regarded them. Yet it should be understood that we do not make the claim that the Hebrews through processes of conscious thought came to the *conclusion* that there must be only one God. On the contrary, the Hebrew patriarchs, beginning with Abraham, were told by Yahweh that him alone must they worship, and in later centuries Moses and then all the prophets taught that there *was* only one God. But this was an inspiration given to these men by Yahweh himself, and one of its purposes was to prepare men for the coming of the self-conscious ego. Elijah's experience that God was not in the earthquake, or the whirlwind or the fire, but in the inner being of man (I Kings: 19) was a fundamental one, coming as it did at the end of the age of the sentient soul, and prefiguring what would come to be a primary experience common to the majority of men in the age that was to come. Monotheism was acceptable to the intellectual soul but not to the sentient soul; it was because the configuration of the soul changed that monotheism came into being. The concept was not, and could not be worked out by the sentient soul peoples themselves. When Akhenaton, ahead of his time, tried to change the Egyptian religion to one that was virtually monotheistic, he brought upon himself the wrath of all the polytheists of his era and his religion did not survive his death.

The Egyptian records make it clear that the early Pharaohs were guided wholly by inspiration, an inspiration explained by Steiner as due to overshadowing by higher beings. But by the end of the Old Kingdom the Pharaohs—and this is equally visible in the historical record—had lost this inspiration. The Sumerian leaders who founded Mesopotamian civilization received their inspiration through dreams, which originally they were able to interpret for themselves. Their successors, the Babylonians and Assyrians, lost their power of interpreting them. But in the case of both the Egyptians and the Mesopotamian peoples a tremendous treasure survived from the past into times when men were no longer naturally clairvoyant and had lost the art of interpreting dreams. Clairvoyance could still be acquired by initiation into the mysteries, at least in Egypt, and all these peoples were still able to celebrate the great cultic rites and festivals of the past, even if they had no longer the key to understanding their meaning. The Babylonians and Assyrians compiled dream books that were carefully preserved for centuries, in which were recorded the interpretations given by their predecessors; they also developed new methods for discovering the will of the gods that had not been available to the Sumerians, as, for example, through astrology, which required careful observations of the heavens.

Although in the centuries following 2000 B.C. direct inspiration was gradually lost, this did not mean that the myths that had been based on such inspiration were abandoned. The so-called myth of the Divine Kingship in Egypt had been based on actual reality during the Old Kingdom. At that time the Pharaoh was indeed ensouled by a higher being, as was true also of the earliest Sumerian leaders. It is no accident that all the great inventions of the sentient soul epoch were made during this early period. These inventions did not come into being by trial and error. They were actually inspired by higher beings who were working at this early period at the task of preparing man for his future life on earth. As long as the people were able to perceive supersensible beings with a greater clarity than they could perceive the earth and *its* beings, they were unable to orient themselves enough to earthly life to be able to make earthly inventions for themselves.

About 2200 B.C. the Old Kingdom of Egypt came to an end when the Pharaoh Pepi II lived to the age of almost 100, and apparently lost both his power and his relationship with the higher worlds on which Pharaonic power at that time was still based. What followed would in our time be thought of as a true revolution, but it was described in a peculiar and highly significant manner by the Egyptians. They state categorically that *Ma'at* had disappeared from the land, and this word in this context signified the disappearance of the established order and harmony of the universe. "He who never had a plank is now sleeping on a bed," the chroniclers complain, "he who never wove for himself is now the owner of fine linen, the former owners of fine robes are now in rags. Maidservants make free with their tongues; when mistresses speak it is burdensome to their servants. . . . The land spins around like a potter's wheel. The king's might can no longer be seen." Although foreigners did penetrate into the Delta region of Egypt, it does not seem to have been they who forced the monarch to leave his capital and take up his residence in a small city, from which he ruled with lessened and always uncertain authority; though nobles ruled in other cities and they may have played some part in the revolution, they seem merely to have moved into what we should now call a power vacuum. In other words the authority of the Pharaoh, which was apparently previously exercised with a minimum of force, was lost during this revolution, and it was never thereafter wholly recovered. When the interregnum was at last brought to an end and a new Pharaoh from the South took over the throne and reunited Egypt, it was proclaimed that Ma'at had been restored. But the old easy confidence was never quite regained, and it is difficult to resist the conclusion that the interregnum marked a turning point in Egyptian history. Thereafter the Pharaoh ruled with the aid of the priests, as had not been necessary for him when he was truly overshadowed by divine beings, and needed no priest to interpret his inspirations.

Although in later times Egypt built an empire, and the myth of the king-god was carefully fostered, it is difficult to think that the myth was now fully believed. But it remained a useful myth, from a political point of view, especially during the empire—as we can see from the texts in which rebels are warned of the danger of resisting a god's authority, since he has a god's power to punish. Whereas in earlier times it was a Pharaoh's duty to take his servants with him into the hereafter during which he would continue to care for them as on earth, now first the nobles and then the common people began to arrange for funeral

42

ceremonies for themselves that would ensure them a blessed hereafter. Such ceremonies naturally enriched the priests and enhanced their power. They sold suitable spells for use in the hereafter, and provided their clients with formulas to be repeated verbatim in the judgment hall of Osiris after death. All this does not mean that *only* corruption flourished among the priests. They did still possess a detailed knowledge of the nature of the afterlife, but the influence of Ahriman had permeated Egyptian wisdom, and however much we may admire the wisdom concealed in the texts, the decadence of the mysteries by the middle of the second millennium B.C. cannot be denied.

The actual mystery teachings that were revealed to those who had undergone the necessary tests are not known to us except from what Steiner has told us about them. As later in the Greek mysteries, ordinary people were given the truths of their religion in the form of myths, while what lay behind these myths was revealed only to the initiates who kept them secret. But Steiner does tell us that it became ever more difficult for the priests to receive any new knowledge from the spiritual worlds. Clairvoyance was disappearing, and only through certain magical practices connected with the mummies could contact be made with higher beings, and these were of a Luciferic or Ahrimanic character and might thus as easily deceive as enlighten them.* Characteristically enough, in the last years of Egyptian independence in the first millennium B.C. there was no new literary or religious writing of any importance, but hundreds of ancient texts were discovered and copied, and it is to the diligence of the copyists that we owe most of our knowledge of the work of earlier periods. Thus all creativity came to an end as the Egyptians passed over from the age of the sentient to that of the intellectual soul. All their inventions and all their religious literature had been based upon the spiritual knowledge accessible to the sentient soul, and they could not come to terms with

---

* See especially his lecture cycle *Supersensible Influences in the History of Mankind*, six lectures given in Dornach in September and October 1922 (London, 1956).

the new soul impulses of the new age. In the fourth century B.C. Alexander, one of the greatest figures of the age of the intellectual soul, conquered Egypt, and for many centuries thereafter all creative work in the country was performed by the Greek immigrants.

Meanwhile the enigmatic Pharaoh Akhenaton, to whom reference has been made earlier, had sat on the throne for the few years in the middle of the second millennium B.C., and singlehandedly set in motion a religious and artistic revolution that included what amounted to a virtual monotheism. But he himself was the sole inspiration for the revolution, and his successors abandoned his work. Indeed his very name was obliterated from the royal records. It is just possible that Moses was aware of this "monotheistic" tradition but there is no historical reason to think so; it may be best to consider the appearance of this Pharaoh in so apparently untimely a manner as an unexplained element in world destiny on which it would be impertinent to speculate.

The other leaders of the sentient soul epoch, the Sumerians and their Babylonian and Assyrian successors, did not found any great and long lasting civilization comparable to that of the Egyptians, and once the innovating and creative Sumerians had ceased to exist as a separate people, the priests do not seem to have inherited any great treasure of esoteric spiritual knowledge. The achievements of the Sumerians themselves, however, are the equal of those of the Egyptians, and their influence, even into our own times, must be considered even greater than that of their Egyptian contemporaries. Steiner (in Lecture 4 of his 1910 lectures published under the title, *Occult History*) tells us that the task of the Sumerians and their successors was to "lead the spiritual world down to the physical plane. Their fundamental achievement was the invention of writing, and the translation of thoughts that were, in them, still living, into symbols capable of being understood by the human mind." It is worth noting that experts in the Sumerian language, who are even today few in number, have emphasized the great difference between Sume-

44

rian and all other subsequent languages. As one such expert (J. S. Cooper of Johns Hopkins University) has remarked, "Not only is Sumerian totally different in structure from all Semitic languages, but it has never been successfully related to any known language, ancient or modern."

Steiner draws attention to the occult fact that at this time "a tone or sound evoked a definite feeling, and the soul was bound to express unequivocally what was felt in association with a particular thought and at the same time with a particular sound" (*Occult History*, p. 65). This language "bore a quite definite character and was intelligible to one who listened to it simply because of the nature of the soul." It may be imagined therefore what an extraordinary feat it was in these circumstances to create a written language, and it is perhaps not surprising that the language that resulted could not be inherited by subsequent peoples. Indeed, a text exists from a later Babylonian epoch where the writer remarks how difficult it is even for him (about 1800 B.C.) to understand Sumerian. The story of the Tower of Babel recorded in the Bible (Genesis: 11) tells us how the common language of mankind (presumably the original language spoken by the Sumerians but not the language as it was developed in order to be committed to writing) was "confounded," and how the various peoples thereafter spoke only their own tongues.

Scarcely less important was the creation of units for measurement based on cosmic phenomena. The unit 60 used by the Sumerians and Babylonians was not arbitrarily chosen but was obtained by multiplying the twelve signs of the zodiac and the five planets. By comparison, the 10 on which our decimal system is based is entirely arbitrary (to say nothing of being less *useful*, since 60, unlike 10, can be divided by 3). This people was the first to divide the circle into the 360 degrees we retain to this day, as we have also retained the 60 for measurements of time (minutes and seconds). Indeed, the fundamental belief of the Sumerians was that the earth is the microcosmic image of the macrocosmic heavens, and even the governmental forms used

45

on earth were believed to be the exact copy of those used by the gods in the heavens. It was thus no accident that when the Babylonians and Assyrians wished to know what to do on earth they studied the movements of the heavenly bodies, which if properly understood indicated what was to be done on earth. This astrology, which long preceded astronomy, nevertheless in time became a true astronomy. This was an achievement of these very peoples, but at a time when humanity had moved into the age of the intellectual soul, and they were aided in the task as we shall see by the intellectual soul people par excellence, the Greeks.

It may be noted here in parentheses that the Egyptians of the Old Kingdom were equally skilled in the practice of measuring, and they had a profound knowledge of the relationship between the microcosm and the macrocosm. These things were perceived intuitively in the epoch of the sentient soul, and, as Steiner says, experienced within their own organisms. Hence the Egyptians could build the pyramids, and even erect the obelisks as a picture of man as a being who stood upright, and do all this with the utmost "astronomical" precision. But it was not the task of the Egyptians, as it was of the Sumerians, "to lead the spiritual world down to the physical plane." Hence it was the Sumerians who gave writing to the world and the Sumerians who transmitted their systems of measurement to subsequent peoples.

The Egyptians, whose Pharaoh was regarded as a god who "knew the hearts of men," felt no need until late in imperial times for a written law to govern their social relationships. All law was made by the Pharaoh who, at least in theory, could from his own knowledge of Ma'at alter it at will, and his appointees gave judgments in accordance with their intuitive knowledge of the truth. By contrast the Sumerians, in accordance with their mission, did not rely on their dying clairvoyant knowledge, but wrote down their customary law for subsequent generations to use and modify as times changed. Many compilations of laws are extant from Mesopotamia, both laws of the Sumerian cities and then of the Babylonian empire. The famous

46

Hammurabi Code of the early second millennium B.C. was compiled by a foreign conqueror who, as might have been expected, claimed to have received the laws from the Babylonian god of justice, thus giving them a divine sanction. But the code is in fact derived from earlier Sumerian codes, to which he added laws of his own, as has been done by all lawgivers since his day.

Lastly, the story of Gilgamesh, recorded in an epic that continued to be reedited down to Assyrian times in the first millennium B.C., throws a considerable light on a change in consciousness that was already beginning in Sumerian times. It is surely no accident that in the ancient king-lists of the Sumerian cities all kings down to and including Gilgamesh himself reigned for what we must think of as improbably long periods, whereas Gilgamesh's son who succeeded him reigned for only thirty years and his immediate successors for even shorter periods. None of the later kings is credited with reigns of more than a hundred years. This peculiarity of the king-lists, when taken in conjunction with what we are told of Gilgamesh, strongly suggests that only at this period did man become truly aware of death, and experience it as a sorrowful event cutting man off from the fullness of his life on earth. In one ancient Sumerian poem the gods tell Gilgamesh on his deathbed that they have given him glory and power on earth, with which he must be content and not look for immortality also. In the famous Epic of Gilgamesh itself, which was not of Sumerian origin in any of our copies, Gilgamesh on the death of his friend Enkidu (called Eabani by Steiner and earlier scholars) suddenly comes to the full realization that men, including himself as well as his friend, are not immortal. Thereupon Gilgamesh sets out on a quest for the plant of immortality, which at last after many dangers and trials (an initiation) he finds, only to lose it again so that he cannot bestow it, as he had intended, on his people. The relationship with Enkidu in the poem is also highly significant. Enkidu is shown as a wild man who was hairy and lived close to the animals until he was seduced by a prostitute sent to him by

47

Gilgamesh, thus entangling him with the earthly plane, whereas before, according to Steiner, he had been clairvoyant. After this episode Gilgamesh and Enkidu wrestle together, but neither prevails. They therefore become friends, and go forth to kill a monster protected by the goddess Ishtar. They vanquish the monster, whom Gilgamesh wishes to spare. But Enkidu insists that it be slain, thereby incurring the wrath of Ishtar, who demands Enkidu's life in return. It was Enkidu's death that started Gilgamesh on his own initiation (his search for the plant of immortality), but Enkidu, whose own clairvoyance was atavistic, had to die while Gilgamesh went on to perform his task as ruler for the next hundred years—an initiated ruler but not one ruling through direct inspiration by higher beings.*

The continuity of Mesopotamian culture from the time of the Sumerian city-states onward is unmistakable, but nevertheless subtle changes have been pointed out by scholars, which, if rightly interpreted, mark the ending of the epoch of the sentient soul and the beginning of the intellectual soul, with its fuller incorporation of the human ego. What is most noticeable is the evidently declining ability of traditional religious beliefs to satisfy the by now personalized religious aspirations of the people. It appears clear from the records that from early in the first millennium B.C. individual Babylonians were becoming conscious of having personally "sinned" against the gods, and that they attributed their sufferings (as the Hebrews did later) to having in some manner disobeyed the gods. There is no indication that they were made unhappy or in any way criticized

* The above is an interpretation by the author of the *Epic* taken in conjunction with various Sumerian documents as they have come down to us. It should be noted that Steiner in the third lecture of his cycle *World History in the Light of Anthroposophy*, given in Dornach on December 26, 1923 (London, 1950) gives a different version of the story of Gilgamesh, which is presumably based upon the true facts behind the legends that have come down to us in so many different versions, but makes substantially the same interpretation. The difference between the surviving versions of the *Epic of Gilgamesh* and the story as told by Rudolf Steiner is especially interesting for the light it throws upon the relationship of popular legends to the esoteric truths they so often conceal.

48

themselves for their moral failures, but they did associate their sufferings with acts they had committed or duties they had failed to perform that had angered the gods. But the extraordinary thing that emerges from the many "penitential" psalms that are extant is the difficulty the Babylonians experienced in reconciling their new "moral" consciousness with their inherited beliefs in a polytheistic universe. One prayer is addressed to all the gods whom the sinner may have offended, including gods and goddesses whom he "knows or does not know!"

In one important document Marduk, the god of Babylon, is clearly regarded in much the same light as Yahweh was regarded by the Hebrews, that is, as the enforcer of justice on earth, with the crucial difference that in this case the sinner is totally unaware of how he has offended because in his view he had never failed in his religious observances, and, like his Hebrew prototype Job, was in all respects a righteous man. The same problem is adumbrated in several of the Hebrew Psalms, most notably Psalm 73. This consciousness of a personal relationship between man and God demonstrates clearly enough the change in consciousness that was beginning, and gives weight to our contention that monotheism is a necessary element in the intellectual soul, by contrast with the sentient soul, which felt itself at home in a polytheistic universe.

Parallel with this religious development in the last phase of Babylonian history we find advances in Babylonian mathematics marked by the ability to deal with mathematical abstractions, an ability that is absent in the earlier period. At the same time the old Babylonian astrology, which had amassed astronomical observations for centuries, while not disappearing, became closer to the scientific astronomy, which, in part with the aid of Babylonian thinkers, became a serious astronomical science in Alexandria after the conquests of Alexander. Thus the intellectual soul, which, as will be remembered, began about 747 B.C., and reached its full flowering among the Greeks, had a visible influence also in Mesopotamia as well as among the Hebrews, as will be discussed in the next section.

The above discussion has carried us forward a long way in time, making it necessary now to retrace our steps to the beginning of the world mission of the Hebrews, to which a brief reference was made earlier. The task of the Hebrews, according to Steiner, was to prepare the way for the full incorporation of the human "I," which in the third post-Atlantean epoch was not yet entirely within man, and did not enter him fully until well on into the period of the intellectual soul. The higher self of man, which made possible his future evolution as a morally free being capable of fulfilling the destiny envisaged for him by the gods, entered mankind only with the Christ; the preparation of a body capable of receiving the Christ spirit was a part of the Hebrew mission.

Moses lived at a time when the ancient Egyptian clairvoyance had disappeared, and perception of the spiritual worlds had long been darkened. Such spiritual knowledge as remained was locked up within the Egyptian mysteries, but even this could no longer be fully understood, even by the priests and initiates. Moreover, it had for centuries been corrupted by Ahrimanic influences, giving rise to all kinds of magical rites and practices. Yet on the other hand it was still too early for any human beings to bring to birth any new knowledge of the spiritual worlds from within themselves. Thus if a new impulse was to be given to mankind it was necessary for it to be given by direct revelation to persons who could be prepared to receive it, and for this purpose spiritual beings of great power had to concern themselves with this task. The spiritual being who undertook it was called by the Hebrews Yahweh or Jehovah who belonged to the hierarchy of the Spirits of Form, or Elohim (the fourth hierarchy above man).

The first revelation of this being was to Abraham, who was instructed to institute his worship, and he revealed himself also to Isaac and Jacob, Abraham's son and grandson. Jacob spent the last years of his life in Egypt, whither his son Joseph had preceded him. The Hebrews who went with him into Egypt and settled there stayed together as a people, retaining their worship of Yahweh, until the time came for them to settle in the land of Canaan. For the purpose of leading the exodus from Egypt a Hebrew, who had been brought up in the household of the Egyptian Pharaoh and been initiated into the secret mysteries of Egypt, was chosen. Moses received a direct revelation from Yahweh, who in answer to his question gave himself the significant name of the "I am," thus announcing the truth that the higher ego, or self, of man, was of a divine nature. This higher self, however, could not yet be born *within* man. It was given to him only through the incarnation, death, and resurrection of the highest spiritual being who concerns himself with man, the being to whom the name of Christ was given. Already, as Steiner tells us, this being was preparing for his incarnation and gradually approaching the earth, influencing already the earth and man from his dwelling place in the spiritual sphere of the sun. Yahweh or Jehovah, working from the spiritual sphere of the moon, reflected the Christ-Light from the sun, while preparing the Hebrews to receive the Christ when the time came for his incarnation.

The manner in which the Hebrews fulfilled their mission is, or used to be, one of the most familiar of all stories to Westerners, and its details need not concern us here. But when considering Hebrew history from the point of view of the evolution of human consciousness certain features of that history need to be stressed. The Hebrew task was the preparation for the coming of the Messiah, the Christ, or the true higher self of man, while at the same time through the observation of certain religious practices and rituals a suitable earthly vessel could be prepared through the generations for his incarnation on earth. In preparing for the full incorporation of man's "I" within him, it was first necessary for men to be told how this "I" would act when it was indeed incorporated. This was the purpose of the gift to the Hebrew people of the Ten Commandments, which consisted of a series of moral principles, which man was as yet incapable of evolving for himself from his own inner being. But once the Commandments and the rest of the Law was given, men could

51

act as if the moral principles were their own, and the Hebrew leaders could enforce these laws, see that they were obeyed. It was only later, during the age of the intellectual soul that these principles could be interiorized, so that men would feel they were *sinning* when they disobeyed any of the injunctions. But when Christ taught on earth, claiming indeed that he was only re-proclaiming "the Law and the Prophets" he actually gave to his disciples only two commandments, both positive, and incapable of being enforced: Thou *shalt* love the Lord thy God with all thy heart, and thou *shalt* love thy neighbor as thyself. Love of this kind cannot be compelled but only offered as a free gift, and it can be offered only by a morally free (and indeed Christ filled) "I." The possibility of developing *this* "I" came only with the Christ. The relation between the Mosaic Law and the two positive commandments of Christ was well understood and explained by St. Paul, who called the Law a "schoolmaster" (literally, *paidagogos,* or child-leader) to lead us to Christ (Galatians 3:24). After the coming of Christ, Paul says, all men had been given the possibility of freedom, and were no longer "in bondage to the Law," adding later in the same epistle (Galatians 5:14) that "all the Law is fulfilled in one word: Thou shalt love thy neighbor as thyself."

In the works of the great Hebrew prophets we can see the gradual recognition of the truth that the time was coming when men would assume full responsibility for their acts. We have noticed earlier how Elijah came through an inner experience to the understanding that God was within him and was not to be perceived in any outer phenomenon. The most striking statement of the truth that mere obedience to the Law was to be transformed into full inner recognition of moral responsibility is to be found in the prophesies of Jeremiah, who lived more than a century after the dawning of the intellectual soul. In a prophesy of the Messianic age of the future, Jeremiah, in the name of Yahweh, proclaimed a "new covenant," not like the covenant made with the Hebrews when he led them out of Egypt. In this new covenant Yahweh would "put my law within them and write it on their hearts" (Jeremiah 31: 31–33), a promise that was in fact fulfilled through the resurrection of Christ, as will be discussed in due course.

It should not be thought that the Hebrew prophets, even those as late as Jeremiah, were in any sense *thinking* out their ethics, as a Greek philosopher might do. They remained under the direction of, and inspired by Yahweh. Indeed, Jeremiah himself tells us (Jeremiah 1) that he had not wanted to be a prophet. When he received the summons from Yahweh, he pleaded that he was only a "child," and had no talent for speaking. Yahweh rebuked him for his faint-heartedness, telling him that he had been predestined for the task. Yahweh had known him while he was still "in the womb," and had set him apart to be a prophet before he had been born. Then, according to Jeremiah's account, he "stretched forth his hand and touched my mouth," saying, "See I put my words in thy mouth," and gave him "authority over the nations."

Similarly with the other late Hebrew prophets, who were specially summoned by Yahweh. But at the same time there was a growing literature among the Hebrews that is not prophetic in nature, and this it seems reasonable to ascribe to the intellectual soul, since it shares many of the characteristics of work performed by contemporaries in other countries where the new consciousness of the intellectual soul had come into being. This is the so-called Wisdom literature, of which *Ecclesiastes* is an example among the canonical books of the Old Testament, although most of its more important examples were relegated by the early Church Fathers to the Apocrypha. The Talmud and other Hebrew works of exegesis and learning are typical products of the intellectual soul. But it was above all the Greeks who brought this new consciousness to birth in its most characteristic form, and we shall devote considerable space to Greek culture and thought as typical products of this consciousness. Before coming to the Greeks, however, it is necessary to try to characterize this consciousness of the intellectual soul, which was attained by man at the mid-point of his earthly evolution.

This was no ordinary period in human history. During this epoch man completed his "descent" from the spiritual worlds and became fully incarnated as earthly man, and received the possibility of "ascending" again into the spiritual worlds, retaining his earthly consciousness that he had just acquired, but adding to it a consciousness of the spiritual worlds that it is his task to acquire for himself by his own efforts. The possibility of this ascent was provided by the entry of the new impulse into earth evolution that we call the "Christ impulse," a deed performed by a God, who became man and died as a man, and was resurrected, having thus linked himself for all eternity with the destiny of man. It is impossible to grasp the significance of the age of the intellectual soul without having at least some notion—inadequate though all that we can say here must be—of the meaning for human evolution of the deed of Christ.

From the eighth century B.C. onward the ancient clair-voyance and direct perception of the spiritual worlds, which had at one time been universal, were becoming increasingly dark-ened among at least the leading peoples in world evolution. Among various peoples far from the main stream of Western civilization some remnants of natural clairvoyance persisted even into the Christian era, and in various mystery centers it was still possible for initiates to acquire some clairvoyance of their own after suitable preparation, as well as receiving instruction in truths that had been preserved from earlier times by the priests of the mysteries. Some individuals here and there were also for a part of their lives overshadowed by higher beings and thus able to be inspired by them. But ordinary men now felt themselves fully at home on the earth and no longer directly aware of higher worlds and spiritual beings. They were in principle free to believe or disbelieve in them, and in any event to act as if they did not exist. But in fact Skeptics, Cynics, Sophists, Epicureans and other emancipated non-believers must have constituted only a small minority of men, even in the height of the Roman Empire, so great remained the weight of religious tradition and the social importance of religious ceremonial. Or, to put it another way, the human "I" was as yet so little accustomed to being on its own, it was so new in the world, that it could scarcely stand on its own without aid, and in any event the human soul sensed, however dimly, its links with the spiritual worlds. Faith, even though now unaccompanied by knowledge or direct perception, remained strong. The divine powers, in short, were preparing to let men strike out on their own in the world, but remained ready to give them all the help they could accept compatible with their freedom, to the end that they should not fall helpless victims to the lures of the hindering evil powers whose wish it was to prevent mankind from reaching its goal.

This danger was, and is, a real one. Loosened from the bonds linking them with the spiritual worlds, men could have plunged ever deeper into matter, and from having worshipped the gods because they were directly aware of them, they could have totally forgotten their divine origin and taken simply to worshipping *men*—deifying them either in their lifetimes or after their deaths. This was in fact the path chosen by the Romans when they began to deify their emperors and institute cults for their worship. But just at this moment the possibility was given to men to take the upward path back to the spiritual worlds, no longer as unfree beings, but as beings who, knowing both good and evil, can from their own intuition choose the good, and who in the fullness of time can come to a *conscious* knowledge of the spiritual world that they will have acquired for themselves by their own efforts.

Steiner tells us many times and in many different contexts that what he calls the Mystery of Golgotha, the death and resurrection of Christ, was a deed of the divine worlds performed on the human stage, and that it can never be fully understood by men. How indeed is one to understand an event by which the earth itself was changed, so that to spiritual sight it appeared to *shine,* from the moment that the blood from the pierced side of Christ penetrated the earth? More will be said on the nature of the Christ impulse in Chapter 5, and all that need be said here is that with the resurrection the possibility was given to man to fulfill the mission originally purposed for him by the gods and to become a truly free being. As long as men had an actual perception of the spiritual worlds and knew from their own experience and knowledge that they were guided by higher beings, then they could not be truly free. It was necessary that this knowledge should be taken away from them and the spiritual worlds darkened if they were to find within themselves their own higher being, which, from the time of the Mystery of Golgotha, had become capable of being filled by the Christ. St. Paul had an accurate realization of what had happened, when he wrote to the Galatians (2:20), "I am crucified with Christ, nevertheless I live; yet not I but the Christ liveth in me, and the life which I now live in the flesh I live by the faith of the Son of God."

Yet it is a part of the mystery of man's freedom that the Christ, who can, as St. Paul says, live within man from the time of the Mystery of Golgotha, does not take away man's own autonomy. When man performs a good deed it is his own, as also are his evil deeds. It is not the Christ who performs the good deed, but it is man's task to become aware of the Christ within him and invite his aid. Such aid is increasingly necessary in our time because the evil powers are in no way inhibited from interfering with man's freedom—both Lucifer, who tells him that he can be a god if he makes the effort and follows him, and Ahriman, who tells him that he is *only* a man, that he himself is the lord of the earthly world, but that he can reveal all its secrets to men if they are prepared to listen to him.

The Mystery of Golgotha took place at the very center of earth evolution, at a point in time that coincided with the first deification of the Roman emperors, and it should be recognized that the upward evolution of man following the Mystery should continue slowly until the end of earth evolution. As Christ told his disciples after the resurrection, "Lo, I am with you always even to the end of the world" (Matthew 28:20). He entered earth evolution at this moment in time, but he will remain until its end, and though the possibility for upward spiritual evolution was then given to man, the evolution of human consciousness was not thereby suddenly speeded up. The age of the intellectual soul, which was only a third completed, continued to its appointed end in 1413 A.D., when it was replaced by the consciousness soul, which at the present time has also been one third completed. It is now necessary to attempt to characterize these two soul configurations, just what they are and were in themselves and in what respects they differ.

It is a specially difficult task to try to describe the intellectual soul because it possesses several facets of more or less equal importance. This diversity is indeed reflected in the three different names Steiner gave to it, none of them giving us any precise concept when translated into English. The word intellectual or mind soul emphasizes the fact that for the first time in human history man became capable of thinking for himself. One consequence of this possibility was the creation of philosophy. Man in the age of the consciousness soul (unlike the sentient soul, which preceded the intellectual soul) also thinks and philosophizes, but he does so in a different manner, as we shall try to show. There is, indeed, a characteristically intellectual soul method of thinking, and a characteristic consciousness soul method. Another name given by Steiner to this soul is the "understanding" soul, and a third name is the "responsive" soul. Although, to the author's knowledge, Steiner did not specifically explain these two alternative terms, the German word for the last named soul, translated in English as "responsive," was *Gemütseele*, which includes the typically German concept of the *Gemüt*, which has no English equivalent. When a series of lectures given by Steiner and entitled *Anthroposophy and the Human Gemüt* came to be translated, the translator offered two alternative renderings: (1) the mind warmed by a loving heart and stimulated by the soul's imaginative power, and (2) the soul in a state of unconscious intuition arising from the working together of heart and mind. This second meaning perhaps comes close to what Steiner meant by the "responsive" soul, and it was

57

indeed a prevalent soul mood during the height of Greek civilization, and also in the Christian Middle Ages, the two civilizations that begin and end the intellectual soul epoch. Few would claim that we are now living in an epoch suffused with this particular soul quality, and indeed it would hinder the attainment of that "objectivity" that is so greatly treasured in our modern age.

It seems to me that the "understanding" soul has also a strong element of intuition in it. Today we are inclined to think we have "understood" something when we have discovered how it works, and what are the parts that compose it—perhaps also when we believe we have understood its historical antecedents, or what we think are causes. But in earlier epochs such information would not have been considered sufficient for understanding a phenomenon. Aristotle, in particular, required the investigation of what he called a final cause, which is akin to purpose. At all events it seems scarcely to be doubted that we understand in a different manner from our historical forbears, and our intelligences are satisfied by different kinds of explanations from those accepted by the Greeks and medieval Christians. By giving the term "understanding soul" to the epoch preceding ours, it seems to me that Steiner was indeed suggesting that these men, though *knowing* incomparably less than we, yet may have *understood* more, difficult though it may be for us to accept this possibility.

By contrast, the consciousness soul is characterized especially by objectivity, which results from the ability of the self in this age to withdraw completely from the subject he is studying. For this reason Steiner has also spoken of this soul as a "spectator" soul. While earlier peoples felt themselves to be integrally linked with the external world, which was indeed not seen at all as a separate entity until comparatively late in history, to us the world is seen as totally separate from us, and therefore as something to be understood in itself, apart from man—hence the importance of the modern philosophical problem, how can the subjective "mind" know the objective world? To some extent

58

modern men can also view *themselves* objectively, and in any event are always making the effort to do so. Hence our new fields of study: The analysis of the human soul (psychoanalysis), human behavior (psychology and anthropology), and the like. Most important of all, are our practical efforts to make use of our acquired objective knowledge to change the external world and man in accordance with our subjective ideas. In this modern age our self-consciousness has increased immeasurably as well as our consciousness of the external world, so that there is little need to explain the use of the term "consciousness soul" to describe our present epoch.

None of the names given to the intellectual soul (the name we shall be using here, as the most widespread term in English) stress one of its most important features, though the entire history of the evolution of human consciousness as it has been discussed in this chapter will explain it. The ego had so recently been incorporated in the human being that few men by the eighth century B.C. had begun truly to experience themselves as "I." Throughout the entire epoch of the intellectual soul that ended, as we have mentioned, as recently as 1413 A.D. not many men or women did come to experience themselves in this way. Throughout this period the consciousness of being a member of a group was far stronger than the consciousness of being an individual. We shall call this pre-ego consciousness a "group soul" consciousness. Clearly enough it persists to the present day in most peoples of the world, and even in the West where on the whole consciousness has evolved the furthest; the feeling called "nationalism," an emotional awareness of belonging to a particular nation, may often lead to the complete submersion of the individuality, to say nothing of the forgetting of all awareness of being also a member of humanity. Even now, isolated individuals truly emancipated from "tribal" or group soul feelings, and able to act with complete inner and outer independence are extremely rare, and in the intellectual soul epoch can scarcely be said to have existed—with one single exception in ancient Athens, Socrates, who was in this respect so

59

exceptional that a full discussion of him will be given later. This will reveal much about not only the consciousness of his own day but wherein ours differs from it.

The Greeks were the people above all who brought the impulse of the intellectual soul to mankind, and although most Greeks for a long time continued to live within the sentient soul, it is to the work of the leaders of all aspects of Greek culture that we must look to discover the nature of this new soul configuration. Since our primary task here is to indicate how the older consciousness gave way to the new, we shall give a little attention to each of the main aspects of Greek life and culture in the attempt to reveal this change, subtle as it often was and slow as it had to be.

It has always been recognized by historians that the Greeks did not think and act in the same way as their predecessors, and they have always drawn attention to the Greek interest in all kinds of novelties, and to the manner in which they so largely freed themselves from traditional thinking. It is usually pointed out that the Greeks, unlike the Egyptians or Babylonians, were oriented toward this world and this earthly life. For this reason they have often been considered to be a people less religiously inclined than their predecessors. There is some truth in each of these propositions, but what must be recognized is that the ego or self was now for the first time becoming fully incarnated in at least the leading Greeks. Indeed, all Greeks to a greater or lesser extent experienced themselves as separate from the world around them, a world that could now be apprehended with reasonable clarity through the senses. Whereas Homer, who lived at the beginning of the new age, still had some difficulty in distinguishing colors as we do (this fact has often been pointed out), and allowed none of his characters in either the *Iliad* or the *Odyssey* to take action independently of the gods, in later Greek poetry the gods were more distant, and by the time of the Sophists and Euripides in the fifth century B.C. they were even being criticized by leading Greek thinkers. A few centuries later their very existence was being denied. It seems worthwhile, however, to draw attention to the fact that Homer chose for the hero of his later poem, the *Odyssey*, a man who was always singled out by his fellows for his cleverness, and his capacity for thought. Such qualities belong to the intellectual soul, and it is no accident that the greatest Greek poet, whose work ushers in the new epoch, should have glorified them. Though Odysseus is always advised by the goddess Athena (who sprang from the *head* of Zeus), he is more strongly individualized than any of the heroes of the *Iliad*, is less dominated by his emotions than a half-divine hero like Achilles, and is more emancipated from his group soul than the Trojan hero Hector.

It would clearly take us too far if we were to attempt to discuss all aspects of Greek life and thought, even those that have a definite bearing on the new consciousness of the intellectual soul. But it is hoped that the relatively few indications given here will stimulate other students to examine other aspects of Greek culture for themselves, thus enabling them to come to their own conclusions as to how this new soul manifested itself in the various individual Greeks and in the different aspects of their culture. Here we shall deal only with a few.

Political Life. Whereas the ancient Egyptians, Babylonians and Hebrews, peoples of the sentient soul, were all in greater or less measure guided by higher beings during the earlier phases of their development, and in later years retained the same form of government that had been appropriate at an earlier time, none of the Greek city-states remained long content with retaining the traditional monarchy of the sentient soul. Though most did not go so far as to install democracies of the Athenian type (or if they did install them they did not for long retain them), all went at least as far as to replace the monarchies by oligarchies. Indeed, the Greeks regarded the Macedonians and Persians as notably backward because they clung to their monarchies.

This political change is of the highest significance. Absolute monarchy had rested on the unquestioned belief of the people in the infallibility of the monarch, which he owed to his possession of divine attributes. Oligarchies and democracies of the Greek type are based on the implied belief in a collective wisdom, whether the wisdom of an aristocratic minority or the entire citizen body. Greeks regarded inhabitants of other cities as alien foreigners, but their devotion to their own city-states was unbounded. Exile was always regarded as a fearsome punishment, scarcely less severe than death. For this reason many exiles who had been banished for political reasons from their cities either by a particular oligarchic group or by the people as a whole intrigued constantly in the hope of overthrowing the government that had banished them, so that their sentence might be commuted and they themselves be permitted to return. Away from their particular city all Greeks felt in some measure lost. Thus, in effect, government by the gods through a single inspired ruler gave place to a kind of government by group soul through the collective will of the citizens, or of a group of citizens. The group soul patriotism characteristic of the Greek cities remained the norm throughout the fourth post-Atlantean epoch, and it has been and remains one of the tasks of the consciousness soul age to transcend it.

From Religion to Philosophy. In the entire history of human thought nothing is more crucial than the transition in Greek thinking from the traditional religious notions accepted without any real questioning by all previous peoples, including religious explanations of earthly phenomena, to the skeptical attitude of mind characteristic of the various thinkers of the third century B.C. onward. The explanation for this epoch-marking change is, of course, the gradual incorporation of the human ego. But it remains extremely interesting to perceive the manner in which this incorporation manifested itself over the centuries.

Throughout Greek history there were always two different forms of religion, the mysteries, with their secret teachings, and the popular religion and myths, which in no way contradicted the mystery teachings, but were a kind of external picture of them. These teachings could not be *understood* without the aid of the key given by the mysteries, but could be accepted into the human feeling, thus satisfying the religious longings of the majority of the people.* The content of the mystery teachings must on no account be divulged to the populace. Yet probably all the great dramatists had been initiated into the mysteries, and it was their task to convey the hidden truths through their art in such a way that the audience that participated in the tragic drama (given in Athens at the festival of Dionysus, the god who was the patron and hidden teacher of the mysteries) obtained an experience of *katharsis* or purgation (itself a kind of religious experience) without actually being able to *understand* the truths that lay behind the myths reenacted in the tragic drama.

The tragic drama was therefore through and through religious, even the drama of the most skeptical of the three great Athenian dramatists, Euripides. Indeed, the influence of the intellectual soul is clearly to be seen in the work of Euripides, especially in his questioning attitude toward traditional religious teachings. Throughout his plays is the spoken or unspoken but implicit question—if the gods are as we have been taught, then surely they are, by human standards, unjust. If this is so, Euripides implies, then human beings are the helpless victims of divine injustice. Whereas Aeschylus and Sophocles portray the grandeur of human beings in the grip of a malignant destiny, often through little apparent fault of their own, Euripides takes pains to show them exactly as they really are in life, suffering misfortune with despair, resignation or complaint, as the case may be. This contrast is especially noticeable when Euripides treats the same subject as one or both his great predecessors. His Agamemnon in his *Iphigenia in Aulis* is a scheming ambitious man who is willing to sacrifice his daughter to ensure a favorable wind for the expedition to Troy for no higher reason than his desire to remain its leader, while the Agamemnon of Aeschylus' trilogy, though ruthless and overbearing enough and too proud for his own good, certainly does not lack elements of grandeur,

---

* The relation of the mystery teachings to the popular religion forms one of the major themes of Steiner's book *Christianity as a Mystical Fact.*

and his murder by his wife and her lover is clearly a part of the tragic destiny of his whole family. But perhaps the most important contrast is one often referred to by Rudolf Steiner because it marks the beginning of conscience and the first use in any language of a word for it.

Orestes, the son of Agamemnon and Clytemnestra, is told by the gods, especially Apollo, to avenge his father's murder. This entails the killing of his mother, a crime regarded as one of special horror in ancient Greece. For such a crime the murderer was pursued by beings known as the Furies, irrespective of the provocation for the crime, and even of the commandment laid upon the murderer by the gods. In Aeschylus' play the *Eumenides*, Orestes is pursued all over the earth by the Furies until at last he takes sanctuary in the temple of Athena in Athens, where the Furies can no longer touch him until he has been tried before the goddess Athena for his sacrilegious act. In this trial Orestes is defended by Apollo, but he does not win a clearcut verdict, since the votes of the jury are equal, leaving Athena herself to make the final decision. Before she can free Orestes she has to find a way of pacifying the Furies, which she does by converting them from Furies to tutelary spirits of Athens or "Eumenides." Then Orestes is freed from the consequences of his sin.

In Euripides' play the *Orestes* there are no external beings who pursue the murderer, but he wanders nevertheless all over the earth as before, until he reaches Sparta where his uncle Menelaus gives him hospitality, and tries to commiserate with him. "Why are you suffering?" he asks the unfortunate man, and Orestes replies, "It is my conscience (*synesis,* which etymologically means a kind of intuitive knowing) because I know (the same word in its verb form) that I have done terrible things." No longer were there external, if non-physical, beings to pursue the murderer, but an internal mentor that told him of his wrongdoing and persecuted him for as long as he lived. In the early fifth century, when Aeschylus lived and wrote his plays, the human conscience had not yet become incorporated within the human being. By the end of the same century Euripides used a word for it, and no doubt had a personal experience of it, while Socrates, the close contemporary of Euripides was describing a not dissimilar, but in fact significantly different internal mentor that he called his daimon.

Socrates and Euripides were both born into and worked in an intellectual milieu dominated by the Sophists, a group of men who in effect abandoned all traditional religious beliefs on the grounds that, as Protagoras, one of the first Sophists, expressed it: "Man is the measuring rod for all things, of things that are that they are, of things that are not that they are not." Whatever Protagoras himself may have meant by his dictum, it was interpreted, as Plato tells us (*Cratylus*, 386), to mean that there is no objective reality, that "wisdom is indistinguishable from folly," and that because "what appears to each man is true to him one man cannot be wiser or even better than another." "Things do not have a permanent essence of their own."

From such premises as these the Sophists concluded that all traditional beliefs and morality were no longer to be taken seriously, and they used their newly awakened intellectual capacity to criticize them unmercifully, in the process using the most ingenious, not to say outrageous arguments. Many of them became teachers, training especially the young to enable them to win cases in the lawcourts and influence policy in the Assembly through dazzling displays of verbal expertise.

All this was most distasteful to the conservative upholders of tradition, and the Sophists made many enemies. Nevertheless it was an important step toward human progress and intellectual freedom when men began, particularly in Athens, to teach their fellow citizens to question all long held assumptions, even though in the process they committed many excesses. It was against these excesses that Socrates set himself, and, unlike the Sophists, he was not prepared to go forward all the way to skepticism, even though no one criticized more severely than he the conservative tendency to defend indefensible assumptions just because they had long been accepted as eternal verities. The famous Socratic method, known as the dialectic, consisted in reducing such assumptions to absurdity through rigorous questioning, following this destructive work by an equally rigorous attempt to find what really did exist in the human mind that was true and beyond any questioning. He held that such knowledge was innate, and that it was his task to "bring it to birth" by means of the dialectic, in this acting as he said, as a "midwife of knowledge." Such true knowledge had, of course, nothing to do with perceptions of the outer world, which would appear different to different people and might be subject to illusion; on the contrary it consisted of universal ideas, such as beauty and goodness, and indeed all abstract ideas, none of which, he held, could be derived from sense perceptions. They must therefore have been already existing in the soul at birth.

How much of this epistemology was actually held by Socrates can never be known, since he himself did not write a word, and it was Plato who ascribed it to Socrates. According to Plato the soul had perceived these ideas in the heavenly world before it incarnated in the "prison-house" of the body, and it was one of man's tasks to become conscious of them, which was the purpose of the Socratic dialectic. Since it was therefore possible to come to a knowledge of the good, the absolute good that was a spiritual "form" or idea, men did not necessarily have to accept traditional ideas of the good. At least philosophers could determine the good for themselves and pursue it, as long as they did not allow their emotions to deflect them from their chosen path. Thus, in effect, Socrates and Plato were trying to repair the damage wrought by the Sophists by providing their fellow Greeks with an ethical system that could replace, at least for philosophers, the traditional morality inherited from their forefathers. For the purposes of our study it should be noted only how completely this system is dependent upon the intellect, and one should not miss the assumption that if the good is known, (*to the mind*), it can be pursued, as long as reason allows the pursuit through keeping a tight rein on the emotions. It may also be noted here that Plato defines courage as "the *knowledge* of what ought and what ought not to be feared," surely a definition that would scarcely occur to a modern man, though not unexpected in a Greek. Few Greeks of the fifth and fourth centuries B.C. were as emancipated from tradition or as fully individualized as Socrates. Whereas Plato, as a mystic, often filled his dialogues with knowledge taken from the mysteries, Socrates does not appear to have been a mystic at all, though Plato shows him in several of his dialogues making allusions to the mysteries as if he knew something of their content. But Socrates did speak of his own personal *daimonion* or little daimon who accompanied him and always told him what not to do while refraining from advising him on any positive action. Such a being would seem to be of the nature of a guardian angel of whom Socrates was aware, and not to be merely a figurative description of that conscience of which Euripides had been aware. The daimonion of Socrates did not counsel him against evil deeds in particular, but against acts that were morally quite neutral.

Rudolf Steiner in his book *Christianity as Mystical Fact* (Chapter 2) has thrown some light on the daimon as it was understood in the mysteries. Several writers indeed have referred to the daimon in relation to the mysteries, but without further explanation. Steiner speaks of it as the higher self of man, who is awakened through initiation, and in a striking passage even refers to it as the "son of God" that was born freshly in each human soul during initiation. If Socrates himself had indeed been initiated, he would scarcely have dared to refer openly to this secret of the mysteries when he referred to his own daimonion. He was indeed criticized by his enemies for "making new gods" when he spoke of his daimonion, but was never, as far as is known, accused of betraying the mysteries.

What seems to have been true of Socrates is that he was a highly developed man, with his "I" fully incorporated within him, perhaps the first of such men to be incarnated in the Greek civilization, who discarded all traditional moral teachings in favor of what his own inner being dictated to him. Having lived

67

an exemplary life, which included the performance of all his formal religious and civic duties, he was finally accused by his enemies, who no doubt resented his total independence of thought and action, of corrupting the youth, and in effect, of being an atheist. Plato in his *Apology* provides us with a moving account of how Socrates defended himself to the jury by explaining what he had done throughout his life and his motives for doing it. The jury condemned him to death, and though he could have gone freely into exile, he took the position that he was an Athenian citizen and, as such, had no right to break Athenian laws. Nor should he now behave at the age of seventy as if life were the most important thing and his integrity of lesser importance. So he accepted the sentence, and, as he was awaiting the executioner with the poison for him to drink, he discoursed to his disciples on immortality, making it clear that in his belief he was simply moving from one life to another, a better one, for which exchange there was no reason for them to sorrow. Such words, spoken while his death was imminent, show that his life and teachings were a true unity, and had an evidently most potent effect on his auditors, who included Plato among their number. Or, to put it another way, that at this moment of death he and his daimonion were one, and he had in effect become an initiate without having passed through the mysteries. The daimon, or higher self, (or Son of God) had been born within him.

This was as far as mankind could progress until the advent of Christ on earth, for, as we shall see, after the resurrection Christ himself became the higher self of man. In the beginning of the fourth century B.C. when Socrates died, Christ himself was in fact approaching the earth, making it possible for Socrates to have the experience of the higher self within him in the manner in which it would be possible for all men to have it during the centuries since the resurrection.

Plato, by contrast, was certainly an initiate, and from past lives had reached a high degree of spiritual development (as was the case also, of course, with Socrates). But Plato's teachings, deeply spiritual as they were, were not perfectly suited for the age of the intellectual soul as it was to develop. His theory of ideas, for example, was not specially helpful for the intellectual road that had to be followed in the future, nor was the search for "perfect ideas" of beauty, truth and goodness likely to lead to a usable ethics to replace the now outdated traditional ethics that were in the process of being abandoned by Greek intellectuals. What was needed was indeed for spiritual truths to be brought down to the earthly level so that they could be understood by men who were not initiated. The newly achieved power of creating abstract ideas and thinking abstractly (which had not been possible in the age of the sentient soul) had to be understood and made intelligible. Platonism would always be a philosophy for the mystic and would-be mystic, but it did not really provide *explanations* for earthly phenomena, including human thought processes, however fully it provided nourishment for men's souls. Plato's account of creation given in the *Timaeus* is mythological, not metaphysical, and the developing intellectual soul was deeply interested in metaphysics. It was Aristotle who provided this soul with its new material for study, and, as has always been recognized, brought so many of Plato's teachings down to an earthly level.

Nevertheless, Steiner tells us that Aristotle was himself a great initiate and a highly developed individuality who had already passed through important previous earth lives. It was precisely because of this spiritual background that he was able to perform his difficult task of transmuting the living ideas and thoughts of his predecessors into material satisfying to the analytical mind that was coming into existence, the kind of mind, indeed, that Aristotle himself possessed in a highly developed form. So Aristotle invented the science of logic, which deals with the correct relationships among ideas, and he proposed a theory of knowledge, close to that of Plato, but with a refinement that totally changed its orientation. Whereas Plato had held that abstract ideas, or archetypes, are exclusively of a spiritual nature, and can be attained by man only by "bringing them to birth" within him, so that all such knowledge is really recognition of what had been experienced before birth, Aristotle taught that the human mind can draw forth (ab-stract) the universal ideas from the sense perceptible objects, precisely because these objects contain both a physical element (perceptible to the senses) and a non-physical element (perceptible only to the non-physical mind or Nous). The student of Rudolf Steiner's philosophy will recognize the similarity of this theory to Steiner's own epistemology, as explained in his *Philosophy of Freedom*.

Whereas Plato in his *Timaeus* gave an account of creation drawn from the mysteries, Aristotle considered the question of creation from a philosophical point of view. His theory expressed in his *Metaphysics* that all motion was communicated by one object to another required logically the postulation of a First Mover, himself unmoved; the metaphysical principle that everything in the world is caused by something else logically required a First Cause, itself uncaused; while the principle that everything in the world is contingent, that is, it might not have been there, requires a Necessary Being. These three principles were used in the High Middle Ages by Thomas Aquinas as his first three proofs for the existence of God (*Summa Contra Gentiles*). By even the fullest deductions from them, however, Aristotle did not feel it possible to posit a creation in time, even though he did equate his First Mover and First Cause with God. Indeed, he was still too much impressed by the argument of his predecessor Parmenides that Nothing was inconceivable, to suppose that there ever could have been a Nothing, before there was a Something—the world. Thomas, following him in this respect, concluded that Creation could not be *proved*. But since the Bible had given the true story of Creation, it could be *believed*, as a revelation inspired by God.

These metaphysical proofs for the existence of God are typical of the intellectual soul, and Thomas Aquinas, who was born at the end of the intellectual soul period was perhaps the most distinguished representative of this soul at its furthest development. Such proofs differ from those acceptable to the conscious-

70

ness soul mainly because no proof is adduced from the outside world. The activity of pure thinking, without the need for evidence, was sufficient for intellectual soul philosophers, and when some medieval thinkers began to feel the need for reinforcing knowledge with evidence, even experimental evidence (as, for example, Roger Bacon) this was an indication that the age of the consciousness soul was approaching. Indeed, it is interesting that Thomas did not think much of his own fifth proof for the existence of God, namely, that the world was so marvellously designed that it presupposed a divine intelligence behind it. Such an argument, by contrast, was found much more satisfactory by more recent philosopher scientists, as for example Isaac Newton, and by the eighteenth century deists.

As a last example of the kind of "terrestrializing" of knowledge performed by Aristotle, his ethics may be adduced. Whereas Plato and Socrates had held that individual men must so develop themselves that they can come to a knowledge of the good, and Socrates, at least, had held that if one knows the good one can pursue it, Aristotle in his *Ethics* went into much detail as to how men were diverted from their ethical goals by the various passions, while at the same time propounding an end for man that was no abstract Good, but happiness. This led him to consider the nature of happiness, how it differed from pleasure, and the like. He concluded that true happiness consisted in the *intellectual* contemplation of truth—a perfect conclusion for the pioneer of intellectual soul thinking.

Science and Scientific Philosophy. The earliest Greek thinkers who lived long before Socrates already gave unmistakable indications of the change of consciousness that was beginning to operate in Greece. Unfortunately, we know little of what these men thought and wrote; indeed, most of our information about them comes from Aristotle himself, who in the first book of his *Metaphysics* has given us a kind of history of early Greek philosophy. It is therefore not at all certain exactly what they themselves actually meant, since their ideas were filtered through the sophisticated mind of Aristotle, who lived so much

71

later than they. Moreover, the Greek language did not as yet possess any abstract nouns capable of expressing philosophical thought; most of these were actually created by Plato and Aristotle, who also made use of existing nouns but gave them new meanings.

The great question posed by Thales of Miletus and his immediate successors was: "Out of what did all things come?" At least, this is the literal translation of their question as they formulated it. Both in Greek and English the question is ambiguous—out of what material, or from what beginning? Thales gave the answer "water" or wateriness (literally, the wet things!), Anaximenes suggested air or airiness, Anaximander limitlessness, and Heraclitus forthrightly proposed fire. A little later Anaxagoras spoke of "seeds or germs, infinite in number," Empedocles of four elements, earth, air, fire and water, and finally Leucippus and Democritus suggested atoms that floated around in the void.

Numerous scholars have tried to interpret all these suggestions, and to give reasons why this or that substance was preferred. For our purposes here it is important only to note that, in the first place, this *kind* of explanation is quite new in history. Hebrews and earlier Greeks would never have thought of giving purely material explanations for "coming into being" and for "changing appearances." Barely a century before Thales, Hesiod was still explaining such things in mythological terms, and indeed much later Plato in his *Timaeus* gives his mythological account of creation, showing little or no interest in the kind of explanation given by his older contemporary Democritus. These pre-Socratics may have been speaking of some primeval substance, or some primeval condition of form; in any event they were no longer speaking of anything so vague as the Greek chaos or the Hebrew formlessness. With the exception of Anaximander they wished to go back in thought to a real material substance that existed in the beginning and gradually changed its form.

A second important characteristic of these explanations is to be found in almost all science of the intellectual soul period, right down to the end of the Middle Ages: the theory cannot be checked by experimental evidence, and the thinker does not propose his explanation in such a way that it is even in principle verifiable. The primary requirement of intellectual soul explanations is that they be satisfying only to the intellect. They should preferably be elegant, and whether or not they are true or can be verified by evidence is seldom of much interest. Still less is there any question of practicality; knowledge in the age of the intellectual soul did not have to be useful. This is not to say that the Greeks did not observe well. Greek astronomy was based on a great number of careful observations, made both by Greeks and by Babylonians. But there were never enough observations to be able to support a convincing theory. In short, it was a Greek trait to jump prematurely to conclusions, some of them marvellously elegant, but always arrived at by the sudden mental leap that we call intuition rather than by painstaking observation and experiment as a result of which compelling and convincing conclusions might have been reached. This applies even to Aristotle, by far the most empirical of the Greek scientific thinkers of the classical age who did carefully study at least the world of birds and animals. Even so, almost all his mistakes were the result of premature generalization and explanation.

It must be conceded that the Greeks as a people had an astonishing gift for striking generalizations (almost always, in our view, premature and on the basis of insufficient data). We may think of Thucydides, the Athenian historian, writing about the nature of *all* revolutions on the basis of the handful he had observed; of Aristarchus proposing, contrary to the evidence of the senses, that the earth moved around the sun, more than a millennium before the mathematics necessary to support this hypothesis was invented; or Democritus proposing his atomic theory of matter, and describing the size, shape and movement of the different atoms, without having performed the very least experiment or calculation, or having even thought it necessary to

73

produce evidence for his theory. In the light of these observations it will seem quite natural that the Greek science par excellence should have been geometry, not the practical geometry at which both Egyptians and Babylonians excelled but theoretical geometry, which is, after all, a mental construction. Thales of Miletus is credited with having proposed the first theorem—that in *all* triangles the angles subtending equal sides are equal to one another (as we should express it). Thales had not seen *all* triangles, or, if it comes to that, he had never even seen one perfect triangle, since perfect triangles cannot be constructed by man. But his proposition was true for theoretical or ideal triangles. Similarly for all the theorems compiled by Euclid about the turn of the third century B.C. The proofs for the various propositions are always based ultimately on one or more axioms. But these axioms are mental constructions that the mind (or, at all events the intellectual soul) feels compelled to accept. All are generalizations, but scarcely premature ones, since they at least are based on numerous approximate observations. Greek plane geometry has therefore never had to be abandoned, or even modified by later knowledge. All modern mathematicians have done is define the kind of space (Euclidean space) to which the propositions are applicable.

Greek Art. According to Rudolf Steiner the Greek artists were still able to experience their own etheric bodies, at least until the end of the fifth century B.C. It is this faculty that accounts for the exceptional, even unique, beauty of Greek statuary, and it enabled the artists to work without models, out of an inner experience of their own life forces that they were able to build into their statues. The great statues of the gods, however, are types, for the excellent reason that the etheric body is not differentiated like the physical body, and the gods are always shown as if in the prime of young manhood, because the etheric body does not grow old. Even Zeus, the father of gods, is shown in early manhood in the early Greek statuary.

As time wore on, however, the divine element in the statuary becomes humanized and individualized, even as early as the

74

fourth century sculptor, Praxiteles. Whereas in the fifth century Parthenon friezes the figures of the young riders are static and without noticeable individuality, the later sculptors began to strive to portray ideal manhood, idealizing the individuals who were their models, as in the case of the statue of Alexander the Great attributed to Lysippus. By the next century the gods themselves have become ideal human types, as is the case with the famous Aphrodite of Melos, a most recognizable woman, quite different from any of the early statues of Athena. These sculptures of the Hellenistic age are often full of movement, even strain, as in the famous Laocöon group. By Roman times this art, taught to the Romans by the Greeks, portrays and is intended to portray the human being just as he is in life, warts and all, thus reflecting the full incorporation of the self and the supreme Roman interest in personality and character. Roman imperial sculpture was at least partly stylized, and had to be to some extent flattering, but even the busts of Roman emperors almost always show the character of the individual emperor as seen by the sculptor, and the unflattering appearance of so many of them suggests that even emperors had a healthy respect for Roman realism.

Lastly, a word should be said on the Greek temples. The Greeks, as has been indicated, were the first people who felt themselves really at home on the earth, and the world of the afterlife was a dim abode for insubstantial shades. Whereas the Egyptians, at least the later ones, seem to have felt that the afterlife was an improvement on this life, traditional Greek thought held that, as Achilles had told Odysseus in the *Odyssey*, it was "better to be the slave of a poor man in the upper world than a king in the realm of shades." Greeks made no special preparation for the afterlife, and Socrates' teaching about immortality is virtually unique in Greek literature. Human and earthly life was experienced to the full, to the virtual exclusion of any thought of life before birth or after death, and even the gods were not supposed to be far away. Early Greek thought placed them on Mount Olympus, not a highly exalted peak, though few

75

in later centuries believed this. But they did believe that the gods needed a home on earth, and the Greek temples were therefore built as homes for the gods to whom they were dedicated. The Parthenon, dedicated to Athena and built for her, had a cella, or upper chamber of the temple, as her own dwelling place, and here was placed her statue, as the great, but unhappily lost statue of Zeus by Phidias was placed in the all-Greek temple of Zeus at Olympia. The Greeks therefore did not go to the temple as Christians go to a church, to worship at a service performed by a priest. On certain days the Athenians thronged to the Parthenon for a festival in honor of the goddess, but no congregation was necessary for fulfilling the purposes of a Greek temple. The god's presence was enough, and it was always there, once the temple had been built and dedicated.

The conquests of Alexander spread Greek culture into Egypt and the Near East. But Oriental culture was strong enough in itself not to be overwhelmed by Greek innovations, and it in its turn influenced the Greeks who immigrated into the newly conquered lands, which were ruled by Macedonian Greeks until they were in turn conquered by Rome. The resulting amalgam of Greco-Oriental culture (usually known as Hellenistic culture to distinguish it from the earlier classical culture known as Hellenic) was virtually confined to the new cities, but in these new cities the configuration of the intellectual soul as described in the last pages, is visible. The forms of the democratic government as established in Athens were imitated in the new cities where the immigrant Greeks were in the majority and knew how to make use of them, while the kings who were overlords of the cities but did not much interfere with them, were absolute monarchs, who, like Alexander himself, received divine honors—a hold-over from the typical sentient soul political system.

The new major philosophies of the post-Alexandrian world were Cynicism, Stoicism, Epicurism, and Skepticism. The founders of all these philosophies were Greeks, although Zeno, the founder of Stoicism, was born in the island of Cyprus but taught in Athens. Stoicism is closer to being a religious philosophy than Aristotelianism, and reflects far more than does Aristotle's public work, the new universalism that followed the conquests. All the philosophies, however, owe much to the Greek philosophical tradition, and were taken over by the Romans who had no original philosophers of their own. The use made, in particular, of Stoicism by the Romans will merit some attention later.

Alexander himself is a somewhat enigmatic figure. He was tutored by Aristotle, and his conquering expeditions always reflected the scientific interests of his master. But Alexander's vision of a great empire peopled by Greeks and Orientals, especially Persians, where the two peoples would be equal, was totally unlike anything apparently favored by Aristotle in his known works. But there has always been a tradition in Western civilization that Aristotle gave much secret instruction to Alexander, and various pseudo-Aristotelian works are extant, not least a peculiar document known as the *Secret of Secrets*,* current in the Middle Ages, in which Aristotle is presented as a teacher not only of political science and the art of rulership but of alchemy and astrology. Steiner tells us that Aristotle did indeed give much private instruction to Alexander, but it remains difficult to point to any evidence that Aristotle, who died the year after Alexander, approved the conquests and the mingling of Greek and Oriental culture.

There can be no doubt at all, however, that Aristotle's scientific interests were shared by Alexander, and the conquests ushered in a real scientific renaissance, especially in the Egyptian city of Alexandria (one of seventy bearing his name). Here the Museum was founded by the Ptolemies, Macedonian successors of Alexander in Egypt, as a center for research and with a great library. Here worked all the great Greek astronomers, who were now able to make use of material collected over

* This work was well known to the medieval Arabs and translated into Latin in the thirteenth century. As far as I know, no English translation exists.

more than a thousand years by the Babylonians, enabling the Greek and Babylonian astronomers to build up a theoretical astronomy quite distinct from astrology. Some of the scientists in the Hellenistic world made some practical inventions, such as a fire engine, and various other contrivances that made use of water power, compressed air, and steam, all invented by Hero of Alexandria. Most distinguished of all the Hellenistic scientists was Archimedes of Syracuse who discovered specific gravity and made numerous inventions, some of which he used in the defense of Syracuse against the Romans. Archimedes is an exception to the general statement made earlier that the Greek scientists did not try to prove their hypotheses, but he was typically Greek (and intellectual soul) in his lack of pride in his practical work. He commanded that his greatest achievement should be recorded on his tombstone. This was his discovery of the ratio of the volume of a cylinder to that of the sphere inscribed in it, for which none of his successors has honored him, unduly, and even the Greeks and Romans of his own time would not have shared his judgment.

The traditional date of the founding of Rome is 753 B.C., but the true historical date, according to Rudolf Steiner, was 747 B.C., the year given by him for the beginning of the age of the intellectual soul, in which Greeks and Romans were equally pioneers—although their contributions were different in character. In almost all realms of culture the Romans were dependent on the Greeks; only in the political and legal realm was the work of the Romans truly original. Their achievements in this respect are the result of the deeper penetration of the ego into the physical bodies of the vast majority of Romans—indeed almost all Roman achievements, good and bad, stem from this deeper penetration of the ego. One of the consequences of this penetration is to be found in the stress laid by the Romans upon character and individuality, especially during the early years of the Roman Republic. The untranslatable Roman word *gravitas* was regarded as the most desirable of qualities, for which an old Roman most won respect. Seriousness is the nearest English equivalent, a quality that no one would have thought of attributing to the average Greek (for whom the word volatile might be more appropriate).

Many of the Roman heroes celebrated in historical legend may well have been mythical or never performed the heroic deeds attributed to them. But it is significant that the Roman people extolled as heroes such men as they did. Horatius at the bridge who with his few companions held the enemy at bay even though apparently hopelessly outnumbered; Q. Mucius Scaevola, who thrust his hand into fire to show his lack of fear; Lucius Brutus who, after driving out the Tarquin usurpers and founding the Republic, killed his own sons when they plotted to restore them; even Q. Fabius Maximus, who persisted in his policy of wearing down the Carthaginian Hannibal when all Rome criticized him and demanded that he should give battle; Cincinnatus who saved the city and then retired to his farm, refusing all offices and honors; even Lucretia who stabbed herself after being dishonored by a Tarquin, thus bringing on the rebellion that led to the Republic. All these men and women were heroes to the Romans, and all were remembered because of their *characters*, whereas it would be difficult to point to any Greek, with the single exception of Socrates, a special case, who is remembered for his character rather than his talents. It is noteworthy that portrait busts of the Republican period likewise stress character, as it may be observed in the face, whereas Greek statues and busts give little attention to this feature. Lastly, it is most significant that the Hellenistic philosophy of Stoicism, when taken over by the Romans, stressed qualities of will, endurance and refusal to submit to oppression. Even in the early years of the Empire it was the Stoic philosophers, in particular, who preferred to die rather than submit to the imperial will, falling on their swords or opening their veins in the bath as their last act of the will.

Roman law was the first to grant legal rights to individuals, whether they were citizens or foreigners. In early centuries the Romans followed Greek practice and recognized the rights only

79

of full citizens, foreigners remaining without rights of their own. But as the Romans extended their empire over foreigners their legal notions evolved; they granted some special rights to foreigners, and then extended citizenship itself to ever increasing numbers of foreigners. By the third century A.D. all freeborn persons born within the empire became automatically citizens. All then enjoyed the same legal rights, which inhered to them as persons, making them entitled to protection by Roman authority even when traveling outside the bounds of the empire. Steiner on several occasions drew attention to the fact that the Romans were the first people to recognize individual wills, that is the right of the living to make provision for inheritors, so that their "will" was enforced even after their deaths. This statement is true only in the sense that the Romans received the right to leave their possessions *as they wished,* whereas the wills of earlier civilizations, for example, the Babylonia of Hammurabi, allowed provision to be made only for surviving members of the family. By contrast, the Romans could leave property *outside* their families if they wished, and indeed a profession of "legacy-hunting" (*captatio*) grew up in the late Republic and in the early Empire, whose practitioners paid court to numerous wealthy men in the hope of receiving legacies at their deaths. Many Roman emperors insisted on inheriting from their leading courtiers, who would have lost favor with them if they had refused to draw wills naming their masters as their legatees. Thus in a peculiar way the Roman state recognized the unfettered right of individuals to dispose of their property and wealth as they saw fit after their deaths—a right that is no longer recognized as absolute in those countries, like France, which suppose themselves to be ruled by Roman law, whereas Great Britain and most of the states of the United States continue to allow parents to disinherit their children if they wish.

By our standards Roman religion seems extremely unsubstantial. Most of what passed for religion among the Romans was derived from the Etruscans, a people from Asia Minor who settled in Italy and for a time ruled Rome. The religious

80

inheritance from the Etruscans consisted of various cults that had fallen into decadence, and practices of divination that had been taken over from the Babylonian-Chaldean epoch. Throughout all Roman history a college of augurs existed that watched for omens and interpreted them for the benefit of the state. The Sibyls were also an inheritance from this epoch. As far as the Romans themselves were concerned they had little of their own except some primitive tutelary deities who looked after each Roman family; they had no systematic group of beliefs and no philosophy that was not Greek in origin, and their main gods were simply the Greek deities under Roman names (Jupiter for Zeus, Juno for Hera, and so on).

As soon as they began to conquer other peoples, however, the Romans tried at the same time to assimilate their gods, adding whenever feasible to their own pantheon. With the gods, Rudolf Steiner tells us, were also brought their mystery cults, which were indeed of great interest to the more modern and sophisticated Romans—to the great disgust of conservatives like the Elder Cato. From time to time, indeed, the conservatives were powerful enough to banish foreign cults and foreign philosophies from Rome, but in time they always returned. In spite of such innovations it is certain that the average Roman maintained his devotion to the family and state gods, and to the old Roman cults, all of which had been inherited from the sentient soul epoch, and thus had a powerful hold on the emotions. Loyalty and devotion to the state itself likewise took the place of the personal religious striving offered by what we think of as the higher religions, all of which by contrast belong to the age of the intellectual soul (including the Hebrew religion which evolved into a true religion during that epoch).

Toward the middle of the second century B.C. traditional religion clearly began to lose its hold on the Roman people, especially, of course, their leaders. In the last century of the Republic individualism ran riot, and in a thousand different ways men began to pursue their own personal ends with little attention given any longer to the old patriotic virtues. Such individual military leaders as Marius, Sulla, Pompey, and finally Julius Caesar are all outstanding as individuals, but no true patriotism nor ethical sense can be discerned in any of them. Family ties weakened, divorce could be had for the asking, even the mysteries were betrayed and parodied by dissolute aristocrats like Clodius and his even more notorious sister Clodia. The utterly corrupt government of this century could not survive indefinitely, and in due course Julius Caesar destroyed the last remnants of the Republic before he himself was murdered in 44 B.C. The task fell to his great-nephew and heir, Caesar Augustus, to try to restore an acceptable government, which in future would be presided over by absolute rulers, with their absolute power decently disguised for a time, but real enough and not likely long to remain concealed from the people. By the time Augustus died in A.D. 14 Jesus of Nazareth was already a young man living in Palestine, and the long duel between Romanism and Christianity was about to begin.

For what follows it is necessary to rely on what Steiner has taught,* since he alone gives the key to some of the curious events known to history, while providing other information that is not known to history at all, or only embedded in legends that are usually regarded as simply apocryphal. According to Steiner, all the Roman emperors from Augustus onward up to but not including Constantine (except presumably those who ruled for too short a time) insisted on being initiated into various mysteries, which had hitherto been reserved for those who had undergone suitable preparation. These emperors had not been so prepared, but the priests did not feel able to resist their authority and power, and initiated them in spite of their often weak characters. Evil forces were able to take over the personalities of the weakest among them, especially Caligula, who has always been regarded as a madman, and Nero, who, according to Steiner, really did set Rome on fire in the hope of destroying

---

* See especially his *Building Stones for the Understanding of the Mystery of Golgotha* (London, 1972), lectures 6 and 7, and *Three Streams in the Evolution of Mankind* (London, 1965), especially lecture 6.

the whole world by fire, thus fulfilling too soon an old Sibylline prophecy. The characters of the older and more stable emperors did not suffer too greatly from this forced initiation. According to Steiner, this was especially true of Augustus, who, however, conceived a scheme that would have kept mankind from fulfilling its destiny, and would have thrust the Romans back into the age of the sentient soul so that they could never have either acquired fully the intellectual soul or been able to accept the impulse of Christ.

History tells us that Augustus made a serious effort to reform the Roman religion, and to overcome the irreligion and skepticism of the Romans by restoring the old cults in all their ancient beauty and power. The various decrees he made to try to inculcate moral ideas and foster moral behavior have also come down to us. It is said that he himself did not wish to be worshipped, although he did deify Julius Caesar, his predecessor, as part of a state cult. Instead, he permitted the people to worship his "genius," the tutelary spirit that guided him, thus drawing attention to the inspired quality of his reforms. What Steiner adds is that what Augustus wished to restore or institute were "sublime powerful rituals that had proved effective in earlier times before people had acquired intelligence, and when the cults of the gods had arisen out of the sentient soul, so that men should not be left without gods. These were great rituals, full of significance, designed to take the place of reflection—rituals which, according to old atavistic customs, were to arouse the soul in a half hypnotic condition to a living experience of the gods and of blissfulness through the divine." * This conscious archaism on the part of Caesar Augustus was, according to Steiner, a conscious effort to oppose what was soon to be brought to mankind as the Christ impulse. It was not in itself successful, but among the rituals restored by Augustus may be found the germ of what later became the Catholic Mass. Augustus's intention that the people should experience deeply

---

* *Three Streams*, p. 109.

83

but not think was carried out by the Catholic Church, so much of whose ritual stems from the era of the sentient, and not of the intellectual, soul.

Tiberius, the successor of Augustus, was likewise initiated, and it was during his reign that Christ was crucified. Steiner tells us that through his initiation knowledge, as soon as he heard of the crucifixion and resurrection (some early Christian stories explain his knowledge by his understanding of the "eclipse" that took place at the crucifixion, which was not to be expected according to natural laws and could only be accounted a miracle) he proposed to the Senate that Christ be accepted into the Roman pantheon as one of the gods, thus strengthening the position of the emperor and empire. Other emperors later made the same proposition. But always they met with serious opposition from those who claimed that Christians were and must always be unassimilable, and that it would never be possible for them to accept the divinity of the emperor, which soon afterward became an accepted fact in Rome, with its attendant cults for each emperor, living and dead. Even the emperor could not force the Senate and people to accept Christ as a god, so the effort foundered, to be replaced by sporadic persecutions of the Christians.

In our discussion of Christianity, which now must be attempted, it should always be remembered that as time went on the emperor cult became the leading state religion in Rome and throughout the Empire. Thus Christianity, founded by a God who incarnated and took on the body of a man, was faced by the greatest temporal power the world had yet seen, headed by emperors who claimed to be living gods themselves or became gods at their deaths, thus adding to their power as emperors all that could be added by religion—in this respect returning to the Egyptian model of an absolute monarchy headed by a king-god, and to rituals that equally belonged to the early age of the sentient soul. This was a great effort of Lucifer to turn the clock backward and divert man from his goal.

In Chapter 5 we shall discuss Christianity from many aspects, including its place in history, and a short introduction to Christianity was given at the beginning of the section in this chapter on the intellectual soul. Here therefore we shall only indicate in the most summary manner the effect of the entry of the Christ impulse on the evolution of consciousness. The Christ event occurred at the middle point of the post-Atlantean epoch (the fifth of the great ages of earth evolution and at the same time at the middle point in the history of man as an earthly being). During the first two of the seven great ages (Polaric and Hyperborean) man was not yet an earthly being. The first age during which he took on physical form was the Lemurian, which was followed by the Atlantean age, which was in turn followed by the so-called post-Atlantean, our present age, in the middle of which occurred the Christ event. Two more such ages are to come before the end of earth evolution. Lastly, it should be remembered that earth evolution itself is in the middle of planetary evolution, with three planetary conditions in the past (Old Saturn, Old Sun and Old Moon) and three still to come (Jupiter, Venus and Vulcan). Thus from every point of view the incarnation, life, death and resurrection of Christ Jesus are central to the whole evolution of man. Indeed, according to Rudolf Steiner, the Christ is that spiritual being who has always been and always will be the most intimately connected with man, and it was his earlier sacrifices before that on Golgotha as a man that made man's evolution and man's freedom possible.

This chapter has thus far dealt with the gradual releasing of man from divine tutelage, and the gradual loss of his ability to perceive clairvoyantly the spiritual worlds. It has been shown that he could not have attained freedom without the full incarnation of his ego and the consequent darkening of this consciousness. During the reign of Caesar Augustus (31 B.C. to 14 A.D.) this process of human estrangement from the divine worlds reached its nadir, and without the entry of a new impulse mankind would either have regressed into the past (the solution of Augustus himself, as has just been explained), or sunk more deeply into matter, substituting man-worship (the imperial cult) for God-worship—in effect the negation of all religion and final separation from the spiritual worlds.

But, as has been explained earlier in the chapter, man was to be given the opportunity by the divine worlds to achieve his spiritual freedom, after which he would himself direct his own further evolution. It was as yet too early for the final victory for man's soul to be won by the hindering powers, but their threat was strong enough for their leading adversary to find it necessary, personally, as it were, to take the field against them. From the very beginning the Christ being had purposed to give man the possibility of overcoming and fulfilling his task, and this could be done only by himself becoming man, suffering death as a man, and then returning to the spiritual worlds through his resurrection and ascension. Through this deed the impulse of Christ became permanently linked with man's future evolution, as was described earlier.

Although the possibility of upward evolution, through which man is to come consciously to a new knowledge of the spiritual worlds was given by the entry of the Christ impulse, it will be realized that this was only a possibility, because from now onward to a certain extent man has to take his own evolution in hand. Without any effort on man's part the age of the intellectual soul would give place to the age of the consciousness soul in the early fifteenth century, as the consciousness soul in turn will give place in the sixth post-Atlantean epoch to the spirit-self, if man survives so long and does not destroy himself by abusing the powers entrusted to him. As long as man continues to exist on the earth higher beings will continue to devolve new powers on him, and this does not depend on human volition.

But it is also true that men spend only a relatively small part of their total existence clothed in their earthly sheaths. They continue to have different experiences in the spiritual worlds between death and rebirth, as they also have different experiences during their earthly incarnations. Such experiences are different from what they were before the Mystery of Golgotha, not only because the earthly world in which they spend their

86

incarnations has been at least partly Christianized, but because the Christ has had a different role in the spiritual worlds also. Thus human beings who pass through the gates of death and birth undergo certain experiences of which they are naturally totally unconscious, but which nevertheless influence their subsequent lives, and especially their soul configurations. In the nearly two thousand years since the Mystery of Golgotha few men have not been incarnated at least twice, but such spiritual advancement as most of us have made has been exceedingly slow, as has the spiritual evolution of mankind as a whole.

Thus the possibility of coming to a conscious relationship with the spiritual worlds to replace the unconscious relationship of the pre-Christian era was not an immediate one. Indeed, the old clairvoyance had yet to be fully extinguished, and this did not happen in the West until the end of the intellectual soul period. Steiner mentions the thirteenth century as the time when almost no one in the West had any direct clairvoyance capable of perceiving and distinguishing between the spiritual beings. But many of the early Christians had some direct knowledge of the spiritual worlds, as is visible from their writings, while others acquired a measure of clairvoyance through Christian initiation, or in the Greek or other mysteries that still survived in a decadent form. Gradually this knowledge died out, and a great and profound thinker like Thomas Aquinas had no clairvoyance at all. Indeed, when he wished to write about the spiritual hierarchies, he confessed that he had no knowledge of them beyond what he derived from the writings of his predecessors, to whom he paid tribute. For Thomas there had once been true revelation through inspiration, and this now had to be *believed*, taken on faith, to add to the knowledge acquired through logical thought.

Even when the intellectual soul epoch came to an end most men continued to sink down further into materialism, which was perhaps at its strongest in the nineteenth century, as will be discussed later in this chapter. It was Rudolf Steiner's task, however, to show men the way in which they could come to a conscious spiritual knowledge, a task that he claimed had been laid upon him by the spiritual worlds precisely because of the danger that they would sink so far into materialism that they could not be rescued. A part of Steiner's task was also to reveal to men the results of his own investigations in the spiritual world as a modern initiate, because by absorbing and pondering on this true picture of the spiritual worlds man makes progress in his own spiritual development. But the work of the consciousness soul is by no means confined to the acquisition of spiritual knowledge. As part of his effort to win his freedom and take charge of his own evolution it was also necessary for man to acquire an entirely different attitude toward the external world. This he did indeed acquire, without being aware of the reasons for the change, when the consciousness soul began to work in him. This different attitude toward the external world was to result eventually in modern science, but, as we shall show in Chapter 7, it must in time come to be permeated by the Christ impulse if it is not to result in the destruction of humanity. That modern science is not, to say the least, an unmixed blessing, is due to the failure of men to allow the Christ impulse to breathe its warmth into their work, while on the other hand, the hindering powers have offered them all the kingdoms of the earth if they will fall down and worship them, and this is a standing temptation of supreme attractiveness.

In the millennium following the Mystery of Golgotha Christianity as a religion became thoroughly systematized and organized by the Catholic Church, with a legal and administrative system that was essentially Roman. The hierarchical organization with its autocratic and absolute head was directly inherited from the late Roman Empire as established by Diocletian, and by Constantine I, the first Christian emperor. Canon law, the law of the Church, is founded directly on Roman law. It was the strength of its organization after the fall of the Empire in the West that enabled the Church to absorb the Germanic invaders of the fifth and sixth centuries and introduce them to Latin civilization. Its religious monopoly preserved for posterity both the sentient soul ritual that it had inherited from pre-Christian times and the intellectual soul law taken from the Romans. Its monopoly of learning preserved the Latin tongue as the universal language of the educated, and even the vernacular languages of southern Europe, including France, bear a strong Latin impress. Christian theology, though of course partly based on the Hebrew tradition, was from the time of St. Paul onward greatly influenced by Greek philosophy, and the Western Fathers of the Church were imbued with Roman traditions. Thus, in essence, the Church was a creation of the intellectual soul, and it has had the greatest difficulty in adapting itself to the consciousness soul, which took over from its predecessor in the early fifteenth century. By contrast, the Protestant Reform of the sixteenth century had far more consciousness soul elements in it, even though it retained intellectual soul elements also, as was to be expected at that early period.

Steiner tells us that the intellectual soul as it developed in southern Europe did not have within itself the possibility of absorbing the new consciousness of the consciousness soul as a regular evolutionary process, or, to use his own words* "the stage of the soul among these particular peoples is not such as to have in it a living seed, which could properly evolve *out of itself* the consciousness soul," and "it is as though this consciousness soul were not something that came out of the particular personality of the Greek and Roman, but rather something that was implanted into him from without." These peoples were not able to come to a living relationship with the Christ impulse, nor could they come to a new understanding and experience of Christianity as required by the consciousness soul epoch, in which a *conscious* knowledge of the spiritual worlds has to be acquired. Christianity for the southern European peoples was something that came to them from without, and so had to be based on the historical events of Palestine only, and on finished

---

* *Letters to Members, 1925* (*The Michael Mystery*) No. 28. (Included in *Anthroposophical Leading Thoughts*, London, 1973.)

teachings that were given to them as the content of their faith. The New Testament and the teachings of the Fathers of the Church, as elaborated by later popes and councils, had to be the content of the faith of these southern peoples, whereas the Germanic peoples, who had never truly passed through an intellectual soul development, accepted Christianity in a fresh way as something that filled above all their feelings, their life of soul. Thus, when the consciousness soul age dawned these peoples were, in a sense, ready for it through inner preparation, and it would have been possible for them to have come to a new direct relationship with the spiritual worlds. Even though in fact in the early centuries of the consciousness soul men's attention was directed more toward the earthly world, and they acquired a new relationship with it, and made some social and political advances out of this new soul configuration, the possibility remained for the northern European peoples to obtain a new knowledge of the spiritual worlds. It is, of course, no accident that Steiner himself incarnated in one of these peoples, nor that his message was initially largely heard by Germans.

Over several hundred years the leaders of the Catholic Church were greatly concerned by the necessity, as they saw it, of proclaiming a true Christian doctrine, which should be distinguished from untrue doctrines that were proclaimed heresies. But such a task was in fact beyond even the best Catholic theologians because men were no longer able to perceive the spiritual world, and had to rely on their simple powers of intellect to discern the difference between the true and false, an impossible task for it. The truth, therefore, had to be proclaimed by popes and councils simply because diversity of belief was unacceptable to the Church, and it was not impossible that the truth proclaimed by one council should be overturned by a later one. But in time at least the Roman Catholic Church came to agree on a set of beliefs that had to be held by all Christians (although some of them differed from those held by the Eastern Church). Among those beliefs proclaimed by Rome was one that Steiner often emphasized—that man is a twofold, not a threefold

90

being, consisting of body and soul, but not of body, soul, and spirit, as had been held by theologians in earlier centuries. The threefold or triune belief was condemned as heresy by the Eighth Ecumenical Council held at Constantinople in 869. The actual Council records pay little attention to this clause, which does not seem to have aroused any particular controversy, but Steiner points out that it was, from a spiritual point of view, a crucially important decision, reflecting, as it did, the disappearance of the true knowledge of man from the Church, and a victory for those hindering powers that wished to sever man from his divine origin and close off from him all knowledge of it.

As far as the ordinary believing Christian was concerned, his beliefs were relatively few, and the Church was not interested in encouraging him to think about his religion. As early as Pope Gregory I (590–604) Christians were informed by the papacy that it was especially meritorious to believe as an act of faith something that could not be proved, and the same viewpoint was again put forward in the thirteenth century by Pope Gregory IX, who told some of the early Dominicans that the study of systematic theology might lead them into the deadly sin of pride and divert them from the simple faith that was all that was required of them. For several hundred years there was scarcely any theology worthy of the name, but the Church was nevertheless able to take care of all the religious needs of the people through its ceremonies and its simple teachings enshrined in its few (mostly incomprehensible) dogmas.

But the age of the consciousness soul was approaching, and it cast a long shadow before it. By the eleventh century the speculative spirit was stirring, and some churchmen thought it might be a good idea to try to *prove* the existence of God by the use of reason. The initial effort by St. Anselm of Canterbury, an archbishop, was found so interesting by generations of churchmen that a real theology gradually grew up, which reached its height in the thirteenth century, with Albertus Magnus and Thomas Aquinas. Not only was it thought possible to prove the existence of God, but also to prove almost all the dogmas of

91

religion simply by careful reasoning. It would take us too far to retrace this extraordinary theological effort, and it is not necessary here to enter into details. All that needs to be pointed out is that the *kind* of thinking engaged in is entirely of the intellectual soul variety, but that the effort itself to give the human mind more material to work on shows that the time for the awakening of a new kind of human thinking was at hand, even though these first efforts reached a dead end. The central characteristic of intellectual soul thinking, that it is self-sustaining, needs no evidence from the outside world, and thus is "unscientific," is typical of this theology and of all medieval thought until late in the Middle Ages. One example will illustrate the kind of thinking, based on the Greek models of Plato and Aristotle, of even a rather forward-looking man of the thirteenth century who was interested in science.

The Englishman, Roger Bacon (c1214–c1292), who was at the time a professor of philosophy in the faculty of arts at Paris, was asked whether a plant could feel. For a modern man of science the question, if it could be answered at all, would be answered with reference to the plant itself, whether or not it had a nervous system, whether it gave external signs of being affected by the proximity of something else. It would, in any event, be impossible for the modern philosopher or scientist to offer any kind of proof, since it would be recognized that an analogy would have to be drawn between man's subjective knowledge of how he himself feels, and how he shows his feeling externally, and the visible changes in the plant. For Bacon the problem could easily be solved. Aristotle had long ago laid down the dictum that "nature does nothing in vain"; there is a sufficient reason for everything in the world, everything has its purpose. Now the purpose of feeling is to enable the feeling subject to escape danger or pain, and to move closer to what attracts him and he finds pleasurable. Now the plant cannot move toward or away from anything; it is stationary. Therefore, the ability to feel would have been given to it uselessly; it could not have done anything about the feeling. Therefore, nature, which does nothing in vain, would not have given the plant a useless capacity. Therefore, as a conclusion and answer to the question, the plant does *not* feel.

In essence this kind of thinking, which has here been characterized as belonging to the intellectual soul, stems from Greek geometry, perhaps the greatest achievement of this soul. There are certain truths that cannot be doubted, axioms, as they are called by Euclid. Further truths can be deduced from the axioms, and an infinite number of propositions can be "proved" by reducing them, through the use of Aristotelian logic, to the simple propositions. In Bacon's time Aristotle's dictum that "nature does nothing in vain" was believed to be of the nature of a mathematical axiom, and thinkers did not consider how Aristotle had arrived at it (whether by empirical means or by pure thinking). Thomas Aquinas (1227–1274) engaged in much more rigorous thinking, and questioned all his theological premises, concluding that there were certain truths that were beyond questioning, as, for example, that God could not have been created, or he could not have been truly God. Therefore, a suitable definition of God was that he was a self-subsistent being—from which it was possible to deduce numerous further truths. Indeed Thomas believed that he could prove the existence of God by logical thinking based on indisputable axiomatic truths. When he had to answer the question of how the human mind could know that the fundamental axioms were true, he answered that God had placed these truths in human hearts, just as he had placed the truths of mathematics—a Platonic thought that did not, however, lead Thomas back to the notion, logical to Plato, that such truths had been perceived before birth in the spiritual worlds.

It is this kind of self-sustained logical thinking that rarely if ever needs to be linked with anything in the outside world that we have here characterized as intellectual soul thinking par excellence. It can be recognized long after the consciousness soul had been awakened. Descartes (1596–1650) used similar arguments when he insisted that the mind in coming to "clear and distinct ideas" knows that they are true. This notion was extremely influential, particularly in French thinking. But, as we shall see, in modern times France had the task of recapitulating the intellectual soul during the early centuries of the consciousness soul, so it was only to be expected that the same kind of thinking would prevail for a long time in France.

The thinking of Thomas Aquinas and a long list of medieval philosophers has never been equalled as a sustained effort of pure logical thinking. Its purpose, as has been suggested, was to stimulate the reawakening human mind by posing certain questions of great importance, which could not really be answered truly in that epoch, although in time the consciousness soul might be able to find the answers. In the Middle Ages the only kind of thinking available was that of the intellectual soul. The fact that none of the powerful thinkers of the Middle Ages could transcend this kind of thinking is, to my mind, the clearest evidence that Steiner was right when he placed the beginning of the age of the intellectual soul in the eighth century B.C. and its end at the close of the Middle Ages in the West, in this opposing the views of almost all historians who regard the Middle Ages as a totally distinct period from antiquity, and usually treat it as the early stage of the history of Western man. Even those who still think of the Renaissance as what its name implies—a rebirth— no longer think of it as a rebirth except from a cultural point of view, the rebirth of the Greek and Roman culture and way of life in early modern Italy among the Italian aristocratic and bourgeois classes.

It would take us too far afield to detail all the signs that an old age was passing away and a new one coming to birth in the fourteenth and fifteenth centuries.* All over Europe except in

* For example, space does not permit us to deal here with the important medieval mystics who were, in a sense, transitional figures between the intellectual and consciousness souls, possessing elements of each. They may be studied in an early work of Steiner (1901), *Mysticism at the Dawn of the Modern Age* (Englewood, N.J.: Rudolf Steiner Publications, 1961), also available in paperback format from the same publisher under the title *Eleven European*

Italy where the new movement was beginning, religious life was in utter decay. The papacy had moved to Avignon from Rome in the early fourteenth century; when a pope tried to return to Rome the French cardinals elected another one, thus beginning the Great Schism. At the Council of Pisa in 1410 a third pope was elected, but the other two refused to resign. This schism was settled a few years later at the Council of Constance, the Council that also burnt Jan Hus, one of the great precursors of the consciousness soul (the age of which began, as will be remembered, in 1413). In France the Hundred Years War was raging and the country was utterly devastated with no end in sight. The mission of Joan of Arc, which was to separate England and France for good, began in the decade following the Council of Constance. Through much of the fourteenth century the Black Death raged, with the effect of not only greatly reducing the population of Europe but of bringing stable government, such as it had been under the feudal system, virtually to an end in many areas. Its religious effects are not negligible. The cult of death spread through Europe (this is the century of Hieronymus Bosch and other painters of the macabre), the flagellants marched through Europe calling on sinners to join them. Blasphemy against all the sacred symbols, including the Mass, was commonplace, and indeed the Black Mass was often celebrated during these years and in all parts of Europe. These and many other features of the collapse of medieval civilization are well documented in the classic by Jan Huizinga, *The Waning of the Middle Ages* (Anchor).

Lastly the feudal and manorial systems of the Middle Ages, typical of an age before the freeing of the "I," during which each man had his prescribed rights and responsibilities in relation to his fellowmen, slowly disintegrated over the succeeding centuries. By the fifteenth century the process was already far

Mystics (1971). The long detailed introduction by Paul M. Allen on the lives and work of these mystics forms a useful supplement, while Steiner's own introduction, which is one of the most concise statements he ever made as to the nature of anthroposophy, will be recommended in the reading list for the next chapter.

advanced. In particular the serfs in most countries were being gradually emancipated, and servile labor was being replaced by free labor contracted for and paid for in money. It was, however, well into the age of the consciousness soul before the feudal system came to an end, and some of its vestiges have remained to this day.

The Age of the Consciousness Soul. Some preliminary references to the nature of the consciousness soul have been given earlier in the chapter (see pp. 58–59). Here we shall be more specific.

In individual man the consciousness soul appears at the age of about 35, an age at which the second half of life begins. What may be called the unconscious development of the human soul is now over, and if a man is to increase in wisdom and reach a true maturity he must now take his own development in hand, expecting no further unconscious growth, as he could expect when one stage gives place automatically to the next up to the age of 35.

It is the same with the historical epoch of the consciousness soul that began in 1413 A.D. Man is no longer dependent on the divine world for guidance. He has won his majority, and from this time onward he takes his own evolution in hand. If he makes mistakes he will suffer the consequences, and, it may be hoped, benefit from them. There is not even any automatic certainty that mankind will reach its goal. Help is available for man if he wishes to avail himself of it, and indeed this help is quite different in kind from what was available before he was granted his freedom, that is, before the death and resurrection of Christ.

The resurrected Christ has now become the higher self of man in the sense St. Paul used the words quoted earlier: "Not I, but the Christ in me." But Christ does not usurp the place of the ordinary self of man; the "I" that passes from incarnation to incarnation remains an individual "I," but the Christ power is present in man, ready to permeate his thinking, feeling and willing, *if man lets it.* The Christ impulse is always at man's

96

disposal, but he is not compelled to recognize and welcome it, least of all can he be *compelled* by it to any action since, as was explained at the beginning of this chapter, man was from the beginning destined to be given the opportunity to become free. But, as was also explained, this opportunity to become free implies the existence of alternatives. Man can do evil as well as good. The evil is embodied in two forces opposed to man's true development, as well as opposed, in a certain sense, to one another. These forces are called Luciferic and Ahrimanic and if they were eventually to prevail, then mankind would not reach its goal. Unlike the Christ, these forces can take up their abode in man's astral body, his body of desires and emotions, and thus exercise a strong influence on him from within, whereas the Christ can work only through man's "I," which in effect means that the struggle is by no means an equal one. Man's "I" has to so develop itself that it can in time learn to recognize and resist the manifold "temptations" offered by Lucifer and Ahriman. In developing this central core of his being man can call upon the forces of the Christ that are within him. But the opposing powers have many weapons at their disposal and they do not give up easily. The whole of the rest of man's time on earth will be taken up by the task of transforming himself through the Christ impulse. It is therefore not to be wondered at that so little progress has thus far been made—less than two thousand years since the Resurrection, and less than six hundred years since the beginning of the consciousness soul.

In this age of the consciousness soul the power of the hindering forces is greater than in any previous time, since they are no longer held in check, except to a limited degree, by the beneficent higher powers that guided man's unconscious evolution. It is therefore now necessary to go into more detail than was necessary earlier on the nature and powers of these forces, or beings, and especially to differentiate them from one another. To use the briefest possible characterization, let it be said that Lucifer is the being who tells man that he is "like the gods, knowing good and evil," as the Book of Genesis puts it, and

Ahriman the being who tells man that he is "only man," with no divine element in him, but as man, able to turn to his own use the entire world and everything that is in it. As lord of creation he can even penetrate the far spaces of the universe, and there is no limit to the knowledge he can acquire.

Lucifer is above all the master of *delusion*. It is he who tempts men to believe they are "godlike," more powerful, more effective, more beautiful, more benevolent, more admired than in reality they are. Ahriman is the lord of the earth insofar as it is material, and is therefore responsible for man's materialism (which says that matter is all that there is), his love of power and possessions. A person (or nation) who falls prey to any Luciferic delusion of the kind described, will be an easy prey for Ahriman who will give him (or it), the power, wealth, resources, etc., to try to make the delusion into a reality. By contrast, when the search for material goods has ended in a feeling of satiation, even disgust, the new anti-materialist is ripe to fall prey to the delusions of Lucifer, who will introduce him to all the delights of his "pseudo-spiritual realm." Thus, the two forces work in harmony at the present time, even though they appeal to different instincts in man. Rudolf Steiner in creating the great Group statuary to be seen in the Goetheanum in Dornach, showed Christ, or, as he called him, the Representative of Mankind, in the center, holding in balance Lucifer on the one side and Ahriman on the other. The two forces, tempters though they be for man, have nevertheless positive tasks to perform, and the gifts of neither (especially art in the case of Lucifer, science of Ahriman) are to be shunned. But the true path for mankind is to steer a middle path between the two, and not to be seduced by either.*

---

* What has been given here in the text is a brief picture of the present activities of Lucifer and Ahriman and their helpers (usually called by Steiner simply Luciferic and Ahrimanic beings), insofar as they are powers who try to hinder man's progress and divert him from the goal willed for him by the divine powers led by the Christ. It should be recognized, however, that Lucifer deliberately chose to make it possible for man to be free, and for the Luciferic beings this was

Lucifer appeals above all to man's pride and ambition, making him think he has no limitations, trying to reach the heavens, as the biblical tale of the Tower of Babel expresses it, or as numerous Greek myths expressed it in varied images, including that of Icarus who flew too close to the sun. At the same time Lucifer wishes to keep mankind from developing. He thrusts man back into what Steiner calls his "cosmic childhood," before he had the responsibilities of his freedom. Lucifer wishes men to retain those clairvoyant powers he had in earlier ages, to cling to old religious forms that appeal to his emotions and his unconscious, to old philosophies like those of ancient India that sprang from a far earlier consciousness than man has today. Yet Lucifer himself did start man out on his path to freedom, as related in the story of the Garden of Eden in the Bible, and throughout history he gave man all kinds of gifts, including his love of beauty and art. But he does not want man to be truly conscious, nor to acquire an egohood independently of himself.

Ahriman is in this age of greater significance than he was in the past simply because the consciousness soul has to acquire a knowledge of the earth, which is Ahriman's realm, insofar as the earth is material. He is infinitely clever. Knowing all about the workings of the earth and how to make practical use of such knowledge, he is constantly whispering information to man, and constantly suggesting new machines for "man" to invent. By

a sacrifice that hindered their own upward development. Before the Mystery of Golgotha almost all the gifts man received from the spiritual worlds were brought to him by Lucifer. But since that time it is our task to follow the path of Christ and not the path of Lucifer; if we do this, then in the fullness of time we shall help to restore Lucifer to his true place in the cosmos. For the positive aspects of Lucifer and his destiny as they were described by Steiner, especially in the years before World War I, information on which is scattered through numerous lectures, a small pamphlet consisting of two lectures given by Adolf Arenson in Stuttgart in 1933, entitled *Lucifer* (London: 1934), which is available in most anthroposophical libraries, should be consulted. For the activities of Lucifer and Ahriman as hindering forces in today's world, see the cycle, *The Influences of Lucifer and Ahriman*, five lectures given in Dornach and Bern in November, 1919 (London, 1954), and several important letters to the members written in October and November, 1924, published together in *The Michael Mystery*, especially 4 through 9 for Ahriman, and 10 for Lucifer.

contrast with Lucifer, Ahriman wishes man to advance at breakneck speed, long before his ego and moral nature are ready for such advances. He tells man that the future is already here and the sky is the limit, that man can and should create an earthly utopia here and now. He wishes to foreshorten man's development so that he will never reach his true goal, only a false goal of enjoyment and endless material possessions. He wishes to develop in man a cold razor-sharp intellect, capable of understanding one aspect of the world to the exclusion of all others. The scientist, the engineer and the inventor are Ahriman's natural prey, but all intellectuals can easily fall victim to his blandishments. Wherever there is egoism and love of power, entry is made easy for him, and few leaders of mankind can resist him.

It is necessary in the age of the consciousness soul that men should be able to work with and understand the external world, as it was not necessary in earlier ages. But when Ahriman tells man that the material world that he reveals is all that there is, then he lies. It is with this lie that Ahriman hopes to prevent man from reaching his goal. It is not *predestined* that Ahriman and Lucifer will be defeated. Though it is the *wish* of higher powers that men should reach their goal, nothing can in future be predestined because the goal itself must be reached, if at all, only in freedom. It is therefore clear that the possibility cannot be ruled out that men will succumb finally to the temptations of Lucifer and Ahriman, and other opposing forces who will show themselves in later epochs. With their command of the resources and inventions revealed to them by Ahriman modern men already have it in their power to destroy the earth and everyone in it. The divine powers will try by every means *short of coercion* to prevent man from doing this, but in the last resort they cannot coerce.

It was and is the proper task of the consciousness soul age to come to terms with the material world. To do this man has to be able to observe it objectively, that is, stand as it were a short distance from it and observe it. The laws of the external world reveal themselves only to the seeker who does not allow his emotions to cloud his judgement. The most serious accusation to be made (and correctly) against a scientist is that he is "subjective." Yet this withdrawal from the world in order to look at it carries with it a certain danger. The objective observer can, and too often does, become cold and loveless in relation to what he sees. Steiner has pointed out how the developing intellect of the consciousness soul age was *at first* necessarily cold, while the ability itself was being acquired. Thus the intellect was inclined to fall into the power of Ahriman, who is in fact the lord of cold thinking, the kind of thinking we admiringly call "objective." But Steiner also emphasizes that this attitude must not continue too long. On the contrary, man should *warm* his thinking, but this must be by his own deed. This attitude will be dealt with elsewhere in this book, and we need not go further into it here, except to state flatly that love must come to be a means of cognition. The human being will connect himself with the outside world *by his own act,* and this act takes place not only in the realm of feeling (loving the world) but of thinking. Eventually, this will make possible the perception of the supersensible element in all things, that is, the beings of the hierarchies who work within them. The consciousness soul must acquire the ability to perceive the spiritual worlds (as the sentient soul still perceived them without any effort of its own), but it cannot do this without self-development, including total selflessness. Then the external world reveals itself to the earthly senses, while at the same time what lies behind the external world reveals itself to the spiritual senses.

It now becomes necessary when dealing with the consciousness soul to be explicit about a feature of all evolution that has thus far only been touched upon. This is the law of recapitulation, which should on the one hand be distinguished from mere repetition, and on the other from the notion, once widely held, that evolution is always in one direction, if not at a uniform pace. According to Steiner, all evolutionary processes take place in well-marked time stages, and all have a mid-point at which time a notable change occurs and a kind of reversal of direction of the evolutionary stream. The clearest example of this is the change that took place in the center of our post-Atlantean epoch with the Mystery of Golgotha. Up to this mid-point man had been moving ever further away from his primeval consciousness, when he perceived spiritual beings, but was scarcely at all aware of the earth. Not long after the Mystery of Golgotha man's natural clairvoyance virtually disappeared, and man began to regard the earth as his true home, eventually denying the existence of the spiritual worlds altogether. Thus, the intellectual soul era came to an end. Whatever knowledge existed of the spiritual world was taken from books and ancient tradition and held on faith.

It is the task of the consciousness soul era to recover the perception of the spiritual worlds that was still strong in the sentient soul era, the era of the Egyptians and Babylonians. But this knowledge will not be reacquired in the same form as before. It will be reacquired, if at all, *consciously,* and the ability to perceive the earth and to understand it from a material point of view will not be lost. So man will have regained everything that the sentient soul had in its time, if the consciousness soul achieves its goal. But there is also a tendency to sink back into the experience of the sentient soul, without acquiring anything new. Our inclination to live in, and value especially highly the human emotions; our unfortunate political inclination to sink back into one-man rule, especially of "god-like," almost infallible leaders like Hitler and Stalin; our delight in pictures and images; even our great interest in ancient Egypt itself, are all part of this recapitulation of the sentient soul picture-consciousness of the ancient Egyptians and Chaldeans—even though naturally at the same time we do undertake some of the tasks demanded of us in the age of the consciousness soul, as for example moving toward equality of rights and political democracy.*

* The same recapitulation is to be observed in the life of the human being, as will be discussed later in the book. At the mid-point in the ordinary life of man is the

It should also be noted that there is another kind of recapitulation, different from the one just described. This is the recapitulation of previous evolutionary stages at the beginning of a new one. Thus, Steiner tells us that even at the beginning of Old Sun, Old Moon and Earth evolution all the stages that had been lived through in previous planetary evolutions were repeated before the new evolutionary development proper to the new planetary embodiment could begin. At the beginning of the consciousness soul age in 1413 a similar recapitulation of the two previous soul configurations took place. Only after two leading Western peoples, the Italian and the French, had brought the sentient soul and the intellectual soul respectively to maturity, summing up in themselves the achievements of these souls in the past, while at the same time making use of the newly strengthened ego of the consciousness soul, could the latter begin its true mission.

It may seem at first sight that these soul nuances are exceptionally difficult to grasp, but if modern and even present day history are to be understood, the attempt should be made to grasp them. The subtle differences between peoples are explainable primarily in terms of their different missions, and their different soul development in recent times. As a historian, I have personally found the key offered by Rudolf Steiner to be of great value, and in my view there is abundant historical evidence to show that his insights were correct. But in view of the judgments we so often make about the different peoples of the world it is always wise for us to remind ourselves that we incarnate among a particular people because of the needs of our destiny, and that in our next life on earth we shall surely reincarnate in a different one.

---

age of the intellectual soul, from 28 to 35, when the "I" is fully incorporated within him and should be in full charge of his activity. The age of the consciousness soul, from 35 to 42, follows, and is a recapitulation of the age of the sentient soul, from 21 to 28. The next age, that of the spirit self, in turn recapitulates the age of puberty from 14 to 21, and similarly with the other two ages which recapitulate the first two ages of childhood, 7 to 14 and 0 to 7. (See pages 148–149 below.)

In the Italian Renaissance we see the Italian people living through a sentient soul development in the age of the nascent consciousness soul, and because of their inestimable achievements at this time and the influence they exercised for two centuries over all Europe, they achieved their particular mission. But at the present day they remain, as a people, still inclined toward the experience of the sentient soul, finding it somewhat difficult to take the necessary leap forward into the consciousness soul. It is not impossible for Italians to make this leap, but it is more difficult than it is for others, with the exception of the peoples of the Iberian peninsula who in their different ways lived in the sentient soul during these centuries, while nevertheless colonizing America and Asia in accordance with the needs of the consciousness soul.

The Italians, living in their feeling life primarily at this time, could not bring forward the new thought of the consciousness soul. Renaissance thought, for this reason, is Luciferic, that is to say, it looked backward to the thought of the past, especially of the Greeks and Romans. Renaissance thinkers called themselves "humanists" and were deeply interested in man himself. But they could come to no new ideas about man for the excellent reason that they had lost all knowledge of his spiritual nature.* Indeed, even to this day no people has had any truly consciousness soul knowledge of man, while the earlier intuitive knowledge of man that had, according to Steiner, been instilled in men by spiritual beings in the past, was now lost. But the *interest* in man was awakening in Renaissance Italy, an interest that had been scarce in the Middle Ages when he was more viewed as a candidate for salvation than as he actually was, as an earthly

---

* Steiner's words on this matter are well worth pondering. "Man looks with his fresh opening intellect at nature . . . he gains a picture of the external non-human world, but he loses the picture of himself. He looks at himself, and he has no possibility of arriving at any insight into what he is." "There arose in man's consciousness all that his physical and etheric bodies could tell him about the physical and etheric in nature . . . There sinks from before his vision what his astral body and "I" could tell him about themselves." Letters to Members (Michael Mystery), 1924–1925; 13.

being. Even in the fourteenth century one of the Renaissance pioneers, Francesco Petrarcha, showed a self-consciousness about himself that was new in his time, and could be matched in the past only in the person of that strange figure St. Augustine, who was called by Steiner the first modern man because he embodied in himself through his destiny many elements of the consciousness soul as it was to appear later. The Italian painter Giotto first began as early as the thirteenth century to humanize his madonnas and use real life models, and in the next centuries all painters took their subjects from life, becoming much more interested than before in external nature, an interest that had been far less in Italy than in the Low Countries.

But the great religious works of the Renaissance in Italy, though spiritual through and through, did not look forward to the future and did not emanate from the consciousness soul. According to Steiner, in the letter just quoted, these painters were in fact inspired by spiritual beings for the purpose of helping to warm man's soul at a time when there was a danger that man's view of himself and the world would become coldly intellectualized, losing the feeling element of the intellectual (responsive) soul and not being able to acquire so soon the new relationship needed by the consciousness soul. Aside from the arts, the Italians during these first two centuries of this new soul led the world in business innovations, and their spirit of enterprise was unequaled. When the new science began to spread through Europe in the wake of the Copernican theory, the Italians had their share of the new scientists, most notably the supreme scientist of his age, Galileo Galilei. If the whole history of Europe in this age is considered, and the way in which culture was transmitted, there is abundant evidence for the ascendancy of Italy. Every monarch sought to employ Italian artists and craftsmen, however glorious the local tradition, as in France, might be; no business could hope to survive if it did not make use of the numerous Italian business inventions, from the bill of exchange to the cheque, to merchant banking and double-entry bookkeeping. Nevertheless the Italians did not themselves develop the characteristic institutions of the consciousness soul. Their task was to lead Europe into the new age, but in doing this, recapitulate only the sentient soul age of the third post-Atlantean epoch.

Quite suddenly, in the seventeenth century, France became the cultural leader of Europe, and everyone began to look to France as a model. Many foreign courts spoke French in preference to their own language (for example, the Dutch and Russian); after the building of the palace of Versailles by Louis XIV nothing would suffice for other courts but to have, if not a major Versailles, at least a little Trianon. French formal gardens became the norm elsewhere (except in England), and by the eighteenth century, through which French cultural ascendancy lasted, leadership in almost all arts (with the notable exception of music) had largely fallen into French hands. Most important of all, French philosophical thought in the person of René Descartes, inventor of analytical geometry, became far more influential on the European continent than any other thought of the period (first half of seventeenth century), and largely retained its influence in Western Europe until the nineteenth century in spite of the newer philosophy of the Germans.

The French Revolution at the end of the eighteenth century, followed as it was by the ascendancy of Napoleon, seemed at the time to be spreading French influence even more widely than before. But it was not really so, and this influence remained superficial. The ideas behind the Revolution proved abortive, largely because they were never understood by either the French or anyone else. In the nineteenth and twentieth centuries France was no longer in the forefront of Western evolution in spite of numerous distinguished individuals and the memories of past glory that still shed some effulgence in the new age, and, more importantly, attracted talented foreigners to the world capital of Paris.

For in fact France was not to be the great leader and innovator in the age of the consciousness soul. It was and is extremely difficult for the French people to move out of their

106

intellectual soul thinking in which for two centuries they had excelled, while recapitulating in the consciousness soul epoch the intellectual soul epoch of the Greeks, Romans, and medieval Europeans, and the first millennium of Christianity. The thinking of Descartes and his followers was only a repetition of the thinking that had been up to date in the time of the great Greeks, as modified by the newer mathematics. His metaphysics in no way improved on Aristotle or Aquinas. What he did do was pose the great question: How does the subjective mind know the (presumably) objective world? This problem cannot be solved by the intellectual soul thinking of Descartes or even of Kant, who in the eighteenth century devoted most of his extremely powerful and subtle thought to its solution. Yet it must be solved eventually by the consciousness soul, and part of the next chapter will be devoted to Steiner's own solution. The so-called "geometrical" spirit and method of Descartes has always had a remarkable appeal to the French mind, which still today analyzes problems in a Cartesian manner, prefers an intellectual education based on Cartesianism, and, it may be added, loves orderly gardens laid out on the best Cartesian (geometrical) principles!

During these four centuries of recapitulation, the true bearers of the new age of the consciousness soul were quietly preparing for their task. Without giving any real thought to what they were doing for the rest of mankind, they developed the major institutions that could be used not only by themselves but by others who took them over with few changes from the British. As long ago as 1215 in the High Middle Ages the first steps were taken toward the enforcement of equal rights for all men, and the system of representative government developed by the British, under which representatives were elected, chosen by the voters for the purpose of speaking for them and influencing the government, is essentially a creation of the consciousness soul—presupposing as it does a confidence in the deputy that he will use his free judgment (his ego capacity) in the interests both of his constituents and of the country as a whole. The British

107

civil war of the seventeenth century, which eventually resulted in a constitutional monarchy, was a serious and principled struggle, quite different from the contemporary risings elsewhere (in France) or even from such an event as the German Thirty Years War. On the continent most of the struggles of this epoch, even those with apparently religious causes, were fundamentally between different clans and families of noblemen backed by their respective retainers, whereas in England "freedom of conscience" was always an issue. The Puritans who fought against the established Church of England objected most of all to its insistence on uniformity of worship and belief, and on retaining its episcopal hierarchy and all its weapons for ensuring uniformity and obedience. The religious toleration that eventually emerged from the struggle in the eighteenth and nineteenth centuries was unique in Europe of that time, and is clearly a product of the new consciousness soul. Like British political institutions, this tolerance was diffused from Britain to other nations, especially those of northern Europe, whose soul configuration was similar to the British. Even the empirical nature of British science and philosophy of these centuries is derived from the consciousness soul, whose task is to view the world as external to itself and come to an understanding of what is actually there, thus escaping from the "pre-judgments" typical of the intellectual soul.

The nineteenth century is thus a British century as the preceding centuries had been French and Italian. Again it may be seen how for this period Britain, in spite of her relatively small size and population, led the world in almost all fields of endeavor, spreading not only her newly arisen industrial civilization but also much of her political system. But the century, nevertheless, did not belong to Britain alone, as the preceding centuries had been almost exclusively French. By the end of the nineteenth century she was already suffering the severest of competition, even in the fields she had hitherto dominated, from a power that had been of no importance at the beginning of the century. It did not escape the world's attention that newly united Germany under Wilhelm II was beginning to edge Britain out of her leadership, and herself provide cultural models to the world (as, for example, to the American universities). In fact, Rudolf Steiner tells us that the British and the Germans have had complementary tasks to perform in the present age.

The Germans did not have a "spiritualized instinct for developing the consciousness soul," as did the British. They had, and still have, to win it for themselves, whereas those whose life task included having to work with and develop the consciousness soul tended in this period to incarnate among the British people* who possessed this *instinct* for it. What the Germans did have as a task was to bring the ego itself to full fruition, to reach the highest possible degree of self-consciousness, especially through the development of creative and original thinking, at which pursuit the British scarcely excelled. In a remarkable tribute to the German philosopher, Johann Gottlieb Fichte, (*The Spirit of Fichte Present in our Midst*, given in Berlin in December, 1915, London, no date) Rudolf Steiner chose in the depth of World War I to draw attention to the positive task of the German people, which had never been accomplished so fully as by Fichte. He spoke of Fichte's *Addresses to the German People* delivered after Berlin had fallen to Napoleon, in which the philosopher "tried to communicate to the German people what he had, so to speak, overheard in his meditative conversations with the world spirit," hoping "to arouse in their souls whatever can be aroused out of the deepest sources of the German being." "Power and energy combined with profound introspection—such were the qualities in which this soul strove to take his place in world evolution."

Fichte devoted his life to trying to arouse through his own

---

* The direct quotation comes from a lecture entitled "The Innate Capacities of the Nations of the World" given on December 8, 1918 at Dornach, published as lecture 6 of a cycle called *In the Changed Conditions of the Times* (New York: 1941), page 109. The whole lecture is of great importance, as is the rest of the cycle.

teaching the "I" of his pupils, and he often changed their lives thereby. The other great German philosophers contributed their share of this task, and there is no other thinking to be compared in modern times with this so-called German "idealism." The German soul is always striving ceaselessly with a dynamic energy,* and the typical German nature in its most extreme form may be seen in the figure of Faust in Goethe's drama. Likewise, German music above all other music seems to have been a creation of the striving self, powerfully directed from within but constantly battling, as was archetypally true of Beethoven. Indeed, Rudolf Steiner in his description of the hierarchy of the arts (see Chapter 6 below) attributes music to the "I," so that it is in no way surprising that the people whose task was the development of the "I" should also have been the undisputed leaders in music.

The contrast between Faust and almost any character in Shakespeare will illustrate the difference between the British and Germans in a striking manner. Shakespeare's characters (and indeed almost any character in English literature—Dickens and Jane Austen at once come to mind) are all strongly individualized as people. One might hope to meet and recognize them at any time from their descriptions, even though all are different. But Fausts one cannot expect to meet ever, even in Germany— nor, if it comes to that, may one ever expect to meet such a perfect and flawless young girl as Margaret. The "idealist" Germans, in short, perceive the universal ego, the spiritual "I" before it has been embodied on earth, while the "empirical" English see only the "I" as embodied in individual people, and differently embodied in each.

The major weakness in the German ego-character in this age has been the difficulty the German has in harmonizing his

---

* These terms and the general picture of the contrast between the British and German missions in this age have been taken from or suggested by a stimulating little book by D. E. Faulkner-Jones called *The English Spirit* (London: Anthroposophical Publishing Co., 1935) especially pp. 123–130. This book is strongly recommended to readers if it can still be found.

thinking with his feeling and with his forces of will, the tendency of this ego to degenerate into egoism, and, worst of all into the will-to-power. The German has too often reacted to his experience of the ego by becoming over-satisfied with himself, certain that he, as a German, is superior to all others, an attitude that has too often been followed by contempt for these others and utter disregard for their interests. The consciousness soul cannot be attained along this path. Yet the virtual disappearance of creative German thinking for decades after the advent of Hitler to power left a gap in the thinking of the world that has not been filled by others. In a sense, it is the German's task to do the world's thinking, and no other people can do it. For a time, indeed for centuries, from Luther onward, other countries received new ideas from Germany that often proved to be more fruitful than in their country of origin. But no one has ever copied German *institutions*, whether political, military or economic, except to their ultimate undoing.

It need scarcely be added that the Germans, by submitting to Hitler, even if not already by the part they played in launching World War I, betrayed their mission—as indeed many enlightened Germans saw was happening in the age of Wilhelm II.* By contrast, the British undoubtedly fulfilled much of their task in the nineteenth century and earlier, but it has always seemed to me that in the empire that they built, with so little conscious forethought, they missed a "heaven-sent" opportunity by reacting too favorably to their own enterprise after it had been built. Their self-satisfaction blinded them to the needs of their imperial subjects, whom they scarcely saw as persons at all—and this is a sin perhaps even more unforgivable than materialism for the consciousness soul, which, as already noted, has the task of building the bridge from one person to another consciously by true perception and recognition of the "I" of others.

Even if the British and the Germans had completely fulfilled

---

* See especially Fritz Stern, *The Politics of Cultural Despair.* Anchor.

their missions in the nineteenth century, there can be little doubt that the full development of the consciousness soul in the twentieth century would have been led by the United States, and the twentieth century should have been the American century, as was indeed widely thought by both the Americans themselves and other peoples throughout the world. The British and Germans were two of the principal ethnic stocks forming the population of the United States, and by the time of World War I, when the Americans should have been ready to assume their world task, immigrants from all over Europe had combined with them to create a virtually new people. Meanwhile a federal constitution had been formulated more than a century earlier by a remarkable group of foresighted men, which had been amended throughout the nineteenth century in such a way that it was by this time eminently fitted to serve the development of the consciousness soul. Similar constitutions were promulgated by other countries of the American continent and by the United States Asian colony of the Philippines, in much the same way as the European nations had imitated the British constitution in the preceding century.

But if the American mission were to be fulfilled and a task similar to (but naturally differing insofar as this was now a post-Christian era) that of Rome in the fourth post-Atlantean epoch carried out, two things were essential. Internally it would have been necessary for the immigrant peoples to have been fully assimilated so that a really new people, all of whom had absolutely equal rights, duties, opportunities and responsibilities, could have taken over the task. Externally, in foreign policies, the United States would have had so to conduct herself that she would have been a model for the world, to be freely imitated, giving leadership where it was called for and needed, but always with the consciousness soul attitude that all men are of equal worth, that truth is not revealed but must be sought selflessly, and that, as the Bible puts it, "from those to whom much has been given shall much be required." Neither Roman might nor Roman ideas could be of any use to America in

performing her mission—though it would always be a temptation to use them. What was needed was a higher ideal to bind
together her own people—all of the different streams including
the African—an ideal that the nineteenth century president
Abraham Lincoln, a true representative of the consciousness
soul, had glimpsed, and a world ideal by which the United
States, a state founded upon a non-national principle, should set
an example to the national states of the world to show them how
nationalism can be transcended.

It was especially unfortunate that at the most important
moment of the First World War the United States should have
had a president whose thinking was dry and without warmth,
abstract and conventional in the worst sense of the word.
Woodrow Wilson was also personally both arrogant and self-
righteous, and at the same time obstinately attached to his own
ideas. At the end of the war the entire world looked to him for
leadership simply because the American time had come, and
America possessed both the material and moral resources to give
it, or so it was supposed. What was wrong with his brain-child,
the League of Nations, for which he was prepared to make every
sacrifice, was not that his countrymen refused to take part in it,
thus leaving it in the hands of the other victors in the war, but
that the *idea* of such a league was itself still-born, based upon
intellectual soul principles, such as the principle of nationality,
and lacking all imaginative vision of the form that the world
should take in the new age.

Yet the world still continued to long for an American lead. As
World War II drew to an end President Franklin D. Roosevelt
enjoyed a power and prestige accorded not even to Woodrow
Wilson at the end of World War I. He was expected to give the
world a new lead along the paths of peace. But he died before
the war's end and, although some of America's world tasks were
performed well in the years that followed, it is also true that the
shadow side of Rome—the willingness to coerce, the Roman
sense of superiority and Roman self-satisfaction, and the
Roman conviction of manifest destiny—tended to take posses-

113

sion of too many American leaders. In an age when almost unlimited means were available to an industrial scientific civilization for the purpose of enforcing its will, such qualities presented a great danger to the world. Perhaps it was only a matter of time before these means would be used in the attempt to coerce some smaller, weaker and totally different civilization to behave in a manner acceptable to Americans under "free and democratic" institutions *imposed* by the victor. If the effort involved the physical destruction of a large part of the enemy's country through the use of the latest scientific technology, the maiming and death of at least a million foreigners and more than fifty thousand Americans, at least the war aims were good ones, and it was indeed unfortunate if the enemy insisted on continuing to resist, thus bringing their destruction on themselves and their own people! As the Latin proverb puts it *Corruptio optimi pessima*, or, to quote the Roman Tacitus, who puts the words in the mouth of a British chieftain "They make a desert and they call it peace!" (*Agricola*, 30)

Nevertheless, such was the readiness on the part of the Western peoples to accept American leadership, even in the second half of the twentieth century, that whenever a small ray of hope appeared that a world leader had arisen on American soil they reacted to it with all the extravagance of hope deferred. John F. Kennedy was young and handsome, he had a young and charming wife, and had a good war record behind him; he could also voice mankind's hopes with considerable eloquence. But, objectively, there was nothing in his own past history, and nothing happened during his presidency to give the world the impression that he possessed the leadership qualities and the greatness of soul needed for the dangerous age in which he lived. Though he himself and many of his aides may have been idealistic in the conventional sense of the word, no new vision was displayed by any of them, nor were any really new policies initiated, though many of the old bad ones were intensified. In the end only the style and the rhetoric were different—and rhetoric, it may be worth remembering, was a Roman invention.

114

Yet when President Kennedy was assassinated there was such an outpouring of the world's grief as had seldom if ever been seen before. This grief was a measure of the continuing expectations of the world from America in the second half of the twentieth century, but if there are still many who believe in Lincoln's words that America is the "last, best hope of man," there are surely few in the 1970's to believe that this hope will now be fulfilled.

All this is in no way intended to suggest that other nations are in any sense morally superior to the United States, and certainly not because their material resources are so manifestly inferior. Indeed, there are surely more individual human beings already born into the American culture who are able to develop the consciousness soul with a minimum of obstacles to overcome than there are now in any other people. It is also worth noting that in the case of any great catastrophe anywhere in the world the Americans are the first to recognize that they must out of their own wealth help those less fortunate than themselves—and even the United States tax system favors philanthropy more than does any other system in the world. All this is a consequence of the mission that it was intended for the United States to fulfill in the twentieth century. But I think at the same time it must be said that in proportion as the opportunities are greater, so are also the temptations to which the leading people at any stage of history are subjected. There is no need to discuss the nature of these temptations here, nor to fill this chapter with any further descriptive information about the two "tempters" Lucifer and Ahriman, who will be often enough referred to in the course of the rest of this book.

Having brought our historical study of the evolution of consciousness up to the present day we can now turn our attention to the nature and tasks of the consciousness soul from many different points of view. But one historical question may yet be touched upon to conclude this chapter since it is likely to be asked by all readers: what of the Russians, the Soviet Union, the leading political rivals of the United States? To this question

Steiner has given a definite answer. The epoch following that of the consciousness soul, during which further especially spiritual qualities have to be developed (the epoch of the "spirit self"), was intended to be led by the Russians and other Slavic peoples. The sixth post-Atlantean age should be one in which Christianity truly enters into the human will, and human life is to be guided for the first time by the principle of brotherly love. Since we are now almost one-third way through the age of the consciousness soul the next stage is already being prepared, and its precursors may even be expected to appear among the Russian people in order to prepare the soil, the territory on which the new impulse will reach fruition.

But what has happened is that the subconscious impulse toward their mission was seized upon by Ahriman, who whispered, as is his custom, that the future is already here, and that there is no need to live out the long period of the consciousness soul, slowly evolving as it is toward the spirit self. The era to be marked by "brotherly love" can be forced into existence by the use of power, Ahriman's special gift and special temptation. Thus Bolshevism, Communism, State-ordered Socialism, whatever the Soviet system may be called, is an Ahrimanic illusion, a horrible doppelgänger of what is to come into existence in the sixth age, and which *cannot* be brought into existence by coercion, but must arise out of an evolution of the human soul and a further stage of human consciousness. Because the true sixth age is to be a fulfillment of Christianity it became the first task of the establishers of the new system to root out Christianity, and substitute atheism and "dialectical" materialism.

Yet many Russians have indeed been seized by the true ideal of brotherly love through Christianity, and it has been impossible to root out the deeply religious spirit of the Russian people. So, slowly, the ground *is* nevertheless being prepared through *opposition* by those Russians with the greatest soul development to their state imposed tyranny. Thus, if humanity avoids destroying itself in this fifth age and survives into the sixth, the

Russian land will have been prepared by its pioneers for its task. What appears now as a scarcely mitigated evil will have been turned into good through opposition to that evil by those few remarkable men and women who have struggled and are still struggling, apparently hopelessly in this age, against that tyranny.

SUGGESTIONS FOR FURTHER READING

FOR CHAPTER 2.

Almost any work of Rudolf Steiner has some bearing, however slight, on the subject matter of this chapter. But, unlike the other chapters in this book, Chapter 2 is based on much research and a long period of teaching and writing history on the part of the present author. He has therefore himself used innumerable works of Steiner as well as a few books by others in order to write this chapter and adduce evidence from the external historical records that seems to fit well into the framework that is drawn from Steiner. A few books that throw special light on some of the subjects covered in the chapter are mentioned in the footnotes. Unless these works are also of a general interest their titles will not also appear in this reading list. In all the reading lists the works by Steiner will appear first. The dates given are the dates for first publication in German, if they are books; for lectures the dates of delivery are those given, in most cases simply the month and the year. For other authors the usual publishing information is given.

Works by Rudolf Steiner.
An Outline of Occult Science. First published in 1909, but frequently revised by the author, for the last time just before his death in 1925. The latest edition in English, translated by Maud and Henry B. Monges, and revised by Lisa D. Monges, made use of the latest German revisions (New York, 1972). Besides

comprising, as Steiner states in the preface, "a complete outline of anthroposophy" this book is the main source for the history of the various planetary stages of evolution, the work of the hierarchies, and other material from the Akasha Chronicle, though it may be noted that there is an important short cycle on the same subject, consisting of five lectures given in Berlin between October 31 and December 5, 1911 entitled *The Inner Realities of Evolution* (London, 1953). This cycle is profound and contains deeply esoteric knowledge but it is not difficult for the serious student. For the nature of the Akasha Chronicle itself the reader is referred to pages 38–41 of *Cosmic Memory* (Englewood, N.J.: Rudolf Steiner Publications, 1959 available from the same publisher also in paperback since 1971), as mentioned in a footnote in the text, and also to Lecture 2 of a helpful early cycle given in Stuttgart in August and September, 1906, and published under the title, *At the Gates of Spiritual Science* (London, 1970). While *Occult Science* was in preparation Steiner gave a valuable series of lectures at Stuttgart in August and September, 1908, published under the titles, *Universe, Earth and Man* (London, 1955), and *Egyptian Myths and Mysteries* (New York, 1971). The first named deals with the early evolution of man in an exceptionally clear manner, and the latter takes up the same subject again, but with special reference to the age of the sentient soul.

Only one other strictly historical lecture cycle will be recommended here. This is published under the title *Occult History: Historical Personalities and Events in the Light of Spiritual Science* (London, 1957) and consists of six lectures given in December, 1910 and January 1911. These lectures throw much light on a number of different historical epochs, but Lecture 4 on the Chaldean-Babylonian civilization and that of the Sumerians which preceded it is especially recommended.

On the three phases of the soul that are dealt with in detail in this chapter, the fundamental work is *Theosophy: An Introduction to the Supersensible Knowledge of the World and the*

Destination of Man, first published in 1904 and revised in 1922 by Steiner. It is available in English in a translation revised by Gilbert Church, Ph.D. (New York, 1971). Chapter 1 of this book gives the most systematic account of these three soul configurations, and it is indispensable for an understanding of what is meant by these souls and how they are to be distinguished from each other. A helpful supplement to this book is a guide written by Carl Unger, entitled *Notes on Steiner's Book, Theosophy* which will throw much light on the book for serious beginners (London, n.d. about 1938).

On the nature of the consciousness soul and its tasks in the present age a lecture given by Steiner in Berlin on October 28, 1909 called "The Mission of Religious Devotion" and published in a collection entitled, *Metamorphoses of the Soul* (London, 1934), is extremely valuable and vital for our understanding at the present time. The two previous lectures in the collection are also helpful. For the evolution of consciousness references are scattered throughout numerous lectures, but a series of three lectures given in Stuttgart in September, 1923 under the title, *Man in the Past, the Present, and the Future: The Evolution of Consciousness* (London, 1966) are among the most helpful, although they presuppose a basic knowledge of anthroposophy.

Lastly, one of Steiner's fundamental books should also be mentioned, *Christianity as Mystical Fact*, first published in 1902 and revised by the author in 1910 (New York, 1972). Its chapters on the mysteries are essential for an understanding of the Greek mysteries referred to in this chapter, and their relation to Greek philosophy. Another, earlier edition of this work should also be listed (Blauvelt, N.Y.: Rudolf Steiner Publications, 1972), because it is the only edition that is fully annotated, with the many quotations taken directly from the classical authors instead of translated from the German edition, and with numerous cross-references. The book was edited by Paul M. Allen and has a fine introduction by Dr. Alfred Heidenreich.

N.B. Here it should be noted that most of the single lectures

119

by Rudolf Steiner were never given titles by him, and even some of the major cycles were given their titles only after his death. When, as has sometimes happened since, a series of lectures on a single subject, but given at different times, has been published in a single volume, the editor has given his collection a new title that he has naturally tried to make as descriptive as possible. One result, however, has been that titles are sometimes far from indicative of the true content, and can even be misleading. A cycle called *World History in the Light of Anthroposophy* might well be thought by an unwary reader to be a summary of the content of the preceding chapter. This, however, is far from true, and in fact this cycle given from December 24, 1923 to January 1, 1924 at Dornach, is not being recommended here because it presupposes too great a knowledge of anthroposophy and of other cycles to be suitable for beginners. Another cycle, entitled, *The Evolution of Consciousness*, thirteen lectures given in August, 1923 at Penmaenmawr, Wales, should, in spite of its title, be placed in the category of unsuitable for beginners. In general the reader of this book may safely assume that when a title that would seem suitable because of its title is not recommended in these reading lists, it is because the author has come to the conclusion that the book or cycle in question ought not to be studied at too early a stage. These lists are intended to be as helpful as possible to beginners, not as comprehensive bibliographies of the subjects studied in the preceding chapter.

Works by other writers.

Wachsmuth, Guenther, *The Evolution of Mankind* (Dornach: Philosophic-Anthroposophic Press, 1961; original German version 1953). A stimulating and ambitious pioneer effort to present in a systematic way the early history of mankind, with many interesting illustrations and some extraordinary charts. Although making use, primarily, of Steiner and various anthroposophical writers, the author makes also some effective use of the work of other scholars, even if he usually interprets their data in a manner that would have been astonishing to them.

Van Bemmelen, D.J., *Zarathustra: The First Prophet of Christ; Zarathustra's Gathas with Introduction* (Zeist, Netherlands: Uitgeverij Vrij Geestesleven, 1968). Two original works in the English language that provide as much information as can be gleaned from non-anthroposophical sources, interpreted in the light of Steiner's teachings, on the second post-Atlantean cultural epoch.

Hiebel, Frederick, *The Gospel of Hellas* (New York: Anthroposophic Press, 1949). An original and stimulating interpretation of Greek culture by a noted anthroposophical scholar.

CHAPTER III

Individual Spiritual Development
and Human Freedom

In this chapter we shall try to give a brief explanation of Steiner's concept of freedom, and how the human being can so develop himself as to be able to perform deeds that are truly free. This is a peculiarly difficult task because Steiner's book, *The Philosophy of Freedom*, in which he demonstrates the possibility of freedom is not a book to be read like other books. It is through the experience of reading it and working with it that we gradually prepare ourselves so that eventually we can understand what a free deed is, and at the same time become capable of performing deeds that are free. As Steiner himself says of this book, "We have to read it with a soul attitude through which we become aware that we thereby enter into a completely different manner of thinking and a different way of looking at the will."

It may be admitted at once that this is a pretty large claim to make for any book, and it is a claim incapable of being proved except insofar as the person making the attempt and working thoroughly through the book believes he has proved it for himself. In this sense reading the book and working with it is a spiritual exercise, and the effectiveness of any spiritual exercise can be proved only to one's own satisfaction, never to the satisfaction of anyone else. For the purposes of this book all that we can do is simply to state, as we have just done, Steiner's claim for it, and try to extract from it what Steiner says about the nature of freedom and what he means by free will. These things should be reasonably comprehensible to others who have not tackled the book itself. But we should emphasize, nevertheless, that the major purpose of working with this book is to acquire the ability to think livingly, to attain to what Steiner called "living thinking," the kind of thinking that alone can comprehend the living, organic world. We shall have to refer again to this kind of thinking when we deal with science in Chapter 7. It is a thinking also called "Goethean" after the first great modern master of this kind of thinking—although Goethe simply practiced it, offering no systematic analysis of it, nor did he explain, as Steiner tries to do, how it is to be attained.

We have called this book, first published in 1894, and revised in 1918 *The Philosophy of Freedom*, but the English word freedom is by no means identical in meaning with the German word *Freiheit* (free*hood*, or condition of freedom), a fact of which Steiner himself was well aware. He therefore proposed as an alternative title for the English translation *The Philosophy of Spiritual Activity*, and it was under this title that the book was always published in English until the seventh English edition translated by Michael Wilson and published in 1964. Wilson in an invaluable introduction on his use of various English words to convey the meaning of the various German concepts makes the perfectly true remark that "spiritual activity" in English is not a precise concept, and may well be confused with some religious, (or even mediumistic!) activity—whereas freedom is a word that at least has certain well-defined meanings in English. What Steiner undoubtedly had in mind was that working through the book is in itself a truly *spiritual activity*, since it is an activity of the *self*, or "I," and a part of this activity is the freeing of oneself from all preconceptions and prejudices that arise from our life of soul, our life of feeling. The "I" is the spiritual core of

123

the human being, and in Steiner's writings the "I" and the spirit are often virtually synonymous. Working with and through the book tends to make us aware of this central core of our being, and if we ever attain to truly "living thinking," if only for brief periods at a time, then we are exercising the spiritual part of our being. Wilson's definition of freedom, however, as the "inner conquest of outer restraints" is an excellent working definition for freedom as it is understood and described in this book.

In order to understand Steiner's philosophy of freedom it is essential to have some grasp of his theory of knowledge, and just what he means by thinking, since his philosophy rests upon them. Indeed, the first half of his book consists of cogently and elegantly argued chapters leading up to the demonstration that there are in fact no necessary limits to human knowledge. Only in the second half of the book does he tackle the question of human freedom, and it may be noted in parentheses that no reader should attempt the second half of the book without having at least made a serious effort to work through the first. It is the mental effort required for following the arguments dealing with the nature of thinking that prepare us for the sustained effort to grasp the essence of freedom, what it is, and what it is not.

It may not be immediately apparent why we should come to an understanding of the true nature of thinking before we can consider the possibility of free will. But the emphasis should not be surprising if we stop to consider how we could, even in the theory, ever come to perform a free deed. Clearly such a deed would have to be willed by us—which, in effect, means that we must control our action, not perform it involuntarily. The instrument for control is obviously not the will itself, whatever that may be, but our thinking, which at least *appears* to be under our control, whereas few would claim that our feelings, our emotions, are even slightly under our control in the sense that we can decide what we will feel and whether we shall be sad or happy. But we can refrain from doing something we should very much like to do, and if we do so refrain it was as the result of reflection, thinking about the action before we decided to take it.

But it is precisely this ability to think freely that is denied by so many modern philosophers and psychologists, and if we cannot think freely we clearly cannot act freely. Many of them say that there is and can be no such thing as a truly free act because we have been *conditioned* to think and behave in a certain manner by the whole of our past life and our previous experience, to say nothing of the influences exercised on us by our social class and culture. We refrain from performing a particular act because we were told in childhood that it was wrong. In later life we may pretend to ourselves that we have a conscience, but, at least according to Freud and numerous other psychologists, this conscience itself was imposed upon us from without, and all we have done is "internalize" what Freud calls our "superego." To such psychologists the superego is a tyrant that prevents us from acting freely, and our so-called conscious thinking is conditioned, if by nothing else, by our unconscious feeling processes, by elements in our subconscious of which we are unaware, as well as by our family and cultural environment.

It would be idle to deny the truth of most of these observations. Even if we do not accept what psychologists tell us about our supposed subconscious motives (after all they too have their own problems with the subconscious) we must surely be ready to acknowledge that almost all our actions are indeed the result of our conditioning and our previous experiences, and it may not be going too far to say that most of us have never performed a truly free action in our lives. But this is not to say that we *could* not perform such an action if we knew how to go about trying to win our freedom. All we shall try to do here is to demonstrate that it is not philosophically necessary to suppose that all our thinking (and therefore our willing) must always and inevitably be unfree. What we must demonstrate is that thinking—real thinking, not our usual habit of merely letting various thought processes pass through our mind—is a self-sustaining activity that is under the control of the real self, or "I," of man. This is what Steiner tries to do in the first half of his book, *The*

125

Philosophy of Freedom, to which the reader is referred, and the most that can be done here is to summarize the central arguments.

For several centuries the one great problem in the field of the theory of knowledge (epistemology) has been how the subjective "I" can perceive the world, how it can even know for certain that the world exists at all when all that it really knows and perceives is the "representation" or mental image of what exists in the outer world. This representation, existing as it does only in a man's own mind—so it is held—may be a totally false picture of what is actually there in the outer world. Indeed, some philosophers have held that there can be no proof for the existence of the outer world at all except insofar as we must believe that *something* at least *causes* us to have a representation of an object in our mind. The distinguished philosopher, Immanuel Kant, held that there were three elements to be taken into consideration in any act of perceiving: the subjective viewer, the object as it appeared in his mind, and the object as it was in itself, which last could not be known at all, and was thus called by Kant the "thing-in-itself."

This particular aspect of the theory of knowledge did not interest either the ancients or the philosophers of the Middle Ages. Their interest lay rather in the question of how we come to know ideas, what is the origin of ideas, and do they have any reality in themselves? But, as was explained in the last chapter, the consciousness soul separates itself from the visible world, and, as we called it, it is the "spectator soul" and thus capable of studying the world objectively. Hence the nature of the outside world and how we come to know *it* has become a *problem*, whereas to the intellectual soul the *nature of thinking* and the proper objects for *thought* were of paramount importance. Being unable to solve the problem posed by Kant and others in the form in which they posed it, other modern thinkers have bypassed the problem, and turned to a solution that does not leave them helpless in the face of their ignorance, but allows

126

them to make use of their perceptions for the purpose of creating a scientifically acceptable body of knowledge, even though when pressed they will admit they do not *know* anything for certain. This epistemological substitute is pragmatism, which in effect permits us to ask questions of the external world and have them satisfactorily answered, that is, to our practical but not theoretical satisfaction.

Much simplified, the system works in somewhat the following way. The scientist or philosopher proposes a hypothesis about the world that cannot be immediately tested in the world of extra-mental reality. The hypothesis will, however, obviously be based on previous knowledge in the field of speciality of the proposer. Various deductions must now be made from the original hypothesis, using a logic that must be correct. Eventually some consequence of the hypothesis will be reached that *is* capable of being tested experimentally or that can be observed. When enough such consequences have been tested, then the hypothesis is promoted to being a theory, which will probably be published so that all other scientists and philosophers can try to pick holes in it. If they do not succeed, and evidence piles up in favor of the theory, it will be accepted as provisionally true. But it can never be accepted as unconditionally true because at any time some philosopher or scientist or plain man may find a logical consequence of the theory that can be shown by experiment *not* to be true. In this case the theory has to be modified to take care of the new evidence, or abandoned.

Einstein's theories of relativity are not held by scientists, as a rule, to be absolutely true, at least not in the form in which they were originally stated. But two important logically deduced consequences of the theories have indeed been tested. One could be tested at the total sun eclipse of 1919, when a prediction of Einstein was shown to be observable under the right conditions. The other, more famous (or infamous) conclusion expressed in the form of the equation $E = Mc^2$ led practical scientists to see if they could make use of the relationship between mass, light,

127

and energy to release energy to make a so-called "atomic bomb." They were successful, thus helping to confirm the theory.

Under this system of reasoning the major practical consequence is that "what works" is held to be true until it is disproved. To a large extent men of science have ceased to ask questions that are, even in principle, unverifiable—as, for example, if the soul (if there is a soul) is immortal. Furthermore, they have ceased to care about what the external world really *is,* as such knowledge is meaningless, mere definitions. For example, is that object that we see in the meadow (if it is a meadow) a relationship between elementary particles in a four dimensional space-time continuum, or is it a flower? Which of the two definitions is more or less true than the other is a question that cannot be answered, but which definition is to be used can be chosen easily enough, depending on the purpose of our investigation.

Steiner cuts through all this kind of argumentation by drawing attention to the fact that we are not justified in denying ourselves the possibility of knowing anything except our representations of an unknown external world, and our reflections about such representations, because we do have one completely self-sustaining activity—our thinking when it concerns itself with our own world of thought. This thinking has no connection with the (unknown) outside world, but only with our (known) inner world. From this elementary observation Steiner leads us gently on, step by step, in his *Philosophy of Freedom* to the recognition that in every object in the outer world there is a conceptual element that belongs to *it,* just as fully as does the perceptual element. Confronted with an object, we *conceive* of it by an "intuitive" act, just as much as we *perceive* it through one or other of our senses. A flower or a rock simply cannot register on our senses without at the same time having some impact on our thought. Thus, "intuition and observation are equally the sources of our knowledge. An observed object of the world remains unintelligible to us until we have within ourselves the corresponding intuition which adds that part of the reality which is lacking in the percept. To anyone who is incapable of finding intuitions corresponding to the things, the full reality remains inaccessible." (*Philosophy of Freedom*, Wilson translation, page 73.)*

Having now demonstrated that thinking itself can be self-sustaining, and does not, in principle, have to be influenced by anything other than thinking (which would make it unfree), Steiner then goes on to show how it is possible for the human being to think freely. In the process he concedes that our thinking, and our actions based on it, are almost invariably determined by what he calls our characterological disposition, that is, the more or less permanent character structure that we have created for ourselves on the basis of our original natural and inherited endowments. But it remains possible to transcend even our characterological disposition when we engage in those acts of creative thinking that Steiner calls moral imagination and moral intuition.

Here we are bidden to beware because we can be so easily deceived into believing we are thinking and acting freely when we are not. Steiner gives several illustrations of the kind of self-deception we all indulge in at (almost) all times. Let us say that we are trying to overcome our conscious egoism or self-seeking, that we wish to transcend our natural wish to pursue what is directly pleasurable to us.** We try then to relate

---

* It is interesting to note that Aristotle in his *Posterior Analytics* came to a similar conclusion. In trying to solve the problem posed by Plato of how the mind can form abstract or universal ideas, he concluded that the Nous or mind can grasp the universal element in objects, while the senses perceive the particular elements (Book II, ch. 19). Thomas Aquinas and other medieval philosophers reached the same conclusion but greatly refined Aristotle's arguments. For Thomas the fact that a non-physical element in man existed that was capable of grasping the non-physical element in objects was one of the arguments in favor of immortality.

** In this connection it is still instructive to read what Aristotle had to say about the pursuit of pleasure and happiness, and how to distinguish between means and ends in this pursuit. The discussion occupied the whole of Book X of his *Nicomachean Ethics*.

our actions to a set of moral principles, necessarily abstract, and received by us from someone or something accepted by us as an authority, for example the state, social custom, the authority of the church, or divine revelation. When these commands have been "internalized," we are guided by what we call our "conscience." If we do not acknowledge any outer or inner authority but try to act out of original moral insight, we may accept as motives for our actions such notions as (a) the greatest possible good of mankind purely for its own sake or (b) the progress of civilization or the moral evolution of mankind toward ever greater perfection.

Steiner analyzes (*Philosophy*, Wilson trans., 130 ff) these motives by first remarking that to follow them "a man will try to find out the requirements of the moral life and will let his actions be determined by the knowledge of them." But where does he acquire such knowledge? He must make use of a mental picture provided by either someone else or by himself. Such a mental picture is not achieved as a result of pure thinking, in the sense in which Steiner speaks of pure thinking. The imagined mental picture must have a percept attached to it in the form of particular experiences of a concrete nature. If, for example, we wish to further the advance of civilization, we must have some definite perceptual idea in our mind as to the nature of this advance. We may try to promote perpetual peace, or an earth free of industrial pollution, or any other of an infinite number of goals we favor and should like to achieve. They may all be entirely admirable in the sense that few seriously inclined persons would consider them undesirable. But they are all in one way or another *concrete* goals that call up in our mind particular things, and on all concrete goals some men will be found who differ on them and whose judgment will be different from ours. But in Steiner's (difficult) analysis the "highest conceivable moral principle is one that from the start contains no such reference to particular experiences, but springs from the source of pure intuition, and *only later* seeks any reference to percepts, that is, to life." In such a case our "action is neither a stereotyped one which merely follows certain rules, nor is it one which we automatically perform in response to an external impulse, but it is an action determined purely and simply by its own ideal content. Such an action presupposes the capacity for moral intuitions. Whoever lacks the capacity to experience for himself the particular moral principle for each single situation, will never achieve truly individual willing" (*op.cit*, page 133).

So we return to the question of how to attain living thinking so that each single situation is perceived in all its living and moving reality. Through this living thinking men will then come to create the appropriate intuition, in all the particularity of a particular instance, and not by making use of any universal idea or moral rule, however admirable. The moral intuition, the free act, is created *to fit* a particular living situation as it reveals itself to the living thinking; it is not *determined* by the situation in accordance with any universal moral rule or any particular moral precedent, not even by one that one has previously made oneself for a different situation. It is perhaps instructive to realize that modern existentialism, itself a product of the consciousness soul era and greatly preoccupied with freedom, comes to a similar conclusion, though naturally by a different path of reasoning.

Thus it follows that ethical individualism, as it may be called, is seen to involve nothing that in any way resembles an ethical *science,* such as some modern scientific philosophers are seeking. The seeker after moral rules and moral laws will find himself, in Steiner's term, faced with nothing but a "natural history of morality," that is, moral deeds that have in the past been freely performed by free men, from which deeds it is impossible to make generalizations. Willing and thinking must, in effect, be simultaneous: I carry out the action as soon as I have grasped the idea of it, and it is this simultaneity that makes it truly *my* action. The existentialist will also recognize this conclusion. If I think about the action and then try to relate it to some moral principles before performing it, then I shall, after all, be acting like a moral automaton even if I tell myself that my action, objectively speaking, is "Christian, humane, or seemingly un-selfish." I can, concludes Steiner, act freely only if "I find in myself the ground for my action, my love of the action. I carry it out because I love it."

Obviously, this line of argument can be easily attacked on the ground that we cannot be making such free acts constantly, and that if we make such an effort every time we act, we shall be unable to act at all or will do the first thing that comes into our head, which may by ordinary standards be an immoral one. Steiner meets this argument by saying that moral standards must, of course, be observed *while on the path to freedom,* but deeds performed in accordance with accepted moral standards, while admirable, are not free. What he is trying to do in this book is to demonstrate the *possibility* of free deeds and explain what they are; the only way of attaining this freedom is to raise ourselves to the "intuitive" world of ideas. "Only an act of will that springs from intuition can be an individual one."

It would take us too far to attempt even to summarize the crushing retorts Steiner makes to those who suggest that his system represents a license to immorality if every man creates his own morality for himself (pp. 137 ff.). For example:

The blind instinct that drives a man to crime does not spring from intuition and does not belong to what is individual in him, but rather to what is most general in him, to what is equally present in all individuals, and out of which *a man works his way* by means of what is individual in him. What is individual in me is not my organism with its instincts and its feelings, but rather the unified world of ideas which lights up within this organism. My instincts, urges and passions establish no more than that I belong to the general species *man;* it is the fact that something of the idea world comes to expression *in a particular way* within these urges, passions and feelings that establishes my individuality. Through my instincts and cravings, I am the sort of man of whom there are twelve to the dozen; through the particular form of the idea by means of which I designate myself within the dozen as "I" I am an individual. Only a being other than myself could distinguish me from others by the difference in my animal nature; through my thinking, that is, by actively grasping what expresses itself in my organism as idea, I distinguish myself from others. Therefore one cannot say of the action of a criminal that it proceeds from the idea within him. Indeed, the characteristic feature of criminal actions is precisely that they spring from the non-ideal elements in man. An action is felt to be free insofar as the reasons for it spring from the ideal part of my individual being; every other part of an action, irrespective of whether it is carried out under the compulsion of nature or under the obligation of a moral standard is felt to be *unfree*.

To those who ask how a social life is possible if everyone is striving only to assert his own individuality, Steiner offers a more sophisticated argument, based this time on his earlier proof that the world of ideas is a real one, and that there is only one such world of ideas. It is a unity, but every free man uses his own intuition to take what he can from it. If my neighbor and I are both morally free, and both "conceive out of the idea and do not obey any external impulses (physical or spiritual), then we cannot but meet one another in like striving, in common intent. A moral misunderstanding, a clash, is impossible between men who are morally free." It need scarcely be added, since history so convincingly demonstrates it, that the reverse is true when men follow a particular moral standard. My neighbor then may well have a different standard, which he wishes to force me to obey, or we may have the same standard but he thinks I am too lax in observing it. In both cases clashes are inevitable.

Lastly, to the argument that such free men do not exist in real life, as we may easily see by looking around us, and that for this reason some authority must be established capable of enforcing a moral code providing mankind with at least a minimum of acceptable social behavior, Steiner replies that he is not talking about present-day society anywhere in the world. Almost all men, he agrees, for one reason or another are always unfree in their actions, but he insists that "in all the welter of customs, legal codes, religious observances and so forth there do arise men who establish themselves as free spirits." "Which of us can say that he is really free in all his actions? Yet in each one of us there dwells a deeper being in which the free man finds expression. Our life is made up of free and unfree actions. We cannot, however, think out the concept of man completely without coming upon the *free spirit* as the purest expression of human nature. Indeed, we are men in the true sense only in so far as we are free" (Wilson translation, p. 140).

There we may leave this fundamental book of Rudolf Steiner, which, as he repeatedly explained, laid the foundation in philosophy for all his later work. Although written almost eighty years ago nothing in modern philosophy has really superseded it. The problems Steiner met head on are still with us, though numerous present-day thinkers bypass them, or airily dismiss them as meaningless exercises in futility by comparison with the analysis of meaning that has dominated most modern philosophy. Perhaps what has been said here, oversimplified as it has had to be, will persuade some readers that it is still worth their while returning to this source in order to understand the nature of thinking and willing and what is meant by freedom of thinking and willing, in short, of that freedom of which we all talk so much and understand so little.

It is worth noting here that more than a quarter century after *The Philosophy of Freedom* Rudolf Steiner, in a series of three lectures on medieval philosophy, returned to the subject of the nature of thinking, including especially an explanation of why so many medieval thinkers denied the possibility of attaining to spiritual knowledge through their own thinking. In the course of these lectures* Steiner devotes several pages (pp. 106 ff) to a summary of the main conclusions of the *Philosophy of Freedom* and his other philosophical works of the period, showing how consistent they were with what he now tells us, namely, that the ethical individualism of the earlier book was in reality founded

---

* Given in Dornach May 22–24, 1920, last edited and translated by A. P. Shepherd and M. R. Nicoll under the title, *The Redemption of Thinking*.

134

upon the Christ impulse, although this was not expressed explicitly in the book. Thomas Aquinas, to whom the greater part of two of the lectures was devoted had, in particular, felt forced to insist that the two realms of faith and reason (see below pp. 140–142) must forever remain separated, a gap that was explained by earlier Christian thinkers as a result of original sin and the Fall of Man.

Although Thomas could not accept that explanation because of his reverence for the faculty of thinking as the highest part of man's nature, Steiner in what must seem to be a rather startling manner to most readers, in effect agrees with the earlier Christian thinkers, telling us that the possibility of penetrating into the spiritual world through thinking was indeed a result of the sacrifice of Christ, and that thinking filled with love, and acts performed for the love of the acts themselves, as described in *The Philosophy of Freedom*, are the result of the Christ impulse working in us.* This possibility, however, did not really exist in the era of the intellectual soul when the ego of man was not yet developed far enough to be able to unite itself with the Christ impulse. Thus Thomas Aquinas in fact could not have spiritualized his own thinking, as has become possible in our age with the development of the consciousness soul. This section may therefore fittingly close with a quotation from the third of these lectures in which the mature thinking of 1920 comments on the still somewhat skeletal thinking of 1894.

[Ethical Individualism] . . . is based upon the free spiritual activity that man achieves by changing ordinary thinking into what in my book I called "pure thinking." This pure thinking then raises itself to the direct experience of the spiritual world and derives from it the impulses to moral behavior. This is due to the fact that in the spiritual activity of pure thinking the impulse of love, which is otherwise bound up with man's physical nature, spiritualizes itself, and when the moral imagination discovers the ethical ideals as

---

* This subject will be elaborated further in Chapter 5 in our discussion of the Christ impulse.

135

actual realities in the spiritual world, this spiritualized love becomes the power by means of which they express themselves (p. 110).*

A greater contrast between this necessarily austere moral philosophy and the customary hedonism of the present age can scarcely be imagined. Freedom as defined by Rudolf Steiner has obviously little in common with the pursuit of pleasure. Although the American Declaration of Independence has enshrined the notion that the pursuit of happiness is one of the "unalienable" rights of man, it should be clear enough that happiness as such can hardly be pursued as a goal or aim in life. If a man is thought of as happy, this usually means that he is satisfied by the general conditions of his life, including his personal relationships and the work that fills his waking hours. He may also be temporarily filled with a kind of bliss, which he may define to himself as happiness, as a lover may be happy with his loved one or a mathematician when he has just found an elegant solution to a problem that has been puzzling him. But in the nature of things, such "happiness" lasts for a strictly limited time, and it must be thought of as an ephemeral condition of being rather than as a possible aim for one's whole life.

As will be understood from what has been said in this chapter no one who follows the path indicated by Rudolf Steiner can be said to have an actual concrete and definable aim in life. Ethical individualism, as has been seen, lays down no goals to be pursued any more than it lays down norms of conduct. The self

* As the anthroposophical writer and philosopher H. E. Lauer has pointed out the great German idealist thinkers, Fichte, Schelling and Hegel, were on the same path insofar as their philosophies were all based on the development of the ego as a spiritual entity that experienced itself not through experience of the sense world but through a living and creative thinking that experiences its own unity with the universal spirit. All emphasized that thinking tied to the brain is a dead thinking, as Steiner also held. See, for example, the chapter called "Redemption and the Remission of Sins" in Lauer's book *Die Anthroposophie und die Zukunft des Christentums*, of which a translation exists in French, but not as yet in English. Steiner himself commented on these three philosophers in this same sense in his *Vom Menschenrätsel*, not translated into English.

136

is required to engage in pure morally creative thinking on the basis of the concrete situation with which it is confronted—or, in other words, it will produce for itself the concept corresponding to the percept in the outer world.

We must therefore in concluding this short chapter refrain from trying to lay down any general or specific guidelines for human behavior, and not say what man ought to do with the freedom we have attempted to define. But in the next chapter in which we describe the human being as he is viewed by anthroposophy, including his relations with spiritual beings in the higher worlds, we shall hope to lay a groundwork of knowledge, on the basis of which every man can perceive the way in which he can pursue his path in life in a way that will be constructive for himself and helpful to his fellowmen and to the world. No one has any right to dictate to others, but neither can any man really know what to do with his life without having a minimum of necessary knowledge about his true self, which alternates in time between life in the physical world and life in the spiritual. It is, indeed, the absence of this kind of knowledge that has left modern men so disoriented in the world they know through their ordinary consciousness. Some of this knowledge we shall supply in the next chapter.

SUGGESTIONS FOR FURTHER READING
FOR CHAPTER 3.

The two editions and translations of the major work dealt with in this chapter are, *The Philosophy of Spiritual Activity*, translated by Rita Stebbing (Nyack, New York: Rudolf Steiner Publications Inc., 1963) and *The Philosophy of Freedom*, translated by Michael Wilson (London, 1964). The last named edition was that used for quotations given in the text, but it is not necessarily superior to the former, both editions having their particular virtues. The Stebbing translation also contains an essay by Steiner called *Truth and Knowledge*, formerly called *Truth and Science*, which was in effect Steiner's doctoral dissertation at the University of Rostock, as revised by the author for publication. This work discusses other philosophers in more detail than was necessary in the later work.

Fundamental to all Steiner's epistemology is the valuable little book published under the title, *The Theory of Knowledge Implicit in Goethe's World Conception*, originally published in 1886 and revised by the author in 1923, translated by O. D. Wannamaker (New York, 1940). Most of the themes later handled in more detail in *The Philosophy of Freedom* were adumbrated in this work written by Steiner in his twenties. It is therefore of great help for understanding the evolution of his thought.

The lectures on Thomas Aquinas discussed in the text were given at Dornach, May 22 to 24, 1920. They were originally published with some helpful notes and an extensive commentary by Dr. Roman Booz, but this edition has long been out of print (London, Percy Lund, Humphries and Co., Ltd., 1932). The title of this work was simply, *The Philosophy of Thomas Aquinas*. Another translation with many notes and an extensive epilogue and useful appendices was published under the title, *The Redemption of Thinking*, tr. and ed., A. P. Shepherd and M. R. Nicoll (London, Hodder and Stoughton, 1956).

For other works dealing with Goethean thinking see the Reading List for Chapter 7, where this subject is again discussed in relation to Steiner's contributions to science.

Before closing this short reading list for this chapter, mention should be made of three works, all of which are of great importance for the understanding of Steiner's concept of freedom, and of his philosophy in general, even though the subject matter of each is different. First should be mentioned the beautifully concise twenty-three page introduction to *Mysticism at the Dawn of the Modern Age* (1901) in which Steiner in effect epitomizes so much of what he said nearly a decade earlier in his *Philosophy of Freedom*. A paperback version of this work is available under the title, *Eleven European Mystics* (Blauvelt, N.Y., Rudolf Steiner Publications, 1971), as well as the original under the title given above, published in 1960. The same publisher issued in 1960 a hardcover version of an early work (1895) of Rudolf Steiner under the title, *Friedrich Nietzsche: Fighter for Freedom*. Lastly, also in 1973, has appeared for the first time in English Steiner's monumental work, *The Riddles of Philosophy* (1914), which is a kind of history of philosophy from Greek times onward, written from Steiner's special point of view, sympathetic but critical and always trying to show how each man thought in relation to the consciousness of his time (New York, 1973). The book concludes with a chapter previously translated and published in the 1953 *Golden Blade* under the title, "From Philosophy to Anthroposophy," which sums up Steiner's findings on earlier philosophy, and shows how philosophy needs supersensible consciousness if it is to fulfill its task and solve its problems.

CHAPTER IV

Man in His Life on Earth
and in the Spiritual Worlds;
Reincarnation and Karma

In Chapter 2 a brief allusion was made to the medieval
distinction between two different kinds of knowledge: ordinary
knowledge obtained by the human reason, and what was
thought of as knowledge "above reason," which could not be
acquired by man's own efforts, however acute his powers of
observation and mental capacities. Such knowledge had to be
revealed by God, and it was this kind of knowledge that was
embodied in the Bible, both the Old and the New Testaments,
and was revealed in a more limited way to the so-called Fathers
of the Church. The minds of these men were illuminated, so it
was held, by the Holy Spirit, as had happened also to the
apostles at the first Pentecost. The writings of these men carried
a little less authority than the sacred scriptures themselves. The
scriptural writings and the teachings of the Fathers of the
Church had therefore both to be accepted on *faith,* even though
the knowledge itself was true.

In the early Middle Ages, during which few men in the West
were able to understand Greek or Latin philosophy, when only a
tiny minority were even literate and fewer still could be
considered educated, the realm assigned to faith was much

wider than that assigned to knowledge, and it was quite customary to explain ordinary natural phenomena in the light of one's religious beliefs; relatively little effort was made to apply reason either to religious teachings or to the phenomena observed in the outer world. People knew how to carry out their earthly tasks and occasionally made innovations in technique, but for many centuries there is little evidence of the application of reason even to improvement of their earthly lot. It is a measure of the intellectual accomplishment of the Middle Ages that by the time of Thomas Aquinas educated men now believed that reason could be applied even in the realm of theology, and, as we have already noticed, proofs were offered for the existence of God. Some truths were still thought by Thomas to be above reason, or to be unprovable by reason, but the domain of faith had nevertheless been greatly shrunken. Such a religious proposition as the triune nature of God (the Trinity) remained an example of the truths that were "above reason," and would presumably always remain so. Similarly, the creation of the world by God in six days could not be proved by reason, but because the Bible proclaimed this to be the truth, it could be accepted on faith. The creation of the world out of nothing by God, or by what Aristotle had called a First Cause could not be proved by the unaided human reason, according to Thomas, because it was also possible that the First Cause had *always* been operating, and that the world had therefore existed from all eternity. Thus the Bible in stating that "In the Beginning God created the heavens and the earth" was confirming one of two equally possible hypotheses. Thomas also held that it was perfectly legitimate to try to *understand* all the truths received by revelation, and even such mysteries as that of the Trinity could be meditated upon, thus deepening the thought and feeling life of men who attempted it. So by the end of the Middle Ages there was a considerable theological *science,* as it was thought to be, which received the name of theodicy, and comprised all the religious truths that could be attained by man through the unaided use of his reason. There was a much smaller realm of

141

knowledge consisting of theological truths such as that of the Trinity, that had to be held by faith for lack of the possibility of arriving at them through the unaided reason.

Now at first thought it might seem that the knowledge of the supersensible worlds revealed by Rudolf Steiner is of the same nature as the theological truths received by revelation, as defined by such men as Thomas Aquinas. But in my view there are three essential differences between medieval revealed knowledge and anthroposophy. It must be conceded that for almost all people today the knowledge given out by Steiner does indeed constitute a "revelation" to which they themselves have no access. But Steiner in his major works explains the systematic exercises and training that *may* be undertaken by anyone, and which if faithfully followed may lead to the kind of knowledge won for himself by Steiner. The very first sentence in his major book on spiritual training, *Knowledge of the Higher Worlds and its Attainment*, (New York, 1947) states categorically, "There slumber in every human being faculties by means of which he can acquire for himself a knowledge of higher worlds." In other words, all of us have the capacity, insofar as we are human beings, but we have not developed it. Yet *in principle* it is capable of being developed, and those who have taken even a few steps along the road are led, even by taking these few steps, to the conclusion that there really *is* something in what Steiner has said, thus gaining the hope that if we persist we may achieve *some* results, even if we have not been prepared by previous lives to reach the degree of seership attained by Steiner. Medieval thinkers, even those as advanced as Thomas Aquinas, held that no new revelations could be attained by men, nor did any training exist that could be used to help men attain knowledge of the higher worlds.

Secondly, in the last chapter we gave at least some indications of how Steiner sets about laying the groundwork for the recognition that there are not, in truth, two separate realms, one of knowledge and one of faith, nor is there even a true dichotomy between the subjective self and the objective world.

On the contrary, thinking itself when developed is capable of grasping equally well both the sensible and supersensible worlds. Thus there are no necessary limits to knowledge, and we do not, in order to increase our knowledge, have to await a revelation given to us by God.

Thirdly, as indicated in the first chapter of this book, the "revelations" of Rudolf Steiner can sometimes be tested against facts in the outer world in the same way that scientific hypotheses put forward by scientists can be tested against the experimental evidence. It is also conducive to belief when we recognize how consistent within themselves all his teachings are, how many of them serve to explain so much of the world as a whole, and the course of historical evolution to the present time. By contrast numerous Biblical passages if interpreted literally not only contradict each other, but do not conform at all to what the human mind regards as reasonable. This is perhaps even more true of the supposedly revealed and authoritative teachings of many of the Fathers of the Church.

There is no obvious reason why our own present inability to see into the supersensible world should lead us to deny its existence—an attitude characterized by Rudolf Steiner as "negative superstition"—nor why we should refrain from studying for ourselves the results of another man's researches, as we should be willing to study Einstein's findings even if we do not have the qualifications to contest or prove them. But there is another reason why all those who enter upon a path of training, at the end of which they may themselves be able to attain supersensible knowledge (and thus help to *prove* Steiner's so-called "revelations"), should study what he did give out in his lifetime. According to Steiner the best possible preparation for individual perception in the spiritual worlds is to study what has already been given out by others. The study of his books and lectures therefore prepares our souls for attaining of higher knowledge for ourselves. Nevertheless, Steiner insists time and time again that no student should adopt an attitude of blind faith toward what he imparted. He should simply hold it as a hypothesis, not believing it but also not unreasonably *dis*believing it. Then he may come to see that the teachings, as we say, "make sense" even if they cannot be proved. Such an attitude is close to that of pragmatism, the modern philosophy to which reference was made in the last chapter (p. 127). If we cannot always see whether an anthroposophical teaching "works in practice" (and therefore may, according to pragmatists, be held to be temporarily true), at least we can use our healthy power of reasoning and understanding to see if it makes sense and is reasonable, and helps to explain what we already know from observation. This therefore should be the attitude to be taken by the reader to what follows in this chapter about the nature of man, not only in his life on earth but in the spiritual worlds between death and a new birth (reincarnation).*

Life Between Birth and Death. We have spoken in Chapter 2 of the four separate but interwoven constituent elements in man, the physical, etheric and astral bodies, and the ego, or "I," and explained that the physical body is held in common with the mineral world, the etheric or life body with the plant world, the astral body with the animal world, while the "I" is peculiar to man himself, and is indeed the element that distinguishes him

---

* Steiner himself often mentions "good will" and "healthy common sense" as the most necessary prerequisites for the grasping of anthroposophy. But it is also worth mentioning that when in the last year of his life he wrote a series of leading thoughts or guidelines for the benefit of members he made the remarkable statement that "only they can be anthroposophists who feel certain questions on the nature of man and the universe as an elemental need of life, just as one feels hunger and thirst." (*Anthroposophical Leading Thoughts*, London 1973, p. 11) This statement may at first sight seem startling, but the more experienced one becomes in anthroposophy, and especially in working with newcomers, the more does its truth become apparent. The casual enquirer simply cannot become a serious student of anthroposophy. There must be some questions to which his whole being demands an answer. One cannot really approach anthroposophy as a dilettante taster of cults, beliefs and philosophies; there must be a desire truly akin to that of "hunger and thirst" and this desire in fact derives from our personal karma. We should thus all of us beware of trying to *convince* anyone that anthroposophy is true, and especially not by the use of *arguments*. We are brought by our karma toward a door that opens out on anthroposophy. But it is for us, not the doorkeeper, to make the decision to enter.

144

from the rest of the natural world (a truth that was recognized by Aristotle when he *defined* man as a "rational animal"). In sleep the "I" and the astral body leave the physical and etheric bodies asleep on the bed, and themselves return to the spiritual world for the period of sleep. The etheric or life body remains with man throughout his entire life on earth, leaving only at death; indeed, it is the departure of the etheric body that constitutes death. Left without the etheric body (called also more awkwardly but more descriptively the "body of formative forces") which has given it form during life, the physical body, left to itself, decays into its mineral elements. The astral body of the animals also leaves them in sleep. Animals and men both have a waking day consciousness because the astral body is united to the etheric body, and it is the etheric body that mirrors the experiences of pain, pleasure, desire and so on that fill the astral body.

The astral body contains within it all the senses, the usual and universally recognized five, and other more subtle "senses," a description of which lies outside the scope of this chapter; they include such "senses" as that of equilibrium, warmth, and "sense of the other person" that are not ordinarily classified as senses. Through these senses the astral body conveys the impressions of the outer world to the etheric body. It also has yet other undeveloped "senses" that are present only in potential in the astral body. Indian thought based on ancient clairvoyance has always recognized these spiritual senses, calling them chakras or wheels, or lotus flowers, the term preferred by Rudolf Steiner because of the way they present themselves to clairvoyant vision. In the course of self-development through appropriate training, especially as described in *Knowledge of the Higher Worlds and its Attainment*, these lotus flowers begin (not necessarily all at the same time) to revolve, and through them while still in a waking state the developed clairvoyant can transmit impressions of the spiritual world to the etheric body in the same way as the ordinary "given" senses transmit impressions of the outer world. It will be recognized therefore that it is

145

not the astral body itself that gives us our consciousness, but the interaction between the astral and the etheric bodies. When the activity of the astral body calms down at the end of the day, we lose consciousness, that is, we fall asleep, and the astral body and "I," by leaving the etheric and physical, allow the etheric (life) body to repair the ravages wrought on the physical organism by the daytime activities of the astral. Incidentally, we do not dream while we are actually asleep, that is, while the astral body and "I" are outside. We dream when we are *half*-conscious, that is to say either when the astral body and the "I" are leaving at night, or when they are returning in the morning.

Now the physical, etheric and astral bodies can be actually *seen* by the clairvoyant; the "I" as such cannot be seen by another person, however clairvoyant he may be. But Steiner states that within the astral body as seen by the clairvoyant there is an "emptiness" that may in a sense be compared with the blue sky. The blue sky appears blue to our eyes because light in front of darkness has a blue tint. So the "empty space" in the astral body in which the "I" incarnates likewise appears blue to the clairvoyant, but there is not even a suspicion of "cloudiness" in this blue to indicate the presence of such an "entity" as the "I"; the central and inviolable sacred core of the human being is veiled from all other eyes, and can be experienced only by the individual self who is its "owner."

Steiner calls these sheaths of the human being "bodies" because they are, with the exception of the "I," at least potentially visible. This is not the case with the elements that compose the threefold, sevenfold or ninefold man as Steiner describes him in detail in the first chapter of *Theosophy*.* There is, of course, no contradiction between the different descriptions of man. None is intended to be a comprehensive definition; all

---

* Although this chapter of *Theosophy* (1904) contains a brief description of the "bodies" just described, the account is much fuller and probably better understood by the beginning student in Chapters 2 and 3 of *An Outline of Occult Science* (1909).

are characterizations from different points of view. Man as a threefold being is composed of body, soul and spirit, and it is extremely important in anthroposophy to understand the difference between soul and spirit, especially in view of the fact that the Catholic Church has for over a millennium denied the existence of spirit as a separate element in man, allowing only that the twofold human being made up of body and soul has some soul qualities of a spiritual nature.

Without attempting to go into too much detail here, let it simply be said that man's soul is his; it belongs to him during his life between birth and death; after death, as will be explained later, it gradually dissolves and ceases to exist as a separate entity. Not so the spiritual part of the human being that passes into the spiritual world after death and is indestructible. It passes in that world through spiritual experiences, and when the time again comes for it to incarnate, it forms new astral, etheric and physical bodies as needed for its new life on earth. Thus when, in the book *Theosophy* Steiner speaks of the human being as made of body, soul and spirit, he is referring to three clearly defined entities, and not to some vague religious concepts that can scarcely be defined.

By "body" in this context Steiner refers to the sheaths we have already called "bodies," the physical, etheric and astral bodies. By soul he refers to those three souls that we described in Chapter 2 as successive stages of consciousness, the sentient soul, the intellectual soul and the consciousness soul. It is the "I" working within the three sheaths of man that metamorphoses them into these three souls. The lowest of these souls, the sentient soul, is still closely united with the body, whereas the consciousness soul, the highest of the three, is closely united with the spirit, and at its most developed allows the spiritual to shine directly into it. In between these two souls is the intellectual soul, which, as we mentioned in Chapter 2, was developed in that historical epoch that represents the center of human evolution, the epoch in which the Christ incarnated.

Thus, we have the three "bodies," the three "souls," and

147

above these are yet higher stages of consciousness known to anthroposophy as spirit self, life spirit, and spirit man, which need not concern us here except to note that the historical epochs to come will be required to develop these spiritual elements also, as our own epoch has the task of developing the highest form of soul, the consciousness soul. From this point of view, therefore, man is seen as a ninefold being, or, if one wishes to speak of the three souls under the collective name of the ego or self, since it is this self working in the other sheaths that develops these souls, man may lastly be thought of as a sevenfold being. Man's life on earth unfolds also in stages of seven years. At the beginning of each new period of seven years new possibilities unfold for him that were not possible before. The first seven years are devoted to the building of the physical body, the next to the etheric body, the next to the astral body. This is the period of puberty, so difficult for all human beings, since the desires and emotions now find their means of physical expression in the body while the self, which has to bring these elements under its control, has not yet been born. It may be noted here that Steiner education, which will be discussed in a later chapter, is based primarily upon these fundamental insights.

Between the ages of 14 and 21 the human "I" is not yet fully within the bodily sheaths, and it is only at 21 (always, traditionally and correctly, considered to represent what was so beautifully called "coming-of-age") that it really incarnates. Its first task is then to master the astral body and live consciously through the life of feeling and emotion that was simply uncontrollable in any real sense before. At about 27 to 28 the human being now has the opportunity to develop the intellectual soul, and at 35 the time has come for the incorporation of the consciousness soul. If these stages have been passed through constructively, and the new potentials to some degree at least realized, then a man may be thought of as having reached the threshold of maturity, after which he should now be able to act as a mature human being. Nevertheless, new possibilities arrive

148

with each seven year period, and all the transitional years are of special importance, 42, 49, 56 and 63, until, at 70, in a certain sense life development is over, and all the years that follow present the opportunity for placing the wisdom acquired at the disposal of the world, and preparing in consciousness for life after death and the new incarnation that will eventually follow. To attempt to discuss these ages in any detail would require an entire book in itself, and the attempt cannot be made here. All that is worth pointing out and emphasizing is that all through our lives new potentials are awaiting us that are provided for us by higher powers if we will only use them. The ideal life would make full use of each new gift as it was offered, be ready for the next when the time came for it, and thus ever grow in wisdom and maturity and ability to place the fruits of this mature wisdom at the disposition of our fellowmen—especially from the age of 35 onward, when we should no longer be so much concerned with the development of our personal selves as we were *entitled* to be during the first half of life. During the first half of life we *should* be engaged in developing the instrument that is to become our mature self, even while performing the tasks that fall to us in co-operating with our fellowmen. During the second half (35 to 70), when we are in that half of life illuminated by the spirit rather than tied to the body, our *first* duty is toward others rather than to ourselves, while after 70 we should be *wholly devoted* to the welfare of others, and any new wisdom and insight, any new spiritual enlightenment to which we can attain will be for others, and be of no interest, as such, for ourselves, even though they will in fact bear fruits for our next life.

Life after Death. When man has finally lived out his life, his ego, astral and etheric bodies pass out into the spiritual world leaving the physical body tenantless and thus subject to decay. The etheric body, which has recorded within itself everything that has ever happened to us in the life just finished in the form of unconscious memories, remains attached to the astral body and ego for approximately three days, and then dissolves itself

149

and becomes a part of the universal ether from which it originally came. During these three days the life just completed passes before the ego and astral body in a great panorama, which unfolds itself in space, and not in time—or at least it appears to unfold itself in space. The experience itself should not be thought of as lasting for three days in the sense that it will take three days to bring back to conscious memory all that had been stored in the etheric body. Time as such does not exist for the etheric body and the panorama appears instantaneously in its entirety. When we say that it lasts for three days it should be recognized that the entire instantaneous picture lasts for three days until the etheric body is freed from the astral body and ego, and returns to the etheric "world" whence it came.

Like all the pictures that will have to be presented in this chapter of the experiences after death, this one just described can and must be regarded only as *analogous* to what is experienced on earth. It is essential to try to *imagine* the experiences but not to take them too literally as if they were just like earthly experiences. Above all we must rid ourselves of the quite natural belief, due to the inescapable limits of human language, that there is such a thing as a spiritual *world*, in the same sense as there is an earthly world. The spiritual world is not a *place*, up above the sky or anywhere else. It is perhaps best thought of as a condition of being that can be imagined only by thinking away entirely everything connected with the physical or bodily world. Space and time are earthly concepts, and they cannot exist in the spiritual world. Yet we can describe spiritual experiences only in terms of what is familiar to us on earth, and in some matters that we have to discuss it is indeed quite legitimate to speak in terms of time. The etheric body is not freed from the astral and ego until three earth days have passed. The period spent in kamaloca, which we are about to describe, does occupy about a third of the time occupied by the life just past. It is not experienced in the spiritual world in the body-free condition as so many years because time is not experienced in the spiritual world. Nor is kamaloca a *place* because space does not exist in the spiritual world. But the astral body does take about twenty years of earth time to dissolve if the life just lived lasted for sixty. These time periods are important for those who are on the earth who wish to help the dead in ways that Rudolf Steiner indicated, since the living should know to what condition of being in the spiritual world their dead friend has attained. Lastly, although the "I," which passes from incarnation to incarnation, does not experience time or space in the spiritual world, there will be a finite number of earth years between its incarnations, and these can naturally be counted by earthly measurements of time.

The panoramic unrollment of the past life experienced immediately after death has been experienced also by many persons who have been in danger of immediate accidental death, but have been saved and lived to tell the tale. Numerous persons in danger of drowning have reported that their whole past life suddenly appeared before them, and for some who were rescued the experience remained indelible, in some cases convincing them of the existence of life after death. It is an experience of extreme importance for the man who has just died since it engraves itself on his astral body, which will be surviving for many more "years" yet, while it and the "I" pass through what is usually given the oriental word, "kamaloca," a recognizable if seriously inaccurate picture of which has been preserved in the Catholic Church under the name of purgatory.

As has been noted, the kamaloca experience lasts for about a third of the time occupied by the life just lived, for reasons that will shortly be explained. Every night in sleep we have what may be called a brief kamaloca experience, which differs from the real experience after death because, though the astral body and "I" are outside the etheric and physical bodies, they have not fully deserted them. The "I" and astral body remain linked to the etheric and physical bodies by fine spiritual threads. In any event, we remain alive because our etheric and physical bodies are still together, as they are not after death.

According to Rudolf Steiner, there are two major kamaloca

151

experiences. Because we still possess our astral body in which all the desires and emotions were embedded, we continue to experience these desires and emotions. But since we no longer have a physical body through which they can find expression and be satisfied, we suffer from this deprivation in proportion as our desires and emotions were strongly attached to the physical during our lifetime. By living through the experience of unsatisfied desires our astral body is purged of them until in the end, after a third of the lifetime has been passed, it is purified; like the etheric body a few days after death, it can be dissolved. The second major kamaloca experience is that we live through our past life in a backward direction from death to birth. But instead of experiencing it just as we did on earth we experience what Steiner calls "the other half" of our life experiences, that is, what our fellow human beings and even animate and inanimate nature had to undergo because of our deeds. Everything we ever did on earth had its consequences, and these consequences are now lived through by us in kamaloca. Perhaps most important of all, every deed, good or bad, that we committed in relation to our fellow beings is now experienced *as if we were* that other person or being. At the same time higher beings "pass judgment" upon our earthly deeds. To use Steiner's wonderful description, these beings "rain down their sympathies and antipathies" so that we are within a kind of "spiritual rain." When they rain down their sympathies, it means that they pass judgment on our deeds as good and retain them in the universe. When they rain down antipathies, it means that our deeds are bad for the universe. They will have to be compensated for and, as far as possible, righted in later lives on earth. What was good will also bear fruit for us in later lives, but it also helps the earth fulfill her mission.*

It is the second experience of kamaloca just described that fills our hours of deep sleep during our lifetime. But, aside from our

* For this aspect of kamaloca Steiner's cycle of lectures given in February, 1924, called *Anthroposophy: An Introduction* (especially Lecture 8) should be used as well as the standard early account that appears in Chapter 3 of *Theosophy* (1904).

distorted dream pictures experienced while going to sleep and waking up, we have no conscious knowledge of the fact that we are living again through the deeds of the day just past, both as they were experienced by those with whom we have been in contact and as they are regarded by higher beings. Nevertheless, the experience, in spite of our total ignorance of it, takes place, and what we experience after death is the experience of our sleeping time when on earth, but *in full consciousness.* Since ordinarily we spend about a third of our life between birth and death in sleeping, kamaloca necessarily lasts for about a third of our life on earth; in effect kamaloca consists in reliving the experience of our nights spent in sleep. There is, however, one supremely important consequence of this nightly experience. Without our being in any way aware of it, we are laying the basis for the evolution of our *conscience,* even in this present life. Aside from the occasional experience of a vivid and meaningful dream, we do sometimes become aware during the night of something that aroused the "antipathy" of higher beings, something that was objectively wrong and for which in time we shall have to compensate. If through our awakened conscience we become aware of some wrongdoing we have committed and try consciously, *in this life on earth,* to compensate for it, our karma is proportionately lightened, and our experience in after-death kamaloca alleviated.*

It should be emphasized that the experience of kamaloca should not be regarded as in any sense a *punishment* for deeds committed on earth, nor does anthroposophy speak of anything resembling the traditional religious notion of the "last judgment," followed by condemnation to hell or reward in heaven. In the strictest sense of the words, we do not even pass judgment on ourselves, but rather we perceive the objective results of our deeds. This, after all, is the one way in which such perception can be valuable both for ourselves and for the world. By

---

* It is for this reason that Steiner gave one of his most valuable exercises—that of picturing our day backwards before going to sleep each night. Through this exercise we ourselves do some of the work consciously that we shall later be doing unconsciously during the sleep.

experiencing in ourselves what we have done to others we really come to *know* what we have done. From this point of view it does not matter whether we did it intentionally or unintentionally, maliciously or thoughtlessly, or whether we thought we were conferring a benefit or knew we were inflicting an injury. Thus, on the one side the deed is completed by experiencing the other half of it that we did not know in life, and on the other side we know from the attitude of the higher beings whether the deed was objectively good or bad, a judgment impossible for our finite minds to make, ignorant as we must always be of the longterm results of our deeds for the world. When we have done good to a fellowman, given him joy, helped him over a difficulty, performed any act of love toward him, this too we experience in ourselves and know also the judgment of the higher beings on it.

This experience in kamaloca is of an inestimable value for us in that it provides us with the strongest possible incentive for us to wish to do better in our next life on earth, and to compensate others for the evil we have done to them. It must be remembered that though we may act in a conscienceless manner in our earthly life this is no longer possible in our life between death and a new birth. When the astral body with its desires has been dissolved our "I," or self, continues to pass through the various realms of the spirit world, the description of which may be found in Steiner's various works, especially, but by no means exclusively, *Theosophy*. At this stage it is no longer entirely the same "I" that incarnated at the beginning of our last earth life, for it has been enriched by the good fruits of the life just lived, and bears within it what Steiner ordinarily* calls an extract of the astral body, in fact that part of it that has been transformed by our "I" into spirit self. This "I" *chooses* to compensate for its evil deeds on earth, *chooses* to compensate those whom it has wronged, and, in general chooses its future environment and decides that it will live its next life among the same individualities with whom it worked before. But even the ego as it is in the

---

* See also *Anthroposophy, An Introduction*, p. 127.

154

spirit world is unable without aid from beings higher than the human level to choose just how it is to compensate for a man's deeds, so that the evil he did before will in time be turned into good. No knowledge simply on a human level could possibly plan out the life to be lived next time in such a way that it will be as fruitful as possible, and will provide us with the necessary opportunities for doing what in the life between death and rebirth we have *resolved* to do. But the resolution was ours, the work of our own higher self. It does not derogate from our human freedom that our free resolution required for its fulfillment that a certain kind of body (male or female, weak or strong), a certain set of parents and life circumstances, should be chosen for us by higher beings. Indeed, it could not be otherwise. We need an earthly framework for our coming life, and we cannot have the wisdom, the knowledge of the kind we need to be able to make such choices, nor could we conceivably plan the way in which our lives will interact with those of the others with whom our life tasks will lie. But we can in the depths of our own higher being make the resolve that we wish to make right the wrong we did last time, and we can freely resolve to accept those circumstances that will be chosen for us when the particular individual higher being called in Christianity a guardian angel guides us down to earth for our new life. These circumstances are collectively known by the ancient Indian word *karma*, and we cannot but be glad in the depths of our "I" that we have this karma allotted to us as the one way of working out fruitfully what was unfruitful before. How many times in earthly life have all of us wished that we might have a second chance! Higher wisdom has decreed that we really do have this second, and indeed subsequent chances, even though we do not in our next earthly life possess the consciousness that can recognize them.

Karma. The whole subject of karma is so vast that we can scarcely make a dent in it in a book of the present scope. But one or two points that often cause misunderstanding may be mentioned. As we have said, the resolution to make good what

155

we did before is made by our own higher self, and this amounts in effect to saying that we wish to make progress in our spiritual development. It would be, in fact, impossible for our "I" in the spiritual world to make a different choice, and resolve to hinder the progress of mankind and ourselves by doing evil. Such a resolution can be made only when we are on earth, and when we have an astral body, which on earth is always more or less influenced by Lucifer and Ahriman and their attendant beings. When we have left kamaloca and are in the spiritual world, we no longer have our astral body, and it is after leaving kamaloca that we make our resolution on the basis of our experience in it. So, in the last analysis, it is we who with the highest part of our being have willed our karma. Whenever we bemoan our destiny on earth and complain of our ill-fortune, we are railing against *our own choice,* not the choice of some arbitrary god or gods who have done us a bad turn. In consequence, the one vice from which no one with knowledge of karma should permit himself is *envy,* either envy of anyone else's life situation, or of his talents, fortune or friends. For we have what we have chosen and earned, and what is good for us. Here our earthly freedom begins. We can, as we say so truly, "make the best of" our circumstances; we can fully accept them in the knowledge that they are what we need for our spiritual progress. We have built our house, and now it is our task to live in it.

A second point that is often misunderstood by those who have not studied karma closely and mistake it for fate or destiny is the scope of a man's karma, and how far it acts as a determining factor in his life, thus detracting from his freedom. Karma should never be thought of as an iron destiny, forcing us to do one thing or another. As we have said, we choose the general framework of our destiny, the parents that will help us to fulfill it, the kind of body we have, the people with whom we shall meet, and the like. The karmic threads that bring us together with those with whom we are linked are often of such intricacy that it seems inconceivable to our minds that they could have been *planned*; indeed, we human beings could not have planned

156

them. But somehow the pattern is formed, and we should clearly recognize that at the moment we meet someone with whom we are linked the element of destiny is at an end, and we are both from that time onward on our own. All that stems from our relations with one another in our previous lives remains to be worked out in this (and even subsequent) lives. We are able to act freely because at this stage of historical development we are in our waking life unaware of the details of our earlier relationship, and this enables us to come to totally fresh insights in this life, based on our perception of one another as we are now. It is worth remembering, however, that in our sleep we are aware of our destiny together. At all times our guardian angels who accompany us through our earthly lives as they lead us also through the spiritual world and back to rebirth are equally aware of it, and the angel of our friend or enemy has his own relationship with ours.

By contrast with this freedom that we enjoy in relation to people with whom we are karmically connected, the *events* that occur, even quite late in our life, may well be karmic results of deeds in our previous lives, as predisposition to certain diseases are also the result of certain moral deficiencies in previous lives, perhaps several lives in sequence. These events and illnesses we may indeed not be able to avoid, but since we know nothing about them in our consciousness, our subjective freedom is in no way limited by this inability. At the same time it is also true that numerous important events in our later life are *not* the result of past deeds but a preparation for the future. The friends we make in the later part of life may also be quite new ones for us, with whom our task is to prepare a fuller relationship in the next life. If we have to endure, by earthly standards, a hard life, there is just as much of a possibility that we are preparing for the future by having to undergo certain trials as there is that we are in some way "atoning" for past deeds. We always are situated midway between the past and the future, and karma acts both to allow us to complete what was left uncompleted in the previous life, while at the same time ever new experiences may be in store

157

for us that *create* karma for the future, whether good or bad. If we die from a painful or lingering illness at quite an advanced age of life, it is far more likely that we are preparing our future life by enduring the illness with fortitude than that we are bringing our life to an end in this way because of karma prepared for us in previous ones. It is never possible for us, with our finite minds, to know the inner reason for such events, and even a high initiate may not be in a position to discover the truth. But higher beings know, and it is they who lead us to the illness, and they who determine whether it brings our life on earth to an end, or whether we recover and have the rest of our earthly life thereafter changed by the experience.

Before leaving the subject of karma and continuing our description of life after death, it may be wise to explain the difference between the ideas of reincarnation and karma put forward by Rudolf Steiner and the traditional Hindu and Oriental teachings on the subject. This is especially necessary because it is so often said that anthroposophy "borrowed" such notions from the Orient, and it is also said that the ideas of reincarnation and karma are contrary to Christian thought and indeed incompatible with it. It is true that reincarnation has never been a Christian doctrine though many early Christians held it, but anthroposophy holds that if the doctrine of the Redemption is properly understood the notion of karma is inseparable from it. It was one of Steiner's principal tasks to make Christianity itself comprehensible by throwing light upon it from the science of spirit that included his teachings about reincarnation and karma. Their relation to Christianity will be discussed in the next chapter.

We have already spoken in Chapter 2 of the fact that in the first post-Atlantean cultural epoch mankind was still clairvoyant, as it had been in Atlantis, and was only just beginning to become oriented toward the earth. For this reason the ancient Indians were actually able to perceive through their clairvoyant faculties the fact of repeated earth lives. When the Persians and Egyptians took over the cultural leadership of mankind in their

158

turn the peoples of the Far East, including both India and China, retained their belief in reincarnation and karma, even though in the second and third epochs direct clairvoyance itself was rapidly dying out. The Indians, in particular, committed their beliefs to writing, and they became part of the traditional religion of India, as it has persisted to this day.

But what was not known to the ancient Indian—nor indeed is it even yet in most of the Orient a matter of direct experience—is the reality of the human "I" as an individual entity; so he could not conceive of an "I" that passes from one incarnation to another, making spiritual progress. Yet from early times the Indian was aware of the law of karma, and knew that the acts of his life were judged by higher beings after his death and would have to be compensated in subsequent lives on earth. He himself played no part in this judgment, and thus he had no share in determining what kind of life he would live next time. Least of all did he have any choice in the matter. So when he did return to earth for another life it was his karma that drove him to reincarnate, and thus it had been since the beginnings of man on earth. By incarnating in the first place he created a load of karma that would have to be expiated in later lives, and it was this karma that gave him that "thirst for existence" that is so prominent in Hindu thought. What man therefore had to try to overcome was his thirst for existence, thereby increasing the amount of karma he still had to live through. If the thirst were ever to be completely overcome, as it was by Gautama Buddha after his enlightenment, then he need no longer incarnate and could live in his true world, the spiritual world, out of which he had "fallen" when he first incarnated as man on earth. Buddha's teaching that all life is suffering is therefore easily comprehensible because life *is* suffering, and only suffering, if man is bound to the wheel of fate, as Hinduism holds. He does not have a true self except in the spiritual world. The "I" that man acknowledges when on earth is a Maya or illusion, as is the world itself. Indian thought holds that man's position in life is indeed determined by his previous life. But since he knows nothing of it, and no progress can be made, it is not really important what kind of a life is lived, nor is there any special obligation to help one's fellowmen. Buddha taught compassion and pity, but not that one's earthly life could or should be improved. What man had to do was to overcome the thirst for existence over the course of many lives, and one of the means for achieving this was the recognition of the illusory nature of earthly existence. Perfecting oneself could never mean making moral progress, as the term is understood by a Westerner, but becoming enlightened, in seeing through the earthly covering to the inner spiritual reality.

In a certain sense the first incarnation of the first man brought into being the first thirst for existence and the first karma. For the Oriental this was the equivalent of the Hebrew concept of original sin. But it was not in fact a sin. No devil tempted the first man to commit a moral sin, not even the sin of disobedience to God. Incarnating was just *something that happened* for which no man, not even the first one, was responsible. This notion of man's moral irresponsibility is ingrained in all Oriental thought. Evil is of course recognized by the Indian, but as something that belongs to the body; it results from the fact that man has a body. It does not stem, as in Western thought, from man's soul. In short, almost all Indian thinking on the nature of evil, on karma and on reincarnation, takes on its present form because the Indian cannot yet recognize the "I" as a permanent entity that *itself* reincarnates, and *itself* creates and bears its own karma. If the Indian should begin to experience himself as he should during the age of the consciousness soul, then his ideas could easily be fitted into those of anthroposophy and of Christianity as anthroposophy presents it.

Life in the Spiritual World and Preparation for Rebirth. When the ego has at last passed out of kamaloca, it is now freed from the astral body, and the time of "purification" is over. It enters into what Steiner in the earlier part of his lecturing life used to call Devachan, which originally he divided into higher and lower Devachan. Later he abandoned the use of the Sanskrit terms in

160

favor of what may best be translated simply as spirit-land, or the spiritual world, which he divided into various "regions." These regions are fully described in his *An Outline of Occult Science*, the last edition of which was passed for publication by Steiner himself two months before his death. All that he said there is thus unchanged, but in *Anthroposophy: An Introduction*, a series of lectures given to members of the newly founded General Anthroposophical Society in February, 1924, the material of the earlier books is discussed again but, as Steiner himself tells us, from an inner viewpoint. In this section we shall make more use of this latest work as well as some important cycles given in the intervening years between the first edition of *Occult Science* in 1909, and 1924. No further mention will be made here of the separate "regions" of spirit-land, each of which has its own characteristics and is therefore experienced differently by the self that passes through them.

As we have seen, by the time we enter spirit-land we have experienced the counterpart of all our deeds that during our life on earth was unknown to us, we have seen what the deeds wrought on earth meant to others and their significance to the world, and all this is now engraved into our "I." As Steiner puts it, we and our experiences are now wholly one (or, as he expressed it earlier, the fruit of our past life has been incorporated into the "I") and we move fully away from the pull of the earth. The "world" in which we live now has nothing in it of an external nature, nothing that is now connected with the earth, but it is peopled by other human souls. We ourselves become specially aware of "those souls who died before us and to whom we stood in some kind of relationship, and then the individualities of higher beings." Previously, in kamaloca, we knew only the sympathies and antipathies of these higher beings toward our deeds, but now we live and dwell with them in their atmosphere and are filled with their spiritual forces. Instead of feeling their sympathies and antipathies, we feel the *"gaze"* of these higher beings upon us. This is a new experience that actually endows us with a kind of *consciousness*. Our conscious-

161

ness diminishes as the result of the antipathy of these higher beings toward our deeds; it is enhanced in proportion as we know from our experience with them that our deeds have been good for the world and in accordance with their wishes.

This experience with higher beings in our life between death and rebirth is of supreme importance not only for us but for the higher beings themselves. In Chapter 2 we quoted Steiner's overwhelming statement that "man is the religion of the divine beings." This was not simply a figure of speech, emphasizing only the interest of the gods in man and their desire that he attain his goal, that this earth should become the planet of love. When man in his life between death and rebirth enters into the planetary spheres belonging to the various ranks of higher beings they, as already described, perceive his deeds, and, in a certain sense, judge him. But they also fill him with new forces, as they themselves pour into him their picture of what Steiner calls the Ideal Man, man as he should be. This ideal, as they pour it into man's self between death and rebirth corresponds in a certain way to what man himself feels (or may feel) toward the gods in his earthly life. Where man pours forth his love toward God (or the gods) in his own religious devotion, the gods in their turn pour forth warmth into man. In this warmth lives the picture of the Ideal Man, which man absorbs into himself for his use later when he will again be clothed with a body.

Steiner gives many other descriptive sketches of the spiritual world, but the picture just given, being such a striking one as well as so fundamental, will be the only one we shall give here of life in the spiritual world prior to the midpoint between death and rebirth, a point that corresponds in earthly life to a similar "midnight hour," which occurs at the age of 35, though of course no period in heavenly time can be assigned to it.*

As we approach the so-called cosmic midnight hour we gradually begin to lose our awareness both of the spiritual

---

* The description just given and much of what immediately follows is taken from the lecture cycle given in Vienna in April, 1914, and published under the title of *The Inner Nature of Man and the Life between Death and Rebirth*.

beings and of the other human souls with whom we have been mingling. Our association with these beings becomes ever darker, but at the same time our inner being becomes richer as we retreat into a kind of spiritual solitude—although, as will be explained in the next chapter, we do not lose the Christ who accompanies us to, and increasingly in the future will take us beyond, the midnight hour. At the midnight hour itself we have, as Steiner tells us, "the strongest inward life, but do not have the soul force that enables us to illumine our spiritual environment." We do not even have memories; all that we have is an "infinite inner life" and a "longing for a positive creative power." It is at this moment that this concentrated *longing* of ours does in fact create for us an "outer world," at this precise moment when we are in fact furthest away from both our former and our future outer world. This outer world that we create is a vision of all our previous earthly incarnations spread out before us in a tableau. At the same time a glimmer, as it were, of light appears from the future, the same light that illuminates our past. It is this, so to speak, *beckoning* light that Steiner speaks of as the Holy Spirit, sent to us by the Christ who has led us hitherto—thus giving one part of its profound meaning to the ancient Rosicrucian saying, *"Per Spiritum Sanctum Reviviscimus"* (Through the Holy Spirit we are reborn). It is at this moment, when we perceive the past more fully than at any time hitherto, and are on the point of beginning the task of creating the future, that we finally make all those decisions that will take effect in our karma in the life that is before us.

As soon as the midnight hour is passed we begin to work on the creation of our future body, which has to be built in accordance with the needs of our karma. Although a brief mention of it was made before it should now be explained more fully that in his progress toward the cosmic midnight, when we experience the result of our deeds and the judgment of spiritual beings upon them we are actually passing through the planetary spheres, each with its own higher beings associated with it. Eventually we pass right out beyond Saturn into the realm of the fixed stars of the zodiac, and we return by the same path after the midnight hour. In the building of the "spiritual seed" of our future physical body these beings of the various planetary spheres again play their part.* "Nothing that you can ever do on earth," Steiner told his audience in November, 1922, "can be as great and manifold as what you have to do when from the starry worlds you build this temple of the gods, the human body." This "seed" of the future body is formed in exact accordance with what was experienced on the outward journey through the cosmos during which the results of our deeds were experienced. The various parts of our body will be formed with the aid of certain planetary beings as we pass through particular constellations of the zodiac. This is the truth behind one of the well known aspects of astrology that certain planets and certain constellations are not only connected with the various parts of our body but also play a part in our earthly destiny.

While the spiritual seed of the physical body is being prepared in accordance with our karma, our karma itself is becoming woven into what will be our next astral body, which is indeed called "astral" because it is formed by higher beings in the starry or astral world. As long as this astral body is being prepared we retain a certain degree of consciousness and of intermittent awareness of the higher beings who are working upon it. But when the astral body is completed, this consciousness is lost and we turn definitively toward the earth. We no longer have any power to influence the creation of our sheaths to be used on earth, and higher beings take over the task completely. Under their guidance the spiritual seed of the physical body on which we worked so long finally leaves us and descends to the parents whom, with their aid, we have chosen to receive it. As soon as this seed has left us we feel within our soul-spiritual being, which is now within the sphere of the moon, the overwhelming urge to unite ourselves with this seed. As a result we begin to gather

---

* This description and the quotation that follows are taken from Lecture 6 of a series of lectures given by Steiner in London in 1922, and published under the title of *Man's Life on Earth and in the Spiritual Worlds*, p. 107.

toward ourselves from the total world of the etheric formative forces those life forces needed to give life to the seed that is now enclosed within the womb of our future mother. At the moment when this etheric body for our coming life has been formed, life stirs within the womb.

While still in the moon sphere and just as we are forming our etheric body, we have one last overwhelming experience that corresponds exactly to the tableau that passed before our vision after death while the etheric body was dissolving. This time, however, we have a prevision of the earthly life that faces us, not in all its details as in the vision after death, but in its general outline. This is the life we have planned for ourselves, including all the compensations for former wrongs that we now intend to right, and perhaps great but painful deeds that we intend to perform for the sake of humanity and future lives on earth. It sometimes happens that at this last moment before incarnation the vision gives our soul-spiritual being such a shock that we draw back in horror from what faces us. If this should happen it too often means that we shall not fully incarnate into the body we have prepared for ourselves, and thus be born with some "prenatal" defect, or without the possibility of full control over our organism, as is the case, for example, with epileptics.

While this failure to incarnate fully is, for understandable reasons, especially common in our time, it is also true that the experience of creating an etheric body is itself different from what it was in previous centuries. This is due to the fact that, as will be discussed in the next chapter, the Second Coming of Christ has already taken place with his increased activity within the etheric world in which he now dwells. All that need be said here is that since about 1930 the soul-spirit about to be born has gathered together its etheric substance at a time when this substance has already been permeated to a greater or lesser degree by the Christ. As may be imagined, this great deed of Christ has opened the way for numerous possibilities for the future development of mankind at a moment in time when the evil forces have likewise gathered together their greatest power to oppose him. This is one of the spiritual reasons for the numerous crises of the twentieth century.

Karma and World Population. Although much more could be written on the subject of human nature and life between death and rebirth, for further information on these matters the student is referred to the quite extensive reading list that follows this chapter. But there is one subject that is so often raised that it is worth while attempting an answer here, especially since Steiner himself, as far as this writer is aware, did not ever give an explicit answer to the question. The question in itself is perfectly justified, and deserves at least an attempt at an answer, taking into account a few indications given by Steiner in the course of his life. If everyone, it is asked, who is now on earth has at some time or another been incarnated before, and almost all of us have reincarnated at least once during each cultural epoch, how can we account for the relatively sudden increase in world population, an increase that shows no signs as yet of coming to an end, and that is naturally accounted for by modern scientists and sociologists as the result of entirely physical causes? Why did so few souls wish to incarnate in earlier times when population was so much smaller than now? Is there any truth in what pessimistic demographers suggest, that world population before another century is over will have outrun the resources available to nourish it? It is conceded by demographers, of course, that the average age of the world's population is higher than in the past as a result of the spread of modern medicine and the improvement of sanitation, and that this, in itself, constitutes a problem. But it is also true that more people are being born than at any earlier period of history known to us.

Steiner has repeatedly told us that we do not make spiritual progress in the spiritual world, but only on earth. We can *learn* nothing, strictly speaking, in the life between death and rebirth except the consequences of our earthly deeds, and, as in sleep, in a certain way we refresh ourselves before plunging into another incarnation. It is therefore important for us to learn all we can from each earthly incarnation. One of the ways of learning

166

about the world from a contrasting viewpoint is to be reincarnated in the opposite sex, and, as a general but by no means universal rule, our incarnations as man and woman alternate. Even now we are partly bisexual at all times, since if our physical body is male our etheric body is female, and vice versa. It is also important for us, however, that the world shall have changed sufficiently between our incarnations for a renewal of the experience to be truly worthwhile. In earlier periods of history when the tempo of world change was extremely slow there was no necessity for us to reincarnate after only a short interval in the spiritual world.

This is no longer true. In earlier times there might be at least a thousand years between two incarnations, at all events, two incarnations in the same sex. But with the present pace of change the earth is different indeed from what it was even a century ago; hence a quick reincarnation would provide much more to be learned on earth. It may also be worth noting that Steiner on several occasions explained that the materialistic world culture of the present time tends to tie human beings to the earth more closely than was true in earlier times. Thus, they often have a positive thirst to come back quickly to the earth, and this thirst prevents them from spending as much time in the spiritual world as might perhaps be desirable for them, even needed by them.

But it is surely true that the world population cannot go on increasing indefinitely even though the interval between incarnations constantly grows shorter, and it seems probable that catastrophes and wars, combined with man's willingness to control his reproduction (or, in anthroposophical terms, refuse to provide bodies for souls who are not yet spiritually ready to reincarnate), will intervene long before the dire predictions of demographers are fulfilled. All these factors are already playing their part in the reduction of the rate of population increase in many parts of the world. Population increase, as far as it has yet gone, can be accounted for sufficiently by the shorter interval between incarnations and the value of this for human souls because of the "speed up" in world historical change. Nevertheless, it may be added without further comment that the number of elemental, non-human beings is truly unlimited, and it is not beyond the power of Ahriman to "ensoul" bodies with beings who are subject to him. Such beings would appear externally to be men and women, but would possess no true soul of their own and would be especially without conscience. But at the same time they would be filled with Ahrimanic intelligence, and cleverness to an extreme degree. The possibility that such beings are already on the earth cannot be rejected out of hand, nor is evidence lacking for their presence. As we move into the twenty-first century, when, according to Steiner, many great initiates have been preparing themselves to incarnate to lead the world toward a deepening of Christianity in accordance with the purposes of Christ himself and the higher beings who wish to see man fulfill his true aims and reach his true goal, the forces of evil will also naturally make their greatest effort to defeat the forces making for spiritual progress. A great increase in cleverness, without conscience to moderate it and without a higher spirituality to guide it, would be fully in accord with the purposes of the hindering powers. No good purpose is served by blinding ourselves to the evidence of such an increase in our time, nor to the possibility that the process will continue as we move into the next century.

SUGGESTIONS FOR FURTHER READING
FOR CHAPTER 4.

As noted in the chapter itself, the two fundamental works regarding the nature of the human being are *Theosophy* (1904) and *An Outline of Occult Science* (1909), both books having been frequently revised and clarified by Dr. Steiner up to the time of his death. Chapter 1 of *Theosophy* describes man as a being of body, soul and spirit, and goes on to show in what way he may also be regarded as a sevenfold and ninefold being. Chapters 2 and 3 of *Occult Science* do not speak of body, soul, and spirit, but deal more with the four sheaths of man, the physical, etheric, and astral "bodies" and the "I." The chapters in both books should be read as Steiner's fundamental account of the matter. The outline of the contents of the book *Occult Science*, which is printed at the end of the English edition of 1963, should be consulted for other information on the human being and his nature that is contained in this work.

A book that might be thought to be suitable for reading in conjunction with this chapter because of its title and easy availability is the series of fourteen lectures given in Stuttgart in August and September, 1919, and published under the title of *A Study of Man* (London, 1975), should, in the present author's view, NOT be read at this stage. The lectures were given to prospective teachers for the first Waldorf School and require a considerable knowledge of anthroposophy. Moreover, the lectures are based on a discovery about the threefold nature of man that, according to Steiner himself, he had not felt able to formulate when *Occult Science* and *Theosophy* were written, and none of this preliminary information has been given in this chapter. The book will be recommended for reading in connection with Chapter 10, but not with this one, since at this stage it is more likely to confuse than to enlighten.

For life after death Chapters 2 and especially 3 of *Theosophy* are recommended, which should be supplemented by books already referred to in the text. As noted there, the lectures given in Dornach in January and February, 1924 and published under the title, *Anthroposophy: An Introduction* (London, 1961) are difficult but of great importance, representing, as they do, much of the material given in *Theosophy* from an inner, not an external, point of view. By contrast the 1906 lectures given in Stuttgart and published under the title, *At the Gates of Spiritual Science* (London, 1970) present a simple account of life between death and rebirth (Lectures 2 through 5) that nonetheless contains some information found only with difficulty elsewhere. The following three lectures contain also a simple but clear account of karma. Two important and profound cycles have also been referred to in the text: *The Inner Nature of Man and the Life Between Death and Rebirth*, six lectures given in Vienna in April, 1914 (London, 1959) and four lectures given in London in August and November, 1922, included in a book entitled *Man's Life on Earth and in the Spiritual Worlds* (London, 1952).

For those who are looking for a systematic and extremely detailed presentation of life between death and rebirth, far more detailed than was possible in Chapter 4 of this book, a work by G. Wachsmuth called *Reincarnation as a Phenomenon of Metamorphosis* (English language edition, New York, 1937) may be recommended. This long chapter of almost eighty pages contains numerous quotations from Rudolf Steiner, many of them from books untranslated as yet into English, though the lectures from which they are taken are not referred to specifically. The remainder of the book, written by a man whose primary study was the scientific material presented by Steiner, will probably be found too difficult by beginning students, although it would be impossible to find in English a more comprehensive account of the "physical-corporeal metamorphosis through reincarnation" than the one given by Wachsmuth in Chapter 6 of this volume.

On karma there is an abundance of material in English, beginning with the indispensable Chapter 2 of *Theosophy*. Two early essays were published in New York in 1962 under the title, *Reincarnation and Karma: How Karma Works*, including some questions that are frequently put by beginning students. These essays might be a good introduction to the subject. A detailed account of karma from many different points of view was given by Steiner in a lecture cycle given in Hamburg in May 1910 and published under the title, *Manifestations of Karma*. This cycle (London, 1947) is unequalled for its wide coverage of the subject. A useful compilation of five lectures given in Berlin and Stuttgart in 1912 has been published under the title *Reincarnation and Karma: Their Significance in Modern Culture*, (Vancouver,

1963), and another collection from different periods, including two on a different subject, may also be recommended in its paperback edition. This work is entitled, *Reincarnation and Immortality* (Blauvelt, N.Y. Rudolf Steiner Publications, 1970). In the compilation entitled, *The Mission of Christian Rosenkreutz* (London, 1950), there are two valuable lectures on karma given in Vienna on February 8 and 9, 1912, called "The True Attitude to Karma," and "Intimate Workings of Karma," the first, now available in a new translation, "Facing Karma" (New York, 1975).

Following the foundation of the General Anthroposophical Society at Dornach at Christmas, 1923, Rudolf Steiner began to give many details about the successive earth lives of a number of important historical personages. It is with much hesitation that this series of seven books entitled, *Karmic Relationships: Esoteric Studies* is recommended here (London, 1955–1973) because these lectures, given exclusively to members of the newly refounded Society, represented the very culmination and crown of Rudolf Steiner's life work, and they should *never* be read piecemeal or selectively. It is really essential for any student who wishes to study these lectures to begin with Volume 1 and work carefully through it. This volume gives a wealth of information about how karma works as a whole, whereas most of the later volumes deal with specific personalities, and Steiner on numerous occasions tells us that no generalizations can be made from the successive incarnations of the particular personalities he has chosen. If, after thoughtful study of Volume 1, the student wishes to pursue his study further, he should read the entire series as a whole, the only exception to this being perhaps the second lecture of Volume 3 given on July 4, 1924, which contains a moving and beautiful discussion of the role of the various hierarchies in man's life between death and rebirth, information that cannot be found in such detail elsewhere, and which will supplement the information given in this chapter. This lecture, of course, can indeed be read separately, and is highly recommended.

171

Lastly, two books not by Steiner may be strongly recommended. These are: Hermann Poppelbaum, *Man's Eternal Biography* (New York: Adonis Press, 1945) and F. Rittelmayer, *Reincarnation in the Light of Thought, Religion and Ethics*, (London: Christian Community Press, n.d. (about 1940)). The first named is a beautifully clear and limpid series of three essays by a distinguished anthroposophical biologist, and the second is by a theologian, the founder of the Christian Community, who was also an accomplished philosopher, as can be seen from the first part, especially, of this book that deals with reincarnation from a philosophical point of view. They both are out of print, but are worth looking out for, in case they can be found in libraries or second-hand bookshops.

CHAPTER V.

Anthroposophy and Christianity

Rudolf Steiner never tired of emphasizing that in ancient times religion, art and science were not yet separated from each other, whereas today too often there appears to be no obvious relation of one to the other. Religion is, indeed, usually regarded as the virtual antithesis of science, based as it is supposed to be, exclusively on faith—whereas science is supposed to be based on observation, verified hypotheses and impeccably logical reasoning. It is admitted that art may be religious in content and inspiration, and even in modern times there are some recognizably great and talented artists (for example, Rouault), whose inspiration is religious. But there is certainly held to be no necessary connection between religion and art, and no-nonsense scientists are hesitant to regard any part of their discipline as artistic. Healing used to be spoken of as an "art," as was farming, even history. But the present tendency is for science to make ever wider claims as the only kind of real knowledge. One uses scientific data and reasoning to predict the weather, one makes laboratory tests to diagnose illnesses, one calculates the nutrients necessary to "feed" plants (one no longer needs an "artistic" green thumb), and history is customarily regarded as a social "science" (and much duller in consequence).

But in ancient Egypt and Babylon the only "scientists" were the priests, and their leading science, astrology, was used for religious (and sometimes political) purposes. Of course, artisans in the ancient world had a practical knowledge of their materials, and what they created we today think of as art. But all knowledge that is today regarded as theoretical was held by priests, and indeed most of it originated in clairvoyance. Likewise, there was no art in the world of the Egyptians and Babylonians that was not religious, and even the written symbols used by the Egyptians were called "sacred glyphs" (hieroglyphics). In early Greek times religion and art remained together, but before the end of the Hellenistic age science had become emancipated from art and religion, and with the Romans art became totally secularized.

In our age of the consciousness soul Steiner always insisted that we should by our own efforts begin to bring these three separated realms together. Underlying each of them should be the truths of spiritual science, and a reverential attitude not totally dissimilar to religious awe should inform all our enquiries into nature—of which we can understand really so little if we do not take also into account what is imperceptible to the senses. For art to perform its healing task in modern life it too requires to be suffused with a religious feeling because man, as well as being (apparently) a physical being, is also a supersensible being, and without this recognition none of the separate arts is able to move forward and fulfill the function that it should fill in the future. What is the difference between poster art and a Raphael Madonna, between Mozart's Requiem and a barber shop quartet singing Frankie and Johnny? We know the qualitative difference precisely because we are beings of soul and spirit.

This chapter and the next two will therefore be devoted to each of these three realms separately, religion, art and science, and will discuss what anthroposophy has to contribute to each.

At the end of the discussions the reader may have sensed in what way the three realms are to be brought together in the future through what is common to them all.

Just before beginning his first lecture cycle on the Gospels (on the St. John Gospel, given in Hamburg in 1908) Steiner gave an introductory lecture on Christianity that was translated under the title (now the title of a separate booklet including two lectures), "Christianity began as a religion but is greater than all religions." In order to understand this statement we should recognize Steiner's definition of the word religion, based on its Latin etymology, meaning to "bind back." Steiner explained that the task of religion is to make the connection again between man and the supersensible worlds, bind the two together. In Atlantean times when all men, being clairvoyant, were aware of the supersensible worlds, there could be no religion, since Atlantean man *knew* the spiritual through direct perception. But when clairvoyance began to die out the connection between man and the supersensible worlds had to be re-forged by the human being himself. Thus arose the revealed religions that were given to men by initiates who still possessed clairvoyant knowledge. Those who were not initiated and had no longer any clairvoyant knowledge necessarily had to accept the content of these religions on faith. In the far distant future when man will again have become consciously clairvoyant through his own efforts, and when he can again perceive spiritual beings, religion in the sense of the word as just given will no longer be necessary, as it was not in Atlantean times. But it will remain a fundamental human task to create a relationship with the Christ, and religion will consist of man's efforts to create this and express through himself the Christ impulse, both within himself and in the external world. By this time, as will be clear, there will be no other religion than Christianity, and knowledge will have replaced faith.

It should therefore be understood that anthroposophy is not a "Christian" teaching in the sense that it favors Christianity above other competing religions like Hinduism, Buddhism,

Judaism, Islam, or Shintoism. Each of these other religions performed a certain task at a particular epoch of history, and the founders of all these religions communicated some spiritual truths to their peoples, on the basis of which a relationship between them and the gods could be established. These truths they had themselves received through inspiration, but the people who received them accepted them on faith. All religions have to some degree been institutionalized, churches of some kind or another have been founded, and a form of worship established. This was true also of Christianity as it was established by the followers of Christ Jesus. But in the fullness of time, according. to Steiner, there will be no need for any mediation between man and God, no need for an institutionalized religion, and all religious feeling will be directed toward the spiritual beings who will be perceived directly, and especially toward the Christ who will have a unique relationship with man for the rest of earth evolution. However, when a number of Protestant pastors and theological students asked if it was possible to bring about a religious renewal within the framework of Christianity, Steiner drew from the spiritual worlds a ritual known as the Act of Consecration of Man, which became the main religious service of the Christian Community, a new movement entirely distinct from the Anthroposophical Society. Though the Christian Community and its ritual are eminently suited for the present time, *no* form of worship should be equated with Christianity, which in future will come to mean simply a religious devotion to the Christ, who, as he told his disciples, will be with us to the end of the world ages.

Clearly all aspects of Christianity as Steiner revealed it cannot be dealt with in a single chapter of a book with the scope of this one, and indeed Steiner gave so many lectures in which he spoke of the Christ that it would take many large volumes to collect them all together. What we shall do here is to say little or nothing of any of the other religions, even those of which Steiner spoke much, as was the case of Buddhism, but confine ourselves to Steiner's main teachings about Christianity and Christ Jesus. On all the Gospels Steiner gave dozens of lectures in different

176

contexts, explaining that each of the evangelists had been initiated but that their initiations were different. As a result they all wrote their gospels from clairvoyant knowledge but from different points of view, making no attempt to be biographers in the modern sense of the word. They cannot therefore be understood by readers and commentators who have no access to occult knowledge. Even Steiner's lectures on them cannot be regarded as commentaries on the gospel texts but rather as material drawn from the Akasha Chronicle on what actually happened in Palestine at the time, which is then seen to elucidate many obscure texts in the Gospels themselves. All this material will have to be omitted from this chapter, and the reader is referred to the Reading List at the end of the chapter for Steiner's various lecture cycles on the Gospels, which should be certainly supplemented by a reading of the book known as *The Three Years*, written by Emil Bock, one of the founding priests of the Christian Community (to whom, incidentally Steiner gave many personal teachings that are kept within the priests' circle and not made public).

Steiner's teachings on Christianity as they will be expounded in this chapter may be summarized briefly as follows:

1. A distinction must be made between Jesus of Nazareth, a highly developed human being, and the Christ, who lived as the ego of this human being for three years until his death on the Cross.

2. The Christ who dwelt in the three "bodily" sheaths of Jesus was a divine being who from the beginning of earth evolution, and even before, had been preparing for his eventual incarnation. This incarnation took place at the time of his baptism by John in the Jordan. The primary mission of the Hebrew people had been to prepare over the period of forty-two generations from Abraham to Jesus a body capable of receiving into itself the power of this divine being, a power that would have shattered any ordinary body.

3. The incarnation, life, death, resurrection and ascension of Christ Jesus and the coming of the Holy Spirit at Pentecost are

177

all part of the same mystery, which we call the Mystery of Golgotha. Occurring as they did at the midpoint of earth evolution they made possible the ascent of man from the low point of his descent, which was reached at the time of the Mystery of Golgotha. If this mystery had not taken place the forces of Lucifer and Ahriman described in Chapter 2 would have proved too strong for the unaided forces of man to combat. He needed the divine aid received from the Christ.

4. The doctrine of reincarnation is not at present a Christian doctrine, but it was accepted as a fact by the apostles and evangelists, and is implicit in several passages in the Gospels. The Christianity of the future must make the truth of repeated earth lives a central part of its teaching. Indeed, an understanding of karma is essential to the understanding of what is meant by the traditional Christian doctrine that Christ in passing through the Mystery of Golgotha redeemed man from his sins.

5. Since the Mystery of Golgotha, Christ has always been active in the spiritual worlds and in the earth itself. He may be accepted into man's own inner being in the sense meant by St. Paul when he said, "Not I, but Christ in me." In this sense Christ is active as the higher ego in man, and can even "christianize" our thinking. In the future the only way in which we can make spiritual progress will be by allowing our self to be filled with the Christ. This needs a conscious cooperation on our part and a conscious recognition of the Christ. It is thus a free act. Since about 1930, however, coincident with the increased influence in the world of Lucifer and Ahriman, the Christ has begun to manifest himself in the world next to man, the etheric world, where he may be perceived by those who are permanently or (usually) momentarily gifted with etheric vision. This is the so-called Second Coming, a term that is a mistranslation of the Greek word *Parousia*, which simply means "presence."

It will be recognized that the deed of Christ was performed on the world's stage once and for all, and for all men. To be a Christian is to recognize Christ's deed, to try to accept the Christ into one's own self as one's higher self, and then, of course, to live a life consonant with this. It is *not* to accept Christ solely, or even primarily as either a teacher or an example, and thus to obey his "commands" or imitate Christ in one's life. To be a Christian is to be totally free in the sense described in Chapter 3. It follows therefore that it is not necessary for any Christian to be a member of any organized Christian Church. Indeed, all Churches in the course of time will become unnecessary, especially those that, like the Catholic Church, were founded in the form they were because of the special religious needs of the intellectual soul. Nor, it goes without saying, is it necessary for Christian missionaries to spend their best efforts in converting the heathen to Christianity.

The consciousness soul has to learn to be free, and this freedom has been made possible by the deed of Christ. To recognize our relationship with the Christ is now and for the future the whole content of religion in the strict sense of the word. But there may be services of worship, such as that given by the Christian Community, whose ritual was given by Rudolf Steiner, that help to lift our souls toward the Christ. These not only help us as worshippers, but make it possible for spiritual beings to come closer to the earth to work with man, aiding his spiritual growth. The notion of religion and the notion of worship should therefore be kept entirely separate in our minds, incidentally helping us to recognize that all believers in all religions worship the divine in their own way, and that such worship merits in all cases our respect. In the course of time Christianity will become the only religion, but individual and communal worship will no doubt be as varied in the future as human beings themselves are varied. This too will be a part of man's freedom.

We shall now take up in turn the five main headings of Steiner's teachings on Christianity as enumerated above, with the reiterated warning that all that will be said here can be only the briefest introduction to the subject. This apparent schematization is only an attempt, necessarily a dry and abstract one, to present in a small and manageable compass what is in Steiner's own works full of warmth and life, but for this reason could also not be compressed into an account as brief as this one.

Who was Jesus of Nazareth? There is a great mystery behind not only the being of Christ, but also behind the individuality of Jesus of Nazareth, a mystery that has often puzzled New Testament commentators. The Gospels of Matthew and Luke contain the only biblical information about the circumstances of the birth of Jesus, but in almost every respect the two accounts are at variance with one another. In Matthew, the annunciation is made to Joseph (not to Mary), the child is born in Bethlehem, in accordance with the Old Testament prophesy, but no mention is made of the manger or the inn. Indeed, when the "wise men" led by a star visit the child, he is in a "house," which seems to be the regular home of Joseph and Mary. Herod had enquired of the wise men about the star, and asked them to report back to him after their visit. But they were warned by God in a dream not to do so, thereby infuriating Herod who ordered the so-called "massacre of the innocents," which Joseph and his family escaped because he too was warned in a dream and was able to escape into Egypt. He did not dare to return to the land of Israel until after Herod's death, when again he received instructions through two separate dreams, as a result of which he took up his abode, apparently for the first time, in Nazareth in Galilee, in order to remain outside the jurisdiction of Herod's son Archelaus. Lastly, the entire genealogy given in the Matthew Gospel from David to Joseph is different from that in the Luke Gospel. As recorded in Matthew, Jesus was descended from the entire line of the kings of Judah beginning with Solomon, whereas Luke traces the descent through Nathan, the prophet-son of David.

In the Luke account the annunciation is made to Mary, the wife of Joseph, who was already living with her husband in Nazareth. The only reason they had to travel to Bethlehem was because the Roman Emperor Caesar Augustus commanded that all his subjects should go to the city where they had been born in order to be "taxed." While on this journey Jesus was born in a stable and laid in a manger because there was no room in the inn. There he was visited by shepherds and worshipped by them, they themselves having been told of the birth by a choir of angels. The parents and child then seem to have remained in Bethlehem for a short time until the period required by Jewish law was fulfilled, and Mary could be "purified." This ceremony was performed in the religious capital of Jerusalem, and the child was recognized as the Messiah by Simeon, a prophet, who blessed him, and by Anna, a prophetess. After this, the Holy Family returned to Galilee to "their own" city of Nazareth. There is no mention in the Luke account of Herod, the wise men, the massacre of the innocents, or of any journey to Egypt. If Joseph had already been living in Nazareth it would certainly seem pointless for an angel to tell him to go there on his return from Egypt in order to be outside the jurisdiction of Herod's son Archelaus.

There can be little doubt that if these Gospels had been ordinary historical records purporting to tell of the birth of some child who grew up to become an important personage, every commentator would have been struck by the discrepancies in the two accounts and have concluded that either one account or the other, but not both, were true, or that both were mythical. But because they are the only extant accounts of the childhood of a unique being who was regarded by his followers as a god-man and became the central figure in a world religion, the discrepancies are usually simply overlooked, and the Jesus children mentioned in the two Gospels are regarded as one and the same child. The idea that cries out for recognition from the two documents, if they are considered by themselves, that there were two children born at different times, has simply never been given serious consideration because to all Christians there can only have been one Jesus—the Savior and Redeemer. But it remains true, according to Rudolf Steiner, that in fact there *were* two Jesus children, although of course there was only one Christ.

The child in the Matthew Gospel, descended from the kings of Judah, had in a previous incarnation been that great prophet

181

Zarathustra, whose dialogues with the sun-god Ahura Mazda were recorded in the Avesta (see above pp. 33). He had been incarnated already many times and he was perhaps the most highly evolved of all initiates up to that time, but still a human being in the fullest sense of the word. The "wise men of the East," skilled in astrology, knew that the great Zarathustra was due to reincarnate with a new mission on earth to fulfill. Thus, they followed the star to Bethlehem and bestowed kingly gifts on the newborn child. A being with a heritage like that of Zarathustra was born with extraordinary "natural" gifts, but especially with a uniquely great *wisdom,* the fruit of his work in past incarnations.

A great mystery is involved, on the other hand, in the case of the Jesus of the Luke Gospel, descended from Nathan, the son of David (who will hereafter be called the Nathan Jesus, to be distinguished from the Solomon Jesus who had previously been incarnated as Zarathustra). Steiner tells us that this being had never before incarnated as a human being, but his soul and spirit had been held back in what he sometimes called the "mother-lodge of humanity." He thus had no earthly karma, and his sheaths had in no way been contaminated by the Luciferic or Ahrimanic forces. In a series of lectures given just before World War I (see the Reading List at the end of the chapter) Steiner partially lifted the veil further on this mysterious being, telling us that he had previously, while still in the spiritual world, offered himself as a sacrifice to the Christ who with his aid performed three deeds that had saved man in the remote past from falling under the complete control of Lucifer and Ahriman. As may well be imagined, this Nathan Jesus, when at last he was born on earth, was full of the purest impulses of love. But never having previously been incarnated as a human being he had no earthly wisdom at all, and would in our day, no doubt, have been regarded as in a certain way a "backward" or handicapped child. Steiner also tells us on several occasions that when the shepherds saw the heavenly choir after the birth of this child what they were actually seeing, had they but known it, was a

182

mysterious union with the spirit of the Buddha who from the spiritual world also communicated to the child and incorporated in its astral body those forces of compassion of which he had hitherto been the greatest earthly bearer.

That there were two Jesus children and two sets of parents seems to have been known to certain gifted artists of the High Renaissance.* One Raphael Madonna in the Berlin Museum usually called "Madonna and Child with the Little St. John" has a wholly unexplainable extra child with a face showing a wisdom beyond his years. A remarkable painting ascribed to Van Orley of the same period (1491–1542), now in the possession of the Christian Community at San Francisco, likewise shows a third unexplainable child, but in addition shows two sets of parents, as well as Elizabeth with her own son, John the Baptist. The tradition followed by Van Orley that the mother of the Solomon Jesus (unlike the mother of the Nathan Jesus) was no longer a young woman, is confirmed by Rudolf Steiner. Most remarkable of all is the fresco by Borgognone (1450–1523) in the Church of St. Ambrose in Milan of the incident in the temple to be described in the next paragraph, which shows both Jesus children, the one resplendent on a kind of throne and discoursing with the doctors of the Law, while the other child is clearly stricken and, aided by his mother, seems no longer to have his own ego being. This is precisely the situation described by Steiner as having come about during the visit to the temple described in the Luke Gospel. It is no accident, incidentally, that Matthew makes no allusion to the incident in the temple, as there was no reason why he should have known that it ever took place. The Solomon Jesus whom he describes would not have shown so visibly the change that took place in his twelfth year. He had always been full of wisdom, but he now entered into, thus unifying with himself, the love-filled sheaths of the Nathan Jesus.

---

*See, in particular, the really irrefutable evidence given in the German work, Hella Kraus-Zimmer, *Die zwei Jesus Knaben in der bildenden Kunst* (Stuttgart: Verlag Freies Geistesleben, 1972).

The details of the Luke story (2:41–52) are most significant, and are totally explainable if we recognize the fact that two Jesus children, both living now in Nazareth, one several months younger than the other (and thus having escaped the massacre of Herod that took place before he was born), went to the temple at Jerusalem for the annual feast. The Nathan Jesus of the Luke Gospel stayed behind in Jerusalem without his parents' knowledge, and they did not at first miss him but supposed he was with their kinsfolk. When they discovered his absence, they did not find him for three days, and then he was "in the temple in the midst of the doctors, both hearing them and asking them questions. . . . And when they saw him they were amazed." To which Jesus replied, " 'Did you not know that I must be about my Father's business?' And they understood not the saying which he spake to them."

What had happened was that there had been a mysterious change of personality, in that the ego of the Solomon Jesus, the former Zarathustra, had left the three sheaths in which it had previously lived, and occupied the three sheaths of the Nathan Jesus child, which it immediately began to transform. The parents of the Nathan Jesus would not have been so astonished that he was able to discourse with the doctors of the law if they had already taught him about the law, and if he had been a "bright" child. But he was without wisdom, including all the traditional wisdom of the Jews, which the former Zarathustra had had no difficulty in absorbing. Thus, the sudden wisdom acquired by the boy who had hitherto been "backward" was to his parents in the nature of a miracle, although Luke tells us that his mother, although not understanding her son's replies, "kept all these sayings in her heart" while he returned to Nazareth and was "subject to them." Meanwhile, it may be added that the former sheaths of the Solomon Jesus, now bereft of the "I" that had filled them, soon afterward died, as did the young mother of the Nathan Jesus. The mother of the Solomon Jesus thereupon took over her tasks and looked after the boy who now had within him the ego of the child she herself had borne.

The Bible is completely silent about all the events that took place between the event in the temple and the baptism by John in Jordan when Jesus was about thirty years old. Legend, however, has handed down much about these eighteen unknown years and Steiner has given us some details in a series of lectures drawn from the Akasha Chronicle called *The Fifth Gospel.* These need not concern us here, but it should be said that the presence of this extremely developed "I" in the pure love-filled sheaths of the former Nathan Jesus wrought a great change in the young man, and in effect these sheaths became likewise filled with wisdom as well as love. By the age of thirty the young man Jesus of Nazareth was so far advanced that he could bequeath his fully developed sheaths to the Christ. The last preparation for this was made the night before his journey to John the Baptist in the wilderness. His "I," the Zarathustra "I," passed out of him and filled his mother as a consequence of a kind of conversation that can only be touched upon with the greatest reverence and awe, and may not be explained. But Jesus the next day moved, or as one might say, drifted without any real ego present in him until he was seen by John coming toward him. All the four Gospels describe what followed but none of the English translations uses the words that appear in some of the older manuscripts, which were also quoted by the writer of the Epistle to the Hebrews (Heb. 1:5; 5:5). After the descent of the Holy Spirit in the form of a dove, the voice from heaven in fact said, "This is my Beloved Son. This day have I begotten him." This was, in fact, the beginning of the mission of the Christ. The Christ being had now descended into the bodily sheaths of a being specially prepared to receive him, and he was to live within them for three years until he left them at the Crucifixion.

Who was the Christ Being? It has already been indicated on many occasions in this book how profoundly Christian Steiner's teachings were, and it is a fact that scarcely any lecture cycle from his first Gospel lectures in 1908 onward lacks some material, often new to his audiences, on the Christ. It would be impossible and indeed pointless for me to try to sum up such a

185

wealth of information. When I first began to look into Steiner's work, almost forty years ago—and I think that this is likely to be the experience of most beginning students—I had the overwhelming impression that even if much that Steiner had to say on other subjects might be mistaken or erroneous, he simply could not have been mistaken on the *cosmic* nature of Christ Jesus, and that it would be surely impossible for anyone to *invent* such material so far was it from any ideas ever put forward by professional theologians. Most of us have initially a somewhat vague idea of God as a divine being, presumably omnipotent and omniscient, and if we believe in God at all we are not inclined to trouble ourselves with those problems of detail with which traditionally theologians have concerned themselves. After all, we do not have any first hand knowledge of God and never will. But then neither do theologians who speculate about him, mulling over texts that may or may not be authentic and may even represent the speculations of earlier theologians such as St. Paul.

But when we read the details of what Steiner has to say, not about God the Father, but about God the Son, Christ Jesus, who is also a divine being, then at once we come to recognize that what we can learn from the four Gospels is only the smallest part of what man could, indeed should, know about this highest spiritual being who ever involved himself directly, as Steiner tells us he was, with earthly and human evolution. The common picture of the man Jesus, who lived for thirty-three years on earth and was then crucified, is once and for all replaced for us after reading Steiner by the picture of the god-man, or rather the god who became a man, performing an act of significance not only for man but for the earth, and who continued to work on behalf of both from the spiritual worlds after his resurrection and ascension. However little we may read in Steiner's works, at least this impression is surely a lasting one, and it becomes impossible to think ever again of Christianity and its founder in the same way as before.

Reference was made in Chapter 2 (see p. 22) to earlier

186

"embodiments" of the earth itself, called by Steiner Old Saturn, Old Sun, and Old Moon. Even during these embodiments the Christ was active on behalf of what would later become earthly humanity, but I do not believe that Steiner gave us ever any comprehensible details on his activity on Old Saturn. But he does tell us that on Old Sun he was the "planetary being" of the sun, filled with utter devotion and the spirit of self-sacrifice, and a willingness to fulfill whatever tasks might be laid on him. In this respect he may be contrasted with Lucifer who was the planetary being of Venus at this time, but who became filled with pride rather than devotion. As a result, the Christ Being moved upward thereafter in his evolution, while Lucifer moved downward.*

During the next embodiment of what was in time to become our Earth, the period known as Old Moon, Christ had become the highest of the Sun spirits, and was an opponent of Lucifer who was seeking to capture the human astral body that had just been bestowed on man by the Spirits of Motion. Christ set bounds to the influence of Lucifer on the human astral body. Then came our own Earth embodiment, which began, as described in Chapter 2 (see p. 103) with a recapitulation of the former embodiments of the Earth. Thus the Sun, with its beings, led by the Christ, was united with the earth during the so-called Polaric Age and on into the second age, known as the Hyperborean. The Moon was likewise united with the earth. If the Sun and its beings had remained with the earth, mankind would have progressed too far and too fast. The Sun was therefore withdrawn by its spirits, leaving the Moon still united with the Earth. But the Moon's forces were hardening ones. If they had remained within the earth, they would have so

---

* This brief and bare account is the gist of Lectures 9 and 10 of a cycle called *Man in the Light of Occultism, Theosophy and Philosophy*, given in Christiania (the present Oslo) in June, 1912. The cycle is in all respects an extremely difficult and esoteric one, and was given to a small group of intimate pupils who were well acquainted with Steiner's earlier teachings. For Lucifer see the Arenson brochure mentioned in Chapter 2 (p. 99n).

187

hardened man himself that he could not have attained his goal. So in due time the Moon too left the earth, and both Sun and Moon shone on the earth from outside, the Moon with light reflected from the Sun.

When the Sun left the earth not all the exalted Sun spirits left with it. One, the being known as Yahweh or Jehovah, remained with the Moon for as long as it was with the earth. When the Moon in turn left the earth, Yahweh went with it. All the moon worshipping peoples recognized Yahweh as their God though they gave him different names, whereas the sun-worshippers recognized the Christ who was the chief of the Sun spirits. These Sun spirits are also known as the Spirits of Form or Elohim, and it was they who first gave man the "germ" of his "I." At this time the Christ, in his descent toward the earth and his eventual incarnation, had taken on the rank of one of the Elohim, or, as Steiner describes it, he had become the essence of all the Elohim, while Yahweh was a separate spirit of the rank of the Elohim who had likewise sacrificed himself, primarily, as we shall see, for the purpose of leading the Hebrew people onward in their evolution. Naturally, all the Elohim worked together in harmony under the leadership of the Christ, but Yahweh had at this time a special mission separate from that of the others.*

In the far distant past the Christ already knew that one day it would be necessary for him to enter a human body in order to set limits to the power of Ahriman and Lucifer, and to start man on his upward course of evolution through the development of his own "I." It was described in Chapter 2 how this "I" became incorporated within man only by slow degrees, and it was not until after the Mystery of Golgotha that man reached the point where he could become free. This was the result of the deed of Christ. In the first post-Atlantean epoch the ancient Indians, led by the wholly clairvoyant Holy Rishis, of course knew of the being of Christ on the Sun. In the second post-Atlantean age, as we have seen, the prophet Zarathustra held colloquies with a

* See above, pp. 50–51.

188

god he called Ahura Mazda, who dwelt on the Sun. This Ahura Mazda was, as Steiner tells us, the Christ in the Sun, and Zarathustra already knew that he was approaching the Earth and would one day be born on it. In the third post-Atlantean age it may be thought that the "heretical" Egyptian Pharaoh Akhenaton recognized the Sun Spirit in the god he called the Aton, though, as far as I know, Steiner himself never made any reference to this. On the other hand, the Chaldeans, the people from whom Abraham came, were moon worshippers, and Abraham's revelations came from Yahweh. Abraham, indeed, was instructed by Yahweh to worship him only, and to see to it that his children and descendants did the same. According to Steiner, Abraham, as well as receiving his mission from Yahweh in dreams, was visited by a high spiritual being (described by St. Paul as being without father or mother) who had been a great initiate of the Sun mysteries and a teacher of the original Zarathustra, but was no longer incarnating in a human body. This was Melchisedek, called in Genesis, "the priest of the Most High God" who brought him bread and the juice of the grape. Thus Abraham as the progenitor of the whole Hebrew people was told of his mission by messengers from both Christ and Yahweh.*

The primary purpose of the Hebrew people was, according to Steiner, to prepare through forty-two generations that physical body that could be inhabited by the Zarathustra Jesus whose ego was to fill the sheaths provided for him by the Nathan Jesus from the age of 12 to 30. With Abraham had begun something new in human evolution. He had received a brain that was capable of thought, whereas before his time thoughts had not been thought *by* individual human beings, but thoughts had, as it were, passed *through* the brain. This new kind of brain was essential if the human being were ever to be able to make use of his ego, as a free and autonomous being, and the blood of the

---

* See Lecture 4 of 12 lectures on the *Gospel of St. Matthew* given by Steiner at Bern in September, 1910.

Hebrew people had to be kept pure for the necessary number of generations before this vehicle could become perfected. This was achieved at the time of the birth of the Solomon Zarathustra Jesus.* In due course a brain of this kind was bestowed on all men, and it will now be possible to glimpse the reason why it was stated in Chapter 2 that the possibility of bringing the ego to birth within man himself came about only with the incarnation of Christ (see page 86), which will be discussed in the next paragraph. Here it is necessary to draw attention to the fact that when Moses was summoned and given his mission he saw a divine being in a burning bush, whose identity he did not know. When he asked for a name by which he could identify him when he announced his mission to the people of Israel, the voice from the burning bush replied, "I am the I am," and he said, "Thus shalt thou say unto the children of Israel, the I am hath sent me unto you." This being, according to Steiner, was not the God Yahweh, but the Christ, who is the higher self of mankind. It was thus a special revelation from the Christ that set in motion the exodus from the land of Egypt.

There are many great mysteries connected with the human "I," few of which can be touched on here. The Gospels make many allusions to them, though always in cryptic terms, so that a different meaning can also be placed on them by those who do not have access to the key provided by occult science. The higher self of man, as has been said already, is the Christ himself, and man's future evolution is bound up with his willingness to allow this higher self to fill his own personal "I." This personal "I" is in charge of our life on earth, and it alone survives after death, eventually to be reborn in another life on earth, as described in the last chapter. When St. Paul said, "Not I, but Christ in me," he was referring to the working of the Christ, the higher self of mankind, within his own personal self. Now in the Gospels there are many sayings of Christ, especially

* See Lecture 2, entitled, "The God Within and the God of External Manifestation" given in Munich, December 7, 1909, included in a series of three lectures entitled, *The Ego* (London, n.d.).

190

in the John Gospel, where he refers to himself as the higher self of mankind, but they are not translated in order to show this for the excellent reason that the translators were unaware of the fact. When Christ says, for example, "I am the Bread of Life, I am the Light of the World, I am the Good Shepherd, I am the True Vine," if the true meaning were to be conveyed by the translator he would have to add the definite article—The I am is the Bread of Life, etc.,*—meaning in this case both the Being of Christ, and the higher self in man.

In other cases, however, Christ is simply referring to the personal human "I," which he has indeed bestowed on man, but in such cases the context makes clear that it is not Christ, the higher self, which is being referred to. Consider the famous saying, so often quoted as an apparent prophesy of the divisions within Christianity, "Think not that I am come to send peace on earth, I came not to send peace but a sword. For I am come to set a man at variance against his father, and the daughter against her mother, and the daughter-in-law against her mother-in-law" (Matt. 10:34–35), or the equivalent in Luke (12:51–53), "Suppose ye that I am come to give peace on earth? I tell you, Nay, but rather division; for from henceforth there shall be five in one house divided, three against two, and two against three. The father shall be divided against the son . . . etc." These sayings refer, as the context makes clear, to the coming of the human "I." The correct understanding of these passages will best be obtained by reading them with the addition of the definite article—"The I am has come not to bring peace but a sword." Such statements are precisely true of the egoism that is an invariable accompaniment, at present, of the possession of the "I." The separation of one man from another of which the Christ speaks is something that belongs to the modern age more than to any other—especially to those peoples that have in fact progressed furthest, where the consciousness soul is developing, and where the old cozy life of the group soul with its close-knit family life, no longer obtains.

---

* See especially Bock, *The Three Years*, pp. 108–110.

191

The Mystery of Golgotha and the Powers of Evil. Toward the end of his life Rudolf Steiner spent as much time as he could spare in carving a huge sculptured group that now stands in a special room in the rebuilt Goetheanum at Dornach in Switzerland. This group depicts a being called by Steiner the "representative of mankind," holding at bay and setting due limits to the power of Lucifer, and thrusting Ahriman beneath his feet. The representative of mankind is, of course, the Christ, or man as he could become if totally transformed through the Christ impulse. It is neither the suffering Christ of Calvary, nor the traditional triumphant Christ of the Resurrection and Ascension, but a Christ who acts as the helper of mankind in man's struggle against the two powers that threaten him. These two powers have already been briefly described, Lucifer who wishes mankind to return to his "cosmic childhood" before the development of his "I," in this way preventing him from attaining his goal of free selfhood, and Ahriman who wishes mankind to be definitively cut off from the spirit, enmeshed in matter, with an all-powerful technology but with neither soul nor spirit. The two tendencies are all too visible today, both in those who wish to "drop out" of the struggle and fall back into an easily acquired "enlarged consciousness" or an equally illusionary "return to religion," and those who recognize only the material world, regard man as a powerful animal who has reached his present position by his success in the "struggle for existence," and before whom the future stretches, unlimited in its material possibilities as a result of the gifts offered him by Ahriman.

Both these beings are so powerful in today's world that it is difficult indeed to believe that a counterforce exists that could vanquish them, and that man by following the path indicated by the Christ could actually hold Ahriman at bay and banish Lucifer. It is therefore greatly instructive for us to recall how Christ, as related in the Bible, vanquished them at a moment when the Christ force had only just incarnated in the body of Jesus of Nazareth, and had not yet attained the mastery over the body that he attained later. If Christ had himself succumbed to the temptations, he could not have fulfilled his task, but of course he did not succumb, though he could not wholly subdue Ahriman. His conquest means only that his power and help are available for man to use, but he cannot force men to avail themselves of them.

It will be recalled that immediately after the Baptism by John, that is, immediately after the entry of the Christ ego into the purified sheaths offered up to him by Jesus of Nazareth, Christ Jesus was led or "driven" by the Spirit into the wilderness (or solitude) where he was approached by the "devil." Now this "devil," according to Steiner, was not one, but the two beings to whom we have already referred. It must be recognized that as yet the incarnation of the Christ was new, and he had as yet had no contact with mankind. But the Christ power was vital and active within the body to which it had not yet become accustomed. Thus it may be thought of as the exact moment when the tempter(s) might best be able to make his (their) presence felt within him. Ahriman approaches him therefore with the suggestion that he should command "that these stones become bread." If Christ had succumbed to this temptation, he would have been doing something that was indeed within his power. But in doing so he would have given mankind *at once* the Bread of Life, whereas it was man's task to work for himself, long and painfully, and with the aid of all Ahriman's gifts, at last learning not to succumb to their use. Man would never have become the free being that the divine world wishes him to become if he had received the Bread of Life at once, and never learned to turn the Ahrimanic "bread" into heavenly Bread. So Christ did not crush Ahriman, he did not even defeat him. But he resisted the temptation by sternly telling him that "man shall not live by bread alone, but by every word of God," (Luke 4:4) an admonishment already given to the Hebrew people when they in their turn had wandered for forty years in the "wilderness." The material world, Christ was telling man, was necessary for him but not all-sufficient. Thus, man still had left to him the

193

possibility of his own spiritual growth by doing as Christ had done first, that is, by rejecting the temptations of Lucifer and not succumbing to the many stratagems of Ahriman.

Then Lucifer approached him and took him to the summit of a high mountain and told him that all the kingdoms of the earth could belong to him if he would bow down and worship him. He, Christ Jesus, could become a world leader and by his magical power attract all men to him and rule them, thus again giving them in a moment the good for which it was mankind's task to struggle. Man need not then attain the ego for himself, he would be led by a divine being whom he need only worship and obey. Christ resisted this temptation, too, and then both Lucifer and Ahriman escorted him to a pinnacle of the temple, telling him that if he would but cast himself down his angels would bear him up, that is, the earthly power of gravity would be nullified and he would be visible to all as a divine being, while, at the same time, as Steiner points out,* overcoming the fear of death, a fear that comes to man from the realm of Ahriman, the lord of death.

The so-called "temptations" of Christ have been described and interpreted here not so much because of their intrinsic importance for the Christ himself, but because man in his turn has the same temptations to face now that he has moved on to his upward path of evolution, and is, as we described in Chapter 2, no longer under the direct guidance of spiritual beings. Since the Mystery of Golgotha he is on his own, and is becoming increasingly alone, at the mercy of the forces of evil if he does

---

* Steiner interprets these temptations in the last lecture of his remarkable series of five lectures given to some of his most intimate followers in Christiania in October, 1913, and published under the title, *The Fifth Gospel*. See also Bock, *The Three Years*, pp. 37–46, for a much fuller account and interpretation, based, of course, on Steiner. Incidentally, Steiner gives the true order of the temptations as first Lucifer alone, then Lucifer and Ahriman at the pinnacle of the temple, and then finally Ahriman alone, whom he could not defeat—as men cannot defeat him—but could himself only refuse to do as Ahriman proposed. Steiner tells us that the words, "Give us this day our daily bread," in the Lord's Prayer is a direct answer to Ahriman's temptation. Man must rely on the divine world for the Bread of Life, not suppose that Ahriman's bread is all that there is.

not himself make the effort to use the help that is available to him. It is most important that he should recognize the Christ as the source of this help, through the deed that he performed for mankind in passing through the gate of death, something no god had ever done before or will ever need to do again.

After three years of living in the body that had been bequeathed to him, even this, the most perfect of all bodies that had ever existed on the earth, was used up by the tremendous forces that had lived in it and, according to Steiner, the spirit was already preparing to abandon it when he was betrayed by Judas. Indeed, the surprise of Pilate when he learned that he was dead already (Mark 15:44) would have been quite justified if it had been an ordinary healthy man who had been nailed to the cross. But Christ Jesus was already dead when the soldiers came to finish off the three crucified men. This was because the body could no longer contain the Christ ego, a fact that is alluded to in the extremely esoteric Gospel of St. Mark when properly understood (15:34–38). First Christ Jesus cries out, "My God, my God, why hast thou forsaken me?" The Christ spirit has left the body. Then, "And Jesus cried out with a loud voice and gave up the ghost. And the veil of the temple (his body, see John 2:21) was rent in twain from the top to the bottom."

What followed his death is told in somewhat different but substantially the same terms by all the evangelists. Steiner in numerous lectures has explained the immediate sequence of events that show conclusively how each of the evangelists perceived the resurrection from the standpoint of his own particular initiation. The apostle Peter in one of his epistles makes the astonishing statement that Christ also "preached to them that are dead," (I Peter, 4:6) which he did during the period known as the "descent into hell." In fact, according to Steiner, Christ at this time once again set bounds to the power of Ahriman, lord of death, so that in future the experience of men between death and rebirth would be different, and no longer the simple emptiness that had been experienced by the Greeks. Souls thereafter could incarnate again following a different

195

experience between death and rebirth, and so could come to know and accept the Christ in a new life on earth. Or, as the words in the Christian Community creed given by Rudolf Steiner put it, "In death he became the helper of the souls of the dead who had lost their divine nature . . ."

The Resurrection itself was neither a miracle nor a deception. The body that had been inhabited by the Christ disintegrated almost immediately after burial because, unlike other bodies, it had no ties of its own to the earth, having never been incarnated before and thus having acquired no karma. The process of bodily disintegration that ordinarily lasts for years took place in this special instance almost instantaneously. But the spiritual body could and did become visible as a body of light to those who visited the sepulcher on the third day, as man's body will likewise become wholly spiritualized at the end of earth evolution if mankind achieves its ultimate goal. With this spiritual body Christ Jesus again became visible and tangible for forty days, during which, both according to Christian tradition not incorporated in the canonical books of the Bible, and according to Steiner, he gave his disciples his most intimate and esoteric teachings, which could not be recorded in the Gospels.*

These teachings need not concern us here, but the mysteries of the Ascension and Pentecost are of vital importance for the future of mankind, and an attempt will therefore be made here to give a small part of the explanation that Steiner gave of these mysteries, and especially the intimate connection between the two events.**

An allusion was already made in Chapter 2 to the remarkable fact recorded by Rudolf Steiner that when the blood of the

---

* Aside from the many individual lectures on the Resurrection and the teachings of the Resurrected one, the reader is referred for further material on the subject just discussed here so briefly to the cycle of ten lectures given at Carlsruhe in October, 1911, and published under the title *From Jesus to Christ.*

** This account is drawn from a single lecture given in Dornach on May 7, 1923, called "The Whitsun Mystery and its Connection with the Ascension," printed in a compilation of several lectures given at different times, published under the title, *Ascension and Pentecost* (London, 1958).

Christ flowed into the earth on Golgotha, the earth itself was changed and began to shine. The Christ Being at this moment united himself with the earth itself, and for all time to come he will be the Spirit of the earth. At the time of the Mystery of Golgotha Lucifer and Ahriman had acquired such power over the physical body and the earthly substances that compose it that mankind might have even had to die out because the physical substances were becoming too decadent to be able to house a human soul and spirit, in the same way that the body was becoming too hardened while the moon was still united with the earth, thus necessitating the departure of the moon if mankind were to survive.

Christ's death and resurrection put an end to this danger because he united himself with not only the earth itself but with man's physical and etheric bodies, the physical made up of earth substances and the etheric of non-physical substance woven, so to speak, out of the light. This deed was made manifest to the disciples who in a state of deep clairvoyance perceived the light-body of the Christ ascending out of their sight. But as yet they could not understand what had happened and was happening. For them the disappearance of the resurrected Christ out of their sight seemed to mean that he had left them, perhaps forever. But "two men in white apparel" then appeared to them, consoling them with the promise that he would "return in like manner as you have seen him go into heaven."* Then the disciples remembered Christ's promise that the Holy Spirit would soon be coming to "baptize" them, and they prepared to await the event.

The descent of the "tongues of fire" on the disciples at Pentecost marks the completion of the Mystery of Golgotha as far as it was accomplished at that time. The disciples who now received the Holy Spirit into their own soul and spirit, their astral body and "I," received with it the possibility of under-

* Acts of the Apostles 1:11. This last statement on the Second Coming will be explained in a later section.

standing what had happened at the Mystery of Golgotha, including the rescuing of the earth itself and the picture of the Ascension. This understanding is offered henceforth to all men, in order that we may ever more deeply penetrate its truth. But this has to be through our own efforts. Christ accomplished his work for all mankind, but the work is not completed until each man individually, in his spirit and soul (the parts of his being that are under his control) come to recognize what was done then and is being constantly renewed until the end of earth evolution. Or, to use Steiner's own words in the lecture referred to above, "The truth of the Whitsun festival can be grasped only when men realize that the sending of the Holy Spirit is the challenge to humanity more and more to achieve Spirit knowledge, through which alone the Mystery of Golgotha can be understood."

Christianity and Reincarnation. Reincarnation has never been an officially accepted Christian doctrine, even though some early Christian thinkers such as Origen believed it to be quite compatible with the Christian doctrine of salvation. However, if the Christian teaching incorporated into the Apostles' and Nicene Creeds of "the resurrection of the body and life everlasting" is interpreted in a less literal way than it usually is by those (perhaps relatively few) Christians who now believe in it, it fits perfectly into anthroposophical thought—as does the later Christian doctrine of the immortality of the soul, derived from the Greeks. What anthroposophy holds is that throughout the rest of earth evolution, and through many incarnations, men will be engaged in *creating,* slowly and gradually, a spiritual body, which, when mankind has reached its goal, will be similar to the resurrected body of Christ Jesus. With regard to the doctrine of the immortality of the soul, there can be no quarrel with the doctrine as such, but what needs to be recognized is the existence of body, soul, *and spirit,* of which it is the spirit (or ego) that is immortal and passes from one incarnation to another. What is mistaken in traditional Christian teaching is the belief in a single life on earth followed by an eternity in "heaven," and

198

particularly the belief that eternity in heaven is bestowed on man whether because of his good deeds on earth, or because God predestined him for it before his birth, or because of his faith or his ecclesiastical observances, or for any reason connected with his one single earthly life. Such a disproportionate "reward" seems indeed to so many people to be unjust or illogical that they are ready to abandon Christianity itself because they find it impossible to accept such a teaching.

It cannot indeed be denied that the doctrine of reincarnation as understood by anthroposophy appears to be more in accord with human ideas of logic than are traditional Christian beliefs. But this fact does not make it necessarily true. We must emphasize once again that anthroposophy must rest its case on the truth of Steiner's revelations from the Akasha Chronicle, and that his teachings represent in no sense an interpretation of the Bible. Nevertheless, it is worth pointing out that certain passages in the New Testament seem to suggest that the disciples and evangelists were familiar with at least some aspects of reincarnation.

If we take into consideration Steiner's statement that John the Baptist was a reincarnation of the prophet Elijah, several biblical passages take on a new light. In Matthew 11 Christ tells his disciples that among men born of women there has never been any greater than John the Baptist, adding (verse 14), "if ye will receive it, this is Elias (Elijah) who was to come. He that hath ears to hear, let him hear." After the Transfiguration (Matthew, 17) when Moses and Elijah appeared on the mountain in company with Christ, the disciples ask him afterward, "Why do the scribes say that Elias must first come? And Jesus answered and said Elias truly shall first come, and restore all things. But I say unto you that Elias is come already and they knew him not, but have done to him whatsoever they listed. Likewise shall the Son of Man suffer of them. Then the disciples understood that he spake unto them of John the Baptist." In Mark the questions and answers are substantially the same (9:11–13) but the last verse in the Matthew account that tells of

199

the conclusion of the disciples is not included. Mark, however, also tells us that King Herod thought that John the Baptist whom he had beheaded was working through Christ Jesus, while others said that he was Elijah or one of the prophets (6:14–15).

There is also a peculiar passage in the John Gospel, where Christ and his disciples see a man who had been blind *from birth,* and the disciples ask him, "Master, who did sin, this man or his parents, that he was born blind?" Jesus answers that neither he nor his parents had sinned. Although Jews had always held that the sins of the fathers are visited upon the children, the possibility that *the man himself* had sinned before birth is scarcely explicable at all except on the hypothesis that both Jesus and his disciples believed that he might have sinned *in a previous life.* (John 9:1–2)

Nonetheless, anthroposophy would not wish to rest its case for reincarnation as a Christian doctrine on any such evidence. To the contrary, although, of course, reincarnation has always been a fact—as indicated in Chapter 2—it was not possible for Western mankind to accept it as such until after the beginning of the age of the consciousness soul; for this reason, if for no other, it could not be accepted and promulgated by the early Church. As was explained in the last chapter, the Oriental idea of reincarnation is not the same as that put forward by anthroposophy, primarily because the East does not really accept the notion of an individual ego, nor indeed did the West before the Mystery of Golgotha. When the Westerner after the Mystery of Golgotha did begin to acquire full individual self-consciousness, his notion of himself was an extremely simple one: he was born, lived for a limited time on earth and then lived forever in a different form, in a condition of being that was scarcely imaginable, and was always depicted in terms of what was known on earth. Even today heaven is usually thought of (and preached about) as a *place,* where conditions will be as far removed as conceivable from the suffering experienced on earth, where there will be eternal bliss for the saved, and, conversely, eternal torment for the damned. The fact that such concrete pictures are becoming ever less credible to most people in the West is a sure sign of how far the consciousness soul has progressed. Modern men and women are beginning to need to know the truth, and are ready, in their relatively new ego consciousness, to face it. Vast numbers of them are quite prepared, under the influence of scientific materialism, to deny the existence of soul or spirit, and to insist that death means, quite simply, annihilation.

But this notion also is excessively simple, even more simple than the notion of salvation and damnation held by their ancestors. Its simplicity does not make it any the more true than the earlier theory since there is no particular reason to suppose that either man or universe is necessarily simple. In fact, with the growth of human self-consciousness and especially with the relatively new spirit of scientific enquiry, the time seems to have come when men can learn to understand the complex, but logical, and, in a sense, economical teaching of reincarnation, as this idea is explained by anthroposophy. But it would certainly appear at first sight that the other traditional teachings of Christianity would have to be abandoned if reincarnation and karma are to be accepted—if only for the reason that if man had to compensate for his evil deeds in a subsequent incarnation, and not only after death (in purgatory or hell), there would seem to be no place for Christ Jesus as Savior and Redeemer.

We have discussed in several contexts how crucial the incarnation, death, and resurrection of Christ Jesus were for the whole future of humanity and the earth, but his role as savior has not as yet been stressed. In fact this role can be understood only in relation to the teachings about karma given in the last chapter. As we have seen, the deeds of our past life are first reviewed after death, then the decision is made, *by ourselves,* to recompense our evil deeds in subsequent incarnations. These incarnations take the form they do because of our decisions, though we require the assistance of higher beings to enable us to choose our parents and the kind of framework within which we shall perform our compensating deeds. Likewise, we need their help if we are to meet in a new life those with whom we were united before, and with whom we have again a joint karma to accomplish. But these decisions are fundamentally our own, and within our own higher being we would not wish to escape the consequences of our actions. On the contrary we rejoice that we are given the possibility of remedying the evil we have done.

Nevertheless, our deeds, even though subsequently compensated in our karma, *cannot be undone.* They are objective facts, and as such were inscribed in the Akasha Chronicle. Every deed of any kind done by men in some infinitesimal measure has affected the universe, and those deeds that are truly *sins,* have actually harmed the universe. To use Steiner's expression, our deeds are "objective cosmic facts." * What Christ did after the Mystery of Golgotha was that he actually took upon himself the consequences of human deeds *in so far as they affect the earth and universe.* This fact has nothing to do with man's own future lives in which he will make his karmic compensation. But it makes possible the future evolution of the earth, which would never be able to attain its next condition of being (Jupiter) if the weight of human sins were still burdening it. Moreover, man would always have to behold between death and rebirth the evil he personally had done to the universe, which would in time have become an almost unbearable experience. Thus, the mystery of the forgiveness of sins and Christ's role as redeemer is perceived to be much more profound than could possibly be imagined without the aid of spiritual science.

If Christ's well-known colloquy on the Cross with the repentant malefactor is correctly understood, it is the most striking biblical illustration of this teaching. Christ's "kingdom" is not of this world, and it is in his "kingdom" that sins are forgiven and their consequences for earth evolution expunged. But for this to happen it is necessary for man in turn to recognize the Christ, and in due time to acknowledge what his

---

* See especially the third lecture in the series of four given in Norrköping in July, 1914, and published under the title *Christ and the Human Soul.* This lecture explains in detail what can only be touched upon here.

deed has meant for earth evolution. This is precisely what the malefactor does acknowledge when he admits that he himself has been justly punished but that Christ had done nothing amiss. Then he says to Jesus, "Lord, remember me when thou comest into thy kingdom." To which Jesus replies "Today shalt thou be with me in Paradise (that is, my kingdom)." (Luke 23:41–43). The malefactor will have to make compensation for his deeds through his karma, but the objective spiritual result of his deeds will be assumed by Christ when he returns to his "kingdom."

It is often said and thought that reincarnation is an Oriental doctrine, taken over by theosophists and then by anthroposophists from the East. The explanation for the Oriental belief in repeated earth lives is a simple one. There has been a continuity in Oriental culture that has not been the case in the West, and the earliest Hindu civilization (the first post-Atlantean) was based entirely upon clairvoyant perception. Hindus of that period were therefore directly aware of repeated earth lives, and when clairvoyant knowledge faded in later ages the tradition remained embedded in their culture. But the Oriental belief has been deeply affected by the fact that men of that early epoch had as yet no experience of the "I," either on earth, or in the spiritual worlds between death and rebirth. On the other hand, it was known from early times that karma regulated the lives of earthly men, in the sense that the circumstances of a later life were determined by those of an earlier one. For this reason he experienced it as an ineluctable destiny, not determined by himself through a choice made in the life between death and rebirth, but determined entirely by higher beings. He had no doubt that man was essentially a spiritual being, whose true home was in the spiritual world, and that it was his karma that tied him to earthly existence. Far from being grateful to his karma, as modern men should learn to be, and as the true Christian will be when he comes to understand reincarnation and karma, the Oriental feels that the only way to escape from karma and the earthly suffering it entails is to kill out the "thirst for existence" that draws him back again and again to the earth. This can be done, in his view, by tying himself to the earth as little as possible, by this means creating a minimum of karma. Having no notion of personal sin, or indeed of moral evil, the deed of Christ necessarily remains incomprehensible to him. Thus, it can scarcely be said that the anthroposophical notion of karma and reincarnation owes anything at all to the Oriental conception. The relationship between the teaching of reincarnation and karma and Christianity, as taught by Rudolf Steiner, remains an original conception that belongs essentially to the age of the consciousness soul as it is developing and must develop in the West.*

The Christ Within and the Second Coming. We have referred in an earlier section as well as in Chapter 2 to the fact that after the Resurrection the way was opened for the Christ himself to enter into the inner being of man, and we have quoted St. Paul's words, which were true in his own case, "Not I, but Christ in me." In order to explain how it is possible for the Christ to enter into man without at the same time interfering with man's freedom, a more extended explanation is now necessary.

It will be recalled that mankind received its different "bodies" from the beings of the higher hierarchies in the previous "incarnations" of the Earth, known as Old Saturn, Old Sun, and Old Moon (see p. 24). In these three periods man received his physical body, his etheric body and his astral body respectively, although only in germinal forms. In the present earth evolution for the first time he received his ego, likewise originally in a germinal form. This ego would have come to its full fruition about the middle of earth evolution, and this had been the intention of the Spirits of Form or Elohim who endowed man with his ego. But such an ego would not have been free. In order to allow man to be endowed with freedom the divine powers permitted the Luciferic beings to enter man's being in the third epoch, known as the Lemurian epoch. This event is described in

_____
* See also above, pp. 156–160.

the book of Genesis as the Fall of Man. By choosing the tree of the knowledge of good and evil, Adam and Eve were driven out of the Garden of Eden, and the tree of life was taken away from them. This mythical picture describes a real change in the consciousness of man, and the entry for the first time of evil into world evolution, at first the evil brought by the Luciferic beings, and then, in the Atlantean age, the evil brought by Ahriman. By being able to choose between good and evil, as the myth states, man received at the same time the impulse toward freedom.

The primary result of the entry of the Luciferic beings into man's astral body was that he became capable of "egoism." His astral body was filled with all kinds of desires, and he became what we may call self-seeking, gratifying his own desires even at the expense of others. The human "I" also did not enjoy a normal development, for man became self-conscious to a certain extent far earlier than had been planned for him; this is true also of men today. As soon as a child can say "I" to himself at about the age of three, he is already to a certain extent self-conscious, but it is not his real self of which he is conscious, but a false or Luciferic self. It is this Luciferic self that lives in man until the age when he should have received his real self, namely, between the ages of twenty and twenty-one. A great change does take place in man about his twenty-first year, as has always been known, but man still remains under the influence of the Luciferic and Ahrimanic beings who have been living in his astral body and continue to do so. But after twenty-one man is able to work upon his soul elements, as already described, going through the age of the sentient soul between twenty-one and twenty-eight, the intellectual soul between twenty-eight and thirty-five, and the consciousness soul between thirty-five and forty-two. During these periods the "I" is working within these souls, and experiencing its freedom, but it is an uphill task because of the damage already wrought and that will continue to be wrought by the forces of evil in the astral body, that have had their effects even in the etheric and physical bodies.

All this does not mean, however, that the "I" *in itself* is

205

damaged, or is anything other than the divine entity originally bestowed on man by the Spirits of Form. As we have seen, the "I" indeed did not incarnate fully within man until the time of the Mystery of Golgotha; as a result, divine spiritual beings were able to help man even without his conscious cooperation. But when from the time of the Mystery of Golgotha the "I" became gradually fully incarnated within man it became necessary for man to work *consciously* in cooperation with that divine being who had incarnated on earth and had passed through death and resurrection, if he were to make progress upward toward the goal envisaged for him by the spiritual worlds. For the first millennium and a half after Christ he could receive the Christ impulse into his life of feeling, and man's relationship with the Christ during these centuries was essentially that of believing in him, meditating on him, trying to be like him, loving him. But there was as yet no vital need to *understand* him. This need awoke with the beginning of the age of the consciousness soul, at a time when his thinking was becoming increasingly Ahrimanic or materialistic. In spite of this present tendency, the consciousness soul remains the highest of the three "souls," and it is intimately connected with the spiritual, as the sentient soul is intimately connected with the bodily element. The "eternal spirit," in Rudolf Steiner's words, "shines into his inner being" thereby kindling a light in it that is imperishable. "Insofar as the soul lives in this light, it is a participant of the eternal." *

When Steiner wrote this passage in 1904 he was not yet ready to call this eternal spirit shining into man's inner being the Christ, as he called it in later years. One later reference in which the matter is made abundantly clear may be quoted here, from two lectures given in Stockholm in April, 1912, and published under the title of *The Three Paths of the Soul to Christ*. (New York, 1942). Steiner here speaks of how the human "I," feeling within itself the strife of the opposing powers, is not strong enough to overcome them. But then man feels "that there comes

---

* *Theosophy*, 1971 edition, page 24.

'something that I can take into my ego as a force, something that I can take into my consciousness as conviction. Directly from the spiritual worlds comes something that does not reside in me, but that permeates my soul. From unknown worlds something can flow into my soul; if I take it up in my heart, if I suffuse my ego with it, then it helps me directly from spiritual worlds.' This that comes from spiritual worlds may be called whatever we like, that is not important, only the feeling is important." (page 13)

A few pages later Steiner explains how, if someone realizes within himself strongly enough that he is in need of something "that cannot come to him from human culture," then "something can come over him from which he will recognize that, directly from spiritual worlds, something must stream out that penetrates directly into his ego. He does not know that this is called Christ, but he does know that in his consciousness he can suffuse himself with it, that in his Ego he can foster this that comes to him from the spiritual worlds." . . . "Men can have this *inner experience;* without it men cannot live, without it men will not be able to live in the future. They can have this experience, because once, for three years, there lived objectively in Jesus of Nazareth this impulse that came directly out of the spiritual worlds. As it is true that a man can lay a seed in the earth, and that many other seeds can come from this one, so it is true that the Christ impulse was once implanted into humanity, and that since that time there is something in humanity that was not there earlier." (pp. 18–19)

This passage is one of the clearest of many in Steiner's works in which, albeit in still a somewhat veiled manner, he tells us that what may be thought of as the higher ego or self of man is in fact the Christ. Man can achieve just so much through his own efforts, but he cannot expel the forces of evil from his astral body, nor should he try to do any such thing. The forces of evil, or opposing forces, are there in order that man may be able to make a real, and not merely an apparent choice. It is his task not to drive out evil, nor even, as man's task was understood in the East, to follow the ascetic path and shun all temptations arising from his bodily nature. It is man's real task to turn evil into good. But he cannot do this out of his own forces; for this he needs the Christ as his helper. But Christ cannot help if he is not recognized or accepted by men as their higher self. For a long time to come men may not be able to give a name to the Christ impulse when they experience it. But in later centuries when Christianity is universally recognized to be true, and is not regarded merely as one among many religions, men will know who the Christ is, and, as will be explained in the final section of this chapter, may even come to see him in the form in which he is living now.

At this point we may take up in more detail the discussion that appears at the end of Chapter 3, where we referred to Steiner's intimation in his last lecture given on Thomas Aquinas in 1920 that the philosophy of freedom, with its ethical individualism, cannot be brought to full realization and fruition in life without the Christ impulse, although in 1894 when he wrote his *Philosophy of Freedom* he was not yet in a position to make such a statement. In this lecture he states specifically* that "Ethical Individualism is, in reality founded upon the Christ impulse in man, although this is not expressed in the book," and he goes on to say that in all his earlier work he had "laid special stress upon the *transformation* of the human soul and upon the necessity of its being really filled with the Christ impulse, even in its thought-life." In concluding the lecture cycle he explained in words worth quoting in full how the dilemma of Thomas, dealt with also briefly in Chapter 4 (see p. 141) that while most theological knowledge is to be obtained by pure human thinking, other knowledge can be received only through revelation and accepted on faith—is resolved. The knowledge that in Thomas' day was obtainable only in the revealed Scriptures is for the future obtainable by man when he allows his thinking to be permeated by the Christ impulse. In this way the distinction between the two different kinds of knowledge disappears.

---

* Shepherd and Nicoll edition of these lectures published under the title of *The Redemption of thinking*, pp. 109–110.

We must consider anew, [Steiner states], in a completely factual way, the spiritual-psychic content of man, the thought-world that receives into itself the transforming Christ principle, in order that, through the Christ in us, that is, in our thought world, we may discover again the spiritual world. Are we to rest content with leaving our thought world alone at the level to which the Fall of Man has brought it? Shall man's thought world have no part in human redemption? In the thirteenth century no place could be found in the thought world for the principle of Christian redemption and therefore the thought world was regarded as quite apart from the world of revelation. The future advance of mankind will be realized by discovering the principle of redemption, not only for the outer world but also for human reason. The unredeemed human reason could never raise itself into the spiritual world. It is only the redeemed human reason, which possesses the true relationship to the Christ, that can win its way into the world of spirit. To enter the kingdom of the spirit in this way is the Christianity of the twentieth century (pp. 114–115).

The last subject to be covered in this chapter is the so-called Second Coming, which, according to Christian belief, will be accompanied by the Last Judgment. It would take us too far if we were to attempt to deal with the actual end of earth evolution, with its division of mankind into those who have chosen to follow the Christ and those who, in spite of having incarnated many times since the Mystery of Golgotha, still prefer to turn away from him, thus hindering the proper evolution of the earth. Steiner said much on this subject in many scattered lectures and cycles, but what he told us on the subject after all tells us little more about the Christ or Christianity, which are the subjects of this chapter.

It is quite otherwise with the Second Coming. In Chapter 2 reference was made to the end of Kali Yuga or the Dark Age, which took place in 1899 (see page 34). This Dark Age, during which men lost the vision of the supersensible worlds that had once been the possession of all men, came to an end with the beginning of the twentieth century, thereafter opening up

209

the possibility to men of reacquiring spiritual vision. From the twentieth century onward man's latent faculties that had been obsolescent during Kali Yuga can again become active, not only among those who make the conscious effort to develop them, but among others too who have through their karma been born with a soul configuration that makes such vision relatively easy to awaken. Such persons become able to perceive on the astral plane.*

Because the astral plane is a supersensible realm we should make the effort, difficult though it may be, to avoid thinking of it in spatial terms. The Bible makes references to it in a veiled manner as, for example, when John tells how Nicodemus visited Jesus *by night*, that is, outside the physical body (John 3:2). It is the first supersensible realm open to man's clairvoyant vision, but Steiner also speaks of it as being in the "circumference" or "sphere of the earth." It is here that Christ after the Resurrection and Ascension became potentially visible as an etheric form (thus without a physical body), but it required a degree of clairvoyance that was scarcely possible at that time if anyone were to have perceived him there. Instead of perceiving him clairvoyantly, the great Christian mystics, as, for example, Meister Eckhart and Johannes Tauler, experienced the living Christ within themselves; whereas the famous vision of an angel that came to St. Teresa of Avila was the result of an abnormal condition of her soul at the time. None of these persons saw Christ actually as an etheric form.

But there was one man who did see him in his etheric form within the sphere of the earth. This was Saul on the way to Damascus (Acts 9) who was granted this vision as a special dispensation because of the task he was called upon to perform for Christianity. Because of his initiation into the deepest Hebrew secrets, Saul (or Paul, as he was called after the vision)

---

* The two earliest fundamental lectures given by Steiner on this subject were given on January 25, 1910 in Carlsruhe and in Stuttgart on March 6th of the same year. They are published together under the title, *The True Nature of the Second Coming* (London, 1961).

knew that the Messiah would be resurrected, and that thereafter he could be found by clairvoyant vision in the sphere of the earth. Previously, the initiate would have seen the Christ only in the sphere of the Sun, and this is where Paul would have expected to see him. But when he saw him in the sphere of the earth he knew at once that Jesus had, after all, been the bearer of the Christ; from that moment onward he always preached the resurrection and made it the center of his teaching. "If Christ be not risen, then is your faith vain." And he referred to himself as an "apostle called out of due time," or simply (as in I Cor. 1) as "called to be an apostle of Jesus Christ through the will of God." Even Paul's degree of initiation would have been insufficient in that epoch to enable him to see the Christ in his etheric raiment, but, as he correctly says, it was the will of God that he should have the vision, and immediately believe.

This event must be considered unique, however, not because Christ was not in the sphere of the earth, but because it was not possible as long as Kali Yuga lasted for men to see him there with clairvoyant vision. Seeing him "in the clouds of heaven," according to Steiner, means precisely seeing him as an etheric form on the astral plane. Thus, the Second Coming is not a sudden event, but a gradual awakening of the human being to clairvoyant vision, by which men will be able to see, with their spiritually opened eyes, the risen Christ. Men must be prepared to see him, and wish to do so, and then in time the *natural* clairvoyant faculties will develop once again in people prepared for this by their former earth lives. Steiner movingly describes how scattered people throughout the earth from the 1930s onward will perceive the Christ in this way when they may perhaps be least expecting it.

It is true that a certain number of people will see the Etheric Christ, and will experience the event that took place before Damascus, but this will depend on their learning to watch for the moment when the Christ draws near to them. In a few decades it will happen to certain persons, especially to the young—for already preparation is being

211

made for this—that someone arrives in a place and experiences certain things. Then, if he has really sharpened his vision through occupying himself with anthroposophy, he will notice that someone is beside him who comes to help him, who approaches him, but he thinks it is a physical man. Many a one will experience, when sitting silent in his chamber, his heart sad and oppressed, not knowing which way to turn, that the door will open, the Etheric Christ will appear and speak comforting words to him. The Christ will become a living Comforter to men! However grotesque it may seem today, yet it is true, that many a time when people are sitting together and waiting expectantly, they will behold the Etheric Christ. He will himself be there and will confer with them, his voice will be heard in such gatherings. This is something positive, something which as a positive constructive element is entering human evolution.*

Thus, the Second Coming is a continuous event for those men in the life between birth and death who are prepared to perceive it. Between death and rebirth those who have similarly prepared themselves will also be able to perceive the Christ in etheric form, especially if in the incarnation just finished they have sought him, and have tried to develop their spiritual faculties, especially by pondering on the Christian teachings of spiritual science.** As time goes on, ever more human beings should be able to perceive the Christ unless, as is evidently more than possible, Lucifer and Ahriman succeeded in tempting man to fall victim to their enticements, and accept the materialistic viewpoint as the only possible truth. If this should happen, fewer

---

* Lecture given at Basel on October 1, 1911, and published under the title of *The Etherisation of the Blood* (London, 1972), p. 21. In this lecture (p. 24) Steiner also remarks that Christ's etheric body is the only one that can "work in the physical world as a physical human body works. It will differ from a physical body only in this, that it will be able to be in two or three, nay in a hundred, a thousand places at the same time, a condition possible only to an etheric, not to a physical form."

** See especially the first of two lectures given at Leipzig on November 4 and 5, 1911, and published under the title of *Jeshu ben Pandira* (New York, 1942). In this lecture reference is also made to appearances of the Christ in different forms in later ages, a subject that we have not wished to enter on here, if only because of the many supplementary explanations that would be needed.

people will be prepared, and the astral plane where the Christ dwells will become ever more difficult for most men to penetrate. In today's world there are few persons living who can justifiably claim to be Christians. There are some religious men and women who hold a belief in a God like Yahweh as he is depicted in the Old Testament, who is above all a righteous and just God, who will judge men for their deeds, and may or may not temper his justice with mercy. Both Protestants and Catholics, as well as Jews, have too often retained this notion of God the Father as judge and ruler, and no obvious position remains for God the Son, Christ Jesus, except as a teacher (even preacher of revolution), as model for men to imitate, or as a kind of mediator on behalf of man with his all-powerful Father. Few thinking men seem able to accept the traditional belief that it was *necessary* for Christ Jesus to become man and pass through death in order to bestow eternal life on men in the hereafter. Obviously, an all-powerful God could have done this without any such intervention.

Other men and women call themselves Christians because they are genuinely concerned with the well-being of their neighbors, and wish to help them to the best of their ability. They think of their acts as stemming from "Christian" charity. But such ethical behavior may equally well be found in professed agnostics and atheists, to say nothing of adherents of other religions.

Christianity as a religion is in fact in a state of disarray almost everywhere in today's world, for the excellent reason that its traditional beliefs were arrived at in the age of the intellectual soul, and today they have become Luciferic, in the sense that they belong to the past and not to the present age of the consciousness soul, when it has become man's duty to think, question, and no longer to accept on authority. What Steiner has done is to reveal the truth behind so much of what became Christian dogma. The dogma was not wrong, but, being incomprehensible to the human reason, had simply to be accepted on faith. Without the deepened knowledge derived

213

from spiritual science it seems to me that Christianity is doomed to lose all credibility among men and women of the age of the consciousness soul, and this in a not too distant future. Our age demands and needs knowledge and understanding, and what Steiner has taught about the being of the Christ, difficult though it may at first be to accept, can awaken our understanding and lead us in time toward an actual experience of the living Christ as he is today.

Mankind needs religion not only because the soul and spirit of man require sustenance, but because the spiritual development of man, which alone gives meaning to his existence, needs the *cooperation* of men with higher beings, and preeminently with the Christ. Because the divine world willed that man should become free, in this freedom differing from all other beings in the universe, man must play his part. But to play it he needs the fullest possible knowledge of what he is doing and why, he needs to recognize that he is not alone in the universe, and he needs to learn to love and worship those higher beings who have made his unique destiny possible.

SUGGESTIONS FOR FURTHER READING
FOR CHAPTER 5.

N.B. Several important lectures by Rudolf Steiner have been quoted or referred to in the text, and footnote references given. These titles will not be repeated in the following list unless in their totality they are recommended reading for this chapter.

The early book by Steiner (1902) entitled *Christianity as a Mystical Fact* recommended for Chapter 2 should be read as an introduction to all Steiner's work on Christianity, though as far as the present chapter is concerned it should be considered more in the light of background material. Possibly the best introductory reading to Steiner's work on Christianity is his short series of three lectures given at Copenhagen June 6 to 8, 1911, which were revised personally by Steiner himself for publication as a brochure. These lectures were published under the title, *The Spiritual Guidance of Man and Mankind* (New York, 1970). The cycle of ten lectures given in Berlin, March 27–May 8, 1917, entitled, *Building Stones for an Understanding of the Mystery of Golgotha* (London, 1972), shows the central importance of the Mystery of Golgotha. Steiner gave lectures on all the Gospels, all of which should be studied. I personally find it best to study these cycles in the order in which they were delivered because in them Steiner gradually revealed the truths about Christianity, and some of the material previously given is essential for the understanding of the later lectures. In the two cycles on the Gospel of St. John, for example, Steiner chose to say nothing about the two Jesus children, speaking in a detailed manner about them only after these two cycles had been delivered.

The Gospel of St. John, twelve lectures delivered in Hamburg, May, 1908 (New York, 1973), available in a paperback edition.

The Gospel of St. John in its Relation to the Other Three Gospels, Particularly to the Gospel of St. Luke, fourteen lectures given in Cassel, June–July, 1909 (New York, 1948).

The Gospel of St. Luke, ten lectures given in Basel, September, 1909 (London, 1975).

Deeper Secrets of Human History in the Light of the Gospel of St. Matthew, three lectures given in Berlin, November, 1909 (London, 1957). The first of these lectures provides a valuable comparative insight into the nature of the different Gospels.

The Gospel of St. Matthew, twelve lectures given in Bern, September, 1910 (London, 1965).

Background to the Gospel of St. Mark, ten lectures given at intervals in Berlin from October 17, 1910 to June 10, 1911 (London, 1970).

The Gospel of St. Mark, ten lectures given in Basel, September, 1912 (New York, 1950).

Equally important, but supplementary to the Gospels themselves are *The Christ Impulse and the Development of the Ego*

Consciousness, seven lectures given in Berlin at intervals from October 25, 1909 to May 8, 1910 (New York, 1976), and *From Jesus to Christ*, ten lectures given in Karlsruhe in October, 1911 (London, 1973). Of a special nature is the cycle called *The Fifth Gospel*, consisting of five lectures given in Oslo, October 1 to 5, 1913 and two lectures given in Cologne, December 17 and 18, 1913 (Revised Edition, London, 1978). All serious students of anthroposophy should read this cycle, but not until they have acquired a sufficient background in Steiner's teachings on Christianity.

The cycle mentioned in the text called *Christ and the Human Soul*, four lectures given in Norrköping in July 1914 (London, 1972) is an important one for the understanding of much that is given in this chapter, and in particular for the question of how karma is compatible with the doctrine of the Redemption.

For the pre-earthly deeds of Christ see the cycle of lectures given at Leipzig, December 28, 1913 to January 2, 1914, entitled, *Christ and the Spiritual World* (London, 1963), and an important single lecture given at Pforzheim, March 7, 1914 (Vancouver, 1978) entitled, *The Pre-Earthly Deeds of Christ*.

In connection with these cycles and Steiner's teachings on Christianity in general there are several excellent books written by senior priests of the Christian Community. Three, in particular, may be selected: Emil Bock, *The Three Years* (London: Christian Community Press, 1955); Rudolf Frieling, *Hidden Treasures in the Psalms* (London: Christian Community Press, 1954), which shows in a remarkable way how the Psalms find in so many cases their fulfillment in Christianity; Alfred Heidenreich, *The Unknown in the Gospels* (London: Christian Community Press, 1972), a series of lectures published after the author's death, which constitute one of the finest possible introductions to Steiner's teachings on Christianity.

CHAPTER VI

Anthroposophy

and Its Relation to the Arts

In a beautiful lecture given in Berlin on October 28, 1909, called *The Nature and Origin of the Arts,* Rudolf Steiner presented an imaginative picture of two sisters, lost in a frozen waste. One sister, who in spite of the cold was thrilled by the beauty of the landscape, was rewarded by a dream-experience in which she received from the higher worlds all those powers needed for her to be able to give the arts to mankind. The other sister almost froze to death during the night, and received no spiritual experience. At the end this second sister is revealed as Human Knowledge, who was nursed back to life by her sister Art.

This picture underlies all the teachings and all the work done by Rudolf Steiner in the realm of art. To him art is not something for enjoyment, though it may of course be enjoyed; it is not simply an agreeable adjunct to human existence but a vital necessity for men, as vital as science or religion and directed to the feeling or soul element in man. Without it, as Steiner's picture implies, knowledge itself is condemned to a frozen unfruitfulness for human life. All the arts, according to Steiner, originated in supersensible perception, were gifts to men from

217

the higher worlds. Unless they are constantly nourished from this source, they will become sterile, and incapable of sustaining the soul life of man, a soul life that in our day is in constant danger from intellectualism and that can be nourished only by art.

Such a notion will be unfamiliar to most people, even to those who enjoy and appreciate many forms of art, and may perhaps practice one or more of them. It will perhaps be least unfamiliar to music lovers who may well be prepared to agree that the greatest composers of the past received, and living composers may receive inspiration from a superearthly world—especially such a man as Beethoven who was stone deaf when he wrote his Ninth Symphony, and could never hear with his earthly senses either the choir or the orchestra playing his finished work. Nor could he even hear any part of it while he was composing it. But it remains true that it is possible to point to the supersensible element in every one of the true arts, and a substantial part of the present chapter will be devoted to this subject. The remainder will deal with Steiner's actual personal contribution to an understanding of the different arts, and the impulses he gave for each of them in order that they might be able to play their proper role in the development of man's soul life. All these impulses have been found fruitful by his followers, including some who have devoted their lives to the work, which could be little more than indicated by Steiner himself in his own lifetime. Nevertheless, it is true that Steiner was active as architect, sculptor, painter, poet and dramatist, and he actually created the new art of eurythmy, which will be described in some detail later in the chapter. Newcomers to what may be called "anthroposophical" art certainly are not expected to approve immediately Steiner's work in any of these fields. Indeed, its very strangeness may repel many. Even anthroposophists who accept Steiner's teachings in other realms have been known to lack appreciation, to say the least, of his work in the field of art. In this chapter, therefore, an effort will be made to show the relationship between his teachings on art and all his other work, so that it

218

will be possible even for those who do not care for his art to recognize the organic nature of the whole of his work, and why he found it essential to devote so much of the later part of his life to it.

In his work on both art and science Steiner often referred back to Goethe whose approach to the sense perceptible world so much resembled his own. Indeed, in 1923 Steiner explained clearly that among his recent predecessors only Goethe had started along the path that he himself was to chart later, although Goethe was never able to perceive consciously the supersensible world.* Aside from his imaginative ability, which enabled him to write such an esoteric "fairy story" as *The Green Snake and the Beautiful Lily*, Goethe possessed the ability to see the world without the interference of abstract thought. Through what we may think of as a highly developed aesthetic sense he was able to let the world *reveal itself* to him as few of us can do. Thus, he could view it freshly, without preconceptions, and as a result could make some discoveries that had been hidden from more abstract thinkers. We shall deal with this talent of Goethe's more fully in the next chapter, since the theory of knowledge implicit in Goethe's world conception (as Steiner called it) underlies also Steiner's own work in the sciences.

It also underlies much of what Steiner tells us about the art of painting, and the impulse he gave for its future development, because, as we shall see, he accepts Goethe's theory of colors, which was neglected by the greater part of the scientific world of his own day since it conflicted with the theoretical teachings of Newton and his successors. One of Goethe's more famous aphorisms on art is quoted approvingly by Steiner as essentially the view of anthroposophy. "Art," said Goethe, "is a manifestation of secret laws of nature, which without it would remain forever hidden," to which Steiner adds the comment, "He felt what anthroposophists must feel. If one has attained to a

---

* The eighth and last lecture of a cycle published under the title, *The Anthroposophic Movement*, given in Dornach June 17, 1913 (London, 1933).

219

cognitional comprehension of the world, there arises a *vital need* not just to continue forming ideas, but to create artistically in sculpture, painting, music, and poetry." * A little later in the same lecture Steiner gives an example of what he means by this statement, which could hardly be bettered as an illustration of just what supersensible perception can mean for art. The example is taken from sculpture but could be duplicated *mutatis mutandis* in other arts:

Man must again place himself vitally-artistically in the world; must perceive the whole cosmic being and life artistically . . . we must recognize the form through a sensitive *qualitative* immersion in the human being. Then in a marvelous way we shall recognize in the human head, in its arching of forehead and crown, a copy—not just as allegory but inward reality—of the heavenly dome dynamically overarching us. An image of the universe is shaped by forehead and upper head. Similarly an image of our experience in circling the sun, in turning round it with our planet in a horizontal circling, this participation in cosmic movement is felt artistically in the formation of nose and eyes. Imagine: the repose of the fixed stars shows in the tranquil vault of brow and upper head; planetary circling in the mobile gaze of the eye, and in what is inwardly experienced through nose and smell. As for the mouth and chin in man, we have here an image of what leads deeply into his inner nature. The mouth with the chin represents the whole human being as he lives with his soul in his body. To repeat, the human head mirrors the universe artistically. In forehead and the arching crown of the head we see the still vault of the heavens; in eye, nose and upper lip, planetary movement, in mouth and chin, a resting within oneself.

If all this is beheld as living image, it does not remain in the head as abstraction. If we really feel what I have just described, then a certain sensation arises, and we say to ourselves, 'You were quite a clever man who had pretty ideas, but now, suddenly, your head becomes empty; you cannot think at all: you feel the true significance of forehead, crown, eye, nose, upper lip, mouth, lower

---

* In a lecture given in Christiania (Oslo), Norway on May 18, 1923, and printed in a collection called *The Arts and their Mission*, p. 86.

lip, even while thoughts forsake you.' Now the rest of man becomes active. Arms and fingers begin to act as tools of thinking. But thoughts live in forms. It is thus that a sculptor comes into being. (*The Arts and Their Mission*, pp. 90–91.)

It will be clear from what has already been said that Steiner believed that artistic *creation* is an essentially human activity. Indeed, he often used to warn his students that anthroposophical knowledge ought, in principle, to be fertilized by the practice of at least one art, or their very knowledge and study of anthroposophical teachings would tend to become arid, and end in abstraction. Thus, all the schools founded on the basis of Steiner's pedagogy give much attention to all forms of art discussed in this chapter, but always as *doing* and not only as appreciation. Every child in a Steiner school from an early age paints and plays at least one musical instrument, if only simple ones like recorders and flutes. He learns to model and carve in wood, he learns to declaim poetry (if not to compose it, though this too is encouraged); he will take part every year in several dramatic presentations. Above all, from at least the first grade onward he takes lessons in the new art of eurythmy, and all through the school curriculum time is always found for them, even up to the top grades in the school. Those of us who did not have the privilege of being educated in a Steiner school do not necessarily find it impossible to engage in artistic creation, even though what we create will surely be no deathless masterpiece. The important thing is to create for ourselves as well as contemplating the masterpieces of the past. At the same time we may try to understand and enter as livingly as possible into how the supersensible has in certain masterpieces been indeed able to fill the being of the artist whose work we contemplate. For men and women of the present day this experience has been perhaps most marked in the field of music, which is preeminently the art of the age of the consciousness soul. But through the fuller development of our artistic faculties and the use of our imaginations we may greatly enrich our aesthetic experience and

221

thus give our soul the nourishment it so greatly needs in the world of the present ruled by the abstract thinking of modern science and technology.

Architecture. The first three arts with which we shall deal appear, unlike music, to be linked closely enough with the material world. At most some people might be willing to acknowledge that something spiritual or unearthly can sometimes be brought into painting—as, for example, in the work of some of the impressionists or the light in such a picture as Vermeer's "View of Delft," and in many of the landscapes of Turner. But few of us are likely to think of architecture as a spiritual art in this sense, but rather a practical art whose form has depended primarily on the kind of materials available and the purpose of the building. The Greek temple was given its characteristic form because it was to form an earthly dwelling place for the god or goddess to whom it was dedicated. Similarly, the Gothic cathedral had its characteristic form because it was desired to have it filled with colored light, thus necessitating a structure that allowed the maximum of light to penetrate through the stained glass windows. The pointed arch and the flying buttress were therefore "invented" in the twelfth century because of this need (necessity being supposedly the mother of invention!), as the technical difficulties of creating tall spires were overcome by the builders in this and succeeding centuries because of the need to "symbolize" in this way the aspiration of medieval Christians toward heaven. Likewise, the New York skyscraper came into being primarily because of the high cost of land in the city of New York which necessitated the provision of the maximum of office space on the limited land. The possibility of building them was provided by the development of structural steel and concrete, and the fact that the land on which they were erected was made of granitic rock. In short the form of a building has usually—and always at times when architecture has been original and not simply copied earlier models—been determined by its function.

All this is true enough as far as it goes, and it is even true of

222

the two great and original buildings designed by Steiner, the first Goetheanum, constructed mainly of wood that was destroyed by fire on New Year's Eve, 1922, and the second Goetheanum, built on the same site as the earlier one, in Dornach, Switzerland, that is still in daily use. But it does not take into account the changing consciousness of man in the various ages of history as discussed in Chapter 2, which was responsible for the architecture characteristic of each period, nor does it take account of the subconscious element in architectural creation that has been brought to light by Rudolf Steiner. For architecture is the external expression of the laws of the human physical body—as sculpture expresses the laws of the etheric and painting the laws of the astral body. In the physical body the formative forces of the etheric body are always working, and it is the working of these etheric forces in the physical that gives rise to architecture. In Steiner's words:

> If we carry this spatial system of lines and forces (i.e., the activity of the etheric in the physical) constantly active in us out into the world, and if we organize matter according to this system, then architecture arises. All architecture consists in separating from ourselves this system of forces and placing it outside in space. All the laws present in the architectural utilization of matter are to be found also in the human body. When we project the specific organization of the human body into the space outside it, then we have architecture. . . . Here, carried into the space outside us, is the interaction between vertical and horizontal and between forces that react together, all of which are otherwise to be found within the human physical body.*

Now such information, however *true* it may be, is not particularly *useful* to us as long as it remains purely subconscious. Nor is it any more helpful to us when Steiner tells us in another lecture published in the same collection entitled, "The

---

* From a lecture entitled, "Impulses of Transformation for Man's Artistic Evolution" given on December 29, 1914 in Dornach, and published as part of a collection called *Art in the Light of Mystery Wisdom*, pp. 19–20.

Supersensible Origin of the Artistic," that architectural and sculptural works of art can be created by man only because he can relive now in the physical world of the senses the experiences that befell him in the spiritual world prior to conception and birth. "If," he tells us, "we build houses not merely according to the principles of utility, but really make them architecturally beautiful, we fashion their dynamic proportions according to experiences of equilibrium and rhythmically moving forms, which we recall from the time we spent between death and our new birth."

It may be conceded that this kind of information is not apparently useful to us now, but it does at least indicate the possibilities that might unfold for architecture and sculpture when these forces of which Steiner speaks can be consciously experienced through spiritual development. What he himself created from his own spiritual development could be seen, in particular, in the old Goetheanum that was burned, a building that was and surely will always remain unique, and may still be seen now in the present Goetheanum built in concrete. Both buildings had certain functions to fulfill, for which the form chosen was perfectly fitting. We cannot spend much space here on these buildings, but we shall give at least a few indications that will serve to give some idea of what Steiner purposed and achieved in this art.

The Anthroposophical Society, which had been founded as a separate organization during the course of the period from September, 1912 to February, 1913, clearly needed a center of its own, which would include a stage on which the four mystery dramas written by Steiner could be suitably presented and performed. The original intention had been to build this home in Munich where the dramas had hitherto been performed. But many reasons, not least the disturbed political conditions of the period, militated against this solution, so that when the Society was offered a fine plot of land standing high above Basel near the village of Dornach in Switzerland, the decision was made to

224

build there, and the foundation stone was laid in September, 1913. A devoted group of workers from many countries continued the building all through the war under the personal direction of Rudolf Steiner, who had, of course, had no professional training as architect or builder, but was able to bring all his supersensible knowledge to bear on each problem as it arose.

The building, in Steiner's view, had to be suitable not only for staging plays, eurythmy performances and for giving anthroposophical lectures, but should arise out of the artistic impulses proper to the age of the consciousness soul. Nor should it be an imitation of some building of the past (neo-classical or neo-Gothic) as so many buildings used for similar purposes still were in 1913. It should express or try to express also in itself the spiritual strivings of anthroposophy. Every lecture, every performance given in the Goetheanum, as the building was named, ought to gain immeasurably from the surroundings—not simply because of the acoustics or the décor, but because of the total appropriateness of the architecture, sculpture, the paintings and the windows to what was done in the building. That Steiner was successful in achieving, at least in a large measure, what he sought may be attested by such a passage as the following, written by one who worked with him on the first Goetheanum.

Secrets of human existence were whispered to us within its walls, and an urge to *conscious* union with the Spirit was one of the most eloquent messages that it brought home to us. This spiritual impulse of progress toward the ultimate goal of life slumbering within the human soul found expression in various ways in the architecture. As one's eyes followed the lines running through the decorations in the forms of the capitals and in the interlacing of the ground plan, it was in every way as if the static elements of architecture had absorbed new qualities that had awakened them to life. The Spirit of Form had found union with the Spirit of Movement.*

---

* Arild Rosenkrantz, *The Goetheanum as a New Impulse in Art*, an undated booklet consisting of a number of articles originally published in *Anthroposophy*, a quarterly of the Anthroposophical Society in Great Britain. Page references in

The structural forms in architecture, as Steiner pointed out, derive from the forces in the human physical body, and it was his conscious perception and understanding of these forces that enabled him to design the Goetheanum. The same forces, though experienced much less consciously by the Greeks, enabled them to construct their temples. Sculpture, by contrast, originates from forces in the etheric body, and Greek sculpture was as perfect as it was because the Greek sculptor was aware of the forces in his own etheric body; he never used a model for the human body. In the Greek columns with their capitals is mirrored the evolution of the human "I," the Corinthian capital (the latest in time) showing the highest development of the "I" in the intellectual soul. The architraves and columns of the Goetheanum belong to the age of the consciousness soul, and in the capitals of the seven pairs of columns surrounding the auditorium can be traced the newer development of the human "I."

These indications are given solely for the purpose of illustration. Obviously it would be possible to write indefinitely on other elements in the Goetheanum that took the forms they did because of Steiner's supersensible perceptions. What should, however, be emphasized is that nothing in the entire Goetheanum was *symbolic* in the sense usually given to that word. Nothing in it is a symbol of anything else, even the carved capitals do not *represent* the human "I." Symbols are the product of modern intellectualism, they are *thought out*, whereas the Goetheanum was an organic form, and even the decoration was created in the way in which Nature creates, by allowing each form to be the "natural outcome," as Rosenkrantz describes it, of the earlier forms. Steiner indeed explained how it was possible to create organic forms in architecture and sculpture. In view of the destruction of the Goetheanum by fire and the inability of photographs to do justice to it, we shall close

the text refer to this edition, but the articles are also to be found in a work that is mentioned in the reading list at the end of this chapter. This quotation is from page 17.

our discussion of the matter by an important observation by Steiner himself on the construction of organic forms, as quoted by Rosenkrantz (*op. cit.,* p. 22).

If one is able to realize how the human body on one hand is an instrument for thinking and on the other for willing and that both these faculties are held together by the power of feeling; if one understands the whole human structure, the formation of the head, limbs and trunk, with the heart system as centre, then one is *able to construct organic forms oneself also.* The Goetheanum is such an organic form.

After the burning of the first Goetheanum Rudolf Steiner courageously decided to rebuild, but this time in a fireproof material. In a strange way the forms of the old Goetheanum were metamorphosed into a building that at first sight appears to be totally unlike its predecessor. Steiner himself was able to create a model for the new concrete structure, but he died soon after the work had begun. It was completed during the next decades primarily by those who had worked with him on the first Goetheanum, though it was sometimes necessary for them to guess what his final intentions would have been. For the massive building, which seems to grow right out of the rock on which it was built, concrete was used in an entirely original manner that may have influenced later non-anthroposophical architects, particularly Le Corbusier; in any event it marked the beginning of a style for buildings of various kinds designed for anthroposophical purposes. This is especially true of the many Waldorf (Steiner) school buildings in Germany and Switzerland. Perhaps the most obvious feature of the building apparent even to the untutored eye is the way in which the building, for all its monumental nature, fits perfectly into the Jura landscape, as does the striking difference between the east and west faces of the building. The prevalent winds beat upon it from the west. The west façade therefore seems to be ready to absorb these forces, having been shaped, as it were, to receive them, whereas the other face is simply square to the elements, which seldom beat upon it from that side. Inside, the proscenium is surely not as Steiner himself would have wished it, in part because of governmental safety provisions, but it is extremely effective, and the lighting, so important in particular for eurythmy, as well as for the Mystery Dramas, is perhaps unique in the world for the variety of its effects. Since this building still stands and is now almost complete, it can be viewed by anyone who wishes to view it, and we shall therefore say no more about it but proceed to a few supplementary remarks about sculpture in addition to what has been said already in the course of this chapter.

Sculpture. Sculpture is one of the two arts that differ from all the others in that it is possible for the artist simply to copy nature, and reproduce something seen in the outer world with the greatest possible fidelity. Steiner (probably now in common with the great majority of modern artists and art critics) did not regard such copying as art at all, and certainly not in the sense in which he used the word, that is, as a bridge between the physical and the spiritual. As he insisted, it is impossible for man to do the work of divine beings better than they; a living human being shaped by forces of the spiritual world, or a landscape in the external world with all its living qualities simply cannot be reproduced exactly as they appear to the human eye without making the finished product nothing but a dead copy of the living, just like a photograph. To Steiner this was not art. As far as the sculpture of the human body was concerned, it would be possible to work altogether without a model as the Greeks did; when modeling the head of a living person used as a model the sculptor would still have to experience the spiritual forces that moulded the different parts of the head, as was described in Steiner's words earlier in this chapter (see p. 220). The sculptor's task, according to him, was to bring the invisible etheric forces into physical manifestation. But the astral body and the "I" have already moulded the head more than they have moulded the body. Thus, the sculptor uses different powers and works in a different manner according to whether it is the body or the head that he is modeling. But it remains true that in sculpture it is primarily the etheric body that has to be experienced by the artist, and it was because the Greek sculptors were able to penetrate so deeply into what the etheric body is constantly *trying* to form that they created such perfect bodies—not the imperfect bodies that actually had been formed in the external world and that they saw in the world around them. By contrast, the Renaissance artists studied anatomy with the patience of scientists—as was to be expected in the beginning of the age of the consciousness soul—and tried to create perfect bodies not by trying to experience the archetypal form but rather by correcting defects visible in their human models—a totally different procedure that was already intellectual and a harbinger of the later naturalism, rather than intuitive and aware of the supersensible like the sculpture of the Greeks.

Steiner's own great work of sculpture, a work that was saved from the Goetheanum fire, is a group carved in wood showing Lucifer and Ahriman as they are held in check by man at his highest, a being who in the sculptured group is called the Representative of Mankind. Lucifer and Ahriman as they are portrayed, however, are not simply devils incarnate, but are elements in the human being that, if onesidedly developed, take on the strange and distorted forms shown in the sculptured group, which in this group are shown in the process of metamorphosis. The ideal human being holds the balance between these "subhuman" elements, and thus the impression is given that Lucifer and Ahriman are defeated, or, more properly, held in check, by the Christ, which is also a perfectly correct interpretation of the group. Such a sculptured group was not "thought out" by Steiner with his intellect, and it is certainly not a pictorial representation of abstract ideas. It is an imaginative picture of forms that do not, and indeed could not exist in external nature—at all events not now. The dragon and the unicorn were also in their time imaginative representations of supersensible realities. Imaginatively conceived by Steiner and executed by himself and his gifted assistant, a distinguished sculptress in her own right (Edith Maryon), this work is likely to remain unique, but since it is still to be seen in the Goetheanum it needs no further description.

In this particular case we have a first hand testimony as to the way in which Steiner worked in the field of art since Arild Rosenkrantz, whose booklet (pp. 8–9) has been quoted above, tells us that it was in answer to a question put by him that suddenly the idea arose before Steiner in an imaginative vision of the painting that was to fill the small cupola in the old Goetheanum. Later, on the very same day, he was inspired with the vision of what ultimately became the sculptured group. We may therefore fittingly close this brief section on sculpture from Rosenkrantz' description.

. . . In regard to the question of the way in which the figure of Christ should be treated in art . . . he explained how impossible and incorrect it is to experience the figure of Christ today in the way he appeared as Judge to the people of the Middle Ages and early Renaissance. In speaking of the new presentation needed for humanity in the future, he rose from his chair, stretching his left arm above his head and pressing down the right, saying: "You must imagine the central figure of the Christ arising out of the color yellow. Above His head in shades of purple and red, Lucifer seeking liberation from earth bondage; below in orange shades Ahriman bound." This imaginative description, slightly altered, he immediately made into a sketch destined to be reproduced at the east end of the small cupola of the Goetheanum. On the same day he indicated the composition for the sculpture group that he executed with Miss Maryon's assistance, and he also made a drawing for one of the windows where the conquest of Ahriman and Lucifer is expressed. It was as if the whole new conception of the central point of Christianity and the mystery of human life arose as an imaginative vision before him at the time when the Goetheanum attained a stage when he could introduce this crowning expression into it. Here one was brought into touch with true Inspiration, for he seemed to conceive, as if in a flash of the imagination, a composition containing a whole new world outlook.

230

Painting. Rudolf Steiner did not give any specialized course for painters, as he gave for practitioners in most of the other arts. Yet his influence has been great among painters who have been attracted to anthroposophy, and pupils in Steiner schools paint in every class from kindergarten onward. In principle, as we shall see later, the child should eventually learn to read by first painting pictures that gradually develop into letters, and these letters are then written before ever he starts to read.

In the same way that Steiner emphasized that the true sculptor needs no model, and that it is no part of his task to attempt to create an exact copy of some person or thing that exists in the natural world, he insisted that painters must never try to copy external nature. However "lifelike" and exact such a copy may be, it *must* be inferior to what appears in nature, since spiritual beings have created and are constantly weaving and working in the world of nature. Because of their work nature is truly alive, whereas the copy made by the painter must lack this living element, however "beautiful" it may appear to our eyes, and however skilful the technique at the painter's disposal. Our aesthetic appreciation of a painting is derived, according to Steiner, above all from the harmony of its coloring and the way in which this coloring affects our soul nature. Indeed, to him the act of painting itself was primarily the experiencing of the colors, and it was to color that he devoted the greater part of his lectures concerned with painting. Of course, it was the experiencing of color by the child painters in the schools using his methods that was of importance in education, not the finished paintings that the children succeeded in producing.

To Steiner who accepted Goethe's theory of color and elaborated it further himself, as we shall see, color is a living reality, the visible activity of spiritual beings, and each color has its particular quality. The astral (or imaginative) world is filled with color and tone, and we become conscious of and give expression to this world through the arts of painting and music. It is this world that we experience in sleep, and although we may not always be aware of dreaming in colors, we in fact do so, even if our recollection of them when we wake up is only of black and white or colorless dreams. According to Steiner, small children, however, are always aware of color in their dreams.

When we desire to create harmony of color and put color on the canvas, it is this experience (between sleeping and waking) that urges us on. Into our waking physical body we push and allow to flow what we have experienced between going to sleep and waking up. These experiences are within us, and they are what we desire to paint on our canvases. . . . Painting becomes a . . . revelation of the spiritual world that surrounds us in space and thence also permeates us.*

Steiner also tells us that when a clairvoyant sees a plant,

. . . he had before him not a lifeless color-form but variegated colored light glistening and sparkling in the most diverse fashion, full of inward life, so that each color expresses the peculiarity of some spiritual being imperceptible in the world of physical sense; that is to say, to the clairvoyant the color in the material plant becomes the expression of spiritual beings. Now imagine a world filled with such color-forms throwing most diverse reflections and perpetually changing in form and appearance. . . . Imagine this whole sea of interlacing colors—I might equally well say a sea of interplaying tone, taste, or smell sensations, for all these are expressions of psychic-spiritual beings standing behind them—and you have what is called the imaginative world . . . a real world embodying a different mode of comprehension from that of the senses.**

Early in the age of the consciousness soul linear perspective was invented and used by numerous painters in the Renaissance and since. This was a typical aspect of modern consciousness that wished to paint pictures exactly as the human eye sees

---

* Lecture called "The Supersensible Origin of the Artistic," given on September 12, 1920 in *Art in the Light of Mystery Wisdom*, pp. 68–9.
** From the first lecture on *The Gospel of St. Luke*, given at Basel, September 15, 1909 (London, 1946), pp. 9–10.

them, and to achieve this aim had consciously to create an optical illusion. But in fact it is not necessary to use linear perspective to give the impression of distance. If the nature of the different colors is understood, it is possible to use color perspective instead, as the nineteenth century British artist Turner learned to use it in his later life. Drawing is also regarded, especially perhaps by art schools, as a virtual necessity for painting, the outlines being first drawn by the painter and then later filled in with color. Steiner condemned this practice, and refused to allow it to be used in his schools. Only the geometrical drawing of straight lines in order to create beautiful forms was permitted in them. But even this kind of drawing should not be attempted before the age when the child is able to begin to handle abstractions, whereas he should paint from the very beginning of his school life. The straight line, after all, never appears in nature. There is no boundary between one object and another that is visible to the eye. There is only one color shading off into another, as is, of course, most obvious to us when we look at the horizon. The experience of painting the way in which one color shades off into another is one of the most fundamental experiences available to the painter—as long as one regards painting as the experiencing of color, and not producing a finished canvas.

If we give thought to the matter we shall see that in the external world as we see it, there is *nothing but* color. Yet it has been claimed by philosophers that color is a "secondary" quality of objects, something, in the last analysis, that is entirely subjective. It has also been held that the fundamental reality is light, not color, and that darkness is the mere absence of light. In fact we do not see light as such. Light may have certain physical qualities, as Newton and his physicist successors have shown, but it cannot and does not exist in nature except insofar as it is mingled to a greater or lesser degree with darkness; as soon as light impinges on the darkness (as it always does in life) we have a color. This was the fundamental observation behind Goethe's theory of color, and painters have always refused to

233

trouble themselves with Newton's theories, which are useless to them. They may never have been aware of Goethe's theories, which *could* have been of use to them, but in their paintings they at least showed an awareness of how color arises from the mingling of light and darkness. It was Rembrandt's special claim to greatness that he was so consciously aware of this mingling, and thus used light and shade in a uniquely moving way to express what he wished to portray in his paintings.

Goethe, who was an imaginative scientist as well as an artist in words, as a result of his observation of colors not only gave birth to his new and totally different color theory at variance with Newton's, but he pointed out from immediate observation that Newton's observations and his theory based on it must be, at the very least, incomplete. For whereas Newton with his prism supposed he had split up "white light" into its seven component colors (the colors of the rainbow), when Goethe looked at a white wall through his prism, no color at all was visible—as it should have been if Newton's theory had been correct. Newton discovered the "rainbow" colors by looking at a light shape on a dark ground. But if one looks at a dark strip on a light background one sees instead the "darkness," not the "light" spectrum, and this has eight colors, one of which, called "peach-blossom" color, the color of human flesh, does not appear at all, or anything like it, in the "seven" colors of the rainbow. Whereas Newton supposed he had split up *light,* in fact he had merely examined one special example of the light mingling with the darkness. In his fundamental work on color (translated by Charles Eastlake in 1840 and recently made available again by M.I.T. Press) Goethe gave much consideration to the complementary of colors, to their active or passive nature, and to the qualities of each individual color as he perceived them. In general, Steiner accepted the theory but added much to it from his spiritual scientific viewpoint. His three lectures on color given in Dornach in May, 1921 provide the fundamental expression of his views, but since he also gave much instruction directly to painters working with him on the first Goetheanum, it is necessary to turn to other works by his followers, some of which are translated into or were written in English, and are mentioned in the reading list at the end of the chapter.

In his color lectures Steiner drew a distinction, original with him, between "luster" and "image" colors, red, yellow and blue being luster colors, which are active and with a tendency to movement. Yellow radiates from within outward, blue from the periphery inward, while red permeates the surroundings.* Yellow is the luster of the spirit, blue is the luster of the soul, red the luster of the living. The "image" colors are not in movement (Steiner compared them with the fixed stars by contrast with the moving planets, a comparison that we shall find again in connection with consonants and vowels). White is the "soul's image of the spirit," green is the "lifeless image of the living" (i.e., created out of the lifeless substance), peach blossom "the living image of the soul" and black "the spiritual image of the lifeless." It would take us too far to explain what is meant by these definitions (Miss Mayer's book will give considerable help) because their truth has to be experienced by the painter as he works with them. But it may be appreciated, even by the casual reader, how important it must be for painters to be aware of them so that they will be able to know consciously why they have perhaps unconsciously chosen to use such colors in the past and, more important, to learn now to use colors consciously in the awareness of what is inherent in each of them. This is a task that should indeed be undertaken in a consciousness soul age.

It is not at all difficult, even for the complete beginner, to learn to use color in painting in the way indicated by Rudolf Steiner. Persons who have never painted before can with their

---

* The best description known to me of the difference between luster and image colors, aside from Steiner's own somewhat aphoristic statements, is to be found in Gladys Mayer, *The Mystery Wisdom of Colour*, pp. 89–96, which includes exercises in using the different colors and illustrations of what Steiner meant in his general statements.

aid begin to experience colors, and eventually paint pictures that will prove to be an ever deepening soul experience, so that they, to use Gladys Mayer's words (*Colour and the Human Soul*, page 11) may seek "to understand and recreate the divine harmonies in earthly substance, to bring light into darkness, to weave the divine and the earthly together into a new, colourful harmony." The medium used must be watercolor, though pastels can also be used for the experiencing of color. Oils, however, are totally unsuitable because oil is a heavy earthly substance that cannot be expected to mirror the ethereal transparency of the etheric and astral worlds and the mobility of the ever changing world of color as we see it in the external world. The technique used is that of veiling, and beginners, especially children, will probably do best with wet paper, which makes for richer and fuller colors. Color is built up in successive washes, all of the same strength, but each has to be added only when the preceding wash is already dry. Some painters therefore make two or more paintings at the same time. In general, there should be no retouching because this tends to disturb the underlayer.

It will be evident that this kind of painting must be a living experience, and that for a long time nothing will result that can be thought of as a finished picture, giving pleasure to others. But such pictures have been made by artists skilled in the technique and with their imaginations awakened, and they can be as deeply moving as any pictures ever painted. This is as much as needs to be said on the subject here, and the reader is referred to the practical books written by anthroposophical artists. Pages 34 and 43 of *The Mystery Wisdom of Colour* already referred to are especially useful, as are all the colored pictures in the book that are explained in the text, and the technical notes on page 109. This section may therefore fittingly conclude with another extract from this book, consisting of the sentences that conclude it, which may sound forth as an inspiration for those who may wish to try to experience in a new way the world of color as indicated by Rudolf Steiner.

Colour is our guide, and the soul we carry in us wears its many-hued garment, some of it muddy through errors, some of it radiant. The Spirit-man within us guides us to the sources of colour related to the planets, which in their working give the healing power to our souls which is divine power.

The powers of the heavenly world speak through the planetary colours, purifying the star-body, which each of us individually bears. Jupiter speaks through the radiant orange. Saturn speaks through deep indigo blue. The energy of Mars speaks in the red, the spiritual intelligence of Mercury speaks in the yellow, the balance of green with a shimmering peach-blossom speaks of the love of heaven for earth in Venus; the Sun speaks in its whiteness, the Moon in its mysterious violet. The chorus of creative powers of colour echoing in our own souls conjures forth the magic and mystery of painting.

The Cosmic Christ-power within each one of us speaks in the silence, invisibly, yet insistently, calling each and every one to assume the tasks he entered earth to perform. To some it may well be to become a Mercury messenger, a winged messenger of the Gods, bearing through colour the message of spiritual creative freedom to mankind throughout the earth and thus to rescue, through the darkness, the seeds of a future age.

Music. In beginning our discussion of the higher arts, music and song, poetry, speech, and the new art of eurythmy created by Rudolf Steiner, it becomes necessary to speak again of the human being as he may be perceived by spiritual science, this time from a point of view different from that given in Chapter 4, and again different from the way he will be presented in the next chapter. None of these descriptions excludes the others—only the point of view is different. We must now speak of what may be the most difficult of the descriptions, but it underlies all that Steiner has to tell us about art. The human being, according to this view, is himself actually a *musical instrument,* not, of course, an abstractly conceived instrument such as a piano, but rather analogous to such a "natural" or divinely inspired instrument as a violin, a lyre or a harp. There is nothing in the least arbitrary about any of these instruments, nor is there about the human being himself. Only a limited range of sounds can be made by the human being, whether he speaks or sings. It is only because he himself is a musical instrument that man has been able to externalize his own body in the form of musical instruments (the same is true of the machines that man has made, a subject that does not concern us here).

Since these are somewhat difficult concepts that will lead us rather far, it is perhaps best to quote Steiner directly.

> Studying the secrets of music, he tells us, we can discover what the Greeks, who knew a great deal about these matters, meant by the lyre of Apollo. What is experienced musically is really man's hidden adaptation to the inner harmonic-melodic relationships of cosmic existence out of which he was shaped. His nerve fibers, ramifications of the spinal cord, are marvelous musical strings with a metamorphosed activity. The spinal cord culminating in the brain and distributing its nerve fibers throughout the body is the lyre of Apollo. Upon these nerve fibers the soul spirit of man is "played" within the earthly sphere. Thus man himself is the world's most perfect instrument, and he can experience artistically the tones of an external musical instrument to the degree that he feels this connection between the sounding of strings of a new instrument, for example, and his own coursing blood and nerve fibers. In other words man, as nerve man, is inwardly built up of music, and feels it artistically to the degree that he feels its harmonization with the mystery of his own musical structure.*

Granted that man is a musical instrument and that he can make music sound out in the earthly world through instruments that he creates, what is the origin of the music that he composes? Can true music be arbitrary, or *thought out?* To answer such questions as these an effort must be made to give a description of what the initiate philosopher Pythagoras meant when he spoke of the "music of the spheres," for this music, is indeed,

---

* Lecture 3 of the series delivered in Dornach in May and June, 1923, and published under the title of *The Arts and Their Mission*, p. 37.

according to Steiner, a reality. When an initiate enters the world of Inspiration, or the area of the spiritual world known as Lower Devachan, he becomes clairaudient and enters a real world of tone. This same world, needless to say, he enters also after death.

> When we have reached the point after death, when we lay aside the astral body (i.e., in passing out of kamaloca) we also lay aside everything of a musical nature that reminds us of this life on earth. But at this cosmic moment music is transformed into the music of the spheres. For what we experience here as music in the element of air is on a higher plane the music of the spheres. The reflection of this higher music penetrates into the element of air; it becomes denser and is converted into what we experience as earthly music, which we imprint on our astral body, which is given form by us, and which we can re-experience as long as we possess our astral body. After death we lay aside our astral body; then, if you will pardon the banal expression, our musical experience is switched over to the music of the spheres. So in music and poetry we have an anticipation of what is our world and our existence after death.*

Into this world of tone some of the most gifted composers have undoubtedly been able to enter, and to bring down the sounds they heard into the earthly sphere in such a way that they could be sung by human voices or played on instruments created by man. But exactly *what* they were hearing can have been known only very seldom by composers, if ever, and it is here that Steiner makes use of his supersensible powers to enlighten us. The twelve signs or constellations of the zodiac have traditionally been connected with twelve parts of the human organism, as is fairly well known. But it is less well known that they have a similar connection with the original twelve consonants, which in almost all modern languages (not, however, including the Finnish language) have developed fur-

---

* From the lecture already quoted, "The Supersensible Origin of the Artistic," pp. 67–8.

239

ther variations beyond the original twelve. As we shall see later when we come to discuss speech, and as we can easily recognize for ourselves if we give attention to the matter, the vowels sound forth from within through the consonants to create human speech and song. Similarly, and Steiner assures us that he is not merely making an analogy, in the macrocosm the planets play the part of the vowels and sound forth through the fixed stars of the zodiac in the most varied, and scarcely imaginable tones. As man

travels away from the earth after death he gradually goes so far that he is able to see both the planets and the fixed stars from behind. Only he does not then see the points of light or shining surfaces visible from the earth; he sees the respective spiritual beings. A world of spiritual beings is to be seen everywhere. Looking back from the other side at Saturn, Sun, or Moon, or at Aries, Taurus, and the other constellations, it is spiritual beings that he sees. And this seeing is really also a hearing. So when we say that man looks back and sees the Moon and Venus or Aries or Taurus from behind, we could just as well say that he hears the beings, whose abode is in these heavenly bodies, pouring forth sound into the universe. . . . Looking toward Aries you will have the impression of a consonant quality of soul. And behind Aries, Saturn may be moving with its vowel quality of soul. And in this vowel quality of soul there lives the consonant quality of soul and spirit that belongs to Aries or Taurus. So you have the sphere of the planets singing out with vowels into the cosmic space, and you have the fixed stars which fill the song of the planetary sphere with the soul quality of the consonants. Try and imagine this vividly: the sphere of the more stable fixed stars and behind this the moving planets. When a moving planet passes by a constellation of fixed stars, not just one tone but a whole world of tone resounds. When the planet passes on from Aries to Taurus another world of tone starts to sound. And in the background there is another planet, Mars, let us say. So when Mars in turn passes behind Taurus yet another world of tone arises. So the realm of the fixed stars is a wonderful cosmic instrument and behind it are the gods of the planets who play upon this instrument of the Zodiac.*

* From a lecture given at Dornach, December 2, 1922, called "Human

This, then, is what music actually *is*, in its origins. But as man's consciousness has evolved, as described in Chapter 2, his access to the heavenly spheres has gradually been cut off, as was right and necessary in earth evolution since man had as his task the development of his personal "I." Nevertheless, man still is aware of the devachanic world in his sleep, and the tones he has heard in sleep when they have been absorbed by the astral body are impressed on his etheric body.

Although on waking in the morning he is not conscious of having absorbed the music of the night, yet on listening to music he has an inkling that these impressions of the spiritual world are within him. When a man listens to music, the seer can observe how the rhythms and colours flow into and lay hold of the firmer substance of the ether body, causing it to vibrate in tune with them, and from the harmonious response of the ether body comes the pleasure that is felt. The more strongly the astral body resounds, the more strongly do its tones echo in the ether body, overcoming the ether body's own natural rhythms, and this gives feelings of pleasure both to a listener and to a composer.*

It should, however, be noted that in later lectures Steiner always stressed that we do not experience musical notes as such, but our souls create within us the intervals between the notes, what Elsie Hamilton, a long time student of Steiner's revelations regarding the spiritual aspect of music, calls "the spiritual experience in time between the two notes." ** It is this soul activity in the listener that makes listening to music an active rather than simply a passive experience. Indeed, Steiner in a remarkable passage likens sound to "a window opening onto the spiritual

Expression through Tone and Word," published in the collection, *Art in the Light of Mystery Wisdom*, pp. 89–92.
* From a lecture given in Cologne, December 3, 1906, printed in *The Golden Blade*, 1956, under the title, "The Occult Basis of Music."
** In her article, "The Nature of Musical Experience in the Light of Anthroposophy," in L. Stebbing, editor, *Music, its Occult Basis and Healing Value*, p. 28. This is a most valuable compilation from various sources, almost all of anthroposophical inspiration.

world." In the future, he says, "we shall try to penetrate behind the sounds. The important thing will not be to know the sounds as component parts of a melody, but each sound in itself will have a moral and spiritual value. Through sound, as through a window, the soul will enter into contact with the spiritual world. Every individual sonority will unveil its mysteries to a man who will be able thus to penetrate behind it." *

To quote Elsie Hamilton again (*loc. cit.*) as a comment on what I imagine was this passage, "In the distant future we shall be able to experience a whole melody in a single note. Just as in the future we shall not merely behold a flower but also its spiritual counterpart, so in music we shall be able to hear not only a note, but also what is behind the note, its spiritual content. Man will experience a single tone as an opening that the Gods have made into the physical world, and he will rise through the single tone from the physical world of sense into the spiritual world beyond." From her own experience she then—in a passage that should be pondered deeply by all interested in music as it will be in the future—describes the way in which man may rise to the experience of the spiritual world in a different way through the different intervals, culminating in the octave, which we are not able now to experience, but which is given to man, according to Steiner, as a task for the future.** Miss Hamilton concludes this passage with the words:

> With the true experience of the octave, man rises to the experience
> of the ego itself. He must find himself reborn at a higher level. Man
> has not yet found in musical experience the union of his higher ego
> with the physical world. That will only come when the octave is able
> to be truly experienced. It will be the proof to man of the existence

---

* In a lecture not, I believe, available in English. This passage was translated from an article appearing in the French anthroposophical quarterly *Triades*, Spring, 1968, p. 40.
** Steiner's own teachings on the intervals are to be found in the two lectures in the book, *Art in the Light of Mystery Wisdom*, entitled, "The Human Being's Experience of Tone," March 7 and 8, 1923. These lectures were given to the music teachers in the first Waldorf School at Stuttgart.

of the Gods, because he will experience the ego first as the physical ego within, and then as the Spiritual Ego without. All the other intervals are experienced in their relation to the tonic, but quite a different experience appears with the octave, for it really *is* the tonic experienced at a higher level. The octave experience will one day immeasurably deepen musical experience. With every appearance of the octave in a musical composition man will have the feeling I have found my Ego anew; I am raised in my manhood through the experience of the octave.

In this connection it is worth noting that the evolution of human consciousness is to be perceived in the different way in which intervals have been experienced, that is, which intervals have at different times been experienced as harmonious. Steiner tells us that before Atlantis no interval smaller than the ninth could be experienced, but the Atlanteans felt at home fully in the seventh. In the ancient Indian period and until the Greco-Latin epoch the fifth, which to us appears empty (because "the Gods have left it"), was the interval that seemed most harmonious. With the Greeks—and this can be shown from historical records—the fourth came into its own, and since the beginning of the age of the consciousness soul it has been the third, now differentiated into major and minor. The entire process is the process of the contraction of the "I" so that it is now fully within the human organism. The last process of contraction is the second, which to most people remains a discord, but the way upward and out consciously through music into the spiritual world will go back again through the wider intervals up until the octave.

Much more could be written on the subject of the indications given by Rudolf Steiner in the field of music, especially by using illustrations drawn from the works of anthroposophical students who worked with them. Though lack of space forbids any further extensive quotation or explanation, the work of Anny von Lange should be mentioned, especially her book entitled, *Musik, Mensch und Cosmos* (Music, Man, and Cosmos)

(Freiburg im Breisgau: Novalis Verlag, 1957), which has not yet been translated into English, though a digest in French by Germaine Claretie appeared in the Spring, 1957 issue of *Triades*. Such a thirty page digest can scarcely do justice to the larger work, but it at least gives something of its flavor. One of its most striking features, derived, of course, from Steiner, is the author's description of the relation of the various major and minor keys to certain qualities in the human being that are expressed through them, and the connection of these qualities with the twelve constellations of the zodiac. Also from Steiner is her qualitative distinction between the major and minor keys, the major representing the movement of the soul forward toward a world outside itself, and the minor the return of the soul to its own inner world. The author shows, with scarcely the possibility of a doubt, that Johann Sebastian Bach, whether consciously, or more probably subconsciously, was aware of the essential features of these keys. His *Well-Tempered Clavichord* is a perfect demonstration of his understanding, each prelude and fugue being apparently especially designed to demonstrate the particular qualities of each key, including the human qualities associated with each. Anny von Lange analyzes every prelude and fugue in the collection, and it is from a study of these that a student will perhaps best begin to comprehend what Steiner meant when he spoke of the human being himself as a musical instrument and of his intimate connection, as the microcosm, with the great macrocosm that is the universe.

Poetry, Speech and Drama. In a beautiful lecture devoted mainly to poetry* given in Dornach in June, 1923, Steiner makes the at first somewhat startling statement that "primitive art is nothing other than speech itself." Yet it must be that man did use his own personal instrument of the voice to speak before he could have used external tools for fashioning outer objects that we now think of as works of art. Moreover, Steiner's teachings

---

* Lecture 5 of the collection, *The Arts and their Mission*, p. 60.

244

about the evolution of consciousness make it clear that *thought* was an element in evolution that appeared relatively late. If we give some thought to this, and bear in mind also the inspired statement standing in the beginning of St. John's Gospel, "In the beginning was the Word," we may be more receptive to what Steiner then says about the origin of poetry.

Our speech [we have spoken of this earlier in this chapter] is fettered to the material-earthly; it no longer manifests what it was when human beings, feeling transported into the Zodiac, incorporated into themselves from zodiacal constellations the twelve consonants, and from the movements of the planets past the fixed-star constellations, the vowels. At that time human beings did not intend to express through speech what they experienced upon earth, but rather what the soul experienced when it felt transported into the cosmos; which is why, in ancient times, speech flowered into poetry. The last remnants of such poetry are contained in the Vedas and, more abstractly, in the Edda. They are after-images of what, in greater glory, in much greater sublimity and majesty, had arisen directly out of the formation of languages during those ages when human beings could still feel their own soul life intimately united with cosmic movement and experience.

He then tells us that certain aspects of man's communion with the cosmos have been retained, since in all true poetry the prose element, the meaning, has had added to it rhythm, beat and imagination, and some elements of cosmic harmony and melody remain in the poem. Only the prose element is understood by the human being consciously, in his mind. All the other elements are experienced through his astral body, and are not understood so much as felt. Right down into the Greek period the poet continued to look to the gods and goddesses (the Muses) for their inspiration, the tragic poet looking to Dionysus, the god of the nether world who was the patron of the tragic drama, while an epic poet like Homer began, as Rudolf Steiner so often reminded his hearers, with an invocation to the Muse, which was far more than a simple convention. "Sing, O Goddess, of the wrath of Achilles, son of Peleus!" The epic poet, he tells us, looked to the female deities in the heights to inspire him so that he could describe the deeds of men from the viewpoint of a divine being. An epic poem was not the work of an individual human being, but of a goddess speaking through him.* The third type of poetry, the lyric, he speaks of as on the same level as ourselves, with the "dramatic element" rising "like a volcano" and the epic

. . . sinking down from above, like a blessing of rain. And it is right here on this same plane with ourselves that the cosmic element is enticed and made gay, joyous, full of laughter, through nymphs and fire spirits; here that the messengers of the upper gods cooperate with the lower; right here in the middle region that man becomes lyrical. Now man does not feel the dramatic element rising up from below, nor the epic element sinking down from above. He experiences the lyrical element living on the same plane as himself: a delicate sensitive spiritual element which does not rain down upon forests nor erupt like volcanoes, splitting trees, but rather, rustles in leaves, expresses joy through blossoms, wafts gently in wind. . . . The lyrical can tense up into the dramatic lyrical or quiet down into the epic lyrical. For the hallmark of the lyrical, whatever its form, is this: man experiences what lives and weaves in the far reaches of the earth with his middle nature, his feeling nature.**

Rudolf Steiner himself was not a poet in the usual sense of the word. But he drew down from the spiritual world or revived from older mystery teachings numerous meditations to which he often gave a magnificently poetic form. He also wrote four mystery dramas in verse, which include not only the speeches of

---

* From a lecture given in Christiania, May 20, 1923 and included in *The Arts and their Mission*, p. 110. The long standing controversy on the identity of Homer himself is perhaps illuminated by this remark. Homer simply did not regard himself as the author of the poem. Later generations attributed it to an inspired poet named Homer, of whom nothing was known except for the tradition that he was blind (i.e., clairvoyant).
** From a lecture given June 23, 1923 in Dornach, and included in *The Arts and their Mission*, pp. 41-2.

the human characters but also those of elemental and spiritual beings good and evil, all of which require, as he was to explain just before the onset of his last illness, in a course on speech and drama given in September, 1924, subtle differentiations to illustrate the kind of speech used by each of these beings. For this he not only had to differentiate in rhyme and metre but also in the way they used vowels and consonants. For these plays, and for poems expressed in eurythmy, he had to give indications for developing a new way of speaking and declaiming, out of which Frau Marie Steiner, his wife and the first leader of the artistic section at the Goetheanum, created what amounts to a totally new art form. As will be seen in the next and final section of this chapter, which will be devoted to eurythmy, this latter art would not have been possible without the parallel development of the new art of speech.

It would take us too far to describe here the mystery dramas which every few years are performed in their entirety at the Goetheanum, and at least one of which is given regularly in the course of every year.* But it will be worthwhile to give at least an indication of Steiner's views on the origin and historical evolution of drama, and why it had again become necessary to bring the spiritual down to the earthly realm as he did in his mystery plays. What follows is mainly a digest of Lecture 10 of his course on speech and drama, delivered in Dornach on September 14, 1924, entitled "The Mystery Character of Dramatic Art."

All drama, Steiner tells us, originated in the Mysteries, but no primeval drama from the earliest period survives. In this far distant time the only protagonist on the stage was the Chorus, which together represented the divine world—not even as yet any individual god. The participants and audience, perceiving

---

* Albert Steffen, one of Steiner's most devoted followers and his first successor as president of the General Anthroposophical Society, also wrote many plays in which he too made the attempt to bring the spiritual down into earthly drama, and one or more of these plays is also performed every year at the Goetheanum. Steffen was a noted Swiss poet even before he came into contact with Steiner.

the spiritual world clairvoyantly, had nevertheless to experience just how divine spiritual beings play their part in earthly life. Only supersensible events were enacted, "events that had indeed connection with human life on earth but took place among the Gods." In order to make this possible individual actors did not represent the gods, but the Chorus did so, using

> . . . a special kind of recitative that was between speaking and singing and was accompanied by instruments. In this way a form was brought into being and hovered over the stage, a stylized form that was absolutely real and was created out of sound and syllable and sentence, moulded and fashioned with an artistic sensitiveness far surpassing anything known in ordinary life. This form was conjured forth before the spectators, or rather the listeners conjured it forth from the word—the word with all its qualities of music and sculpture and painting. And the listener who lived in these older conceptions perceived—that is to say, did not merely have an idea of what was happening, but saw for himself that these Choruses gave the Gods the possibility of being themselves present, of being present in the musically and plastically formed word. . . . And while it was proceeding, the whole space was pervaded with what we today would call fear of the Divine, awe and reverence in the presence of Divine Being. . . . The human being felt himself to be in the presence of a supersensible world, and that was what was intended.

Time went on, and men began to lose their clairvoyance, and became themselves gradually individualized, and at this time to the Chorus, which continued in a different form, was added the god himself, now represented by a human being. But the actor had to wear a mask or an animal head because it was essential that there should be no visible changing of expression in his countenance. Through word and gesture alone could his divine nature be shown on the stage.

> When in very early times man looked out into the great world of Nature, he felt there the presence of the Divine, with whom he himself was connected; he felt the God in the clouds, the God in the

thunder and lightning. And still more did he feel the God entering into the word, into the artistically formed and modulated word, which the Chorus in the Mysteries placed out into the world as objective created form. And now, as time went on, this very experience led man to perceive another secret. He began to learn that there is something in himself that is Divine, and that responds like an echo to the Divine that comes to meet him from the far reaches of the universe. . . . The perception began to dawn upon man that when the human being presents his own innermost soul, then too he is presenting something Divine; if he can present on the stage the Divine that is in the external world, he can also present the Divine that is in himself. And so, from being a manifestation of the *Gods,* dramatic art became a manifestation of the inner being of man; it presented on the stage the *human soul.* And this inevitably led to the need to bring innermost human experience into the forming of the speech, to bring this same intimate human experience into the gesturing also that was done on the stage.

This was the reason, Steiner explained, why he was in his course giving so much attention to the correct speech and gesture, and why in his own mystery dramas and the other plays performed at the Goetheanum one becomes aware at once that neither the speech nor the gesture is as one finds them in the ordinary theater. Even prose spoken on the stage, Steiner insists, has to be stylized, for man

. . . has to carry into the external world the revelation of his own inner experiences. But for this it is by no means enough that we should behave on the stage as we do in real life. After all, what occasion is there to show that on the stage? We have enough of it around us all the time. No one with artistic feeling will be interested in a mere imitation of life, since life is always far richer than the poor husk which is all that imitation can produce.

I may as a historian point out that what Steiner says here can be indeed seen to some extent in the evolution of Greek tragedy. We know that the great majority of the plays of Aeschylus have been lost, but we do possess the *Prometheus Bound,* in which no

249

human beings appear; all the characters are gods, or demigods, and the Chorus plays an exceptionally large part in the play. But in other plays of Aeschylus human beings appear, often larger than life, but still entirely human. Yet the language of Aeschylus was in later ages criticized for being "bombastic," that is to say, language such as human beings themselves would not have used. Sophocles was an intermediate figure, deeply moving often even to us, especially in his *Antigone*, but none of his characters was exactly as we might expect to find them in real life, whereas Euripides, even when portraying gods, made them usually very human indeed. Euripides, as Nietzsche pointed out in his *Birth of Tragedy*, ruined Greek tragic drama especially by presenting ordinary men and women on the stage, by, in a word, his *naturalism,* which Steiner so often criticized not only in drama but in the other arts, especially painting. Especially interesting is the fact that the great comic playwright Aristophanes, who was at the same time one of the finest of Greek lyric poets, perceived very well what was happening to tragic drama, and disliked it very much. Thus toward the end of his life he wrote a most serious comedy, *The Frogs*, one of his greatest masterpieces, in which he invents a contest in the netherworld between Aeschylus and Euripides, which is judged by Dionysus the god of tragedy. Looked at from the point of view of the change in the drama in the century between Aeschylus and Euripides, and the change in consciousness that it reflects, it may be seen that Aristophanes is really being quite fair to both. Euripides in the play criticizes Aeschylus for his lack of naturalism, for his bombastic language, for the monotony of his choruses and the like, while Aeschylus criticizes Euripides above all for his debasement of the tragic drama by putting ordinary men on the stage, and thus at the same time teaching the Athenians to despise the gods and ruining their moral characters. This argument Dionysus regards as decisive, and awards the palm to Aeschylus.

When Steiner criticized naturalism on the stage, it was not that he had any desire to restore old fashioned heroics, but it was due to his entire conception of art whose "whole secret," he tells us, "lies in this; in art we reveal truth by quite other means than Nature uses. Nature reveals truth more immediately. Truth must be present in Nature; and truth must also be present in art. The truth in Nature shines forth to the spirit; from the truth in art the spirit shines forth. Once we have grasped this fact and made it our own, we shall feel an urgent need within us to discover how art and style can be restored to the stage, and we shall not rest until we find it." *

Steiner took art and its mission with tremendous seriousness, as will be evident from all that has been said thus far. This seriousness may perhaps best be illustrated in a quotation with which we shall conclude this section. After speaking of the abyss between the purely naturalistic world, in which we must always feel strangers, and the spiritual world which is our true home, and of how religion cannot bridge it unless it is fortified by supersensible cognition, he adds:**

Fortunately the abyss on the edge of which man lives, the abyss opening out before him in religion and cognition, can be bridged. But not by contemporary religion, nor yet by a cognition, a science, derived wholly from the earth.

It is here that art enters. It forms a bridge across the abyss. That is why art must realize that its task is to carry the spiritual-divine life into the earthly; to fashion the latter in such a way that its forms, colors, words, tones, act as a revelation of the world beyond. Whether art takes on an idealistic or realistic coloring is of no importance. What it needs is a relationship to the truly, not merely thought-out spiritual. No artist could create in his medium if there were not alive in him impulses springing from the spiritual world. This fact points to the seriousness of art, standing alongside the seriousness of cognition and religious experience. It cannot be denied that our materialistically oriented civilization diverts us, in many ways, from the gravity of art. But any devoted study of true

* From Lecture 8 in the Speech and Drama course, p. 176.
** *The Arts and their Mission*, 4th lecture, June 3, 1923, pp. 44–5.

artistic creation reveals it as an earnest effort of man's struggle to harmonize the spiritual divine with the physical-earthly.

Eurythmy. In the last section of this chapter, which will be devoted to the art of eurythmy, we cannot hope to do more than explain what eurythmy is, how it arose in modern times out of spiritual science, and how it is related to the rest of anthroposophy as it has been presented thus far in the book. For all details on the actual practice of this art, the reader is referred to the major works on the subject listed at the end of the chapter, while any school using the pedagogical methods inaugurated by Rudolf Steiner and every center for the study of anthroposophy including of course its world headquarters in Dornach, Switzerland, will be able to refer the enquirer to any of the various schools for the teaching of eurythmy now existing in many countries of the world. In the summer of 1972 a two week congress on eurythmy was held at the Goetheanum in Dornach attended by over seven hundred professional eurythmists during which nine different eurythmy troops performed from eight different countries. 1972 was the sixtieth anniversary of the first systematic lessons given by Steiner to his first pupil, a young girl of eighteen named Lory Smits.

It was a strange destiny that led this girl to become Steiner's first pupil in eurythmy. Her mother had been interested in anthroposophy and knew Rudolf Steiner, while Lory herself was greatly attracted by the dance. When her father died suddenly, leaving little money, it became necessary for the girl to prepare herself for a profession. Her mother not wishing her to become a professional dancer asked Steiner's advice, and was given a number of exercises for Lory to perform, all connected with movement of the arms and feet in relation to spoken sounds. These exercises were followed for many months from the autumn of 1911 until Rudolf Steiner felt that she had progressed far enough to be given some private lessons in what was to become eurythmy. He therefore asked Lory and her mother to come to Basel, where he was giving a series of lectures on the

Gospel of St. Mark (September, 1912), and this first eurythmist, who soon undertook to teach others what she had just learned, spent the afternoons in a small room in which, she recalled later, there was little space because of the furniture. At the fourth lesson Marie von Sievers, who was soon to become Frau Marie Steiner, was invited to be present, thereby beginning her work with eurythmy. Prior to that time her great interest had been in the spoken word. She therefore became the natural leader of the first eurythmy troupe, doing all the recitations while the girls (for some time all the eurythmists were girls, a condition that is far from true now) did the movements. In August, 1913 the new art was first presented to an anthroposophical public at Munich. When war broke out the following year, Marie Steiner, as she now was, organized a regular training course for eurythmists that had to be held in Switzerland for those who could escape to or lived in that neutral country. All the recitations thus far had been in German, but after the war when would-be eurythmists thronged to Dornach to train in the new art, eurythmy in other languages had to be created. Every week performances were given. Marie Steiner recited, usually in the presence of Steiner himself, who made numerous suggestions as to costumes, lighting, and all the other elements that have since become an integral part of eurythmy. Since 1919 it has been performed by the original Dornach troupe in numerous other countries, while other troupes have been organized in later years in most of the countries where it has been performed.

What makes eurythmy a new art, totally different from dancing, even dancing that makes extensive use of the hands and arms as does much oriental dancing, is that it is speech and music *made visible,* using the human being himself as their instrument. To understand how the human being can become an instrument of this kind it is, paradoxically enough, necessary above all to understand the true nature of the human larynx, the organ that makes human speech possible. When we speak, or when a musical instrument is played, certain movements are made in the air around us, movements that cannot ordinarily be seen by the human eye, though under certain conditions, even in the laboratory, they can in fact be made visible. These air movements, however, are picked up by another organ, specialized for the purpose. This organ is of course the ear, which, as we say, *hears* the air movements.

Most peoples of the world when speaking make gestures with their hands and arms and fingers, these gestures being largely unconscious except in the case of trained actors. But they are intended largely for emphasis and, as a rule, express the emotional condition of the speaker. Although sometimes also beautiful and expressive, they are in no sense a visible speech. What Steiner was able to do was to perceive the forms made in the etheric world by the sounds that originated in the larynx and were carried forth into the air by means of the vowels and consonants, and to translate these forms into movements made by the human body, especially, as in the case of gestures, the movements of the hands and arms.

As we shall see in the next chapter, the center of Steiner's teachings on human physiology, from which has stemmed among many other things, anthroposophical medicine, is that man is a threefold being, consisting of a head system, which includes his nerves and senses and is situated in the upper part of his body; the rhythmic system, which contains the activity of his heart and lungs and occupies the central part of his organism; and the lower part of man, which embraces his digestive and limbs system. The head and senses system is responsible for our thinking and perceiving, and is the only part of our organization that is fully conscious; the rhythmic system is connected with the feeling and emotional life, and is partly conscious. In the limb system the will is active, and is wholly unconscious. We are, indeed, totally ignorant of the actual procedure by which we do such a simple thing as move our finger. All we know is that our conscious being (our head system) appears to convey an order to the finger, which obeys, but all the incredibly complex movements that follow and result in the action remain totally hidden from us. It is in the rhythmic

254

system that all art comes into being, and eurythmy has a right to be considered as the highest art to which man has as yet been able to attain since, as we have said, he uses his own body, and only his own body as an instrument, needing neither stone nor marble, brush nor paint, bow nor strings to create it. Although, as Steiner has told us, *all* art originated in the supersensible, this particular art most clearly does so—as dance, in so many respects similar to eurythmy, usually does not.

The larynx belongs to the rhythmic system, but it is more closely allied than the lungs or heart to the head system, and as everyone knows, it has one great peculiarity. It undergoes a marked and predictable change just at the moment when the feeling life of man is about to come to full expression with the freeing of the astral body at puberty. For no apparent physiological reason the male voice, as we say, breaks; while at the same time other changes, which do not concern us here, take place in the rhythmic system of the girl. All sound is either created by the human larynx or is reflected in it. It is well known that listening to music, and especially to singing, may sometimes give us a feeling of tiredness, even a "sore throat" in our larynx. If, however, we could see supersensibly the movements of the larynx we could perceive the etheric movements in the air around us, and so come to the eurythmy forms that Steiner created and gave to the world.

This is not to say that anyone who views a performance of eurythmy can *translate* it directly, even though each vowel and each consonant has its characteristic eurythmic form, because eurythmy is also an *art,* and involves the element of human feeling. A consonant linked with a particular vowel may be different in one word than another; the feeling of a whole word may be different from the feeling attached to its component vowels and consonants. The feeling of a whole poem, or piece of prose, will naturally dictate the kind of eurythmic forms that will go best with it. For this reason the artist in eurythmy has a great deal of freedom, within the limits of the actual sounds used, to create the most varied forms, and when eurythmy is performed by a group of artists, the movements of all must be coordinated one with another to create a total form that may be extraordinarily complex. Yet there is not in the case of eurythmy an absolute freedom to do anything at all, as there is in the dance. The poem that is to be shown visibly dictates always the permissible form for the eurythmy movements, as does the piece of music that is likewise shown visibly in what is called tone eurythmy, or "visible song," as Steiner used to call it. Moreover, the movements of the feet never vary greatly, for eurythmy is in no sense a dance (a product primarily not of the rhythmic but the limb system), nor are facial expressions of any importance. What is of great importance was not at first made use of by the early eurythmists, mainly for lack of the necessary technical facilities. This is color, which varies immensely from one poem to another, in accordance again with the feeling mood of the poem. Especially at the Goetheanum and in Stuttgart a great virtuosity has been used to make the most varied color combinations, which greatly enhance the artistic impact of any eurythmy performance.

Goethe's famous dictum quoted earlier that "all art is the revelation of concealed laws of nature, which without such revelation would remain for ever concealed" has a special relevance to eurythmy. Since man is, as Steiner called him in another connection, the "hieroglyph" of the universe, a microcosmic counterpart of the macrocosmic universe, everything that is to be found outside in the universe is also to be found within the human being. Human speech, as was described in the last section, has a cosmic origin, as was known in ancient times. It was not only the Christian initiate St. John who wrote at the beginning of his Gospel that "In the Beginning was the Word," but the Egyptian initiates in the Pyramid age also spoke of the universe as the creation by the Word of the great god Ptah. No sounds therefore are arbitrary, and no language—at least not in its early form. Each language has its own genius, and this genius can be expressed by the human body in the way in which it makes visible the sounds of this language. The sacred sounds of the Orient, the TAO and the AUM, when rendered in eurythmy, clearly reveal their particular nature, even though the sounds as such, however beautifully chanted or sung, may make little impression on our materialistic and unprepared Western consciousness. The eurythmic gesture of T suggests creative movement from the heights to the depths, the A relates man to the universe in an attitude of reverence, while with the O he is again enfolded by the universe; the A of AUM places man before the universe to which, as before, he gives reverence, the U bears within it the aspiration toward a spiritual reality, while with the M the protective activity of the universe pours itself into man.

The art of eurythmy seeks to express the macrocosmic word through the instrument of the human body. The laws that regulate the movements of the heavenly bodies are the same laws that are active in man the microcosm, and it is by virtue of these laws that he can utter speech. As Steiner himself put it:

All that can be perceived by supersensible vision, all that can thus be learned about the nature of these forms and gestures of the air, can be carried into movements of the arms and hands, into movements of the whole human being. There then arises in visible form the actual counterpart of speech. One can use the entire body in such a way that it really carries out those movements which are otherwise carried out by the organs connected with speech and song. Thus there arises visible speech, visible song—in other words the art of Eurythmy. When one brings artistic feeling to the study of the nature of speech, one finds that the individual sounds form themselves, as it were, into imaginative pictures. It is necessary, however, entirely to free oneself from the abstract character which language has taken during the so-called advanced civilization of the present day. For it is an undeniable fact that modern man, when speaking, in no way brings his whole human being into activity. True speech, however, is born from the whole human being.*

Unless an organism is defective or the soul cannot effectively

---

* *Eurythmy, a New Art of Movement*, a lecture given in Penmaenmawr, Wales, August 26, 1923, p. 12.

function in the body, we can all speak, but the extension of speech into movement, though it seems to have been known in part, albeit largely or altogether unconsciously, in the Greek Mysteries, required in our day for its revival the combined gifts of supersensible perception and artistic sensibility. Only thus could the hidden laws of speech in relation to movement be revealed. If there had been no Rudolf Steiner the "hidden laws" of this art would have long remained unrevealed, at least until another man was born who combined the two gifts in his own person. Rudolf Steiner always said, even at the end of his life, that eurythmy was still only in its infancy, and it has indeed been greatly developed in the fifty years since his death in 1925. His initial inspiration was, however, essential. In the last year of his active life he gave his most extensive courses on eurythmy, *Eurythmy as Visible Song* in February, 1924 (tone eurythmy) and *Eurythmy as Visible Speech* five months later. Both of these series of lectures, representing Steiner's last word on the subject, contained an immense wealth of new indications for the future, which have only slowly been brought into realization by his pupils. To illustrate the uniqueness of Steiner's own gift, a short passage from one of his first pupils may be quoted.

> Then, finally, came the musical forms. . . . It almost took one's breath away to see the creation of such a form for tone eurythmy. Rudolf Steiner had the piece played to him or simply took the score in his hand, and, while listening to the music, he let his pencil glide slowly, consideringly, over the paper, as if shaping a deeply significant design; and so there arose—often under the eyes of many curious bystanders—drawings, whose legitimate connection with the music was understood only by the eurythmists and musicians in the course of their studies, but whose beauty of line and inexhaustible variety enraptured one at first glance.*

The reader who has accompanied the author through this chapter will perhaps be reminded of Baron Rosenkrantz's

---

* Annemarie Dubach-Donath, *The Basic Principles of Eurythmy*, page v.

description of how the sculptured group, now in the Goetheanum, was first sketched by Rudolf Steiner, as recorded on page 230, and though more, much more could be said on Steiner's conception of and contribution to the arts, and how eurythmy is used in Steiner schools, in therapy, and in curative education, these latter can be left for the chapters on how his ideas have been put into practice throughout the world in the years since his death. It seems fitting to bring this chapter now to an end with these two pictures brought before our souls of Steiner the inspired artist, drawing on the supersensible worlds for his inspiration for the fulfillment and healing of man's soul. In the next chapter we shall turn to his contributions to the sciences, the way in which he studied the external world in the light of his supersensible knowledge, the new methods he brought to bear on this study, and some of the results of his work.

SUGGESTIONS FOR FURTHER READING
FOR CHAPTER 6.

The two major collections of lectures on the arts have frequently been quoted in the text: *Art in the Light of Mystery Wisdom*, eight lectures given at different times and in different cities, translated by Johanna Collis (2nd edit. London, 1970), and *The Arts and their mission*, eight lectures given in Dornach, May 27 to June 9, 1923, and two lectures given in Oslo, May 18 and 20, 1923, translated by Lisa Monges and Virginia Moore (New York, 1979). Both series are difficult for the beginner, especially those in the first named, and they will probably have to be reread and pondered over many times before they yield their full meaning. Much simpler are the "legend" mentioned in the text called *The Nature and Origin of the Arts*, a lecture given in Berlin, October 28, 1909 (London, n.d.), and a lecture given also in Berlin, on May 12, 1910 entitled "The Mission of Art," published in the collection called *Metamorphoses of the Soul* (London, n.d.). This latter lecture provides a good general introduction to Steiner's views on the role of art in human development.

Steiner's views on architecture are to be found in four lectures given in Dornach, June–July, 1914, published under the title, *Ways to a New Style of Architecture* (London, 1927). The small brochure by Arild Rosenkrantz called *The Goetheanum as a New Impulse in Art*, quoted several times in the text, has long been out of print in itself, but it appears also as part of a work called simply, *A New Impulse in Art* by the same author (East Grinstead: New Knowledge Books, 1968). A valuable appreciation of Steiner's work as architect is an article entitled, "Architecture in Accord with Man" by Kenneth Bayes in *The Faithful Thinker*, Centenary Essays on the Work and Thought of Rudolf Steiner (London: Hodder and Stoughton, 1961). Other essays of value for this chapter in this collection are "The Activity of Colour in the Art of Painting," by Alec and Gladys Morrison, and "Colour, Science and Thinking," by Michael Wilson.

On Goethe's Color Theory a sumptuous work with this title arranged and edited by Rupprecht Matthaei has recently appeared (New York: Van Nostrand Reinhold Company, 1971), and Goethe's own book has been reprinted in the old Eastlake translation of 1840 (Cambridge, Mass.: M.I.T. Press, 1970). The theory may also be conveniently studied in an excellent book by Maria Schindler simply called *Goethe's Theory of Colour Applied by Maria Schindler* (East Grinstead: New Knowledge Books, 1978). Steiner himself devoted a full chapter to the Color Theory in his *Goethe's Conception of the World* which first appeared in 1897. The chapter occupies pages 139–168 in the 1928 London edition. His lectures on color given in Dornach, May 6 to 8, 1921, have been recently republished together with a series of extracts from his notebooks. The book is simply called *Colour* (London, 1971). Three books by Gladys Mayer, all published by New Knowledge Books in mimeographed form, constitute the essence of the author's lifelong experience as a painter using the indications of Rudolf Steiner. These are: *Colour and the Human Soul* (1961); *Colour and Healing* (undated, but apparently later than the first named); and, much the fullest, *The Mystery Wisdom of Colour* (1961), which has the added advantage of extracts from other anthroposophical writers on color, together with several valuable illustrative plates. Lastly, from the same publisher is an excellent course on color and painting entitled, *The Creative Power of Colour* by H. Boos-Hamburger.

On music another New Knowledge book may be used to supplement what Steiner himself says on this art, especially in *Art in the Light of Mystery Wisdom.* This is an undated work called *Music: Its Occult Basis and Healing Value,* compiled by Lionel Stebbing from the work of many authors. Rudolf Steiner's early lecture, "The Occult Basis of Music," given in Cologne, December 3, 1906, was published in the *Golden Blade* for 1956, and was quoted in the text.

On poetry the last lecture in the compilation, *The Arts and Their Mission,* is valuable, but beyond all other works on the subject the nineteen lectures given by Steiner and published under the general title, *Speech and Drama* (the course was given in Dornach in September, 1924), should be read and studied. They are full of interesting insights into poetry, speech and drama, and contain also various asides on acting, including acting in the Mystery Dramas. The long passages recited by Marie Steiner during the course to illustrate Steiner's own observations are not the least interesting feature of the book. Almost all are given in the original language with English translations, thus enabling the perceptive reader to gain some insight into the genius of the different languages. Rudolf Steiner's Mystery Dramas themselves are available in four paperbound volumes in a new translation by Hans and Ruth Pusch (Steiner Book Centre, Vancouver, 1973), and there is another translation of the first Mystery Drama available by Adam Bittleston under the title, *The Portal of Initiation* (Englewood, New Jersey: Rudolf Steiner Publications, Inc., 1961).

For eurythmy there exist the two fundamental lecture courses by Rudolf Steiner himself given in February and June–July, 1924 under the titles *Eurythmy as Visible Music* (London, 1977) and *Eurythmy as Visible Speech* (London, 1956) respectively, as well as a number of introductions to eurythmy usually given before performances on the stage. Among the latter are a lecture given in Penmaenmawr, Wales, on August 26, 1923, called *Eurythmy: A New Art of Movement* (London, 1926, and also included in *Eurythmy as Visible Music*), and *Movement: The Speech of the Soul* given at Dornach, April 27, 1924 (London, 1928). Lastly, for the actual practice of eurythmy, the book quoted at the end of the chapter, Annemarie Dubach-Donath, *The Basic Principles of Eurythmy* (London, 1937) is invaluable, while a short article by Owen Barfield entitled, "The Art of Eurythmy," which appeared in *The Golden Blade* of 1954, may be found helpful by many as an effort to inform a member of the audience of a eurythmy performance as to just what he is viewing if he has never seen such a performance before. This article goes into somewhat more detail than the section in the chapter. It is written from the point of view of a connoisseur of human language, who is also an anthroposophist of long standing.

Although we have not considered the matter in this chapter it may be worthwhile to note that Steiner gave several indications on the subject of crafts and handwork, on which there is a book, Hedwig Hauck, *Handwork and Handicrafts from Indications by Rudolf Steiner* (London, 1968), by the original handicraft teacher in the first Waldorf School in Stuttgart.

As a final suggestion it may be worthwhile for the reader to return to Steiner's first lecture on art given to the Goethe Society in Vienna, November 8, 1888, which is entitled *Goethe as the Founder of a New Science of Aesthetics*, a lecture that Steiner revised for publication in a second edition in 1919 (London, 1922). Many things said in this lecture foreshadow what Steiner was to say on art later, and nothing in it in any way contradicts them.

262

CHAPTER VII

The Science of Spirit
and the Science of Nature

It should be clear enough from what has been said thus far that anthroposophy, or the science of spirit, if it is true knowledge, ought to revolutionize all that our modern age has, in its limited way, hitherto regarded as "science." For not only does it put forward propositions regarding man's relationship with the cosmos, past and present, and give us a treasury of new information about the nature of man, but it also speaks about a world that cannot be perceived by the "five" senses, a world peopled by unseen beings and by forces as yet undiscovered by scientists. For this reason even the most open-minded scientists, who are quite willing to admit the degree of their ignorance about the "ultimate truths" of the world and universe and freely acknowledge how much they still do not know, are nevertheless —or perhaps I should say *therefore*—especially skeptical in their attitude toward Rudolf Steiner's teachings, so few of which seem capable of verification, even in principle, by their own standards of proof.

It should be emphasized, however, that scientists, even when

263

they accept fully the teachings of Rudolf Steiner in other realms, and accept his scientific pronouncements as at least reasonable working hypotheses, are in exactly the same position as their non-anthroposophical brethren. As investigators of the outside world they are bound to seek for verification of their ideas in that world, and only relatively few of Steiner's ideas are able to be put to the test in practice. It is, for example, impossible to conceive of an experiment that could ever prove conclusively such a proposition as that the earth itself breathes, exhaling in the morning and inhaling in the afternoon. All that can be done is to show that this proposition explains a large number of observed facts hitherto more or less explained by other theories. Yet the proposition, if true, must be of enormous practical importance, and might well lead on to similar explanations of other still unexplained or imperfectly explained phenomena. The so-called etheric formative forces, whose existence is "postulated" by anthroposophy, likewise provide helpful and fruitful explanations for a wide range of observed phenomena, but skeptical scientists who prefer more materialistic explanations are not likely to change their views as long as their own explanations satisfy them.

The anthroposophical scientist may begin his life work with a faith in the truth of the spiritual science taught by Rudolf Steiner, including what he taught in the field of his own specialty. But if he is to be a good scientist he ought to be as skeptical of what Steiner said as he will be of everything else, at least until he has done what he can to test it. He may expect to find that what Steiner taught in the field of natural science is consistent with his other teachings—one of the criteria for testing spiritual science put forward in Chapter 1. Just occasionally he may find that some remark of Steiner's has later been found to be true by independent scientists and observers—as was the case for Steiner's discussion in the early 1900's of the relation between fluorine and the teeth, and some of his remarks about the physical composition of the moon, which were confirmed when the American astronauts brought back samples.

But if in general he cannot himself test directly much of Steiner's teaching, is there any other way of testing it, aside from the criterion of internal consistency? To this the answer must be that by contemporary scientific standards of "objective" proof no such testing is possible. But the question may also be asked what standards would be applied in the case of a man born blind who is enabled to see by a successful operation. Before the operation it would have been impossible to explain satisfactorily to the man what color is, though he might have been instructed as to the wave length of the different colors, the speed of light and similar items of "objective" knowledge acceptable to physicists. After the operation the man would suddenly become aware of a world hitherto unknown to him, but even so he would have acquired no reason to doubt the objective facts he had heard before. Yet he knows very well that something has been given to him that he did not have before, the ability to see. If now he begins to describe the objects he sees and how they are colored, and this information agrees with what the operating doctors themselves see, then they will know that their operation was successful. The only proof of this is that all those gifted with sight (except the colorblind) will agree with both patient and doctors; all trust their senses, and the evidence of sense perception is enough to cause them to believe they live in a world of colored objects. They do not really need to have this fact proved to them, and indeed it required a considerable intellectual effort to think away the visible reality of color and describe it in terms acceptable to physicists.

The Nature of Living (Goethean) Thinking. The point of this analogy is to drive home the truth that in the last analysis no one can become a creative anthroposophical scientist, or even deal effectively with Steiner's teachings unless he has, at least to a minimal degree, become capable of living thinking, in accordance with what we have called the Goethean method; this kind of thinking is as real, and first hand, as it were, as ordinary sense perception. A biodynamic farmer, an anthroposophical doctor or pharmacist, a curative eurythmist, a curative worker in a

265

home for handicapped or "exceptional" children, even a teacher of normal children in schools using Steiner's pedagogical methods, cannot work effectively simply by *following the rules,* the rules being in this case the necessarily limited information given by Rudolf Steiner himself. Indeed, in almost all these matters there are no rules; there are only individual cases that have to be observed and thought about. To attain to living, or imaginative, thinking is the first great task that the consciousness soul has to undertake, and it is not beyond the abilities of those who have reached the stage of the consciousness soul, and who have, almost as a matter of course, begun to perceive the outer world objectively, as if they were onlookers.

In Chapter 2 when we discussed the beginning of the modern age, we devoted several pages (pp. 96–101) to the nature of the consciousness soul, and we pointed out how, because it looks upon the world as a spectator, it has become able to manipulate and control the external world for the benefit (or detriment) of man. It can be changed to suit man's convenience by the practical scientist, the engineer and the technologist. Man is thus faced with certain moral questions, whether or not he is aware of them. Willy nilly he must himself make the decision as to what is good or convenient for him, and he must weigh certain important and inescapable choices, such, for example, as to how much damage he dare do to the environment in order to attain the good he seeks. Does he have any responsibility for the non-human world, the world of the animals, or do they exist solely for man's benefit (or entertainment)? Could it be that he has some responsibility for the earth itself, its plants and minerals, its fertility? Man's present knowledge is not sufficient for him to be able to give definitive answers to these and similar questions. Most men vaguely feel that they have some responsibility for passing on an unruined earth to their descendants, but meanwhile pollution on the whole grows worse, population is increasing and millions more mouths have to be fed each year. Even those who believe in God cannot be quite sure what God would want—more children and greater consumption of not unlimited resources, or fewer children and perhaps smaller consumption?

In the passage referred to in Chapter 2 we mentioned that man's recognition of himself as separate from the world in the age of the consciousness soul was an essential preliminary condition for the achievement of his freedom and egohood, but with the achievement of freedom and egohood he becomes subject to great temptations. At the same time the world, having become objective, is no longer linked to man as it was in the consciousness of earlier peoples. Man's attitude, in short, becomes necessarily a *cold* one. In winning the ability to change matter at the same time that we come to understand it, we are compelled to make cold, unsentimental decisions as to how to make use of the world we have inherited. In domesticating animals, eating them, shooting them for sport, often without thinking very much about the matter, we exploit them as if they were *things,* not living beings, and when we look upon the whole world and everything in it as *things,* we cease to have any relationship with them in our life of soul. It is the primary task of the consciousness soul to overcome this coldness, to change the cold dead thinking of the intellect into the warmth of living thinking illuminated by the spirit, to abandon our "objective" attitude toward the world in favor of what I should like to label "subjective-objective" thinking, entering with our whole being *into* the world phenomena, not remaining outside them.* It is our task to forge new links with the external world, links that are created by the activity of our own "I," so that we no longer simply *know* the world (or think we know it), but love it. It is an essential part of living thinking that we connect ourselves with it in our feeling life of soul. If we withdraw from the world in order to observe it (as withdraw we must if we are to observe anything

---

* The philosophical basis for this kind of thinking is laid, in particular, in Steiner's book, *The Philosophy of Freedom,* especially in those chapters concerned with our experience of the world as union of concept and percept. It is also developed further by Steiner in his book, *Goethe's Conception of the World,* published three years later than *The Philosophy of Freedom* (1894, 1897).

outside ourselves) and make ourselves receptive to what is before us, then it will *reveal* its secrets to us; they do not have to be extracted from it by main force. Science has made its tremendous advances of the last centuries by treating the world almost exclusively as if it were dead matter and could be understood by the dead thinking of the intellect. No one, certainly no anthroposophist, would deny the tremendous intellectual power that has been used in the acquisition of our new knowledge, nor the immense technical expertise that lies behind our technology and engineering. But it should not be forgotten that, as was also explained in Chapter 2, the world of sub-nature in particular, the world of electricity and atomic energy, is a world that was revealed to man by Ahriman, who is the lord of everything in the world that can be weighed, measured, and calculated. Ahriman tries to persuade man to use what he gives him in ways that will hinder his spiritual development, and it is surely visible enough in today's world that he is succeeding only too well. In particular Ahriman tries to gain control of man's intellect.

Now intellectual knowledge is unable really to understand the living. The intellect prefers to treat the whole that appears in nature as if it were made up of innumerable tiny parts, forgetting that a whole is qualitatively different from the sum of its parts. Nor can the ordinary scientific mentality come to anything that could be called scientific morality for lack of knowledge of the true nature of the world, and the spiritual beings that created it and are always present and active in it. The Christ after his incarnation, death, and resurrection became the Spirit of the earth; the bread and wine, fruits of the earth, are indeed his body and blood. This truth is not symbolic but a fact of complete actuality, and if we are to come to a conscious relationship with the earth, we should know that in building this relationship we are performing what in the highest sense of the word may be called a *Christian* duty.

We can engage in a significant discussion of scientific morality only after we have completed our discussion of what new factual information anthroposophy can contribute to natural science. But at this point we should try to explain more clearly what is meant by living thinking, and why it is particularly important for the study of the organic world as well as being capable of making significant contributions to the knowledge also of what is now thought of as the inorganic. The great pioneer in this kind of thinking was Goethe, though it was Steiner who was the man most responsible for making explicit what was only implicit in Goethe's own numerous writings on scientific subjects.*

In the Middle Ages and antiquity the study of the natural world, organic and inorganic, had been dominated by the idea of purpose, but there was no hard and fast distinction between the two realms, since it was believed that the earth itself was alive, that the planets were the outer expression of spiritual beings (intelligences); that all the mineral substances had their own particular qualities, and that, in principle, it should be possible to transmute baser metals into gold if only the philosopher's stone could be found. Since it was taken for granted that God had made the world, and that everything he had created served some useful purpose, or, as Aristotle put it, "Nature does nothing in vain," one of the tasks of scientists and

---

* Steiner, while still in his early twenties, was asked to act as editor for the scientific material to be published in a new edition of Goethe's works then being planned. His introductions in this Kürschner edition are collected in a book translated into English under the title, *Goethe the Scientist*. In 1886 when he was 25, Steiner published a book called, *The Theory of Knowledge Based on Goethe's World Conception*. Then in 1897, as noted earlier, he published a further Goethean study called, *Goethe's Conception of the World*. All these books, as well as the invaluable work by Ernst Lehrs, *Man or Matter*, will be used for the following discussion of Goethe's scientific ideas. All should be studied in connection with Steiner's fundamental book, *The Philosophy of Freedom*, or *Philosophy of Spiritual Activity*, a title that will reveal its meaning during the course of this chapter.

It may be added that in the footnotes covering quotations from Goethe most references are given to Steiner's works on Goethe and not to Goethe's own, which, with some exceptions, are not easily available in English. Steiner's books cited here, however, do contain the required references to Goethe's works, some of which were edited by him for the first time, and they should be consulted by the interested reader.

philosophers was to discover God's purposes. Far less interest was displayed in learning how to make effective use of what God had provided, or in trying to understand what we might call the *mechanism* of nature.

As we have seen, this attitude changed in early modern times with the coming of the consciousness soul, and the "onlooker" consciousness of modern man. Great efforts were now made to discover the mechanical "laws" of nature, and then give mathematical expression to them. But it was found that what we now think of as the inorganic world was the only part of nature that seemed to yield reliable laws that worked on every occasion and could be shown to work by planned experiments. As Steiner pointed out in his 1886 book on Goethe's Theory of Knowledge, the reason why it is possible to discover such reliable laws of nature in the inorganic realm is because there is no *whole,* no individuality in this world. If a few tons of rock are removed from a mountain it remains a mountain. Moreover this world can be subjected to quantitative analysis; its component parts can be weighed, measured and numbered.

But during the second half of the eighteenth century when Kant and Goethe were active, it was not believed that it would ever be possible to subject the organic world to similar analysis. According to Kant, any laws that man might believe himself to have found in this realm could not apply beyond the particular case; no laws in the organic realm would be of universal applicability. Indeed, Kant insisted that it is part of the very nature of human thinking that it must proceed from the particular to the general, but that this kind of abstract thinking is not possible in the case of organic nature in which every living organism differs from every other. Thus Kant was compelled to fall back upon purpose, that is, the part played by the particular living organism in the entire organic world; this, he said, was all that could be known by man. As Steiner dryly commented, "Kant here, so to speak, established the unscientific scientifically!" (*Theory of Knowledge Based on Goethe's World Conception*, p. 84).

270

Goethe, a younger contemporary of Kant, disagreed with him, as we shall see, but Goethe himself had few followers in this field. In the nineteenth century those methods that had worked so effectively in the inorganic realm began to be applied ever more exclusively in the organic, and with tremendous practical success in some areas. Whole new so-called "life-sciences" have been born, but if such a wide array of knowledge can be dismissed in so summary a manner it must surely be said that the successes have largely been won by *treating the living as if it were dead.* As Steiner was to remark later in another context, blood drawn from a human being and subjected to chemical analysis in a test tube is *qualitatively* different from blood as it circulates within the human body; to Steiner if not to biochemists the distinction is a crucial one. There is, he said, a different way of studying the living, a way that is the only one suitable for the life sciences, and with value even for the inorganic world if we wish to understand more about it than is revealed to us by modern physics and chemistry. This way was first suggested in modern times by Goethe.

The chapter entitled, "The Adventure of Reason," in Lehrs' book, *Man or Matter,* ought to be read and studied by every student interested in this subject, since it deals in detail with Goethe's method, a method that Lehrs follows himself in the rest of the book. Here we can only deal with the matter in a rather brief manner, pointing out a few essentials. In essence the Goethean method for observing the organic world is to follow the evolution of the organism as it proceeds in nature, without inserting one's own thinking, without trying to explain, but resting, as it were, in stillness in front of the object, and letting it reveal its secrets. In Steiner's epistemology, as we have noted in Chapter 3, all objects in the outer world contain a physical perceptual element, and a non-physical conceptual element. Both equally exist in the object itself, and when we as human beings recognize the plant or other object and put it in a certain class, we are, as it were, extracting the conceptual element from the object. But it is possible to do much more than this. The

271

object needs a warm, even loving, thinking if it is alive and is to reveal its secrets to us. This is in a real sense a new kind of thinking that should become characteristic of the consciousness soul, and it has a right to be called living. It is in no sense an illusion, a simple fantasy, nor is it in any way sentimental. It actually reveals what is there but hidden; and in developing this kind of thinking we also learn to think with our etheric body, not through the medium of our earthbound brain. This etheric body is in itself a part of the etheric world; indeed, it is borrowed from the etheric world for our lifetime and dissolves in the three days following our earthly death. It is only through thinking with our etheric body that we can learn to perceive the etheric element that exists in all things living.

Clearly, such a statement cannot be accepted by a reader without having grasped for himself how Goethe (and Steiner) used this kind of thinking, and what kind of secrets actually were revealed. We shall try to defend the statement shortly by making a comparison between the way in which a modern analytical scientist would arrive at his conclusions, and describe the kind of information he will obtain, with what a "Goethean" scientist might hope to discover by his methods. But it may be noted here that Goethe has been credited with a few discoveries even by scientists, though they have not been greatly interested by them. He discovered the human intermaxillary jawbone through his theory of the metamorphosis of all living things, and his theory on the metamorphosis of plant forms is generally accepted. In pursuing thousands of investigations into the world of the living, Goethe began to develop what we have called "living" or imaginative thinking, as anthroposophy understands these words. He entered so deeply into the life of the plants that he was observing, and penetrated with his thinking and observing into the way in which they changed their forms according to the laws he was discovering, that eventually he arrived at what we are justified in calling a *living idea,* since he could really *see* it with the "eyes" of his imagination. When his friend Schiller told him that it was not an "experience" as Goethe had claimed it

272

was, but only an "idea in his mind," Goethe retorted, "I am glad to have ideas without knowing it, and to see them with my own eyes."

What Goethe had "seen" was what he was to call the *urpflanze,* usually translated as an "archetypal" plant. This was a plant that existed nowhere in nature, but from which *all* plants are in some measure derived. In all his subsequent investigations this living idea served him well, as he tried to see how it expressed itself in so many different kinds of plants, all totally different, to our ordinary untrained sense perception. Goethe, however, was not so successful in trying to extend his idea to the animal world, and Steiner often drew attention to Goethe's weaknesses in his observation of the human realm, as also his lack of interest in the processes of his own thinking. What Goethe left undone Steiner did. All his work is a result of his own living thinking, which we have also called "imaginative thinking." This thinking brings us to the lowest realm of the supersensible world, and Steiner insists that the great majority of persons who try to develop this new faculty in our age will be able to do so. Beyond imaginative thinking, however, are the two higher realms, called by Steiner inspiration and intuition. These he himself developed and as a result was able to teach anthroposophy or the science of spirit in a form accessible to human thinking and human understanding. As for the rest of us we may occasionally have what we think of as inspirations, even intuitions, but we do not have constant access to them, nor will such conscious access to them be at all common among men until much later in history, when the consciousness soul will have run its course and a new epoch with new tasks begins.

Now let us return to our two botanists. The first one, trained in analytical methods, will amass a great deal of information about any plant that he is considering. According to the procedures developed by Linnaeus, it will be assigned to a particular plant family, and it will be assigned its correct name, in Latin and the vernacular. Its reproductive processes will probably be studied, whether or not it is self-pollinating, and whether it needs to be pollinated by wind, bee or butterfly. The soil composition that the plant prefers, or rather the kind of soil in which it appears to grow best, will be noted, and the methods of cultivation that seem to be most suitable for it. For almost all other facts that are amassed about this plant it must be torn out of its environment. The number of chromosomes can be counted after a slide has been prepared and a high powered microscope trained on it; the ash of the plant may be analyzed to discover its chemical components, including even so-called "trace" elements. From this kind of information it may be possible to breed new plants with characteristics regarded as more desirable, and the nutritional requirements can supposedly be calculated. No one can deny the usefulness of all this information that could not be obtained by mere observation, however "living" or "warm" and "loving." Yet the student of botany could discover almost all of it from a good text book; he need never have even seen the original plant for himself. A good diagram in the text book will in fact be just as good, if not better. The memory and intellect of the student in botany will be put to full use. But nothing will be asked of his imagination, and perhaps little enough even of his powers of observation; it is more than likely that the study as a whole will arouse little enthusiasm in him of the kind that can, and surely *ought* to be aroused by the study of the living world.

Now let us examine how the same plant would be considered by the Goethean method. We ourselves, first of all, have to become active; we must observe the plant and watch how it unfolds. We shall probably, by our own observation and thinking, recognize, as Goethe did, how the various forms of the plant all represent *metamorphoses* of the leaf, which Goethe calls "the true Proteus, who can hide and reveal himself in all formations. Forwards and backwards the plant is only leaf, so inseparably united with the future germ that one cannot be conceived without the other." As soon as the plant has taken root we see the cotyledon or cotyledons unfold, and immediately

274

thereafter the first leaf makes its appearance, sometimes large and well formed, and sometimes small and insignificant, depending on the particular plant. In any event the entire green part of the plant follows the appearance of the first leaf, and each leaf takes on a somewhat different form as the plant grows upward toward the light. The final leaves change into the sepals of the calyx, or, as Goethe put it, "the stem leaves softly steal into the calyx stage." The sepals then turn into the petals and the flower, and from the pistil and stamens the fruit and seed are formed. This completes the original life cycle.

As the process is observed a certain sequence of stages reveal themselves. Goethe perceived three rhythms of expansion and contraction, which in his view could not possibly be imposed upon the plant by some outside influence, but must be inherent in the plant itself. "In the calyx," he wrote, "the plant form draws itself together, and in the corolla again spreads itself out. The next contraction follows in the pistils and stamens, the organs of generation . . . At this stage of contraction the same force distributes itself into two organs. What is separated seeks to reunite. This happens in the process of fructification." In the union of the male pollen with the female substance Goethe perceives "the force to produce its like," which is to be observed in all living bodies, though he was averse to using the analogy of sexual reproduction taken from the animal and human world. After the last contraction into the seed "the whole nature of the plant appears once more, contracted to a point." He showed also much interest in the varying ways in which plants reproduce themselves. The bud, he remarked, was a kind of plant on a plant, and he was especially interested in observing it since, unlike the seed in the earth, the process of germination could be observed. This happened when suitable external conditions, as for example, the absence of extreme cold, obtained. He also naturally noticed the way in which shoots develop out of the node, and remarked that the seed was only another form of the nodule that develops on the stem, and he was naturally well-aware of and commented on the fact that for many plants it is enough to place the node in the earth for it to develop roots and grow into another plant.

Now it must be admitted that this kind of observation is carried out also by the modern botanist, who also obtains much "hard" information through his investigations on the dead plant. Goethe's method in itself told him nothing about the cells and chromosomes, now observable through powerful microscopes, after the plant has ceased to grow, nor does it tell him anything about the chemical constituents of the plant. What is different about the Goethean observation is that a *process* can be followed both with the physical eye and "in the mind's eye," as we say. In Lehrs' words, when we try to comprehend the plant in this way we "re-create it inwardly," and this is a process that overcomes our tendency to look at the world solely from the point of view of the onlooker. This inward re-creation, in short, is another word for imaginative thinking, and it is the first stage on the path of supersensible perception. We activate our etheric body, and whether or not we are consciously aware of it, we do in fact learn in this way to perceive what we may call the "signature" of the etheric formative forces, the form building forces, in the world of nature.

This example of the Goethean method as applied by its originator, instructive though it may be in itself, ought to have been followed by an example given from Rudolf Steiner's own work, from which we could show how what had been still quite primitive in Goethe himself could be brought to its apogee almost a hundred years after his death by a man who added inspiration and intuition to the imaginative thinking of his predecessor. Such examples do exist, and it is extremely instructive to observe in particular the way in which Steiner inspired the work in curative education for what he called, as translated into English, "children in need of special care" (in German *Seelenpflegebedürftig*). There are now dozens of such centers in the Western world, all of them resulting from the major impulse given by Steiner during the last year of his life on earth. For this series of twelve lectures given in Dornach from June 25 to July 7, 1924 his audience was made up almost entirely of a handful of young people who had already opened a home for these children in Lauenstein, near Jena, Germany, and a few who were working in a branch of the therapeutical clinic at Arlesheim, near Dornach, which had been opened by a close collaborator of Steiner, Dr. Ita Wegman. During the second half of these lectures, Steiner called some of these afflicted children into the Schreinerei (or workshop) where he was giving the lectures to an audience of about twenty persons. Then he proceeded to draw attention in the kindest possible way to characteristics that almost no one else would have noticed, and only he could have interpreted. Later on, he gave the appropriate therapy.

It is impossible here to devote space to even a single complete example, since all cover several pages in the transcript of the lectures. Moreover, in an introductory book on anthroposophy the numerous references to the etheric and astral bodies and what Steiner in his last years called the "ego-organization," and the relations between them would be largely incomprehensible. Most fortunately, the lectures themselves have recently been published in English under the title, *Curative Education.* They are recommended not so much for their specific content as for the value they have as models of how the most minute observation, coupled with thinking developed to the degree of intuition, can reveal so much that would be unnoticed by almost any other observer, or, if noticed, would not be regarded as significant. For Steiner *nothing* was insignificant or meaningless, and this is another lesson we can all learn from him; also, no two cases are ever alike, so that new and fresh observation and living thinking is needed in every single case. What Steiner wished to impress on his pupils was that in spite of their less developed spiritual faculties they could all make the effort to observe and try to grasp imaginatively the inner and outer being of the apparently defective human beings to whom they were to devote their lives. Thus in time, and with increasing experience,

277

they too might hope to be able to diagnose and find the combination of remedies and treatment that would, as Steiner said so beautifully, do for the children in this earth life what otherwise would have to be done for them by spiritual beings after their death—thereby enabling them to reincarnate in a different way than if they had simply been placed in an institution and given little more than custodial care until they made everyone's lives easier by passing over the threshold of death.*

Rudolf Steiner gave us the fundamental teachings that lie behind all anthroposophical science, but as a rule he did not go deeply into details unless he was asked specific questions. Almost all his lecture cycles on scientific matters were given between the end of World War I and his death in March, 1925. Indeed, from the end of September, 1924 he was confined to his bed and could give no more lectures. During these postwar years his lecturing activity was immense, so that several major cycles on specific sciences are available from this time, including the one we have already discussed, several cycles on medicine and a fundamental one on agriculture. But already for some years before his death, and in some instances well before he gave his

---

* Another example may be found in that extraordinary series of fourteen lectures given in Dornach in July and August, 1922, and recently republished in a new translation by A. O. Barfield and T. Gordon-Jones under the title, *World Economy* (London, 1972). In these lectures Steiner presents to his audience a series of what can only be called living insights into how the economy, all economies, function. Nothing in the cycle is what might have been expected, not a single concept is drawn from any economic thinker of the past or present. The present-day reader is simply driven to undertake the perhaps unwelcome task of re-thinking and re-perceiving everything that he has hitherto thought and perceived on this subject in the past—a truly cleansing operation for him as well as revivifying—though it may well be true that nothing Steiner says can be fitted into our deadest of social sciences, what used to be called political economy. But what we do achieve is an imaginative insight into a living and functioning organism, living and functioning as it ought to function if our social order, and especially our economic order, were ever to live and free itself from the dead weight of abstract thinking. Thus, as an example of the thinking we have here called Goethean, there may be nothing better to study in all anthroposophical literature than this course given on what we may initially have thought to be an unpromising subject.

complete courses, a fairly large number of anthroposophical students were engaged in scientific research of various kinds, some of them as the result of questions they had put to him within the fields of their own specialties, to which his answers had opened up totally new fields of enquiry. This first generation of scientists was in fact extremely creative, and some of them have written several most valuable books, in almost all cases stemming from indications given by Steiner from the wealth of his own spiritual knowledge. The reading list at the end of the chapter will mention some of the most useful of the scientific books available in English, and the later chapters of this book devoted to the practical work that has stemmed from Steiner's teachings will give necessarily brief summaries of work done since his time and continuing to be done at the present day. The theoretical work of these scientists, though of enormous interest, cannot be included in any detail in this chapter, and the reader must be referred to the books themselves and the remarks about the contents of each that will be included with the list. The rest of this chapter will be devoted instead to a discussion of a few of the basic scientific teachings of Rudolf Steiner himself, or teachings that enable us to understand the earthly world as it is revealed to the science of spirit. All that will be discussed in this chapter, remote though it may at first appear to be from current scientific preoccupations, has a real bearing on such preoccupations.

The science of spirit, not acknowledging the limits that the science of nature has placed on its own search for knowledge, can by its own methods not only provide solutions to many apparently insoluble riddles, but reveal how the "onlooker-consciousness" of our century can be transcended. In doing this a real scientific morality will reveal itself, which derives from our enlarged knowledge of the world and universe, and is not simply superimposed by some faith or philosophy that is not grounded in scientific knowledge.

Man's Relation to the Universe and Its Beings. It seems fitting to introduce in this chapter the anthroposophical conception of

279

man's place in the universe from a viewpoint opposite to that used in Chapter 2. In that chapter we discussed briefly the tremendous preparations that had to be made by the divine spiritual beings before it was possible for them to create that unique being, man, who is to be the tenth spiritual hierarchy. Here we shall deal with the subject from the point of view of man, who has his own particular place in the universe. In his present form man could not exist without the aid not only of the nine hierarchies above him and of the animal, plant, and mineral kingdoms, which he uses so fully, but of those other beings who are known as elemental beings (or nature-spirits) who are at present invisible to him—although until quite recent times they were visible and have often been described in folk-lore. In the course of this exposition we shall also have to deal with various "forces" that are also invisible and as yet unknown to scientists, although one of their "offspring," electricity, is now, quite suddenly, very well known, and has been made the basis of modern industrial civilization.

Most biologists are ready to concede that there is something with which they have to deal all the time in their work, which they do not really understand. They do not understand the exact nature of the living or organic, and wherein it differs from the inorganic or dead. Although they believe they know the major constituent elements that go to make up the living organism, they are usually prepared to admit that something escapes them, that there is something truly mysterious about the "organization" of living matter, and about the way in which nature seems to "hang together," as I have heard one biologist express it. That branch of biology called ecology is particularly concerned with the interrelationships among the different living creatures, and their environment. As everyone knows, the subject has suddenly become fashionable because it has been found that modern industrial civilization, in spite of its obvious successes, has at the same time polluted the environment and disturbed the "balance of nature." But neither ecologists nor other biologists know just what a true balance of nature should consist of, except that it should be such that a place exists in it for at least the present population of the human world.

Almost to a man, modern biologists believe in the Darwinian theory of evolution, as modified and refined in the years since the publication of Darwin's *Origin of Species* in 1859. The original nineteenth century Darwinian notion of the survival of the fittest in the struggle for existence is no longer believed, as it once was, to mean the survival of the strongest. Instead, the prevailing theory is that the organism best fitted to survive in an ever changing environment did so; the mutant with the greatest survival value did in fact survive and reproduce itself. This theory has the great advantage, in the eyes of most modern scientists, that it not only does not require the existence of any divine being, but it also makes unnecessary any concept of purpose, leaving the only agent of the entire evolutionary process as "chance." By chance a particular mutant comes into being, and it proves to be so successful that it eventually supplants the existing species. Although the vast majority of mutants are inferior to the existing species and, having no survival value, do not survive, once in a very long time one is successful. This is certainly true of some artificially produced mutations, and the fact is regarded as sufficient explanation of how species evolved in the historical past, and explains man as a successful mutation of his animal ancestors.

Now this theory may be and often is criticized, especially by non-biologists, but since no better theory exists that can explain in some manner all the facts amassed by scientists, and can equally well do without "the hypothesis of God," and the notion of purpose, it still holds the field. But, as may be surmised by readers of this book, it is quite contrary to what is revealed by supersensible perception, which not only puts forward a totally different explanation for the evolution of species, and, in particular, the creation of man (see Chapter 2 above, pp. 28–29, which will not be repeated here), but it pictures the universe as filled with all kinds of beings, each, indeed, with its task to perform within the so-called "balance of nature." The anthroposophical conception is indeed much more like the older theory of the Great Chain of Being, derived mainly from Plato and Aristotle by medieval philosophers, and widely held in the West until the great advance of materialism in the eighteenth century. Supersensible perception reveals man as a totally unique being in the universe, and, as we explained in Chapter 2, the plant and animal kingdoms evolved from an earlier stage of what was eventually to become man as we know him today. Here we are particularly concerned with the animal, and it is necessary to make clear how in spite of numerous resemblances to man, it also differs from him in essential ways. It will be recalled that we spoke of the human being as possessing physical, etheric, and astral "bodies," and an "I." The animals possess the first three but they do not have an individual "I." They do have a group ego, however, or group soul. Each species has its own group soul, who is a real being, higher than man, whose dwelling place is the astral or elemental world. The individual animal, having no "I," is not immortal; it has no life either before birth or after death. But the group soul, which does not incarnate, is, like other non-physical beings, immortal; from the elemental world it directs, through what in an animal we call instinct, the individual animals upon earth, including the extraordinary activity of the social insects such as ants and wasps and bees. Such individuality as animals possess on earth is derived from the man who tames or otherwise cares for them. The animal, *all* animals, are specialized for a particular task, as man is not; they possess those capacities that are needed to perform that task. Being directly under control by the group soul, a higher being than man, the animals are in a sense more perfect than man, who has to use his own ego, incorporated within him, to make progress. No man has a sense of balance like a cat, the sense of smell of a dog, the "radar" system of a bat, the speed of a horse or a horse's strength; he cannot fly like a bird. *All* animals also have supersensible faculties, capable of sensing in advance natural catastrophes such as earthquakes, of perceiving astral specters or ghosts, and all kinds of dangers

282

before they occur. Man has many of these faculties in embryonic form, which he could develop. Lastly, when the time comes for an animal species to die out naturally, or be exterminated by men, the animal group soul turns to other tasks, as higher beings evolve no less than men.

Animals are not what they are *because* they have proved to be best fitted among all animal species to survive in a changing world. They are the result of the work of higher beings in earlier phases of the earth, and they are directed now, as we have said, by their own group souls. It is true that they cannot survive when man, or natural catastrophes, have made it impossible for them to do so in their original habitat, and migration to a better one is no longer possible. But they are not themselves evolving to a higher stage of being, as is man's task. On the contrary, all animals are degenerating in a natural manner at a slow or rapid pace as the result of having incarnated too soon (as is the case with animals) or too late (as is the case with birds), thus halting their evolution. Their degeneration, however, can be a slow process. Man can breed what he thinks of as superior species, for example, race-horses, or fast greyhounds, or extremely refined and "intelligent" dogs. But, as animals, most biologists would not consider them to be superior; in the process of being "improved" by man, they have degenerated more quickly by losing many of their original "natural" instincts, and they are likely to be much more subject to disease. The same is true of plants. Hence the ever recurring need to find wild "unspoiled" strains of plants to cross with the degenerated strains developed by man for his own needs.

The animals, therefore, are not, according to the science of spirit, only in our present world because of the survival value of chance mutations. They are as much the result of the work of spiritual beings as is man himself, and the spiritual beings took part in their creation because of tasks the animals, birds, bees and other living creatures have to perform in nature. By contrast many harmful insects have been brought into being by the powers hostile to man, largely as the result of man's own moral failings. The relation of all living beings to all others is a huge subject that has been discussed by Steiner in many different cycles of lectures, and only a few examples can be given here as illustrations of the kind of information he made available to us. Certain animals do, indeed, have as one task the direct nourishment of man, at his present stage of evolution. In digesting their own food these animals provide man with vegetable matter (man's proper food) that is not in its original form. Although, for various reasons that need not be entered into here, it would, for many people, be better not to eat animal food at all, most men today do not have the necessary etheric and spiritual forces to convert plant food directly into all they need to sustain their strength. At the present stage of human evolution only men with strong spiritual and life forces can do this effectively; for this reason most men have to resort to eating animal flesh, which they can use for the simple reason that the animal has already performed a part of the digesting process. The man who eats animal flesh is therefore freed from the necessity of doing all the digesting himself, but if he relies heavily on fish and meat for his sustenance, he does not at the same time make sufficient demands upon those spiritual and life forces through which plant material can be directly digested. He thus becomes inwardly more sluggish than he would otherwise have been.

The work of the animal who sacrifices himself for man's physical nourishment, however, is far from being his principal task. The cud-chewing animals, the cow and the sheep, have an important earthly task in providing manure for the nourishment of the land. But, aside from this obvious earthly task, perhaps even more important is the spiritual task entrusted to them. In essence, this is to bring down cosmic forces into the earth—a process that was known to the ancient Indians when they first began to look upon the cow as a specially sacred animal. The elemental beings called the gnomes, whom we shall be discussing later, and who live beneath the surface of the earth, cannot, as Steiner tells us, see the sun. But they can see the astral aura of

284

the cow, which is penetrated with the force of the sun, and this nourishes them and helps them to perform their task for the roots of the plants. As the gnomes and the undines, who live in the watery element close to the surface of the earth, rejoice in the cow, so do the air and fire spirits, the sylphs and the salamanders, rejoice in the flight of the birds.* The birds themselves, however, have a task allotted to them that is exactly the reverse of that given to the cows and sheep. They carry earthly substance out into the cosmos. This earthly substance has been incorporated into the airy structure of the birds' plumage, and after their death when the "feathers fall into decay . . . the spiritualized earthly matter ascends into spirit-land and becomes changed back into spiritual substance" (*op. cit.*, p. 59). Elsewhere Steiner speaks especially of the song birds whose song ascends spiritually into the far distances of space and nourishes the highest of the spiritual hierarchies, the Seraphim, who pour the song back onto the earth as a blessing for man.

As a last example, we may mention the bees to whom Steiner devoted nine lectures, which were given in 1923 to the workmen engaged in the preliminary work for the building of the second Goetheanum. In these lectures he described the enormous importance of the task the bees perform and the wonderful wisdom that lies behind the bee colony, the relationship of the bees with the bee-keeper, the cosmic tasks performed by the bees (quite apart from their role in pollination), and the unique nature of honey, which is a food of such exceptional value, especially for the aged. Many members of his audience were bee-keepers themselves, and it is extremely illuminating to see

---

* Most of these examples are taken from a lecture cycle given in October and November 1923, at Dornach called *Man as Symphony of the Creative Word*, especially Lecture 3. The marvelous fourth and fifth lectures of this extremely beautiful and stimulating cycle are concerned in particular with butterflies and the meaning of their successive metamorphoses, and how they carry spiritual substance out into the cosmos, and are themselves the gift to earth of the sun and the outer planets. These lectures should not be missed, but they are too detailed to be described here, even in an abbreviated form, which would do too scant justice to them.

how Steiner was able to speak quite easily to them on their own specialty, and enlighten them from the viewpoint of the science of spirit.

In the same way that we found it impossible to discuss the animal world without reference to the all-important, invisible group souls of each species, we cannot understand the plants without reference to the elemental beings who aid in their growth, and we should note that the plants also have a group soul, which resides in a higher realm than the group soul of the animals. While the plant has only an etheric and physical body on earth, it has an astral "body," if we can call such an impalpable entity a body, in the world that immediately surrounds it, the astral or elemental world, in which also the group souls of the animals dwell. Steiner indeed tells us that plants cannot live and thrive if they are not surrounded by an astrality (their "astral body") made up, in particular, of birds, butterflies, bees and those beneficent insects whose task it is to help in plant growth and decay.

The invisible elemental beings could be perceived until recent times by many people, and they have passed into the folklore of every country. They were given names, which we shall also use here. The *gnomes* or goblins are the beings of the earth who work with the roots of plants and have a special affinity for the metals of the earth. The *undines* are water beings who used to be pictured so often as living near springs; they work with the leafy part of the plants. The *sylphs* live in the airy-warmth element, and it is their task to bring the light down into the plants. Lastly, there are the *salamanders* or fire-beings who bring warmth to the blossoms and make possible the formation of a seed that is capable of reproducing the plant anew after the period it has spent within the earth—in the realm, once again, of the gnomes. The metals themselves are influenced, as also used to be known, not only by the gnomes who work with them but by the forces of the planets. The traditional lore that connected Mercury with quicksilver, Venus with copper, Moon with silver, Sun with gold, Mars with iron, Jupiter with tin, and Saturn with lead, is quite correct, and some interesting experiments have been made by anthroposophical scientists that reveal these connections.* Lastly, before coming to the relation of man himself to the cosmos, we may make mention of a fact referred to briefly earlier, that the earth itself is not truly inorganic; it is not a dead planet that is made living only because it can harbor life on its surface. The earth breathes, takes one breath every twenty-four hours, breathing in during the afternoon, and breathing out in the morning. This breathing in fact accounts for the rise of the sap in trees during the morning and the sinking back of the sap in the afternoon. The earth obeys also another annual rhythm, breathing out in the spring and breathing in again in the autumn. It is asleep as regards the external world in mid-winter, but is most awake in its interior at that time. The reverse holds good in midsummer. All these supersensible facts are of the greatest importance in anthroposophical (biodynamic) agriculture inaugurated by Rudolf Steiner, a subject that will be discussed later.

We now come to the position of man himself in the universe, and the unique role that he plays. We shall begin this section with the discussion of a series of striking cosmic rhythms connected with man, that can scarcely be simply a fortuitous coincidence.

When a human being breathes normally, he takes eighteen breaths every minute. He thus takes 1080 breaths in an hour, and 25,920 in a day. Now it is an astronomical fact, well known since the time of the Alexandrian astronomer, Hipparchus, that the equinoxes occur slightly earlier each year, so that the sun

---

* Many of these are to be found in the somewhat colloquial but suggestive book written by L. Kolisko on the basis of experiments carried out also by her late husband, Dr. Eugen Kolisko (who died before the book could be completed): *Agriculture of Tomorrow*; also in L. Kolisko's photographic accounts of the influence of the sun on gold and Jupiter on tin. Throughout the first named book are to be found accounts of numerous ingeniously contrived experiments to show the working of what we shall shortly discuss under the name of etheric formative forces, and of the influence of "unseen" forces in the cosmos on earthly matter.

rises a little earlier, for example, on March 21, the day of the spring equinox. It is not easy to calculate exactly how many years it would take for the sun to rise again at exactly the same moment as it did at the spring solstice of 1973. Astronomers customarily give the period of time as something over 25,800 years. Steiner gives it more exactly: 25,920 years. The ordinary life of man was given by the Hebrew psalmist as threescore years and ten. Steiner tells us that a man's karma has been lived out by the age of 70, and that any years that he may spend on earth beyond that age are to be regarded as given to him by the spiritual powers so that he may use them as a blessing for his fellowmen. At all events they are a heavenly gift; the ordinary life span is then over. Now if we calculate how many days a man has lived by the time he reaches his seventieth birthday, the figure is a little short of 25,920 but more than 25,000. Before he has passed his seventy-first birthday he will have reached this "magic" number.

We are thus given three extraordinary proportions: As a single breath is to a day, so is a day to an ordinary lifetime, and so is a year to a cosmic year, often called a Platonic year because Plato, from his mystery knowledge derived from Pythagoras, spoke in the *Timaeus* of a "perfect" year (*Timaeus* 39d). Each of these proportions is 1:25,920.* The first of these proportions relates man's breathing process, which is usually unconscious and is not with impunity to be disturbed, to the earth's daily movement around the sun; the second proportion discussed here relates the annual procession of the seasons to the actual movement of the sun through the zodiac; while the third relates the daily revolution of the earth to the normal lifetime of a man. On the other hand the normal pulsebeat of a man is propor-

---

* The simplest description of these proportions is to be found in Lecture 2 of a cycle given in Berlin in February, 1917 and published under the title *Cosmic and Human Metamorphoses*, while a far more detailed description appears in a cycle given in April and May, 1920 in Dornach called, *Man: Hieroglyph of the Universe*. Almost all of this last-named cycle bears on the subject under discussion here, but these particular proportions and the Platonic year are discussed in Lecture 4.

tional to his breathing as 4:1. This pulsebeat is not in any particular conformity to any cosmic rhythm, but it is an important sign of illness if this 4:1 proportion is not maintained. Man's blood circulation, which has no relation to the cosmic rhythm, has to be subordinated to the true cosmic rhythm observable in this breathing, and Steiner calls it a "primal healing process that is continually at work in man" that the breathing rhythm be maintained by all the means possible to us.*

Steiner tells us also of numerous other relationships between man and cosmos that will no doubt appear to the modern materialist, like so much that has already been said in this chapter, simply as unverifiable flights of the imagination, which, even if they were true, could be of no conceivable value to us. We shall hope to show in later chapters that this last statement is demonstrably untrue, since in fact these relationships underly not only biodynamic agriculture but also anthroposophical medicine and pharmacy. Curiously enough, some persons who are in all other respects materialists seem to accept some elements of astrology, and may even refer to themselves as born under certain zodiacal signs. They may even consult the popular press, which has not been slow to cater to this form of what, to the anthroposophist, is almost entirely outmoded superstition. There is some truth in astrology, and Rudolf Steiner did, indeed, give some indications as to how a true science of astrosophy could be founded. But this need not concern us here. What we

---

* Lecture 10 of the important cycle already discussed in this chapter, *Man as Symphony of the Creative Word*, given in Dornach, October–November, 1923. It is worth mentioning here that the system of yoga used from ancient times in the Orient and increasingly in the West of recent years, tries consciously to bring the breathing rhythms under human control and wrest them out of the cosmic rhythm to which they were originally attuned. There is no doubt that breathing exercises do have a great influence on the man who practices them, and for various reasons that we shall not enter into here the practice at one time was indeed justified in the East. In the West we are not equipped to deal with the results of such practices. We are intended to use our new-found consciousness and our will forces for other purposes, and it is well for us to be content with the cosmic rhythm incorporated into our breathing.

wish to do is to give one general example of the kind of information Steiner gave about man's relationship with the universe. It may be conceded that this information can never be verified by materialistic science, and it is difficult to suggest the kind of experiment that might be made for the purpose of verifying it. Nevertheless, if true, it may easily be imagined how valuable it might prove to be, especially in medicine, in an age when supersensible perception is taken seriously.

In the cycle just referred to called *Man as Hieroglyph of the Universe* (pp. 74–78), Steiner describes how man's *form* is moulded by forces residing in the fixed stars of the zodiac. This fact was known to the ancient peoples, who believed that each major part of the body is ruled by one or the other of the signs of the zodiac. *Internal motion,* that is, the circulation of the blood and other bodily liquids, is related to the movements of the planets. Those bodily *organs* that are formed by these internal motions, as, for example the heart, which is formed by the blood circulation, and the lungs, formed by the breathing, are also shaped by extraterrestrial forces, but not those of outer space. These organs are formed by forces that live in the atmosphere of the earth. Lastly, in our digestive processes we are entirely enclosed within the earth sphere, shut up, as it were, within ourselves. It is no accident that these least perfect elements of our bodily apparatus are the most subject to diseases, which from the digestive system react on the rest of our organism. It may well be possible for this knowledge to bear fruit in the practice of medicine, even in our own times.

To sum up, man is thus a part of a world in which everything is intimately connected with everything else. He has his position and his role, a role planned for him by higher beings. Over aeons of time higher beings have gradually made it possible for him to come into being in his present form, have conferred upon him the possibility of autonomous action, and made him in large measure responsible not only for his own personal survival but for the survival of the other beings that inhabit the earth and its atmosphere. Some of these beings, as for example the animals

290

and plants, are visible, while others are invisible to man's ordinary sense perceptions. Among these are the elemental beings, of whom a brief description has been given. Indeed, it should be regarded as quite exceptional for beings to be visible to our earthly eyes and audible to our earthly ears, and apparently uninhabited territories like the moon are not necessarily without invisible inhabitants. According to the science of spirit, we have a responsibility toward both kinds of helpers, the animals and plants that we can see and study, and the elemental beings that can be seen only after developing the necessary faculties. We draw attention to these responsibilities here before discussing the unseen *forces* in the natural world, since at the end of the chapter we shall try to outline a scientific morality based on spiritual science. Clearly, we do not have the same responsibility for inanimate forces as we do for beings, seen and unseen, even though the way we deal with these forces may be of the utmost importance to all these beings, including even the hierarchies above man.

The Etheric Formative Forces. The name given by Steiner to these hitherto unknown forces is etheric formative forces, and they are closely connected with what used to be called the "four elements." For reasons that it would take us too far to explain here, these forces are called the life ether (connected with earth); the chemical ether, working in the watery element; the light ether living in the air, and the warmth ether, living, as the name implies, in the element of warmth or fire.

In merely naming these etheric forces we have added nothing to the knowledge of the reader. Yet the scope of the subject is so vast that we do not feel it possible in this chapter to do much more than give a few indications as to the different fields in which the activity of these forces is to be discerned. Nothing in the realm of anthroposophical science has been as fully studied, and the many students of Rudolf Steiner who have devoted themselves to demonstrating the existence of these forces and the way in which their activity explains so many things in the natural world that have hitherto defied any really convincing explanation, have in most cases written books or articles that are easily available. Even one of the modern non-Euclidean geometries (projective or synthetic geometry) has been found, in accordance with Steiner's own suggestion, to be perfectly fitted for illuminating their action.*

We have several times alluded to the fact that all living creatures have etheric bodies. Steiner also sometimes referred to the etheric body as "the body of formative forces." The formative forces in question are those four forces of which we have just been speaking. They are not, strictly speaking, enclosed within the physical body; they act upon it from outside, unlike the physical forces known to science, which act on it from within. They endow it with life, with certain kinds of chemical reactions, including thinking, with form, and with warmth, and they bring all these forces from the planetary realms. For this reason they have been properly called the "architects" of the living, using physical matter as their construction material, and it is their task to organize it. As soon as they withdraw, the organism is dead, and delivered over to the forces of decay that belong to the physical world, and the form bestowed on the physical body by the formative forces is almost at once dissolved into chaos. As soon as a fertile seed or a fertilized egg is ready to begin the cycle again and produce a new organism, the formative forces begin to work again. Indeed, all the forces of the cosmos borne by these ethers unite to bring "order" into the chaos, which, as Steiner observed, always precedes the production of a new organism. It is the life ether which, of the four ethers, plays the crucial part in creating a living organism, but the other three regulate the growth, and model the form. Without the life ether there would be no new and complete organism, able to survive as a separate living entity. The chemical (or sound) ether, working, as we have said,

* See in particular G. Adams and O. Whicher, *The Plant between Sun and Earth* (1952) and O. Whicher, *Projective Geometry* (1972). These and the other major books and articles devoted to the etheric formative forces will be described in a special section of the reading list at the end of the chapter.

in the watery element (as do the beings we have called the undines) regulates the proportions between the different substances of the organism, essentially a chemical process. For this reason Steiner occasionally called this ether the ether of number. The light ether is primarily responsible for the *form* of an organism (as also for the forms of crystals). No organism can live without light in one form or another, even if it is in the form of electricity, which Steiner called "disintegrating light." It should, however, be recognized that the light ether is, like the other ethers, *invisible.* Light itself cannot be seen on earth apart from color, as will be recalled from the last chapter, where we quoted Goethe's correct saying that color comes into existence always as a mingling of light and darkness, or, as he also said, color is "the deeds and sufferings of the light." * If light is to become visible it must come into contact with something, and this something, as far as we are concerned on the earth, is the air, the atmosphere, which by contrast with the light, is dark. It goes without saying that it is the light ether that attracts the plants upward as does also the radiating warmth ether. It is also the light ether that produces the chlorophyll in the plant through the action of photosynthesis.

In a later chapter we shall be dealing with an important facet of these etheric formative forces because of its relevance to education—the strong influence of these forces on young children. Up to the age of seven the child makes more use of these forces than he will do at any later stage of life. The supreme achievement of the etheric body in the first seven years of a child is, paradoxical though it may sound, the creation of the second teeth, the hardest and most substantial part of his

---

* The passage is from Goethe's introduction to the 1810 edition of his *Theory of Color.* It is frequently quoted by Steiner, and Lehrs has a whole chapter in his book (Ch. 14) called "Colours as 'deeds and sufferings of light.'" Steiner's quotations naturally use Goethe's own words just as they were written; Lehrs' work as a translation gives the words as cited in the text. It is interesting (and symptomatic) to note that the latest edition in English of the *Theory of Color* translates the words in a totally abstract manner as "The colors are acts of light: its active and passive modifications" (Matthaei, *Goethe's Color Theory,* p. 71).

whole body. These teeth are expected to be permanent. If they are damaged they can be repaired from outside by a dentist, but they cannot regenerate themselves. Steiner tells us that the etheric forces hitherto used for building up the organism, and in particular for creating the second teeth, are set free as soon as the teeth appear, and are thereafter used for *thinking*. For this reason in Steiner schools the will activities, not intellectual activities, are stressed up to the age of seven, and reading, as far as possible, is not taught until after the appearance of the second teeth. The etheric body makes possible human thinking. We do not think with the brain, which merely *reflects* the thoughts of the etheric body; all that the brain does is therefore to make us *conscious* of our thinking. The brain, as was noted earlier, is fashioned in particular by the chemical ether, and its forms tend to follow those of water, which is the element of the chemical ether.* Thinking, as an *immaterial* activity cannot be dependent on any material organ. The etheric world itself is immaterial, and it is continually worked upon by the sun and the planets and the higher beings connected with them. When we mentioned earlier the exhaling of the earth during the daytime and in the summer, we were referring to the etheric forces that are breathed out then, as they are concentrated within the earth at night and in the winter.

Rudolf Steiner explains that the etheric world is not simply devoid of matter, and in this sense immaterial. It is filled with something that can only be called "negative matter." This concept is too difficult to be explained here, and the reader is referred in particular to the books by Adams and Lehrs in the reading list. Even if we do not try to explain it, however, we should mention that the teachings of homeopathy and the well-demonstrated effectiveness of homeopathy if used in favorable circumstances, are essentially based on this "negative material" aspect of the etheric formative forces. When a

---

* See in particular Theodor Schwenk, *Sensitive Chaos: The Creation of Flowing Forms in Water and Air*, pp. 95–96.

substance is diluted in a regular manner, for a time its effect as a medicament is weakened. But if one continues to dilute it in the same proportion it suddenly begins to become effective again, indeed more effective than before. The procedure is as follows. One takes a medicament, ordinarily used allopathically at full strength, and dilutes it with water in the proportion of nine parts of water to one of the substance. One then takes one part of this substance, and again dilutes it in the same proportion. By this time one has diluted it a hundred times. When one has repeated the procedure six times we have what would be called D 6, one part of the substance to 1,000,000 parts of water. This mixture may well not be effective either homeopathically or allopathically, but if we continue the diluting process we reach a point where, with most substances, the etheric forces begin to penetrate, while the physical forces become negligible. A medicament diluted thirty times, that is, D 30, is often extremely effective. The process, known as potentizing, is used in all true homeopathy, which tries to make use of the etheric rather than the physical forces. Even so there is a limit to the potentizing that is possible, and no further etheric forces can then be added. Indeed, after a certain point they too disappear.*

Lastly a process has been developed and is in regular use in anthroposophical clinics both in Switzerland and in Germany, under which the etheric formative forces can be shown in action in the crystallizing of various substances. All substances when

---

* The process is described briefly by Steiner in Lecture 11, pp. 145–7, of his *Spiritual Science and Medicine*, given in Dornach on March 31, 1920. Numerous experiments are described in L. Kolisko's *Agriculture of Tomorrow* and other works not translated into English. Experiments have been carried out regularly in the last fifty years, and published from time to time in scientific journals. The use of carefully calculated potencies lies at the basis of most anthroposophical therapy, since the main procedure of such new medical procedures is to stimulate the etheric body to heal the organism. By contrast Steiner described allopathic medicine as a kind of "borrowing," justified in certain cases when immediate help is needed, but which ought eventually to be paid back by increased spiritual work. All that allopathic medicine as a rule achieves is the suppression of the most obvious symptoms, making it possible thereafter for the organism to heal itself.

they are made to crystallize in a solution of copper chloride have their own specific form, the result of the etheric formative forces that are at work in the substance, whether it is the sap of a plant or human blood. In disease the typical form changes, thus making it possible to diagnose various diseases—by no means all—and even locate the part of the body in which the disease is centered. Again, on this subject there is a considerable literature, and though it requires considerable experience to be able to read the slides correctly, the technique is constantly being improved.*

The Threefold Nature of Man. Steiner surely regarded as his most important discovery in the realm of what we may call physiological psychology, the true nature of man as a threefold being. When he wrote while in his 40's his books, *Theosophy* and *Knowledge of the Higher Worlds and its Attainment* (both published in 1904), he described man as a being of body, soul and spirit, and spoke of his three non-physical activities as thinking, feeling and willing. The three higher faculties that may be brought into activity during his earthly life, but are not his natural endowments, Steiner called imagination, inspiration and intuition. But it was not until 1917 after, as he tells us, over thirty years of pondering over these threefold aspects of man, that he felt able at last to relate these aspects to the *bodily* nature of man. It was characteristic of Steiner that he should not have announced the discovery in a special lecture or cycle of lectures devoted to the subject—these he was to give three years later in his twenty lectures on *Spiritual Science and Medicine*—but in a

---

* See especially the books by Ehrenfried Pfeiffer in the reading list. Pfeiffer, at Steiner's suggestion, devoted himself for several years to the development of the sensitive crystallization process described above. L. Kolisko developed another process that she called capillary dynamolysis, which also demonstrated the activity of the etheric formative forces. The results of some of her experiments are described in the book already referred to, *Agriculture of Tomorrow*. It may be noted here also that a scientist working at Dornach in the 1930's, Paul Eugen Schiller, made some interesting experiments with flames to show the action of the chemical or sound ether, working through the human voice or such instruments as the violin. Although these experiments were not recorded in a book, several photographs by Schiller have been included in the English edition of Schwenk, *Sensitive Chaos* (Plates 61–70).

manner that was almost offhand, in a note on a sentence he had written many years earlier that he felt needed some elucidation. This precious "note" should not be missed by any student of Rudolf Steiner or any reader of this book, since never again was the essence of the matter presented in such a clear and succinct form.*

Man, according to this description, is a threefold being, consisting of the head or neural (also called head and senses) system located in the head, the respiratory or breathing system, located in the center of the body and mediating at all times between the two extremes, and the metabolic, or digestive and limb system. The neural system creates mental images (or representations), as is of course generally recognized, and contains the sense organs through which the outer world is perceived. What, by contrast, has never been recognized by scientists is that the feeling, or emotional processes of the human being, are intimately connected with the breathing system, and the willing process with the metabolic system. Indeed, the whole notion of willing is scarcely at all understood, even when its existence is recognized by scientists. To quote Steiner directly:

When something is represented [or to use an easier English equivalent, when one makes a "mental picture,"] a neural process takes place, on the basis of which the psyche becomes conscious of its representation; when something is "felt" a modification is effected in the breathing-rhythm, through which a feeling comes to life; and in the same way, when something is "willed," a metabolic process occurs that is the somatic foundation for what the psyche experiences as willing. It should be noted, however, that it is only in the first case (representation mediated by the nervous system) that the experience is a fully conscious, waking experience. What is mediated through the breathing rhythm (including in this category everything in the nature of feelings, affects, passions and the like)

---

* It appears in English as Section VII of a selection from Rudolf Steiner's book *Riddles of the Soul*. This selection was made by the translator Owen Barfield under the title, *The Case for Anthroposophy*, and Section VII appears in this edition under the title "Principles of Psychosomatic Physiology."

subsists in the normal consciousness with the force only of representations that are dreamed. Willing, with its metabolic accompaniment, is experienced in turn only with that third degree of consciousness, totally dulled, which also persists in sleep. . . . (pp. 71–2).

. . . All three forms of activity subsist, not alongside but *within* one another. They interpenetrate and enter each other. Metabolic activity is present at all points in the organism; it permeates both the rhythmic organs and the neural ones. But within the rhythmic it is *not* the somatic foundation of feeling, and within the neural it is *not* that of ideation. On the contrary, in both these fields it is the correlative of will-activity permeating rhythm and permeating the nerves respectively (p. 75).*

To complete the picture, the thinking, which, as we said earlier, is performed by the etheric body, is not only connected with the body through the system of nerves and senses (or, as we said earlier, "reflected" by the brain), but is also able when spiritually developed to reach upward to imagination; when the rhythmic system of the organism is spiritually developed it can receive inspirations (the same word as inbreathing), while the deeply hidden human will when spiritually developed can attain to intuition. Thus, all these various "threefoldnesses" are intimately connected with each other. Steiner was careful to explain that although the metabolic system provides the physiological basis for the will, this does not mean that the metabolic (digestive) system is more fully developed than the neural system. The reverse is the case. The neural system is the most highly developed (elsewhere Steiner tells us that the human head is a metamorphosis of the metabolic and limb system of the previous incarnation), and as a result it can sustain a highly complex and refined system of thinking, while, as he puts it, "the bodily processes associated with willing are only a feeble reflection of willing . . . Real willing takes its course in regions

---

* *The Case for Anthroposophy*, Section VII.

that are accessible only to intuitive vision; its somatic correlative has almost nothing to do with its content." *

In other lectures Steiner frequently draws attention to the fact that the process of consciousness is what he calls a "death process," by contrast with the activity of our limbs and digestive system in which the etheric body is extremely active; and whereas the etheric forces used in the early years of our life to build up our body later become available for thinking (and without which we could not think at all) ordinary thinking and indeed even sense perception have a deleterious effect on the organs of the upper pole of our organism. This is not something to be deplored, since in our age it is essential that we become ever more conscious. But as we become more conscious so do death and degenerating processes lay hold of us more strongly. The living thinking (or imaginative thinking) of which we have spoken earlier, however, does not have the same degenerating effect. It is in essence a "body-free" thinking and thus has a different effect on our organism than ordinary thinking and ordinary consciousness.

Throughout our life the effort should be made to establish as far as possible an equilibrium between what Steiner calls the

---

* A note might be added here on one more threefold relationship. Steiner explains in *Spiritual Science and Medicine* (pp. 77–80) and on numerous other occasions in the years following 1917 how from a certain point of view the plant may be regarded as like a human being upside down, with its "head" in the earth and its "metabolic limb system" up in the air. This fact, as we shall discuss in more detail in Chapter 13, must be taken into account not only in human and animal nutrition, but in medicine. The root system of the plant, the true root plants, should be used to nourish the head system of man, the stalk and leaf system nourish the rhythmic system of man, while the flower, fruit and seed nourish the human metabolic system. Each of our three "systems" should be properly nourished, and we should not unbalance our nutrition by consuming too exclusively from one section of the plant. All should, as far as possible, be kept in balance, though of course this is not done by feeding the same quantities from each part of the plant. Human and animal nutrition is discussed from this point of view in *Man as Symphony* . . . pp. 196–200, and in Lecture 2 and especially Lecture 8 of Steiner's agricultural course given in Koberwitz in 1924 (London: Biodynamic Farming and Gardening Association, 1972).

consciousness pole and the life pole—the nerve and senses system and the metabolic and limb system. In principle this equilibrium should be established or reestablished by the rhythmic system and its central organ, the heart. As he explains, the heart has a double action, situated as it is midway between the two poles. But his description, differing so markedly from the usual medical supposition that it is a kind of pump, is worth giving in his own words, thus bringing this brief section to an end until such time as we discuss anthroposophical medicine in a later chapter.

There is an interaction in the first place between the liquefied foodstuffs and the air absorbed into the organism by breathing. The process is intricate and worth attention. There is an interplay of forces, and each force before reaching the point of interplay accumulates in the heart. The heart originates as a "damming up" organ between the lower activities of the organism, the intake and working up of the food, and the upper activities, the lowest of which is the respiratory. A damming up organ is inserted and its action is therefore a product of the interplay between the liquefied foodstuffs and the air absorbed from outside. All that can be observed in the heart must be looked upon as an effect, not a cause, a mechanical cause, to begin with. . . . We need not stop short at the mechanical aspect if we consider the heart action as a result of these symbolic interpenetrating currents, the watery and the airy. For what is the heart after all? It is a sense organ, and even if its sensory function is not directly present in the consciousness, if its processes are subconscious, nevertheless it serves to enable the "upper" activities to feel and perceive the "lower." As you perceive external colours through your eyes, so do you perceive, simply and subconsciously through your heart, what goes on in the lower abdomen. The heart is an organ for inner perception. . . . The heart is primarily that organ whose perceptible motion expresses the equilibrium between the upper and lower processes; in relation to the soul (or perhaps more accurately in the subconscious) it is the perceptive organ that mediates between these two poles of the total human organization. . . . As long as you do not differentiate between these two poles, superior and inferior, and their mediator, the heart, you will not be

300

able to understand man, for there is a fundamental difference between the two groups of functional activity in man, according to whether they pertain to the upper or the lower polarity." *

The Seven-Year Stages in Human Development. Since we shall be dealing at some length in a later chapter with the ideas that lie behind the pedagogy developed by Rudolf Steiner, on the basis of which more than ninety schools are now in operation throughout the world, a little should be said here on the physiological basis of this pedagogy. Steiner often spoke about the important milestone in a child's development that occurs at the age of about three, the age at which for the first time he calls himself "I," and no longer speaks of himself in the third person. No one teaches him to say "I"; he suddenly starts doing it of his own accord, because it reflects a true inner process in himself. Steiner has also drawn attention to the fact that we cannot in our later lives remember anything that happened prior to this moment, or only rarely, and even then only in the case of a few exceptionally important memories. Up to this time the child should have learned three things quite unconsciously, though with the exercise of a great deal of will power. These three activities are learning to stand upright and walk, learning to speak in his native language, and, through the use of language, learning to think. In a sense, each of these activities arises out of the prior one. The next great step in his life is the freeing of his etheric body from the task that fully occupied it hitherto—the building up of his own organism. This freeing, as has already been mentioned, occurs with the pushing forth of the second teeth, which enables him to use his etheric body for other tasks. Up to this time the child has been especially developing his will forces, learning above all by imitation, and his education should have had little indeed to do with the development of his intellect. It is not impossible to teach a child to read even at the age of three, but such an act will call upon him to make use of etheric

* *Spiritual Science and Medicine* (1920), pp. 24–26.

301

forces that are not yet ready to be used for this purpose. As a result, the whole organism is likely to become prematurely aged and dried up, and it will be difficult to develop the soul and spiritual capacities, for which there is so dire a need in our present age.

From the age of seven onward the emotional life of a child begins to take shape. He is no longer so closely attached, physically, to his mother, and the unfeelingness toward other children and even animals that has so often been remarked among young children comes, or should come, gradually to an end. He now becomes capable of great affection, especially for his teachers, and for this reason in Steiner schools he should in principle be accompanied throughout the entire seven year period up to fourteen by the same teacher, with whom he should have established a firm basis of mutual understanding and affection. At the age of nine a further change takes place in the organism, as the "I" takes a further step forward in the process of incarnation, in preparation for the freeing of his astral body at puberty. This gradual deeper incarnation of the "I" should take several years. But, as the result of one-sided education, premature use of the intellectual faculties, various modern inventions such as television, and perhaps most important of all an unsuitable diet and inability to obtain proper nourishment (as the result of worn out soils and the heavy use of chemical fertilizers, as will be discussed in a later chapter), the astral body is often freed prematurely, and puberty takes place before the time from a physiological point of view most suited for it. Certain intellectual work in Steiner schools is not given to the pupils before the age of fourteen, even though puberty, which should, in principle, mark this age, has been premature. It is fully recognized that puberty is a soul-spiritual process as well as a physical one, and the astral body will not be fully freed in any event before the age of fourteen.

From the age of fourteen to twenty-one the adolescent is going through certain experiences that result from the freeing of the astral body; though it may appear that he already has, in

302

some cases, the power of judgment that accompanies the full freeing of the ego at twenty-one, it remains questionable whether the ego ever really takes possession of the organism fully before the age of twenty or twenty-one, usually nearer twenty-one than twenty. Steiner once pointed out how easily we can be deceived because young people of eighteen and nineteen have so many *opinions* to which they do not hesitate to give voice. When we look back from a more mature age to what happened to us at the age of twenty or twenty-one, so many of us find that after all something did happen to us then, which marked a great change in our attitude toward our own lives. Suddenly we took hold of them, and really felt that we had them in hand, and could come thereafter to real judgments of our own.

It would be possible to go through the changes that occur toward the end of every seven year period thereafter: the living through of the age of the sentient soul between twenty-one and twenty-eight, the intellectual soul between twenty-eight and thirty-five, the consciousness soul from thirty-five to forty-two, and even the ages that follow during which we receive the possibility of developing the three higher spiritual qualities, and we could show how the ages after thirty-five recapitulate the ages up to thirty-five in backward order. Even Steiner himself in the lectures given in 1924, after he had attained the age of sixty-three, spoke of new capacities that he had recently attained that enabled him to make a deeper penetration into certain realms of the spiritual world. All this, which was briefly touched upon in Chapter 4, would form part of a truly scientific psychology based on anthroposophy. But unless it were to be discussed at considerable length and with illustrations from life, its usefulness would be limited. By contrast, the considerations we have already put forward concerning the ages of childhood, seem to us to be fully justified even in a book of this present limited scope, in view of the contributions they make to the understanding of anthroposophical pedagogy.

Nature and Subnature—the Realm and Activity of Ahriman. There is one further subject that requires some elucidation

303

before we conclude this chapter with a discussion of scientific ethics in the light of anthroposophy, on which, indeed, it has considerable bearing. Man's intelligence, which is of cosmic origin, was always administered by spiritual beings until the fifteenth century when it was finally handed over to the control of man himself, so that at last he could become a fully free and responsible being, in charge of his own evolution and destiny. It was above all the bestowal of this gift by the gods on man that marks the new age that began at that time, which we have called the age of the consciousness soul. From this time onward men, who had not hitherto considered that thinking was a purely earthly capacity bound up with the human brain, but was, as Thomas Aquinas had held, an active spiritual principle, began to regard themselves as totally responsible for their own thoughts. Indeed, for the last few centuries there has been much speculation as to the manner in which the "brain" thinks, whether it "secretes thoughts as the liver secretes bile," as the eighteenth century philosopher and medical doctor, Pierre Cabanis, held, and the like.

Now Steiner explained on numerous occasions, and we stressed earlier in this chapter, that only "living thinking" is a true spiritual activity, and that in order to think in this manner man has to develop the capacity for it—which is not simply given to him, as are other capacities, in the ordinary course of his coming to physical maturity. The world as man perceives it was created indeed out of the highest wisdom, and everything in the ordinary world of natural phenomena remains permeated by this wisdom. But spiritual beings are no longer actively at work in it; the world, as Steiner expressed it,* consists of the embodied thoughts of high spiritual beings in the past; they are

---

* For all the contents of this section, the last work done by Steiner on earth, the letters written during his last illness and published under the title, *The Michael Mystery* have been used, especially Letters 4, 5, and 6, from which the quotations have been taken, and the last letter of all, No. 29, called "From Nature to Sub-Nature."

no longer living thoughts, but have to be given life by human beings.

Now, as we have seen especially in Chapter 4, since the Mystery of Golgotha Christ has united himself with the earth, which without his sacrifice would inevitably have belonged forever to the great enemy of mankind, Ahriman. But Ahriman was not thereby made powerless. On the contrary, he now disputes possession of the earth with the Christ, and insofar as man permeates his being with dead, intellectual, materialistic thoughts about the world of nature, so does he fall gradually into the power of Ahriman, and so does Ahriman himself continue to be the lord of the earth. In Steiner's words:

> The Ahrimanic beings are entirely capable of absorbing into themselves all the intelligence that is released from the divine beings. They are capable of uniting all intellectuality with their own being. Thus they become the greatest, most encompassing and penetrating intelligences of the cosmos. (Letter 5)

> They want the cosmic intellectuality absorbed by them to irradiate the whole new cosmos [i.e., a cosmos ruled by Ahriman] and man to live on in this intellectualized and Ahrimanized cosmos. In such a life man would lose the Christ. For he entered into the world with an intellectuality exactly like what once lived in the divine-spiritual, when this divine-spiritual in its essential *Being* still constituted the cosmos. If we speak today in such a way that our thoughts can also be those of the Christ, we oppose the Ahrimanic powers with something which protects us from succumbing to them. (Letter 6)

If therefore we understand or try to understand the world of nature by mechanistic thinking, and regard all the natural realms as devoid of spirit, we already fall prey to Ahriman. But below the world of nature, in which Christ and Ahriman struggle for man's soul and spirit, there is the world of sub-nature, which is the realm of Ahriman himself, into which the Christ does not penetrate. Steiner tells us that to work with this world is of great danger to man. If it is to be used by him, he must learn to understand it as such, and not confuse it with the world of nature that was in the beginning created by higher powers.

305

Subnature can be comprehended only when man rises in spiritual knowledge at least as far toward the extra-earthly, super-nature, as in technology he has descended into sub-nature. The age needs a knowledge extending *above* nature, because it must deal inwardly with a dangerous life-content, which has sunk down below nature. . . . There are still very few people today who feel that significant spiritual tasks are developing for man. Electricity which was hailed upon its discovery as the soul of the natural existence must be recognized in its *inherent* power to lead downward from nature to subnature. Only man must not slip down with it. . . . In a science of the spirit another sphere is now created in which no Ahrimanic element exists at all. And precisely by the understanding reception of this spirituality, to which the Ahrimanic powers have no access, is man strengthened to confront Ahriman in the world. (Letter 29)

It should be clear therefore that it is not a matter of indifference whether we make use of natural or sub-natural forces. However dangerous the former may be when misused by man, they come from a realm that is permeated by the Christ and in which higher beings are still at work. With the latter forces Ahriman hopes to win man's soul and spirit for himself and prevent him from attaining the goal willed for him by the higher beings. It is no accident that in the last centuries, and particularly in the present one, inventions from this realm have accumulated far beyond the ability of man to make good use of them and balance them with the necessary spiritual knowledge and activity. The materialistic scientist who specializes in the field of sub-nature will surely receive from Ahriman every kind of aid that is available to the "greatest, most encompassing and penetrating intelligences of the cosmos," and as he makes himself ever more receptive to the suggestions whispered to him from out the Ahrimanic realm, so will grow his worldly success and the esteem in which he is held (gifts of Lucifer who in this respect acts as a precious aid to Ahriman). While it seems clear that almost every invention from this realm has been and will continue to be used for purposes detrimental to the spiritual development of man, it is certainly true that the first use of so

306

many of them was made in warfare, beginning with the atomic bombs dropped on Hiroshima and Nagasaki, and continuing most recently with the intricate and horrifying weapons used to maim and kill, with the utmost precision and from a safe distance, in Vietnam (including what their inventors called, significantly, "smart bombs").

Science and Ethics. We have alluded in the last paragraph to some elements in spiritual science that lie completely outside the scope of the knowledge of ordinary scientists. Few will make any attempt to distinguish between nature and sub-nature, which will surely seem to them an unreal distinction, and probably the greater part of Western humanity has lost any real belief in evil. To most men evil is simply the absence of good, and even the good it is impossible to define with any precision. To them the very existence of such beings as Lucifer and Ahriman is a childish notion. It was all very well for primitive people such as the Hebrews to picture evil in an anthropomorphic form, and ecclesiastics naturally have a vested interest in threatening their congregations with threats of hellfire. It was also perfectly all right for poets like Milton and Goethe to introduce such beings as Lucifer and Mephistopheles into their works, but educated modern men and women cannot be expected to subscribe to any such beliefs. In short, what scientists say is likely to be given much more attention than anything that may appear in the Bible or be taught by clergymen. Nevertheless, spiritual science must assert the existence of such beings, as also of higher beings. The limitations of scientific knowledge both in this respect and in others, as discussed in this chapter, have had the consequence that it is now impossible for scientists to make any universally acceptable pronouncements on what is or is not ethically justifiable, even in relation to their own specialty. This is not because they lack good will, nor even because of their unwillingness or inability to devote much thought to questions of ethics and morality. Scientists such as the late Robert Oppenheimer were deeply concerned with ethical problems, in his case especially because he had some right to be thought of as the "father of the atomic bomb." The failure of scientists in this realm is simply due to their ignorance of too many crucial factors, an ignorance that is not going to be overcome by the acquisition of more knowledge of the same kind as they have acquired hitherto.

Let us take as an example the ecologist, surely among the most socially aware and the most vitally concerned of men of science of the present day. It is his business to take into consideration all the interrelationships in the world of nature, and there is no ecologist alive who is not appalled at the increasing pollution of the earth and the atmosphere, and its effects on all living things. He may point out that the balance of nature is disturbed by the use, say, of insecticides, and he can point to dozens of short term effects of their use, all of which he may think to be detrimental to agriculture in the area, and even to some long-term effects of equal or greater importance. But for the farmer whose crops are being destroyed by insects all these considerations are of lesser importance than the single crucial one that he *apparently* cannot make a living without using the insecticides. The agricultural scientist who examines closely the insect problem may come to the conclusion that the insects are multiplying so rapidly because they like to feed on diseased or weakened plants, and that the plants have been weakened by the farmers' efforts to obtain higher yields by applying too much commercial fertilizer. To this the farmer will reply that he was forced to use this fertilizer in order to have enough money to pay for his tractor and for the higher education of his children. Is he expected to return to "horse and buggy" days? The ecologist himself must recognize the fact that the population has been increasing, and higher yields or more extensive farming must provide the necessary increase in food. His advice may therefore be that of some distinguished ecologists of the present time— start a crash program for controlling population growth.

Now the science of spirit has indeed much to say on each of these problems, and biodynamic farming on an ever wider scale would surely have some good results. But the most important and surely the most fundamental contribution it can make is not the understanding of any particular problem, but the notion of man himself as a spiritual being among other spiritual beings who *does not have the right* to treat the earth and its non-human inhabitants as if he were really the lord of them all, responsible to no one but himself, with the right to make use of them all for his own well-being (as he understands it), his satisfaction and his enjoyment. At most some men think that they ought not to waste unnecessarily resources that should be bequeathed to posterity. But perhaps the majority even of these take comfort in the thought that human inventiveness will produce substitutes for what is wasted now, and that no damage inflicted in this generation will be irreversible—so clever is man at recovering from setbacks and so prolific and generous is nature at producing suitable mutants capable of surviving in the changed life conditions of the generations to come.

If once we accept and allow to work upon us the truth that we have a responsibility for our heritage and that *we ourselves* will be living again on the planet that we are now so rapidly destroying, then it will be possible for us at all times to have a different attitude toward the external world and everything that is in it. If we even try to exercise living imaginative thinking in relation to the natural world and approach it with our souls full of enthusiasm and warmth, then we can give positive aid to all the elemental beings who are also in need of what human beings can do for them—an aspect that we have not been able to touch upon in this brief chapter. To illustrate what can be done a beautiful passage from one of Steiner's lectures given in 1923 is worth quoting extensively:

One who simply grows up into our modern civilization observes the things of the outer world; he perceives them, forms abstract thoughts about them, possibly derives real pleasure from a lovely blossom or a majestic plant; and if he is at all imaginative he may even achieve an inner picture of these. Yet he remains completely unaware of his deeper relation to that world of which the plant, for example, is a

309

part. To talk incessantly about spirit, spirit, and again spirit is utterly inadequate for spiritual perception. Instead what is needed is that we should become conscious of our true spiritual relations to the things around us. When we observe a plant in the usual way, we do not in the least sense the presence of an elemental being dwelling in it, of something spiritual; we do not dream that every such plant harbors something that is not satisfied by having us look at it and form such abstract mental pictures as we commonly do of plants today. For in every plant there is concealed—under a spell, as it were—an elemental spiritual being; and really only he observes a plant in the right way who realises that this loveliness is the sheath of a spiritual being enchanted in it—a relatively insignificant being, to be sure, in the great scale of cosmic interrelationships, but still a being intimately related to man.

The human being is really so closely linked to the world that he cannot take a step in the realm of nature without coming under the intense influence exercised upon him by his intimate relations to the world. And when we see the lily in the field, growing from the seed to the blossom, we must vividly imagine, though not personified, that this lily is awaiting something. . . . While unfolding its leaves, but especially its blossom, this lily is really expecting something. It says to itself: Men will pass and look at me; and when a sufficient number of human eyes will have directed their gaze upon me—so speaks the spirit of the lily—I shall be disenchanted of my spell and I shall be able to start on my way into spiritual worlds. You will perhaps object that many lilies grow unseen by human eyes: yes, but for them conditions are different and such lilies find their release in a different way. For the decree that the spell of that particular lily shall be broken by human eyes comes about by the first human glance cast upon the lily. It is a relationship entered into between man and the lily when he first lets his gaze rest upon it. All about us are these elemental spirits begging us, in effect: Do not look at the flowers so abstractly, nor form such abstract mental pictures of them; let rather your heart and your Gemüt [defined as the mind warmed by a loving heart and stimulated by the soul's imaginative power] enter into what lives, as soul and spirit, in the flowers, for it is imploring you to break the spell. Human existence should really be a perpetual releasing of the elemental spirits lying enchanted in minerals, plants, and animals.

310

An idea such as this can readily be sensed in its abundant beauty; but precisely by grasping it in its right spiritual significance, we can also feel it in the light of the full responsibility we thereby incur toward the whole cosmos. In the present epoch of civilization—that of the development of freedom—man's attitude toward the flowers is a mere sipping at what he should really be drinking. He sips by forming concepts and ideas, whereas he should drink by uniting, through his Gemüt, with the elemental spirits of the things and beings that surround him . . . Mighty, manifold, and magnificent are indeed the spiritual effects that continually approach man out of the things of nature when he walks in it . . . The elemental spirituality of nature flows into him; it is something that constantly streams toward him as a supersensible spirituality poured out over outer nature, which is a mirror of the divine-spiritual.*

When we come to consider industrial civilization, the world subject to the control of modern scientific technology, there are in particular two questions we must ask ourselves and try to answer in the light of anthroposophy. The first is what is the actual effect on the human being of the various products of this technology, and secondly, how does their use favor or impede man's advance toward his proper goal. Materialistic science can certainly give some answers to the first question that would be quite acceptable to an anthroposophist. Tests, for example, can be made of the effects of street and airplane noises on householders and pedestrians, of television on viewers, of stereophonic music on its auditors, and the like. But even so, certain crucial items of knowledge will remain missing for lack of information about the etheric and astral bodies. The difference between electronically reproduced music, amplified through the use of sub-natural means, and true music played by a pianist, violinist, or orchestra that is taken over by the sound or chemical ether and conveyed directly to the human ear by the waves of the air, is not yet measurable by science, in part

* From Lecture 2 of a lecture cycle given in Vienna, September–October, 1923, entitled *Anthroposophy and the Human Gemüt* (New York, 1946), pp. 21–23.

because it has scarcely interested itself at all in the problem. The effect of sound on flames (see above page 296n) as photographed by P. E. Schiller can be demonstrated, and it would certainly be possible for science to detect the difference. But it would still be impossible for it to explain the difference and interpret it, without reference to knowledge derived from anthroposophy.

The second question, whether or not the use of a particular invention or product favors or impedes man's advance toward his proper goals, cannot be answered, as also in the case of the world of nature, without accepting certain truths about man. If, as is held by anthroposophists, it is essential that mankind should in this age make certain steps toward spiritual development, then it is obvious that the beings opposed to that development will make every effort to deflect us from that goal. A labor-saving device might aid or deflect us; in itself it is probably quite neutral. If we use wisely the time saved for us by it, then clearly it would help us toward our goal. No anthroposophist would wish us to return to the days when men and women were forced to work so hard and such long hours that all they could do at the end of the work was to sleep like a log until the next day when the work started again. The age of the consciousness soul, with all its technical and scientific advances, gave man the possibility of freeing himself—and all his fellow-men—from drudgery, giving him the time and the leisure to undertake spiritual development. But it also, through the intervention of those powers that wish to hinder man's development, gave men the possibility of creating new gadgets that would enable them to amuse and entertain themselves, to consume mightily, often at the expense of their fellowmen, and to hinder the development of political freedom by making it possible for numerous tyrants to wield enough power to keep their fellowmen in oppression. It is scarcely necessary to add that the use of technology has made possible the waging of wars on an unprecedented scale. That all these things have spiritual and karmic consequences that tend toward the continued deterioration of human society and the human race is not understood in detail for lack of the necessary spiritual knowledge, though many sensitive persons certainly recognize at least the spiritual deterioration. The consequences for the spiritual worlds of the First World War, which up to that time had been unequalled for the number of souls suddenly thrust unwillingly and unprepared into those worlds, and the consequences of these things for the living, were explained at some length by Rudolf Steiner in his postwar lectures. He clearly predicted the other wars of the century, but he did not live to speak also of *their* karmic consequences.

Enough has now been said to indicate what kind of a bearing spiritual scientific truths may have on ethics, and no more need be said here, especially in view of Steiner's teaching that all morality in the future must be individual, and that we have to reach our own individual ethic through our own free spiritual activity (see Chapter 3). In this respect all Steiner's other teachings should be regarded only as knowledge thrown on the subject to enable proper individual decisions to be made. Toward the end of World War I he himself recognized very fully indeed—as might well have been expected of him—the changes necessary in the social structures of the world in general and Europe in particular, if men were to have a new opportunity of pursuing their spiritual goals and avoiding for the future a war of the kind that was just ending. The so-called Threefold Commonwealth, to which he devoted so much of his activity in the years following 1917, and which he hoped might be brought into existence, at least in some parts of war-devastated Europe, is surely in 1981 further away than ever from realization. But the ruling ideas of this new social impulse, which Steiner explained had been drawn by him from the spiritual worlds as especially suited for the age of the consciousness soul, are by no means totally outdated, even though they have never, at least consciously, been put into operation fully anywhere. How these ideas can still be reinterpreted to fit our present age, and how some of them at least may still be put to use in our day, will be the theme of the next chapter.

On Goetheanism and "Living Thinking." Rudolf Steiner, *Goethe the Scientist* (New York, 1950) consists of the author's introductions to the different sections of Goethe's scientific work, which accompanied the Kürschner edition. The original publication date was 1883. In 1886 appeared Steiner's first original book on Goethe, *The Theory of Knowledge Based on Goethe's World Conception* (New York, 1965), which was greatly expanded in his 1897 book, *Goethe's Conception of the World* (London, 1928). In the interval had appeared a revised version of his doctoral thesis at the University of Rostock, which was called *Truth and Knowledge* and is printed in one of the editions of his major work on the subject which is discussed in Chapter 3 of this book, *The Philosophy of Spiritual Activity* (tr. Rita Stebbing, Nyack, N.Y.: Rudolf Steiner Publications, 1963). The same book, translated by Michael Wilson, and without the essay, *Truth and Knowledge*, appeared from Rudolf Steiner Press, London, in 1964 under the title, *The Philosophy of Freedom*. Earlier editions of the book carried the title, *The Philosophy of Spiritual Activity*, a title suggested by Steiner himself as suitable for England, the reasons for which should be clear from the preceding chapter, and the accompanying essay was called *Truth and Science*. Lastly, the student is referred to the difficult but extremely interesting account of how Steiner himself in early manhood slowly and gradually developed his ideas in such a way that he was at last able to formulate them in *The Philosophy of Freedom*. This account is to be found in Chapters 3 to 12 of his autobiography written in 1924, *Rudolf Steiner: An Autobiography* (Blauvelt, N.Y. Rudolf Steiner Publications, 1977).

In addition to Steiner's own work the excellent book of Ernst

Lehrs, *Man or Matter* (2nd edit., London: Faber and Faber, 1958) is extremely useful, being based throughout on the Goethean method. All the material is related to Goethe's own ideas more definitely than Steiner was able to do himself in his own much shorter works. Examples of Goetheanism as applied by Steiner in the last years of his life may be found, as indicated in the text, in his 12 lectures given in Dornach, June 25 to July 7, published under the title, *Curative Education* (London, 1972).

On man in relation to the world of animals the fundamental work by Steiner is *Man as Symphony of the Creative Word*, 12 lectures given in Dornach, October 19 to November 11, 1923 (2nd edit., London, 1970). The work on bees referred to in the text was given to workmen at the Goetheanum, Dornach, at intervals throughout 1923, and was last published under the title, *Nine Lectures on Bees* (Spring Valley: St. George Publ., 1975). Among the most valuable books on this subject written by a pupil of Rudolf Steiner are Hermann Poppelbaum, *Man and Animal: Their Essential Difference* (2nd edit., London 1960) and *A New Zoology* (Dornach: Philosophic-Anthroposophic Press, 1961). The second named work has an excellent account of evolution as it is viewed by anthroposophists, including a valuable series of sketches.

E. and L. Kolisko's work, *Agriculture of Tomorrow* (Edge, Stroud, Gloucestershire: Kolisko Archive, 1946) is a mine of fascinating material on the interrelationships between various planets, metals, and plants, as well as containing reports of the system of capillary dynamolysis used by L. Kolisko to estimate the value of various potencies. Part I of this book is concerned with the influence of the planets on plant growth, as are also three separate monographs by L. Kolisko (*Jupiter and Tin*, London, 1932, *The Moon and the Growth of Plants* (London, 1936), and a book of wider scope, *Gold and the Sun* (London, 1936), which is an account of experiments conducted in connection with the total eclipse of the sun June 19, 1936.

As mentioned in the text the February, 1917, lecture cycle

entitled, *Cosmic and Human Metamorphosis* (London, 1926), contains a brief account of the mathematical relations between man and the cosmos in Lecture 2, while a difficult cycle given in April and May, 1920 in Dornach called *Man: Hieroglyph of the Universe* (London, 1972), gives a more detailed account in Lecture 4. The lecture cycle as a whole, however, is not perhaps to be recommended until a good deal of anthroposophy has been thoroughly absorbed, for it is far from being a suitable cycle for beginners.

On the subject of the etheric formative forces it is difficult to suggest any particular lecture or series of lectures by Steiner himself. His references to these forces are scattered throughout his works, but on the whole they are best studied by means of the writings of those of his students who especially occupied themselves with them. The most important single study must surely be the early book by Guenther Wachsmuth, *The Etheric Formative Forces in Cosmos Earth and Man* (London, 1932), originally published in German in 1924. It is a comprehensive and beautifully illustrated book, but unfortunately it has been long out of print. Out of print for many years Ehrenfried Pfeiffer's book on these forces, *Sensitive Crystallization Processes*, which consisted almost entirely of photographs showing the action of the formative forces as they are to be perceived in the blood, was reprinted in 1975 by Anthroposophic Press. A more general account is to be found in Pfeiffer's *Formative Forces in Crystallization* (London, 1936). Lehrs' *Man or Matter,* already recommended earlier in this list, contains a clear account of the forces in general. More specific is Theodor Schwenk, *Sensitive Chaos* (London, 1965), a sumptuously illustrated work on "flowing forms in water and air," which throws much light on the etheric forces themselves. The geometry that demonstrates how these forces work is to be found especially in Olive Whicher's latest book, *Projective Geometry* (London, 1972), as well as in the earlier one written in conjunction with George Adams, *The Plant Between Sun and Earth* (Clent,

Worcs.: Goethean Science Foundation, 1952). As a short introduction to the subject, however, it is difficult to surpass George Adams' lecture called, "Potentisation and the Peripheral Forces of Nature," given to the British Homeopathic Congress on June 1, 1961, and published in that society's *Journal*, and also in the *Golden Blade* for 1966.

On the threefold nature of man the basic statement by Steiner, as mentioned in the text, is to be found in a selection from his *Riddles of the Soul* edited and translated by Owen Barfield under the title, *The Case for Anthroposophy* (London: 1970). Extremely useful on all phases of Steiner's medical teachings, including the potentization of the recommended medicaments is the series of twenty lectures entitled, *Spiritual Science and Medicine*, given in Dornach in March and April, 1920 (London, 1948), and *Four Lectures to Doctors* given during Medical Week in Stuttgart in October 1922 (London, 1928). Steiner's work written in 1924 in conjunction with Dr. Ita Wegman, and called *Fundamentals of Therapy* (London, 1970) is a more brief and general work, with a specially valuable first chapter on the etheric body. Lastly, Steiner's three lectures given at Arnhem, Holland, 17–24 July, 1924, under the title, *Spiritual Science and the Art of Healing* (London, 1950) is an invaluable little work, and represents Steiner's last words on the subject addressed to a general audience.

The classical account by Steiner himself of the various stages in the life of children was given long before there was any question of opening a school, and before any new pedagogical impulse had been given. This account, which formed the substance of many lectures given in various parts of Germany in 1909, has been published separately in English and given the title, *The Education of the Child in the Light of Anthroposophy*. All other books and lectures by Steiner and his followers on the subject of education will be included in the Reading List for Chapter 10, in which education is discussed in more detail. Steiner's systematic course on biodynamic farming was given to

317

a circle of farmers in Koberwitz, Silesia in July, 1924, and was, as noted in the text, never made available to the public until 1972, but was used only by farmers and gardeners themselves. There is now a large literature on the subject that will be dealt with later when biodynamic farming as a whole is given more detailed attention.

CHAPTER VIII

The Social Tasks of the Age
in the Light of Anthroposophy

When Rudolf Steiner was composing his fundamental work on individual spiritual development, first published in sections in 1904 and 1905 in his magazine, *Luzifer-Gnosis*, and later published in book form under the title, *Knowledge of the Higher Worlds and its Attainment* (New York, 1967), he was undoubtedly pondering the important question how the spiritually developing human being can take an active part in social life without betraying his personal ideals. No one knew better than Steiner that man is a social being, that he cannot be an exploiter of his fellowmen on weekdays and a practicing Christian on Sundays; yet present-day society is not so ordered that it is at all easy for men to practice their ideals in their working life, still less to be consistently altruistic in their social behavior. Yet, if it was true, as Steiner averred (*Knowledge of Higher Worlds*, p. 21), that "all knowledge pursued merely for the enrichment of personal learning and the accumulation of personal treasure, leads you away from the path; but all knowledge pursued for growth to ripeness within the process of human ennoblement and cosmic development, brings you a step forward," a similar social law must also exist as equally a matter of spiritual fact. That there is

319

indeed such a law Steiner was to make clear immediately after the publication of the last installment of *Knowledge of the Higher Worlds*, when in the next three issues of his magazine he wrote a series of three articles originally called, *Theosophy and the Social Question*, which when published later after the separation of the Anthroposophical Movement from the Theosophical Society naturally became *Anthroposophy and the Social Question.**

There is, Steiner tells us (p. 32) "a fundamental social law that Anthroposophy teaches us and that is as follows: In a community of human beings working together, the well-being of the community will be the greater, the less the individual claims for himself the proceeds of the work he has himself done; i.e., the more of these proceeds he makes over to his fellow workers, and the more his own requirements are satisfied, not out of his own work done, but out of the work done by the others."

Steiner then goes on to say:

It is a fundamental law which holds good for all social life with the same absoluteness and necessity as any law of nature within a particular field of natural causation. . . . This law only finds its living fitting expression in actual reality, when a community of human beings succeeds in creating institutions of such a kind that no one can ever claim the results of his own labor for himself, but that they all, to the last fraction, go wholly to the benefit of the community. And he, again, must himself be supported in return by the labors of his fellow men. The important point is, therefore, that working for one's fellow men, and the object of obtaining so much income, must be kept apart as two separate things.

The problem of the present day is how to introduce people into conditions under which each will, of his own inner, private, impulse, do the work of the community. No one, therefore, need try to discover a solution of the social question that shall hold good for all time, but simply to find the right form for his social thoughts and

---

* See the reading list at the end of the chapter. The word anthroposophy will be substituted everywhere for theosophy in quotations from this lecture, as in the English language edition.

320

actions, in view of the immediate needs of the times in which he is now living. Indeed, there is today no theoretic scheme which could be devised or carried into effect by any one person, which in itself could solve the social question. . . . There is only one thing that can be of any use, and that is a spiritual world conception, which, of its own self, through that which it has to offer, can make a living home in the thoughts, in the feelings, in the will. . . . It is true that in every man there slumbers a 'higher self' which can be awakened . . . But if one brings men together, without their having a world conception of this kind, then all that is good in such institutions will, sooner or later, turn to bad. With people who have no world conception centered in the spirit it is inevitable that just those institutions which promote men's material well-being will have the effect of also enhancing egoism, and therewith, little by little, will engender want, poverty, and suffering.

These articles are, for the most part, concerned with the famous nineteenth century efforts of Robert Owen to establish ideal small communities. What is important for us, at this point, is to recognize that as early as 1905 Rudolf Steiner was giving serious thought to the solution of social problems, and that from the beginning he rejected any form of government-imposed socialism. He had not, as yet, spoken or written of what during the years of World War I was to become the Threefold Social Impulse leading toward a new social order based on the threefold principle analogous to the threefold principle of the human organism discussed in the last chapter. It should be recognized from the outset that Steiner never at any time had the notion that such a social order as he envisaged could possibly be brought into existence by any governmental or parliamentary body. He was not interested in constitution-making, nor in fostering a "revolution" as a result of which a Threefold Social Order would come into being. What he was doing from 1917 onward was trying to describe for any who would listen the kind of social order demanded by the age of the consciousness soul, which must necessarily be in full accord with the fundamental social law that he had enunciated in 1905. His book, *The Threefold Commonwealth** was certainly in the hands of all the leading statesmen upon whose shoulders would fall the making of the peace; for several years after the war great efforts were made by many of Steiner's followers to make his ideas known, and even on a small scale, to put some of the ideas into practical effect. Steiner himself devoted a tremendous amount of effort to clarifying his social ideas both to public audiences and in numerous written studies. He did this because it is clear that he foresaw many of the disasters that would follow if there were no major changes in the social institutions of the world, and he felt it to be a spiritual duty to do his best to avert them. Nevertheless, it is difficult to see how in the circumstances of the end of the war, even with much more enlightened leadership than was available at the time, so many changes could have been made—or even started—that the full Threefold Order as Steiner envisaged it, would have eventually followed from them. Each element in it is closely related to every other element, as in any organic structure, and if any key elements had failed to yield to the will for change, the entire structure could hardly have failed to be unworkable. For example, one of the key elements in Steiner's economic thought was that no nation state should continue to direct or control its own "national" economy, but that the economic life should be free and independent and self-directing, as we shall see; its sole task should be the supplying of the needs of the other two "domains" of the Threefold Social Order. Indeed, there should be no "national" economies at all; all economic life should transcend national boundaries.

Obviously, at the beginning of 1919 no nation, old or new,

---

* The word "threefold" is in English a rather unsatisfactory and certainly not very enlightening translation of the German *Dreigliederung,* and we are not accustomed to speaking of our social structures as constituting in their totality a "social order." But the reader is urged to take these words in context as they will be used in this chapter, and if he wishes, to try to find better words for himself. Translators of Steiner's social writings into English have always disagreed on the best English equivalents, but it is hoped that the meaning will become clear from the context in which the words are used in this chapter.

possessed a government that would be ready to abandon its self-imposed task of trying to run a "national economy" for the benefit, in particular, of its own citizens. Nor could one expect national governments to be willing, even if able, to turn over the education of its citizens to educators alone. In 1919 the three "domains" of society, the spiritual or cultural domain, the governmental (or jural) domain concerned with the maintenance of human rights on a democratic basis, and the economic domain were everywhere inextricably intermingled. This has remained essentially true to our own time, now more than sixty years later. The emphasis has changed in some countries. The national states and their governments continue to feel themselves responsible for the success of their national economies and act accordingly; the same national states still largely control (or perhaps control more than ever) the kind of education given to their children and adults; the joint stock corporations may be larger and in some cases multinational in scope and occupied with many different and often unrelated products, but they are surely no less powerful than in 1919. The labor unions still bargain collectively for the wage increases granted to their members by the corporations, and now concern themselves also with fringe benefits and in some instances with working conditions. But labor is certainly just as much regarded as a commodity as it ever was, in spite of the many-pronged and eloquent attacks launched by Rudolf Steiner upon the very concept of labor as a commodity.

Yet such minor developments as have occurred, treated cumulatively, have suggested to some students of anthroposophy that the Western world is moving, however slowly, in the directions indicated by Steiner, and it is certainly a worthwhile occupation to try to trace the development of some of his social ideas to see how and to what extent they have been (unconsciously) put into operation. Such an attempt, concerned mainly with Great Britain, was made by R. J. Kirton in an article entitled, "The Threefold Commonwealth," that appeared in the book of centenary essays, edited by A. C. Harwood, that appeared under the title, *The Faithful Thinker* in 1961.* The reader is referred to this useful essay, but as far as the present chapter is concerned, it seems best not to try to duplicate this work even by extending the same kind of investigation to other countries than Great Britain. It seems more helpful to present the leading ideas of the Threefold Order here, primarily as *ideas,* which could be used now or in the future to help our society onward toward fulfilling its task in the age of the consciousness soul, offering occasional illustrations of how they are actually in practice being developed in one or another part of the world. In attempting this, it will be necessary also to point out in what conspicuous ways Steiner's warnings are being and have been disregarded; his warnings and predictions were also a part of his social thought. It was, for example, an essential part of his thought that the spiritual, cultural life of mankind must be free, and freely supported as a spiritual *and* economic necessity by the economic enterprises; in this the state should have no part whatever to play except to enforce equity. Yet in almost every country in the world the state is the actual provider of education, and "free" education, untramelled and uninfluenced by the state scarcely exists anywhere; where it exists it is at the disposition almost exclusively of the economically privileged. This condition of affairs is regarded as natural and, indeed, "democratic" and in all respects desirable, even by liberal thinkers. Yet the result is, to say the least, a partial stifling of the free spiritual cultural life, and an excessive devotion to conservative and established ideas. This is only one example of the consequences of the disregard of one of Steiner's basic social teachings.

Not all of his teachings about modern society, however, are to be found in his *Threefold Commonwealth* and related works of the period immediately following the war. In addition to these he gave a separate lecture cycle (unpublished in English) on

_____
* London: Hodder and Stoughton, 1961.

imperialism, and he constantly warned against the increase of nationalism, and the occult forces that were promoting it. In his last years when he spoke constantly of the working of the Christ impulse, and the task in world evolution that had been assumed by the Archangel Michael from 1879 onward when he undertook the tasks of the Spirit of the Age, he showed how in the age of Michael, nationalism must be transcended if humanity is to progress, even survive, through the rest of the fifth post-Atlantean epoch. It is not possible to give a clear idea of Steiner's social thought if these other elements found in his postwar lectures are not taken into consideration equally with the more specific social ideas from the years he spent in developing the movement known as the Threefold Commonwealth.

Nationalism as an Anti-Christian Impulse. It seems to me that one of the most important, if not the most important key to the essence of Steiner's social thought may be found in his oft-repeated criticisms of President Woodrow Wilson. In the years from 1917 to 1919 Wilson was widely regarded in Western Europe, even in Middle Europe, as the great prospective peacemaker, the one man who, like his own country, was not directly and selfishly concerned with the terms of the eventual peace settlement. Wilson had no material claims to put forward on behalf of the United States. He could afford to be altruistic, to stand above the quarreling statesmen of Western and Middle Europe because, alone among them, so it was thought, he was an idealist. It is true that Wilson favored a non-punitive peace, that he made himself the apostle of self-determination for all peoples. Above all, he it was who fought for the establishment of the League of Nations, whose task was to enforce the peace through "collective action," thus putting an end to wars in the future. The new states would all have democratic governments because, in Wilson's phrase, the world would have been "made safe for democracy," as the war itself had been "a war to end all wars."

American anthroposophists have often been embarrassed by Steiner's consistent and many-pronged attack on Wilson's thought and Wilson's ideals, sometimes even going so far as to wonder whether he did not possess some residue of Middle European patriotism, more especially since, if they have not followed Steiner's arguments carefully, they themselves have tended, like so many of their fellow countrymen, to admire Wilson's idealism, and to take him at his own valuation—a man who was constantly thwarted by self-seeking politicians, first in Europe and then in the United States, so that in the end he suffered a stroke and his country refused to enter the League of Nations. As a result, so they have tended to think, the League of Nations fell under the control of the European victors, and was used in their own interests, whereas if the United States had been a member, the Second World War might have been avoided. Perhaps the experience of the United Nations to which the United States has belonged from the beginning may have made them change their minds over the League. But the question still remains: How could Steiner be justified in criticizing Wilson so unmercifully as if he himself were responsible for the failure of the League?

Steiner's criticism was never directed, it need hardly be said, against Wilson as a man, but against his method of thinking, which in Steiner's view was the quintessence of abstraction. It was abstract and dead, "non-Goethean," and therefore quite incapable of seeing social realities in their living actuality. All his thinking was related to outdated norms and ideas thought by others before him—hence, what Steiner calls his "schoolmasterliness," his predilection for moralizing and preaching little sermons. He had not only never attempted the kind of free creative thinking and moral imagination discussed in Chapter 3, but he had utter self-confidence in his own kind of thinking. This would not have mattered if Wilson had not through his destiny been granted what amounted to leadership of the world in a crucially important moment of time when great changes might have been accomplished by a more receptive, indeed, a humbler, man. All the Peace Conference leaders, as we have noted, had received copies of Steiner's book *The Threefold*

326

Commonwealth, but if Wilson had ever read it, even glanced at it, he never showed any signs of having done so.

Now if positive action for the future were to be taken, certain spiritual realities would have had to be taken into account, which were naturally not made explicit in a book intended for political leaders and the public. One was the different soul configurations of the different peoples. Democracy, so dear to Wilson's heart and so prominent in his rhetoric, had been developed in the age of the consciousness soul by a people in whom the consciousness soul had already been so largely developed; only such peoples could really be expected to administer democratic constitutions without further ado. For an abstract thinker like Wilson democracy was good in itself, the democracies had proved able to defeat the more authoritarian powers in the war, hence if democracy were to be established on a European scale and the democratic powers were to join together to keep the peace, then peace would be assured. The principle that all peoples had an absolute right to self-determination, to independent nationhood, was surely unimpeachable in principle, even though in practice it has proved to lead to numerous new problems as the result of the ethnic multiplicity of almost all nations, new and old. Yet even this principle was criticized by Steiner as actually contrary to what was called for by the spiritual realities of the postwar epoch. What these spiritual realities were, calls for some discussion, even though the matter cannot be entered into in any great detail here.

Reference has already been made to the truth that nationalism must be transcended if humanity is to move forward. To explain this statement it should be recognized that each nation is guided by a real spiritual being of the rank of an archangel, and that the world as a whole is guided in its evolution by a spiritual being of the hierarchy above that of the archangels, the archai, or spirits of personality. The folk spirits who are often spoken of are therefore real beings, as is the Time Spirit, or Zeitgeist. The Time Spirit is in fact promoted from the ranks of the archangels

327

when he has to guide evolution in a particular epoch, and each such Spirit has a particular mission to fulfill in his epoch. From the sixteenth to nearly the end of the nineteenth century Gabriel was the Time Spirit, thus guiding mankind during the earlier centuries of the consciousness soul. He it was who undertook to lead mankind into materialism in the positive sense of that word. As has been explained in several places already in this book, man had to lose his atavistic clairvoyance altogether, and to cease to be able to see at all into the spiritual world. As long as he could perceive spiritual beings, he was unable to *disbelieve* in them, and the possibility of such disbelief was an essential part of man's freedom—in the same way as it was now within his power to deny the reality of the Christ impulse. It was also a part of Gabriel's task to divide the leading peoples of mankind into nations, and to foster the patriotism of their inhabitants.

In 1879, however, Gabriel gave place to the Archangel Michael as Time Spirit, and Michael's task was a different one. He has a special relationship with the Christ and it is now his task to help man to recognize the Christ impulse, bringing men toward a personal free relationship with the living Christ as he is now, in the etheric world, as described in Chapter 5. This is a quite different kind of relationship from that obtaining during the age of the intellectual soul, when men approached Christ and Christianity through an organized Church. It is an essential part of Michael's task to bring men together as individuals, so that they recognize their common humanity and the Christ who lives within each human being. Therefore, from the moment when Michael assumed the leadership of the age, the principle of nationality ceased to be in accord with the spirit of the time. As will be readily understood, however, from that moment onward it became the task of the hindering forces, Luciferic and Ahrimanic, to foster the spirit of nationality, and turn what had been patriotism and a normal feeling of unity with one's fellow countrymen into the evil that we call nationalism. As Steiner clearly explains in a passage that should be studied in detail,* in

---

* Lecture entitled, "Specters of the Old Testament in the Nationalism of the

a lecture cycle given just at the end of the war, the demand for the establishment of new nations based on folk cultures is a retarded Ahrimanic demand, whereas what the Christ impulse calls for is something altogether different, on which Steiner's words are worth quoting in full.

The cultivation of the social life, which in earlier times had its source only in the bonds of blood, does not depend so much upon any sort of socialistic programs, but upon man's becoming a spiritual-social being. But he will become such a being by awakening within himself . . . the deeper forces which can bring to birth within him the capacity for perceiving pictorially the other human being. . . . When we form a picture of our fellow man we enrich our own soul-life, then do we bestow a treasure upon our own inner soul life with each human acquaintanceship. . . . We gain the capacity to have other human beings live in us. But this must be acquired; this is not something born within us. And if we should continue simply to cultivate those characteristics which are born in us, we should continue within the limits of a mere blood culture, not the culture to which could be ascribed in the true sense of the word human brotherhood. For only when we carry the other human being within ourselves can we really speak of human brotherhood, which has appeared thus far only in an abstract word. When we form a picture of the other person, which is implanted as a treasure within our soul, then we carry within the realm of our soul life something from him just as in the case of a bodily brother we carry something through the common blood. This elective affinity as the basis of the social life must take the place in this concrete way of the mere blood affinity. This is something which must really evolve. It must depend upon the human will to determine how brotherhood shall be awakened among men.

Human beings have hitherto been separated. They ought to become socialized in brotherhood. In order that the manifoldness shall not be lost, that which is the innermost element in man, the thought, must be able to take form individually in every single person. With

Present," given in Dornach on December 7, 1918, and printed in a cycle called, *In the Changed Conditions of the Times*, pp. 98–99.

329

Jahve [i.e., in Old Testament times] the whole folk [i.e., the people of Israel] stood in a relationship. With Christ each individual person must stand in relationship. But the fact that brotherhood will thus awaken requires that there shall be a compensation in an entirely different field—that is, through freedom of thought.

This last sentence is the key to one element of the threefold order, the insistence on what Steiner calls the free spiritual life of thought. In the new community of the future the inviolable self, the "I" will remain inviolable in its activity, that of thought, even while the human "I" seeks to come to a new brotherhood with other human beings through "implanting a picture of the other person as a treasure in our soul," or acquiring a true sense of the other person. In our present age the young people in particular, as might have been expected, have a kind of intuitive feeling for this new kind of human brotherhood. But they do not realize the kind of society that would make possible this brotherhood, and they look for it in ways that belong to the past, not the future. The motto "liberty, equality and fraternity" that was brought to expression in the French Revolution has never been understood. It arose out of man's unconscious at the end of the eighteenth century as an advance picture of what was indeed to be sought during the age of the consciousness soul. Its true meaning was revealed by Rudolf Steiner when he explained that each of the three ideals is the aim of one of the three domains in the Social Order: liberty in the cultural spiritual life, that is freedom of thought; equality in the life of rights, in which every man has the same rights as every other, and fraternity in the economic life, in which human economic and material needs are satisfied through a free exchange of goods throughout the world, unimpeded by national boundaries, or other hindrances.

What was wrong, therefore, with Woodrow Wilson's thinking was that it was far too conventional. Not only was he ignorant of spiritual realities, for which he might be forgiven, but on the basis of his limited understanding he had the presumption to try to dictate the future of Europe and the world simply by putting

330

on display again a series of abstract outdated ideas that had in the age of the consciousness soul already become Ahrimanic, and thus destructive; behind these ideas he placed the power and prestige of his country, by this time the most powerful in the world. The notion of self-determination for all peoples is not only impossible to put into practice, as was quickly discovered, but the failure to solve the problem of minorities under the new national regimes played an important role in bringing on World War II. Yet the idea seemed, and still seems to many, a good one that was made to fail between the two wars merely because it was put into effect unwisely. According to Steiner, nations should not as such disappear in the future, but their role becomes much more limited; if it is so limited, it cannot give birth to or foster the growth of nationalism. The Michaelic, Christian, principle of universalism, the overcoming of the bonds of the blood, is *required,* according to Steiner, in our age and in the future. The means by which we move toward it is above all through the recognition of the three domains of the social order—an idea that Wilson could perhaps have sponsored if he had not been so infatuated with his own abstractions. A description of these three domains will therefore constitute the next phase of our discussion.

The Three Domains of the Body Social. We have alluded in the last chapter to Steiner's fundamental insight into the nature of the human organism, that it is composed of three separate "systems" that interpenetrate each other: the nerves and senses system centered in the head, the rhythmic system centered in the heart, and the metabolic and limb system centered in the lower part of man's organism. In introducing his readers to the "threefold" (or three "membered," three domained, three dimensional—the German word, *Dreigliederung,* as we have noted, does not have any obvious and comprehensible English equivalent) nature of the social order in Chapter 2 of *The Threefold Commonwealth,** Steiner began by referring again to this three-

---

* References will be to the translation of this work by E. Bowen-Wedgwood, published by the Macmillan Co., New York, 1922.

fold nature of man himself. But he also made it clear that he was not simply offering a glib analogy, as is done, almost unconsciously, when one speaks of the social "organism," or the "body" social. What he did here was to tell his readers that they would find it helpful to perceive once more how the three bodily "systems" do indeed interpenetrate each other, and then observe the social order with the awakened insight one will have thus gained. In other words, we are back again with the necessity of trying to develop living, imaginative, Goethean thinking as the only capacity able to perceive the social order as a living functioning entity. "The present crisis in the history of mankind," Steiner tells us, "demands the development of certain faculties of apprehension . . . just as each individual has long been required to have a certain measure of education. From now on it is necessary that the individual should be trained to have a healthy sense of how the forces of the body social must work in order for it to live." *

We are therefore warned that we have to do here with an "organism" that cannot be grasped by abstract thinking, only by the kind of thinking appropriate to the living. But at the same time we must not start talking about cells, connective tissue and the like, any more than we should talk about the social order as a mechanism, as is more likely to be done today. What "living" thinking should perceive is the three interpenetrating domains of the cultural or spiritual life, the political realm, the region where human rights should prevail (the realm of equality, as noted earlier), and the economic life. There is a definite analogy to be made here with the nerves and senses system, in which thinking is active; the rhythmic system, which mediates between the upper and lower parts of the body and keeps them both in equilibrium, and the digestive system, which is concerned with the consumption of foodstuffs, their transformation, and their conversion into energy used by the entire human body, a function not unlike that of the economic system in the social order.

---

* *Threefold Commonwealth*, pp. 52–53.

The sickness of the social order, visible enough at the end of World War I and now, in almost all respects, in a far more advanced state of degeneration, is, in Steiner's view, the result of our failure to keep the three realms separate. It is scarcely necessary to elaborate here on the way in which the state or political order (usually called by Steiner by the somewhat awkward term [in English] of the "rights-body") has imposed its authority over the cultural and educational life of every country in a greater or lesser degree; how the economic realm has in the capitalistic countries of the West exercised a dominating influence over both government and culture, while conversely in the socialistic and communistic nations it is the political state that has tried to bend the economic realm to its will. If the cultural-spiritual realm does not exercise an influence over the other realms comparable to that exercised by the Church in the Middle Ages or by the Puritans in more recent centuries, this does not mean that this realm cannot still exercise some tyranny of its own where conditions are suitable. The role played by ideologies such as "Marxism-Leninism," or the thoughts of Mao, to say nothing of some scientific and pseudo-scientific dogmas in the West, should not be underestimated. Such ideas have influenced both the political and economic realms in a manner far different from that envisaged as healthy by Rudolf Steiner, who looked toward a future in which the cultural-spiritual life would be constantly fructifying the other realms with socially beneficent ideas, freely imagined by human beings whose creative capacities would have been newly freed and awakened, once the tyranny of having to think and invent to order (and for economic gain) would have become a thing of the past.

What is important for us today, I believe, is to try to grasp the two fundamental insights of Steiner as given above: that the social order has its three interacting domains, which should be seen to be separate even though every man has his part to play in all three, and that the sickness of our social order is the result of the improper influence exercised by one domain on another.

To these should be added a third, that the individual unit member of the spiritual cultural domain is the single individual person, whose freedom constitutes his essential attribute; the unit member of the rights domain need not necessarily be the state or nation as presently constituted, but could in principle consist of quite a small number of men and women who accept the equality of every member in it and guarantee each other's rights. By contrast there is no natural limit to the size of the economic realm. It is not even inter*national* in scope, but world-wide. In principle, and mostly today in actual practice, material goods flow over the borders of one nation into another. *Any* damming up of this flow, whether by means of differential exchange rates, tariffs, export subsidies or taxes, constitutes a hindrance to the exchange of goods that ought to be free.

By a curious reversal of what most of us are accustomed to thinking, it should be seen that *competition* is the lifeblood of the cultural life, whereas *cooperation* is the lifeblood of the economic life. Any man who has a good idea has the right to test it against other ideas, and it will make its way in this "market-place" only in competition with the thoughts of other freely thinking beings. If it survives in this "struggle for existence" it clearly has some merit, and it would be extremely damaging for mankind as a whole if any obstacle (as scientists have so often reminded us) were improperly placed in its way by, say, the political order through censorship, or the economic order through its insistence that the idea should be financially profitable to some privileged group which might be allowed to exploit it for its own gain. Similarly, it is an obvious fact of the economic realm that the production of all material goods requires cooperation among human beings, and that the so-called division of labor means that each person in the manufacturing process does the task for which he is best fitted. There should be no competition here, since it should not be a matter of opinion but of objective recognition who is the best fitted to perform a particular task. Such competition as there may be here derives, indeed, from the

334

cultural-spiritual realm and is not an essential element of the economic realm itself. In principle each task to be performed has an equal importance for the whole; the managing director will have nothing to direct if there is no assembly line worker to follow his direction.

The question of how each should be remunerated for his work should be decided by the "rights-body" of the enterprise, not on the basis of the greater power exercised by the director nor on the relative scarcity or abundance of the different kinds of talent available to it. Likewise, there should in principle be no need for competition among the various enterprises. The objectively best manufactured object should be the one that is produced, not the one that is advertised most effectively or cuts the most corners and costs in manufacturing. In principle there is no need to manufacture an inferior article, if effective use is to be made of the world's not unlimited natural resources. The consumers themselves should be the persons to judge which articles are most worthy of being manufactured. It is obviously ridiculous, when one comes to think of it, that the manufacturers should make all the decisions (with or without the benefit of market research), proceed with the manufacture, and then have to spend large sums of money in persuading the public that their product should be bought in preference to others.

The Economic Realm. It is for this reason that Steiner proposed that in the economic realm the unit enterprise should be an Association of producers, distributors and consumers who would cooperate with each other, as we have pointed out earlier, in a spirit of fraternity for the good of society as a whole:

> The economic process can only be sound when a wise *self-active Intelligence* is working in it. This can only happen if human beings are united together—human beings who have the economic process within them as pictures, piece by piece; being united in the Associations, they complement and correct one another so that the right circulation can take place in the whole economic process. . . . Something else must be contained in the Associations, and *will* be

335

contained in them once the necessity of such Associations is recognized. There must be in them the *community-spirit*—the sense of community, the sense for the economic process as a whole.*

To complete the functioning of the Associations, an *autonomous* Council should be at their head in which all the separate Associations are represented.

The heart of this proposal for the economic realm is the *autonomous* nature of the economic life and its limited functions, that is, the production, distribution and consumption of commodities. Everyone in society takes part in the economic life, if only as consumer, but neither of the other two realms must *interfere* with the *functioning* of the economic realm. This does not mean that they must leave it severely alone, that they are unconcerned in it. On the contrary the economic realm should be constantly stimulated and fertilized by *ideas*, thoughts that enter it from the cultural-spiritual realm, while the "rights-body," concerned with human equality and especially equality of opportunity and the prevention of discrimination, will have the task of establishing and imposing standards of behavior in the economic realm, including, most certainly, the imposition of a minimum wage, which is an essential element in human dignity.

It is naturally the task of the Associations in the economic realm to provide the workers in the other realms with their sustenance, since the latter do not themselves produce material goods. Steiner has offered some extremely stimulating notions about the role of money, and the different kinds of capital, the details of which lie beyond the scope of this book. It was his thought that money, in itself not a reality but only a medium of exchange, would have to be prevented from accumulating, as it does in the present economic system, in land, pushing up its price accordingly and providing speculators with untold amounts of totally unearned income. Land, Steiner insisted, is

---

* Lecture given in Dornach, August 2, 1922, the tenth lecture of the cycle called, *World Economy*, pp. 206–207.

not in fact *property* at all. What we pay for in land is the right to use, and the right to dispose of the right to use to someone else. Henry George, who wrote about this problem decades before Steiner (*Progress and Poverty, 1879*), wished the state to tax the increase in land values, and tried to show (as his followers still do today) how a single more or less painless land tax would spare governments the necessity of imposing any other taxes. Steiner proposed a money based on some real commodity (such as wheat), which in time would be consumed, thereby automatically extinguishing at the same time the money based upon it. (Such a distinguished economist as the former French prime minister, Pierre Mendès-France, has proposed something not dissimilar in recent times.) Whatever the basis for the issuing of money, Steiner held that the moment in which it becomes most productive is in the last stage of circulation, when the capital has been used to produce goods that have now been sold and produced a surplus (which under the present system would be called profits, and used either for expanding production, payment of state taxes, the establishing of reserves or distribution in the form of dividends). It is at this moment that Steiner proposed that it should do none of these things, but should pass over to the spiritual-cultural body in the form of "gift money." It would then be used by the autonomous spiritual-cultural organization to support education and every kind of cultural activity. The indirect fruits of this gift-money would, in his view, be many times greater for the whole society than it would be if, for example, it were merely used to produce more material goods.

Before passing on to the other realms, it should be noted that Steiner used to repeat in many different contexts his fundamental observation that labor must in no circumstances be regarded as a commodity. If it is not a commodity, then it does not fall into the economic domain but into the domain of "rights," as we shall see. Men should not buy and sell their labor as if it were in any way the equivalent of the goods they consume and produce. Money is to be exchanged for the goods produced by human

337

labor, but only these goods, not the human beings who make them, are to be regarded as falling within the economic domain. From which it follows that the "rights-body" must determine the money to be paid for different kinds of labor, on the basis of needs and abilities, or at all events on some basis compatible with human dignity.

So long as the economic system has the regulating of labor power, it will go on consuming labor power just as it consumes commodities —in the manner that is the most useful to its purpose. . . . The *labor* question cannot find place in its true shape as part of the *social* question, until it is recognized that the considerations of economic life which determine the laws governing the circulation, exchange, and consumption of commodities, are not such whose competence should be extended to human labor-power. New age thought has not learned to distinguish the totally different fashions in which the two things enter into economic life: i.e. on the one hand labor-power, which is intimately bound up with the human being himself; and on the other hand those things that proceed from another source and are dissociated from the human being, and which circulate along those paths that all commodities must take from their production to their consumption.*

It may surely be conceded at once that Steiner was here putting his finger on what is still the heart of what we think of as the major problem of labor—how it is to be remunerated in such a way that human labor is not regarded as a cost of production like the raw materials that enter into its manufacture. It is only fair to recognize that Steiner himself was fully aware of the workers' viewpoint in his own time, having constantly lectured since before the turn of the century at workers' institutes, and continued to discuss their problems with them even while they were building the Goetheanum. He showed himself at all times receptive to their grievances and was able to meet them on a

---

* *Threefold Commonwealth*, pp. 43–44.

man to man basis rare in contacts between "intellectuals" and the working class. He was, of course, well aware of the fact that since the Industrial Revolution the links between the worker and the product, the making of which so often occupies his whole life, were no longer what they had been in earlier times, but were now likely to be simply the tending of a machine that made only a small fraction of the finished product. Moreover, the relationship with his employer was likely to be little beyond the receiving from him of a weekly paypacket. In the preceding feudal system relationships between lords of the manor and their serfs, and in the guild system between masters and apprentices were entirely different from those obtaining in the industrial system. Even in the small scale factories of the early modern period the owner-employer was usually familiar with the lives of his employees, and there was a mutual respect between him and his often independently minded skilled workers who were still scarce in numbers and could easily take their skills elsewhere if dissatisfied.

But, especially in the twentieth century with the coming of the assembly-line, the workers themselves have tended to become, in effect, interchangeable parts, like the parts of the finished product that they spend so much of their lives assembling. Since Steiner's time the problems have become, if anything, more acute, although few sociologists today would diagnose them in just the same terms used by him, namely, that human labor is treated as if it were a commodity. Yet the description remains entirely accurate, and it was expressed in that manner by Steiner because he wished to draw attention to the fact that there are two separate problems involved, and they do not both belong to the same domain of the social order. The first problem is how to produce economic goods as efficiently as possible with a minimum of wastefulness; the second is how to remunerate the workers. The first is an economic problem, the second is a question of human rights, and therefore does not belong to the economic domain at all, but rather to the "jural" or "rights" life, which is administered by the democratically elected "jural" or "rights-body." *

Now it is not self-evident just how human labor can cease to be a commodity, nor how its remuneration can be decided upon by the "rights-body" in such a way as to be both equitable and in accord with human dignity. In different parts of his work Steiner makes different suggestions, which are not so much practical proposals as they are stimulants to further thought on the matter—and as such are still of value today. On page 114 of his *Threefold Commonwealth* he tells us that there should be "a really free contractual relation between the work-director and the work-doer—a relation not resting on barter of commodities (or money) for labor-power, but on an agreement as to the share due to each of the two joint authors of the commodity." Shortly afterward in the same book he remarks that a man with family responsibilities ought in equity to receive more than a single worker. On page 173 he looks toward "the elimination of the wage relation altogether—the adoption of a share-relation, based on contract in respect to the common work performed by the work director and the workers." When Marx used the slogan "from each according to his ability, to each according to his means," he too was concerned with the same problem, but he left the crucial question what is a man's need unanswered—and it must be admitted that the entire problem is one of the most difficult that still faces all social thinkers today. But it seems to me that Steiner's concept of the three separate domains of society does give us some clues as to how the problem might be solved.

Perhaps the most important single observation he made on this subject, and one of the most potentially fruitful, was that the question of what share of the total economic product should fall to each human being in a society should not be decided by the simple working of economic laws, which will inevitably lead to inequities of every kind. The question should therefore be

---

* The old word "jural," though rarely used today might well be substituted for the usual word "rights—" which is after all not an English word at all when associated as an adjective with body.

decided on the basis of equity, of what is fair, by the only body in society that is elected by universal suffrage, the "rights-body" or state government. But obviously such a government could not hand down an equitable decision unless it were totally free from pressures, either by the experts or technocrats who may be supposed to form part of the cultural spiritual life, or by the directors and managers of industry. Nor would the decision be either equitable or enforceable if the elected government were dominated by the manual workers or the bourgeoisie or any other class in society that placed its class interest first. Unless the government really did make a serious effort to place the needs of the whole society above those of any particular sector or any individual or group of individuals, its arbitration would never be acceptable. How does one find such impartial arbitrators?

A part of the answer is to be found in the recognition that the threefold order is a whole, and that no one in the society belongs exclusively to just one of its three domains. Everyone belongs to all three, but everyone's economic needs are supplied by the economic associations because this happens to be their function. The enormous needs of those who are not members of the economic associations have to be met by them, the needs of the government members themselves, of the young, the old, the professors and doctors, the artists. As the task of the economic associations is limited, so also are the tasks of the government or "rights-body." It has the limited task of administering the police and the armed forces, maintaining order in the state, and arbitrating but virtually nothing else, because in no other field should the principle of equality prevail, and in no other fields are democratic principles truly applicable.*

---

* The government will see to it that there are courts, but Steiner was insistent that the administration of justice itself was a function of the spiritual cultural organization. The treatment to be accorded to such anti-social elements as might remain in a society based on the Threefold Order, in which at least crimes against property will become rare, would become the concern of the spiritual cultural domain some of whose members would wish to devote themselves to deciding how best to deal with persons now regarded as "criminals." As for the "criminal" himself, he should have the right freely to choose his judge.

341

In principle it ought to be possible for each man to choose freely in which of the three realms he wishes to spend his working life, or the greater part of it. But, as a practical matter, it will surely be impossible to expect that such a free choice will ever be granted by society as long as the amount of money a man receives is closely tied to the kind of work he does, that is to say, as long as labor even in some slight measure is regarded as a commodity, in other words as long as money is regarded as *earned,* a reward for work. A part of this problem, however, is solved if the possession of enough money to satisfy one's basic needs is regarded as a *right,* something to which everyone is entitled, the amount of which can reasonably be legislated by the "rights-body." Such a minimum wage has been legislated by perhaps the majority of industrial countries and by some others, but it is seldom if ever enough to satisfy even the most basic of needs, even when supplemented by family allowances. The major objection to the minimum wage in practice in our present social order is that it has tended to become the maximum wage in far too many industries, and no fundamental change in society is achieved thereby. Legislation proposed in some countries for a so-called "negative income tax," that is, that the poorer members of society, instead of paying taxes, should receive a supplementary income from taxes paid by others, is a step in the same direction. It is just another way of ensuring a minimum wage, but sparing marginally profitable companies from having to meet the wage bill themselves, and perhaps encouraging others who could afford to pay better wages to allow the general taxpayer to pick up the tab.

But if the rights body, from its own sense of equity and justice, were to raise the minimum wage so consistently that it might come to be widely thought that the possession of material luxuries beyond the satisfaction of all reasonable needs was not a really necessary element in living, then it ought to follow as a matter of course that more attention and more resources would gradually come to be spent on cultural "goods," rather than on unnecessary luxuries. Public opinion, instead of, as is too often the case now, admiring the man who can afford an eye-catching object unavailable to less wealthy neighbors, would begin to look upon him as socially backward—an opinion that he might in time come to share himself. The consumers' representatives in the economic Associations would then begin to report the lack of demand for such luxuries, and they would cease to be manufactured. One result would be that more persons would have the possibility available to them of spending more of their time producing cultural goods, and more producing members of the economic Associations would be able to spend fewer hours at their work—especially, it may be hoped, the kind of work that in an industrial society can scarcely fail to be monotonous. So ultimately it could be possible for every man to be really free to choose in which of the three realms to spend his working life. Monotonous work of the kind demanded by our present industrial society would surely have to be compensated not by a higher wage but by the possibility of spending only a small part of a man's working hours on it, leaving him free to fulfill the other parts of his nature in the remainder of his time.

This kind of scenario may appear utopian and, for many obvious reasons, impracticable. The present writer indeed only puts it forward here as one means by which it might be possible to overcome the almost universally held notion that human beings *ought* to work for money (or for goods that can be bought with it), rather than because it is a need of human nature to be permitted to work constructively in a manner that both satisfies our personal sense of creativity, and contributes to the good of society as a whole. Our social order ought to be such that these two needs can be met, not only for ourselves, but for all members of our society (and of course ultimately for all human beings everywhere). It ought not to be necessary for society in an age of potential abundance to *force* human beings to work or starve, or even to force a large majority of them to work for little more than a bare subsistence; conversely, it ought not to be necessary to reward some of them so much more lavishly than others, and often for work that is far more interesting than that done by the more lowly paid worker. In various countries of the world since Rudolf Steiner's time these problems have been recognized (as of course they were by Karl Marx), and many different efforts have been made to come to grips with them. Although not everyone will formulate the central problem in the way Rudolf Steiner did, namely, that labor is treated as if it were a commodity, it is well understood that some work of a particularly unpleasant kind would never be done at all unless there were some material incentive to do it, and it is widely supposed that material incentives have to be used or men would not work at all. In those countries where attempts have been made to substitute, for example, moral incentives, numerous difficulties have arisen. Either compulsory labor has had to be instituted or the material incentives reintroduced, if in a modified form. In Cuba the leadership self-consciously (and loquaciously) adopted moral incentives because, in its view, the country could not afford material ones, but found they were not enough. In the People's Republic of China, where the social and cultural background of the people was especially favorable for the effort, success may have been greater. In the Soviet Union for a time honors and decorations were substituted for material incentives, with somewhat indifferent success. All the Communist-Socialist states have used some form of compulsion combined with their moral incentives, in part because as undeveloped states trying to industrialize rapidly they simply did not have the material goods available to be able to rely on material incentives. None of these states, with the partial exception of Cuba and China, have been able to bridge the gap between the incomes of the highest and the lowest paid citizens, but the intervention of the state to perform many social services that ought to be provided by the cultural-spiritual domain has somewhat tempered the inequality of incomes.

Experiments along quite different lines with similar aims in view, and more interesting in the light of Steiner's expressed social ideals, have been made in Sweden and Yugoslavia since

344

World War II. In almost all the Western industrial countries the governments have made provision for some worker participation in management, usually in the form of a committee to deal with grievances in which workers and management are represented, and where workers' suggestions are given attention. But this does not go far toward Steiner's ideal of economic Associations in which there would be, in accordance with our earlier quotation, "a really free contractual relation between the work director and the work-doer—a relation resting not on barter of commodities (or money) but on an agreement as to the share due to each of the two joint authors of the commodity." (*Threefold Commonwealth*, p. 114) In Sweden for many years management and workers took part in an annual meeting in which the total industrial product for the ensuing year was calculated, and the possible increase of the share of the output that could be allotted to workers and management was worked out through bargaining. The government, as "rights-body," summoned the meeting, but did not dominate it. This was a good beginning, especially in view of the fact that an increasing minimum wage for all workers accompanied it. In recent times a much more ambitious program has been envisaged, and several parts of it have already been put into effect under which factory workers have been placed on top planning groups, up to and including boards of directors. Alva Myrdal, wife of Sweden's leading economist, Gunnar Myrdal, and herself until recently a cabinet minister, has produced a report in which she asks why an industrial worker should "be content to be part of a hierarchy which is military in nature. The young Swedish worker," she says, "feels this and is now growing impatient with the factory and workplace. After all, these are the people who have gone through schools where they have been treated as equals, and then they are sent out to a factory, where they are ordered about like slaves." *

---

* Paul Dickson, "Sweden's Quest for Equality," *The Progressive* (Madison, Wisconsin), November, 1972.

In Sweden also experiments are now in operation in the factories of the two Swedish automobile manufacturers, Saab and Volvo, in which an attempt is made to overcome the recognized appalling monotony of the assembly line where each worker spends his day doing only one small job, can have no personal satisfaction in his work and can exercise no skill except the single one involved in his task.* Now they are to work in relatively small teams, and each team will by itself assemble a whole automobile, even though the cost of production by this means will almost certainly prove higher than by the traditional system under which each worker performs only one operation.

In Yugoslavia, where there is no private ownership of the means of production, another of Steiner's ideas has been tested, although in conditions far from being the most suitable. Whereas in other Communist states central planning by the state bureaucracy has been the norm for industry, the Yugoslavs have tried to decentralize this planning by handing management over to Workers' Councils. Although the state sets the production quota for the enterprise, it thereafter leaves it alone, and all management decisions, including the wages and salaries of both "work-directors" and "work-doers," are taken by the Councils, which are representative of all elements in the enterprise. Yugoslavian industry also pioneered among Communist states in insisting that each enterprise should make what in a capitalistic state would be regarded as a profit. But this profit should be used as a yardstick to see whether the enterprise was providing goods that could be sold, that is to say, were needed, at a price that showed a surplus over costs of labor and materials

---

* Steiner himself, when he was asked by the German industrialist, Emil Molt, who owned the Waldorf Astoria Tobacco factory in Stuttgart, what could be done about work that was necessarily monotonous, suggested that the worker's part in the whole product should be stressed, and an educational program be introduced that would give him at least some idea about tobacco and its history—in other words that the spiritual-cultural domain be asked to come to the rescue. See Herbert Hahn, "Birth of the Waldorf School from the Threefold Social Movement," in *Rudolf Steiner, Recollections by Some of his Pupils, Golden Blade*, 1958.

and overhead. This notion was also proposed by Professor Lieberman and put into effect in some industries in the Soviet Union. It was one of the reforms proposed by Ota Sik, the Czech economist, at the time of the so-called Czechoslovakian "spring" in 1968 under the Dubček government. Sik also advocated Workers' Councils on the Yugoslavian model. In this connection Steiner had said in Zurich in 1919:

What is it that arises as gain, or profit? It is something that plays the same role in social economy that the rising quicksilver plays in the tube of the thermometer. The rising of the quicksilver shows that the temperature has risen. We know that it is not the quicksilver that has made the room warmer, but that the increased warmth is caused by other factors. The market profit resulting from present conditions of production is only a sign that commodities can be produced that yield a profit. For I should like to know how anyone can possibly discover whether a commodity ought to be produced if not from the fact that when it has been produced and placed on the market it yields a profit.*

That the Yugoslavian ideas and experience have been felt by others to be possibly meaningful to them is being demonstrated at the time of writing by the Peruvian military government led by General Velasco Alvarez, who wished to establish self-governing and self-managing industries while avoiding the mistakes made by the Yugoslavs. He therefore invited some Yugoslavian experts to Peru, and as a result decided to establish a special sector of the economy, distinct from private and state owned industry, to be called "social property." The state is to supply technical and financial aid, but the salaried workers will be the owners and the social property sector is destined to become eventually the principal sector of the Peruvian economy.** Not

* Lecture 2 of a series given in Zurich in October 1919, and published under the title, *The Social Future*, p. 39. The whole lecture is most valuable.
** Although the experiment came to an end some years ago when General Velasco Alvarez was overthrown and his government was replaced by a less socially-minded dictatorship, it seems worthwhile to leave this account in the text as an example of one of the more promising efforts toward the realization of a better social order in the underdeveloped world.

347

every enterprise will be expected to make a profit every year. The profitable enterprises will therefore contribute their profits to make up the deficits of the unprofitable ones. This feature has drawn considerable criticism because it is thought that the right to share in the profits of their work ought to be used as an incentive for the workers. It will be noted, however, that the Peruvian notion of using profits to offset losses is closer to the ideal of the Threefold Order, in which profits, as we have seen, are used as the yardstick to determine both whether there is a need for a particular product and whether the enterprise is being efficiently managed. But the profits as such are not retained in the business beyond what is needed for the expansion of productive capacity; they are as a matter of course used for the upkeep of the state and for the use of the spiritual-cultural domain. The latter, not being part of the economic life at all, cannot charge for its services as if education and other cultural services were economic products.

The notion of so-called profit-sharing to which we have just referred is one of the solutions, offered especially in Europe and North America, to the problem of the "alienation" of the ordinary worker, and his feeling that he is nothing but an interchangeable part who can so easily be replaced by someone else that he loses all sense of his human worth (or, in Steiner's terms, his labor becomes a commodity). The system by which a worker is given a share of the profits of his enterprise, or is allowed to buy (or is given gratis) stock in it on which he will receive an annual dividend, is no doubt a worthy scheme in itself, but it does not really alleviate any of the main grievances of the worker. In Peruvian private industry (not the "social property" sector) the salaried workers already own 15 percent of the stock by law, but they will not for a long time be able to equal the influence exercised by the main stockholders, even when their proportion, as foreseen under the law, rises to 50 percent. Management, so much more concentrated than the individual workers, will no doubt continue to make all the decisions as before. Eventually, however, Peruvian private

348

industry may be expected to become part of the social property sector if the latter succeeds in establishing itself. In other countries the stock held by the workers is in almost every case such a tiny percentage of the whole that the profit sharing should be regarded as nothing but a money bonus paid in proportion to the profit earned. When the state-owned Renault Corporation, the largest French automobile manufacturer, in 1971 instituted a profit sharing scheme by issuing some special stock for the purpose, it scarcely caused a ripple of interest among Renault workers who had been accustomed for years to receiving annual bonuses based on productivity. This was not the kind of "participation" that some of the unions had demanded, and President de Gaulle had favored. But such participation has never been spelled out in detail, although the demand for it once more suggests that something along the lines advocated in the *Threefold Commonwealth* for industry is striving to come to the surface.

Steiner's idea of economic Associations that would engage in producing and distributing all that was needed by a society in the form of material commodities, that would be made up of producers and distributors and some consumers as advisers, and would turn over all their profits beyond what was needed for expansion to the other sectors of society, could be put into operation only if these other two sectors also functioned as intended, side by side with the economic realm. All men, it must never be forgotten, belong in themselves to all three realms, as all men have a three-member physical organism that enables them to live, and that becomes ill when one domain impinges on the realm of another. We are all political men and have a right to political equality and to a truly democratic form of government. We are all economic men insofar as we are consumers of material commodities, and we are all as individuals free, thinking beings, with a right to our own private lives. When Steiner spoke of capital, he often used to remind us that the word is derived from caput, the Latin for head. Capital in the form of ideas is provided by the spiritual-cultural domain for the

349

economic domain, as the latter provides commodities for the thinkers and inventors to consume. There is a constant interplay between these two domains, and in the center, always holding the balance, should be the rights domain, the sphere of equality. Only if these three domains function as they should can there be a society that will be able to fulfill the legitimate needs of the consciousness soul age, and only if at least a beginning has been made and the aims recognized by the leaders of world opinion can the actual forms suitable for the future begin to be worked out further.

We have spent the greater part of our discussion thus far in this chapter on the economic domain, and even so we have been able to touch on only a few of Steiner's ideas in this field. There remains to be discussed later in the chapter the notion of world economy and overcoming nationalism, as we presented the problem at the beginning of the chapter. It is, I believe, to the economic domain that responsible governments and industries have thus far given most of their attention, because it is in this domain that the problems appear to be most severe and in it that the exploited workers have been able to exercise the most pressure. As a result many ideas are in the air, and changes are in progress, some of which we have noted. The cultural life, however, especially education, is probably more firmly under the control of governments than in Steiner's own time, and "free" private education not provided by or dominated by the state seems to be on the wane; while no one would claim that any progress has been made toward relieving governments of their excessive power and influence, and to converting them into mere "rights-bodies" in the sense of the Threefold Commonwealth. We shall therefore now deal somewhat more briefly with these other two domains and Steiner's ideas on their function and composition before returning to the subject that occupied us at the beginning of this chapter.

The State Government or "Rights-body." It will be realized from what has been said thus far in the chapter that the most important single attribute of the rights organization is its independence, on the basis of which it can afford to be impartial. Obviously, if the state provides education for its citizens, or if it owns or manages industry, it cannot be impartial in relation to either education or industry. Conversely, if, as in the United States, governmental bodies are organized with the admirable and legitimate purpose of seeing to it that industries observe the law and act fairly toward the consumer, and if these bodies are then staffed by persons who have spent their lives in industry or in the pay of industry and expect to return to industry after their stint in the regulatory body, the latter can scarcely be expected to give impartial decisions. Nor can members of the legislature be expected to maintain their independence and place the interests of the entire people over those of industry, if the latter pays most of their campaign expenses.

Such comments are not intended to emphasize the special sinfulness of *homo politicus*, but to draw attention to the crucial element in Steiner's thought that the state governments must be strictly limited, and concerned *only* with the administration of rights. This means that we must be clear as to what these rights actually are; in Steiner's thought these do not exactly coincide with the time honored right to "life, liberty, and property," (John Locke), nor, in the words of the American Declaration of Independence the right to "life, liberty and the pursuit of happiness." Indeed, we should never think of them in such abstract terms as these. We should also be clear in what respects all men are "created equal"—we are equal in our right to have our rights respected, and no exceptions can be tolerated to this right. Therefore every adult person in a state has the right to vote for a "rights-body" or government, whose sole aim is to enforce his rights and those of everyone else.

It may be taken for granted that men do indeed have an absolute right to life and liberty, as Locke and the Founding Fathers held, and for the purpose of enforcing this right a code of laws is needed. This code of laws should be based on the common sense of right held by all the people, and expressed

351

through the democratically elected members of the parliament. The government, which should in effect be a committee of the parliament, should maintain order through a police force and will provide for external defense with the aid of such armed forces as may be necessary. As noted earlier the government will not administer the courts of justice, since justice belongs not to the rights but to the spiritual-cultural domain. The other rights are less absolute, and we cannot enter into full detail here. What is essential is that thought should be given to what really *is* a right, and what has come to be considered a right but may be only a privilege not extended to everyone in the state. In Steiner's thought all rights administered by the rights body had to be of universal application. Its task in the spiritual-cultural domain would be solely to ensure that education should be available to all and that this domain should really be free; in economic life its task would likewise be to administer those elements of it that fall within the sphere of rights. For example, every man has certainly a right to be able to support himself and his family, and it would be a duty of the rights body to see to it that he receive a minimum wage to cover this support. It is also possible that some enterprises should be operated by the economic domain, even if they cannot make a profit, as, for example, public transportation. Steiner was not averse to letting the rights body determine to which enterprises the people had a right. But in no circumstances should the government operate such enterprises itself.

The question of so-called "real property" (real estate) was very much in Steiner's mind in the early twenties (see especially Lectures 5 and 7 of *World Economy*) and he gave much attention to the subject, because, in particular, he held that land speculation prevented the free flow of money. One of his most important insights is that it is against the rights and interests of the community for land to be "owned" outright, and bought and sold as if it were movable property. In fact, all land is community property, and the so-called owner has in fact only the right to use and dispose of it for an unlimited period of time and name his successor. He cannot remove his land from one part of the country to another. Since someone has conferred the right to use the land on the owner, Steiner held that this someone in future should be the community, which should decide who is to use the land and on what terms.

Strange as the idea may seem at first, a little reflection will surely convince any impartial person that these observations about the actual facts of landholding are true, and it will then be recognized that the right to use a piece of land should be conferred only on someone who uses it ultimately in the interests of the community, and that if someone who has obtained the right to use the land for a certain purpose ceases to use it, it must be transferred to someone who will do so. Landholding is therefore a relationship in right, and does not belong to the economic domain, though it will, of course, be used by the economic Associations for productive purposes. It follows that there can be no land speculation and no increase in so-called land values, and money needed for the spiritual-cultural life or for productive economic use will never be tied up unproductively in land. Whether or not a nominal rent is paid, a potentially socially valuable enterprise should never be blocked because of the cost of the site to the new entrepreneur. The task of the rights body should always be to *facilitate* movement between the spiritual cultural domain and the economic domain but never to interfere with either, and never to perform itself any of the tasks allotted to them in the Threefold Order.

Obviously, we cannot enter here into much detail and some aspects of the matter will be considered later, but there is one point of great importance that should be discussed in connection with the role of the rights bodies. Because the state's role is so limited in the Threefold Social Order, the area of its territorial jurisdiction can also be limited, and indeed in principle the area of a state could be small indeed without its losing any of its effectiveness as a rights body. A state under the Threefold Order does not have to administer the economy, or an educational system, and, as we shall see, in a world economy such as is striving to come into being there can be no question of imposing tariffs or letting any obstacle whatever stand in the way of the exchange of goods between one part of the world best fitted to produce them and another. Even before such a world economy comes into being there is no reason for an economic area to coincide with that controlled by a particular state. Economic areas can be as large as can be arranged to suit the needs of the economic life of the region. Thus states will lose one important reason for wishing to control others. The way would then be opened to have far *more* but much *smaller* states than there are now. There would be no conceivable reason for the existence of such enormous agglomerations of diverse peoples as the United States of America, the Soviet Union, India, or even China; nor would it be necessary for local patriotisms, which are usually cultural in nature, to be so much discouraged as they are today, in the interests of a larger nationalism, especially superstate nationalism that is always of an artificial nature. Even today there are tiny peaceful states that manage to survive as long as they are out of the range of the strategic interests of the superpowers. A people that feels itself to be one, that has a local patriotism and a common language, could have its three separate interlocking domains, and maintain friendly cultural and economic relations with others. Each would have its own elected rights body, as the tiny principality of Andorra, and the still tinier Republic of San Marino have today.

This kind of local patriotism, which is not exclusive but simply a matter of natural feeling, is, in fact, the very opposite of that diseased nationalism of which we spoke in the earlier part of this chapter that has to be overcome in the age of the consciousness soul. We are part of our own people and part of the world, as we belong likewise to each of the three members of the social order. Group soul nationalism tends to prevent the development of our individual ego consciousness; the shunning of this kind of nationalism does not mean that we must lose our cultural identity in favor of some amorphous yet-to-be-born world consciousness. In a quite small community we can develop our ego consciousness while at the same time learning to place the interests of the great humanity outside our community on a level with our own. But this cannot even be attempted as long as states compete for national prestige and grandeur, as long as national education exalts the achievements of the state that provides it and serves its national egoism and greed, even while it inculcates loyalty and patriotism—with too often the byproducts of national superiority and contempt for those who are smaller and weaker. With the eventual disappearance of the large superstates and the smaller national states that swim along in the national wake of each, it is even possible that the world might look forward to freedom from fear of the sudden nuclear calamity that hangs over us all, and, who knows, perhaps world peace might follow.

The Spiritual Cultural Domain. As we have seen, the jural or rights-body is the mediator between the spiritual-cultural and the economic domains, and its primary quality must therefore be the *impartiality* required of any mediator. The essential element in the spiritual cultural domain of the social organism should be its *creativity*, which flows from its capacity for free and unprejudiced thinking. This domain is in no way aloof from the economic life. On the contrary, it should supply it with the personnel who will keep it on the alert, responsive to new conditions and awake to new impulses, always ready to suggest innovations. Steiner spoke of this domain as

. . . containing everything that rests on the natural endowments of each single human being—everything that needs must enter into and play a part in the body social on the ground of the natural endowments, both spiritual and physical, of the individual. Thus, the first system—the economic—has to do with everything that must exist in order that man may keep straight in his material adjustments to the world around him. The second system has to do with whatever must exist in the body social because of men's personal relations to one another. The third system has to do with all that

355

must spring from the personal individuality of each human being and must thus be incorporated in the body social.*

It is therefore to be expected that in such an order, if it ever were to come into being, men who had worked exclusively within the cultural life would from time to time feel themselves impelled to take an active part in a business in which they could put their ideas into practice. Conversely, men who have spent much of their active life in the economic Associations can retire from it to devote themselves to education. Especially in the English speaking countries there is even now a constant interplay between business and the universities—and indeed many businessmen already lecture in the universities in their spare time.

It will today be agreed by almost everyone that the religious life of man is his personal affair. The only reason a man belongs to a particular religion or sect is because he wishes to do so, and there is nothing to prevent him from changing his religion if his needs and beliefs change. Even today, unless the state imposes an outward conformity to a particular religion on its citizens, religion really is free and independent and little interfered with by the state. But no state at the present time is indifferent to education, and indeed most of its quarrels with religious authorities stems from the latters' wish to impose their own views on education. Almost all states conceive it to be their duty to provide at least a minimum of education for their citizens, and they may or may not tolerate education provided by religious and cultural bodies also. Obviously an omnicompetent state, as presently conceived, which regards itself also as responsible for the proper functioning of the economy and for providing amenities for all its citizens, cannot but be aware that

---

* Quoted in G. Wachsmuth, *From the Basic Ideas of Rudolf Steiner on the Threefold Social Order,* p. 9. Wachsmuth unfortunately did not give any references for his quotations in his valuable little pamphlet, so any other quotes will only refer to the pages in it, where I have not been able to trace the source in Steiner himself.

education is the key to both, and most people who do not give the matter much thought are likely to agree that the interests of the community really do demand that the people receive as much education as the state can afford to give. Education can be provided and controlled by the state at any level—national, provincial, municipal, or local—and it can be varied according to the needs of the body that supplies it. State-provided education does not have to be nationally uniform, as in France, nor as decentralized as it is in the United States. But the principle that governments should see to it that education is provided for at least some of their citizens is scarcely disputed today.

Yet Steiner stated emphatically that the state had no business meddling with education at all, and in his Threefold Order the rights-body was at most entitled to see that education was made available on an equal basis for all. In no circumstances should the rights body attempt to provide it itself. Education in his view belonged exclusively to the spiritual-cultural domain, the domain of freedom, a concept that few in the Western world would be inclined to question as far as the *content* of education is concerned. All Western countries have at least a belief in "academic freedom," but this does not prevent Western governments from laying down educational requirements, certifying teachers, and generally keeping them from straying too far from what they regard as acceptable conduct. This comment applies, of course, especially to elementary and high schools, but even universities have often to be prepared to struggle for their academic freedom, both against boards of trustees or governors and against their appointed administrators.

Steiner, however, went so far as to insist that all curricula should be set up by the teachers themselves, and they themselves should administer the schools in which they teach. Only teachers, he said, can know from their own personal insight what should be taught, or, to quote his own words:

> What is to be taught and how the human being shall be educated in these schools must be drawn solely from a knowledge of the growing

357

human being and his capacities. . . . An educator should devote only such time to teaching as will permit him also to give the necessary time to management. He will thus be able to perform his administrative duties just as well as he does his teaching. No one would be allowed to direct education who was not at the same time actively engaged in teaching and education. No parliament, no person who perhaps at one time had been a teacher but was no longer personally active in teaching, would have any authority.*

Such ideas will perhaps be found especially striking in the United States where school and university administrators have so much power and authority, and where such administration is a specialized profession distinct from teaching. But in Great Britain the public schools (which would of course be regarded as private schools in the United States) were for centuries until recent times completely independent, and the headmaster was almost invariably himself an active teacher. Even now, when so many have had to accept some restrictions on their absolute freedom in exchange for state financial aid, their independence in academic matters is respected by the state. In the better public schools the education is widely thought to be much better than that given in all but the best of the state schools. In Steiner schools all over the world—there are now close to 100—the effort is made to observe his suggestions as to school administration by the teachers, one of whose members usually serves for a limited period as chairman of the faculty rather than principal or headmaster. Steiner education, however, will be left as a subject to Chapter 10, as one of the most successful and widespread among the practical activities stemming from Steiner's teachings, and no more will be said on it here.

All artists, writers and scientists belong naturally to the spiritual-cultural domain. They can do their work effectively only in an atmosphere of complete freedom, but since cultural workers like everyone else must eat, their work at the present time, unless it is subsidized by the state or industry, must at

---

* Wachsmuth, *op.cit.*, p. 10.

some point enter into commerce and be treated as if it were an economic commodity. It is not too easy to see what could be the alternative, even in a Threefold Order. Should a writer, for example, be paid when no one wants to read what he writes, that is, when his book is published (i.e., enters into economic life), and no one buys or borrows it? Should an artist who paints pictures that no one wants to look at, a musician who composes what no orchestra wishes to play, be paid simply because he is, in his own opinion, a creative artist? The question is exactly the same in relation to scientists, but funds are more readily available to them from the state or foundations today, because scientists are more likely to be regarded as contributors to what, significantly enough, is known in the United States as the "knowledge industry."

We must be clear here that a book in itself *is* an economic product, in that it is produced like other commodities, distributed and consumed. But this is not to say that its author should receive his income on the basis of the number of books sold by his publisher, since he cannot fail to be tempted to cater to the interests of the mass consumer, and the economic domain will therefore intrude into the spiritual-cultural. His "spiritual service" thus becomes a commodity. In Lecture 14 of *World Economy* Steiner tells us that the value of a spiritual service can be calculated only on the basis of the time it will take to produce another service of the same kind. So the artist or writer should receive enough gift-money from the economy to enable him to live until he has produced another similar work of art. But as a free being he should calculate this value justly himself, which in today's society would obviously be an impossible burden to lay upon him and upon society.

Obviously, it is a difficult problem, and there may be no ideal solution to it at man's present stage of spiritual and cultural development. But Steiner's solution at least indicates the way in which such questions should be thought through in a Threefold Order. Here we shall refer to a point mentioned briefly earlier in the chapter that has special relevance in this context. The

359

economic Associations should be individually small enough to be manageable, so that each worker, spiritual or manual, should feel himself an integral part of his own Association. Above these relatively small Associations, however, there should be also an industry-wide Council, which would be made up of technically qualified persons from the Associations, and an even larger Council representing all Associations in an area would also have its uses. We have seen that the second member of the social order, the rights state, is elected democratically by all citizens. Likewise, the spiritual-cultural realm should have its free Councils, whose members would be chosen on the basis of their individual abilities. In both Eastern and Western countries organizations in this field exist already. In most universities faculty members are chosen by their colleagues; even where this is not the case senior faculty members will certainly be consulted on new appointments and promotions. Medical associations lay down qualifications for doctors, nursing associations for nurses. Writers and artists could equally well have their own Councils made up of men and women actively working in these fields. But these councils should surely *not* be subjected to political influence, nor should their members be chosen by any outside body, least of all a government. Nor should the members be required to follow a party line laid down by the government, or the Councils will, as in the Soviet Union and Eastern Europe, and in many authoritarian states elsewhere, become caricatures of the kind of council Steiner had in mind—their primary purpose being to stifle cultural freedom, not promote it.

The World Economy and the Overcoming of Nationalism. Several references have been made in this chapter to the way in which a "world economy" is slowly coming into being, that is an economy exactly the opposite of what prevailed in the Middle Ages, when quite small economic units tended to be almost self-sufficient. In our age whose production is dependent on an ever increasing specialization and division of labor, no area of the world can hope to be self-sufficient. In the last of Steiner's fourteen lectures on *World Economy* (1922) already referred to, he emphasized, by no means for the first time, that there is in fact no natural economic unit on the earth except the entire earth itself, as a totality, and in speaking of the earth as a social organism he remarked that states and countries are at most cells in this organism. By making an economic unit co-terminous with the area controlled by a particular government, an artificial excision is therefore made into this single natural unit, and this not only interferes with the natural exchange of goods between the different areas of the earth, but is fraught with the greatest danger for mankind.

Now we have become so much accustomed to thinking of a state as a more or less natural entity, with its main duty that of ensuring the safety and welfare of the people who owe it allegiance, that it is likely to seem meaningless to us to speak of the whole earth as the only true economic unit. In our time the standard of living of a people, to say nothing of the power and influence of a nation, is so closely linked to the possession of adequate resources within its own boundaries, that it is difficult for us to come to the recognition—except perhaps as an abstract moral notion—that the resources of mankind actually belong to the whole of mankind, and not at all necessarily to the particular people that happens to be living where these resources are to be found. We, of course, are willing to recognize that what we use in the course of a day may have come from every continent and from half a dozen countries in each, and we accept the fact that if, for example, we use the oil from an Australian tree or the bark of an Indonesian one to cure our cold, we must have sold the Australians and the Indonesians something of value in return for these blessings. This mutual exchange of goods is taken for granted in our age, even though it simply did not exist in the Middle Ages, or, at most, only on a small scale. Especially in the last century the exchange of goods on a world wide basis has grown at an ever increasing rate, and Steiner in emphasizing the actual fact of the matter was not stating anything new or startling. But as so often, the consequences he drew from his observations seem new, and perhaps not at first obvious, while

361

the spiritual reasons behind the fact and its consequences, to which we have made a brief allusion earlier in the chapter, could have been gained only through the science of spirit. During the present age when Michael is acting as the Spirit of the Time, it is man's task to overcome the blood ties that result in nationalism and racism, and gradually substitute for this a feeling for all humanity, a feeling that all men are brothers, and that, as a consequence, we should act in a brotherly, fraternal spirit toward *all* our fellow men, and not only those of our own nation, creed, color, race, or political persuasion. Now the economic realm is that realm of the Threefold Social Order where there should be a free give and take, where goods from one part of the world are freely traded for those of another, in short, where *fraternity* should rule as there should be equality in the realm of rights and freedom in the realm of culture. Thus, the economic realm, paradoxically enough, is not, or should not be the realm of selfishness, competition, and materialism, but that in which we are, to use Steiner's words, "plunged into the midst of human relationships. Because of this, interests are kindled; precisely in this field of human relations we are able to develop interests which in the true sense of the word are fraternal. In no other realm than that of economic life are fraternal relationships so early and obviously developed among human beings." * In other words, it is in the economic realm that we are called upon to act in accordance with the Christ impulse. In the light of these facts it is scarcely surprising that it is in this realm that the Ahrimanic and Luciferic forces are putting forth their strongest efforts, and, be it admitted, without encountering excessive opposition from mankind.

As we have seen in the early part of this chapter the national

* From a lecture given in Zurich on February 4, 1919, the second of three lectures published in 1950 under the title, *The Inner Aspect of the Social Question*, p. 30. These lectures, it may be noted, were given to members, and they are uniquely valuable in that they give the esoteric side of the Threefold Commonwealth, which at the time was already becoming an active movement in the external world, and supported by thousands who knew little or nothing of what underlay Steiner's efforts to realize the Threefold Order on the physical plane.

state itself is an institution that belongs to the past, but it would be tolerable as a transitional institution likely to lead to something more universal if it were not that it controls a national economy that it uses to further its own power. This fact, together with its tendency to force all its citizens within the same cultural mould, is what makes it so dangerous in our days of increasing scientific and technical advance. As Steiner himself pointed out in the last chapter of *The Threefold Commonwealth*, the nationalities problem in Austria-Hungary could easily have been solved if the "one-fold state" had not formed also "the cultural frontiers for the spiritual life of its various nationalities. Could the spiritual life have been on its own footing, independent of the political state and political boundaries, it would have had a chance to develop regardless of frontiers in a manner befitting the true purpose of the several nationalities; and the struggle that was deeply rooted in the spiritual life, need never have found vent in a political catastrophe." (pp.192–193)

Wars are likewise being fought constantly for the purpose of controlling more land and resources. Such an archetypal war was that between the United States and Mexico in the 1840s, by which the former gained, among other areas, Texas and California, so rich in natural resources. This war was to be followed by numerous others fought by the "imperial" powers in the late nineteenth century in which all the powerful European nations played some part. The great expansion of the United States over the whole North American continent, and the Civil War that made possible the control of such a huge territory by a single government, had the effect in the twentieth century of making the United States the most powerful nation in the world by the time of the Second World War. By similar means in the same period Tsarist Russia came to control all Siberia, and a substantial slice of what had formerly been China, thus bequeathing to the Bolsheviks such a large and rich territory that in due course the Soviet Union became second in power only to the United States.

All present-day elected governments feel that their first duty is to their own citizens, and that if they were to fail in this duty they would never be reelected. If their national economies function badly and provide only a meager living for their citizens, they will be blamed. For this reason they interfere constantly in the economic life of their countries by such measures as offering subsidies, altering the tax rate, protecting industry from foreign competition by tariffs, providing services that citizens desire but which cannot be expected to show a profit, and all this seems quite natural. Even if we recognize in theory that this situation is both dangerous and contrary to any ideals we may hold of the brotherhood of man since the more powerful state can use its power to assert its will in economic as in political matters—it is no accident, for example, that the United States, with some 6% of the world's population produces more than 40% of the world's goods and consumes a proportionate amount of the world's resources—it is certainly not self-evident what can be done to improve this situation.

The Swedish economist and sociologist Gunnar Myrdal in an excellent analysis of this subject published as long ago as 1956* pointed out (p. 63) that international changes in the location of industry (a practical step away from economic nationalism) were unlikely just because the Western European countries were all "definitely committed to defending the standard of living of their citizens," and thus to maintaining home industry in preference to buying the same industrial products from an underdeveloped country in the process of industrialization. He thought then, a year before the signing of the Treaty of Rome that gave birth to the European Economic Community, that "no country in Western Europe is today prepared to accept a significant increase in unemployment or even a serious scaling down of living standards in one industry as the price of economic integration with other countries, even its closest neighbors." In discussing the topic as a whole in his introduction

---

* *An International Economy*: *Problems and Prospects* (New York: Harper and Brothers, 1956).

he concluded that "there does not exist that human solidarity which in the national state is a result of the historical progress toward integration, and which induces individuals and social groups to accept rules and regulations that are not to their immediate advantage." (p. 5)

Here Myrdal of course put his finger on the nub of the problem—*the absence of human solidarity*—and with this comment we cannot but agree. But it should not prevent us from trying to think constructively on the subject. It seems to me that the key given us by Rudolf Steiner is not that we must try to get rid directly of economic nationalism, but that we should look forward toward that element in the Threefold Social Order that makes economic nationalism forever impossible—the substitution of rights-bodies, or state governments as described above, for national states as we now know them. The economic domain will then no longer be co-terminous with the state domain.

Let us suppose, for example, that the cultural units of Northern England, Southern England, perhaps Southwestern England, the Scottish Lowlands, the Scottish Highlands, Wales, Northern Ireland and Southern Ireland all had their own state governments or rights-bodies, but that the economy of the entire British Isles was an autonomous unity, headed by an Economic Council. Would that make so much difference to the ability of the economic sector to provide for the needs of all the people, and to exchange goods with other economic areas outside the British Isles? All the world's economic areas would be closely linked with each other, eventually under a Grand Economic Council for the whole world. However impracticable this may seem for the moment, it is at all events along these lines that Steiner would bid us think for the future.

It is a perfectly legitimate question to ask whether we are now heading in this direction, in accordance with Steiner's statement that the Threefold Order was struggling to come into being, and that it was the only possible order that would enable the consciousness soul to fulfill its tasks.* The year after Myrdal's

---

* In case the statement that "the Threefold Order was struggling to come into being" appears at first sight somewhat startling, Steiner's own words on the

365

book was published the European Economic Community (or Common Market) of six European countries came into being, and at the beginning of 1973 it was enlarged by the addition of Great Britain, Ireland, and Denmark. Its gestation has been difficult indeed, perhaps because it is only an *economic* community as yet, and no major political changes have been involved—nor of course, has it been influenced by any ideas of the Threefold Social Order. The tariff barriers on industrial goods among the original Six have been gradually reduced to zero, and there is a free movement, at least in principle, of labor among the various countries. But the decisions on agricultural policies and especially agricultural prices common to all the component countries have always involved long and harrowing discussions among the governmental officials of each of the member states. All the discussions have finally resulted in more or less unsatisfactory compromises. In effect each of the countries is still running its own national economy, and all that has been achieved thus far has been the removal of some internal trade barriers, thus enabling the Community as a whole to approach the size and economic strength of the United States and surpass

---

subject are worth quoting, given in a public conference in Vienna in 1922. "It is clear," he said, "for anyone who has permitted the social life of Europe of the last thirty or forty years to influence him, without any preconception or prejudice, that what ought to happen at the present time has already been indicated in the unconscious wills of European humanity. Everywhere it is possible to discover the unconscious tendencies in some direction. They really live in the souls of man, and it is only necessary to lend them expression in words. . . .

"It was not really my purpose [i.e. in writing *The Threefold Commonwealth*] to say that I considered one thing or another to be right, but that one thing or another was willed out of the hidden unconscious life. It is absolutely necessary that we shall become conscious of the goal toward which humanity is really striving. The very reason for many of our social blunders lies in the fact that this unconscious aspiration is in conflict with what humanity has thought out in an intellectualistic way and carried over into its external arrangements. As a result, our arrangements actually contradict what is willed in the depth of human hearts." From a lecture given June 11, 1922 entitled, "The Cardinal Points of the Social Question," the last of a series of lectures published under the title of the entire Vienna Congress, *West and East: Contrasting Worlds*, p. 216 of the first English, undated, edition.

the economic strength of the Soviet Union. This limited gain, however, has to be set against the hindrance of world trade resulting from the external tariff against the rest of the world, except those few "developing" countries that have been allowed into an economic association with the Nine. It is therefore doubtful if we should think of the EEC as even a step in the direction of the world economy envisaged by Rudolf Steiner; nor would it be necessarily a gain if the Nine were to organize themselves together into one more superstate to add to the two already existing.

By contrast, quite without any such intention on the part of the nations concerned, "a cloud no bigger than a man's hand" appeared on the horizon that could even yet become a storm that will sweep away the entire structure of national states as "owners" of national resources and managers of national economies. In late 1973 a series of events occurred that made glaringly apparent the anachronistic nature of the present system. The fighting phase of the Fourth Arab-Israeli War finished in the same month that it began (October), but the Arab states that between them owned a large proportion of the world's reserves of petroleum decided to decrease their exports as a means of persuading their deprived customers to put pressure on the Israelis while at the same time increasing the price of the oil they did agree to export. The industrial states suddenly realized how utterly dependent their economies had become on their oil imports that could not be replaced in the short run by any other sources of energy, and in the long run only with great inconvenience and even danger (as if they were to build more nuclear plants). Most of the customers of the Arabs could think of nothing better than to do as they were asked; others considered the possibility of taking possession of the oil wells by force, but were compelled to recognize the immense difficulty involved in exploiting the resources of desert countries whose peoples would certainly sabotage the existing wells and refuse to cooperate afterward with the invaders. To make matters worse for the industrial nations all the non-Arab states decided that an excellent opportunity was presented to them to raise the price of their own oil, which they continued to export. Both the price increases and the threat of decreased supplies were difficult to accept with equanimity in view of the inflation already plaguing the industrial economies.

The repercussions of the astronomical increase in oil prices in the entire world, and not only in the West—not even excluding the Arab countries themselves—raise the quite legitimate question of whether any state *ought* to exercise full sovereignty over its resources when these latter are necessarily limited and perhaps *ought to be* available for the use of the entire population of mankind. Surely, it may reasonably be thought, resources belonging to all mankind should not be disposed of in full sovereignty by those states in which they are found, which may make totally arbitrary decisions with impunity. The rulers of these states can decide to sell or withhold their supplies for reasons that are not necessarily economic, but may, as in this instance, be political. Yet it is equally unreasonable, it may be thought, for the largest and most powerful nation states, which already use a disproportionate amount of these resources, to possess an unlimited right to continue using them up in order to maintain the "standard of living" of their own peoples, simply because these states have the physical might at their disposal to force the "owners" to cede them the right to do so.

The full long-term significance of these events has probably been grasped by few. But it is worth noting that Rudolf Steiner pointed to the problem and even its possible solution especially in the sixth lecture of the cycle called *The Social Future* given in 1919, and the reader is strongly urged to study it in relation to the dilemma we have been able only to touch upon here, which by 1981 was still showing no signs of being solved. The industrialized nations have in general been forced to come to terms with the oil-rich countries and have not only raised the prices of the ordinary goods they export, but have made an all-out effort to export armaments in ever greater quantities, especially to the Arab countries whose economies cannot easily absorb huge imports of more useful products. Meanwhile the poorer nations find it more difficult than ever to meet their energy bills, since the value of their exports has risen only slowly, if at all.

It may be stated with confidence that the peculiar contribution of the United States to the problem of how to organize a world economy is not going to solve it in a way that will be of benefit to mankind. Although there are now many so-called "multinational" corporations that operate in numerous countries throughout the world, the idea for these was American, and most of the corporations are today American-owned and operated. Policy is decided upon almost always exclusively by the parent corporation in America or elsewhere. These multinational corporations have been organized both in the developed countries of Europe and in the "developing" countries elsewhere. In some cases the parent corporation has bought up existing companies, provided them with new capital and furnished them with its own scientific, technical and managerial expertise. This procedure has had two major consequences; they are able to take advantage of the European Common Market, avoiding the external tariff because they are registered in one or the other of the component countries, and they are able to take advantage of the lower wage rates in the countries where they have installed themselves. As a result they are often able to export goods made by foreign cheap labor into the United States itself, and do this in spite of any tariffs that may exist. It is argued that such countries as South Africa, Mexico, Brazil, South Korea, Formosa, Hong Kong, Singapore and others that have proved hospitable to the multinational corporations have profited greatly from the introduction of American capital and business methods.

Even if this were true, which it is not, if only because the advanced technology of the United States will remain indefinitely almost unusable without American technicians to work it, the fact would still remain that most of these countries were chosen precisely because of their low wage rates, which are not necessarily raised by the American multinationals. Not only are their motives in no way altruistic, but exclusively directed toward higher profits and, in some cases, the avoidance of taxes imposed by the United States government, but it is usual that the welcoming countries have themselves granted tax concessions to the multinationals in the belief that they are helping to solve their unemployment problem and that their presence will benefit them. In short, it must be stated that, as in so many other realms, something that is in fact in accordance with world evolution—the creation of a true world economy and the location of industry wherever conditions are most suitable without regard to anything but the most suitable economic conditions—was started under the auspices of that being who is working against world evolution, and in accordance with his suggestions. It was Ahriman who presided over this development and he who still does so, using the incentive for the entrepreneurs of greater profit and power. Meanwhile, instead of profiting from foreign help freely given to them to help them to industrialize, the receiving countries are simply exploited, while their workers continue to receive a pittance. Only the native collaborators with the multinational companies (or fronts for them) grow wealthy at the expense of their own people, for as long as the Americans find their aid useful to them. *Corruptio optimi pessima* is the favorite principle of Ahriman.

Conclusion—Steiner's Social Ideas in Practice. This chapter brings to an end the first and much the longer of the two parts of this book. The remaining chapters will be concerned with the practical results of Steiner's teachings in certain specialized fields such as pedagogy, agriculture, and medicine. Readers of this chapter who are familiar with the social and economic life of the world of the 1970s will surely not expect to find that his social ideas have been put into practice anywhere, at least not on a substantial scale. No country appears to have even moved much closer to a Threefold Social Order. But this does not mean that the social ideas voiced by Rudolf Steiner from 1917 onward have been simply disregarded. Anthroposophists and others influenced by them have been quietly working on what A. H.

Bos has called a microsocial scale by contrast to the macrosocial scale discussed in this chapter, and here—quite apart from the immense value of continued group discussions on the subject—there has been some fruit, although not, in my view, tangible enough to occupy a separate section in Part II of this book. A few words will therefore be said on the subject here to complete this chapter.

Perhaps the best known and useful practical work with non-anthroposophists has been done by the Netherlands Pedagogical Institute, founded by Dr. B. C. J. Lievegoed in 1953. This Institute, staffed entirely by experienced anthroposophists who have familiarized themselves with many aspects of Steiner's teachings, and not only those on the social order, has been self-supporting for many years, acting as consultant in many realms of social life. It has in particular done notable work on what might be called the "humanizing" of the economic organizations that have asked it for help. The staff tries to perceive the underlying realities of each particular industry, and give advice accordingly. As a result, the solutions offered, always tentative and organic, are invariably found *to conform to* the threefold membering of the social organism as described by Steiner, rather than being, as it were, *tailored to fit* the concepts. A great deal of experience in many fields has been amassed by the consultants, and the movement has now spread into several other countries, though the form it takes differs in each. Everywhere that it has spread, however, it is always the meetings of small groups for discussion and criticism, especially self-criticism, that proves to be the real heart of the work.*

From the founding of the first Waldorf (Steiner) School in Stuttgart in 1919 onward, all the Steiner schools where it has been found feasible, organize their work as consciously as possible in accord with the threefold ordering of society. The separate schools, which are completely independent of each

---

* The best description of this work easily available in English is A. H. Bos, "A Dutch Social Initiative," *The Golden Blade*, 1972.

other, allow complete freedom of initiative to the teacher insofar as his actual teaching is concerned. This is the realm of liberty—the spiritual-cultural life as described in this chapter. Schools necessarily also have an economic life. Funds have to be raised, salaries paid, buildings managed and so on, and for this reason usually the first action taken before a school is formed is the creation of an Association, which will be made up of supporters of the school, potential parents, older anthroposophists and the like. This Association will ordinarily remain the legal owner and operator of the school, and its board of directors will bear the economic responsibility for the school. But as soon as the school is formed representatives of the cultural-spiritual life in the person of a number of teachers will become active in the Association, bringing their special expertise to bear on the problems, and in most cases will provide half the members of the board of directors of the Association, but will not occupy the official position of either president or treasurer.

In the center is the College of Teachers, which Steiner called the "heart" of the school. It cannot of course be elected like the democratic parliament of the Threefold Order, but one of its tasks is surely to mediate between the economic and spiritual members of the organism, and among other things, to state, on the basis of equity, what part of the money available to the school should be allotted to each teacher and his family. It should also choose which of its members should sit on the board of directors of the Association, and it has the task of electing one of its members to be chairman of the school itself, a task that ordinarily rotates among the teachers. As a matter of course all members of the College of Teachers are in all respects equal to all other members as regards their rights, but only those who are currently teaching are entitled to participate in meetings and discussions of the College in order to ensure that the school is always managed, and administered as far as this is necessary, by its teachers, who alone have accepted full responsibility for what the school is and does, and without whom, it must always be remembered, there would be no school.

The new movement that is growing, in the United States in particular, for a return to the land and the formation of rural communes, could learn much from Steiner's social teachings, and it may be that if these young people were to pioneer in biodynamic farming, one of Steiner's most important practical realizations, a most important social work could be brought to fruition within the framework of his social ideas. This kind of farming requires a much larger labor force than ordinary farming, as will be discussed in a later chapter, but many non-tangible rewards can be earned by the biodynamic farmer, and its value for the restoration of the land itself has already been amply proved. The farming could then provide the economic underpinning for the whole community, which could have as its other activities a school for normal and another for handicapped or "exceptional" children. These latter would be the spiritual-cultural undertakings of the community as the biodynamic farming work would be its economic activity. Each member of the community would at the same time have his say in the work of the whole through a central rights-body. The new communes, so many of which seem at present to be floundering for lack of those fundamental ideas that would give meaning and purpose to the whole, could surely profit from the application of Steiner's thought to the particular circumstances of their operation.*

These few remarks will conclude the discussion of Steiner's work as a pioneer thinker and teacher of the science of spirit. The rest of the book will now be concerned with how his ideas and his teachings have been put to practical use in the half century since his death.

---

* The Israeli *kibbutzim* have followed a different pattern from that of the Threefold Order, though in some respects resembling it. The Israeli model was in most respects fully in accord with Steiner's fundamental social law (see p. 320 above), and it functioned most effectively in the pioneer stage of development. But with increasing prosperity the older and more prosperous kibbutzim have been faced with certain important problems, some of which (notably the proper disposition of surplus funds) might be solved if Steiner's remarks on the subject were to be given serious consideration. The model is surely of little relevance to present day American or British conditions.

Aside from the three early essays discussed in the text, published under the title, *Anthroposophy and the Social Question* (New York, 1958), Steiner's fundamental work in this field in which he introduced the Threefold Social Order is the book translated under the title, *The Threefold Commonwealth*, published in German in 1919, and for the first time in English in 1922. This translation was made by E. Bowen-Wedgwood, wife of an English Labor member of Parliament who, with her husband, from whom she had separated, had been initially interested in the work of Henry George, but took up Steiner's social ideas with the greatest enthusiasm. In some ways this remains the best translation of several, and I have used this edition for the page references in the chapter. Two editions are now in print: an abbreviated version translated by Frederick C. Heckel under the title *The Threefold Social Order* (New York, 1972) and a complete version translated by F.T. Smith entitled *Towards Social Renewal* (London, 1977).

Although almost everything that Steiner did and almost all the lectures he gave in 1918 and 1919 have some bearing on the Threefold Order, the material is usually scattered throughout the various cycles. Two important cycles for members speak of the esoteric side of what he was teaching exoterically, and these should be studied, especially the first, a series of three lectures given in Zurich on February 4 and 11 and March 9, 1919 translated by Charles Davy under the title, *The Inner Aspect of the Social Question* (London, 1974). The other cycle referred to is concerned with education as its main subject, but in relating the needs of education to the social order he gives many important insights into the latter. This is *Education as a Social Problem*,

374

translated by Lisa Monges and Doris Bugbey (New York, 1969), and consists of six lectures given in Dornach in August, 1919. For the public the six lectures given in Zurich in October, 1919, and published under the title, *The Social Future*, are fundamental as a supplement to *The Threefold Commonwealth* itself (*revised edition*, New York, 1972), but the various mimeographed *Studies in the Threefold Commonwealth*, formerly available, have been out of print for years. It is therefore necessary to turn to such a pamphlet as that of G. Wachsmuth, *From the Basic Ideas of Rudolf Steiner on the Social Order* (New York, n.d.), which makes use of all Steiner's social teachings, with extensive quotations. Two pamphlets by Bernhard Behrens from the same press, *Conditions Vital to the Social Organism* (1944) and *The Economic Essentials of the Cultural Life* (1945) will also be found helpful.

An aspect not dealt with in the chapter, the relationship between the three members of the social organism and the etheric and astral bodies and the ego organization of man, are considered in lectures given in Dornach September 3, 4 and 5, 1920. The first of these, called, "East, West and Middle in Relation to the Threefold Social Organism," was published in a compilation entitled *Ancient Ghosts and Modern Spectres* (New York, 1948), and the other two, published together by the same press in 1944, bear the title, *Interrelationship Between the Human and Social Organisms.*

In 1922 Steiner gave his lectures on *World Economy*, referred to several times in the text. With *The Threefold Commonwealth* itself, these fourteen lectures appear to be the work on social matters of the most enduring interest, as evidenced by a republication in hard and paperback in a new edition (London, 1972). These lectures, given in Dornach in July and August, 1922, bore the subtitle, "The Formation of a Science of World Economics," which is an excellent description of what Steiner was in fact trying to create—a real science based on the application of Goethean method to the economic life of mankind as he observed it. Also from 1922 is one of his best

375

summaries of his work with the Threefold Social Order, to be found in the last lecture of a course of public lectures given in the course of an Anthroposophical Congress in Vienna June 1-12, of that year. The course was later published under the title *The Tension Between East and West* (London: Hodder and Stoughton, 1963), and the recommended lecture was entitled, "Anthroposophy and the Social Question," to be distinguished from the three early essays referred to earlier in this list. The preceding four lectures are also of value for the subject discussed in this chapter.

Although we have devoted much attention to the question of nationalism and Wilsonianism, no recommendations will be given here aside from the lecture referred to in a footnote in the text on page 328. Steiner's references to this subject are always incidental to other matters, and his views have to be gleaned from all that he said on the subject, which occurs in many different contexts, and sometimes in the most surprising places. The entire cycle *In the Changed Conditions of the Times*, now renamed *The Challenge of the Times* (New York, 1979), in which the lecture referred to occurs is well worth reading by serious students who have acquired a sufficient basis of anthroposophy.

PART II

ANTHROPOSOPHY IN PRACTICIAL LIFE

CHAPTER IX

Introduction

In the first part of this book we have tried to present the teachings of Rudolf Steiner primarily in the form of ideas, and only in occasional instances have we spoken much of how they have been brought to realization in practical life. Naturally, the ideas have in greater or lesser degree influenced the lives of those who have accepted and tried to work with them. Our beliefs have changed, we hope that our attitudes toward the world and our fellowmen have been transformed. These changes have been wrought in us as individuals. But anthroposophy, unlike so many philosophies and religions that have affected the inner life of individuals, has also led to practical work based upon its specific teachings about the world and man. Steiner's teachings about the nature of the growing child led in 1919 to the foundation of a totally new kind of school for boys and girls, the Waldorf School in Stuttgart, Germany, by Steiner himself and a group of co-workers whom he appointed to their positions and instructed in the new pedagogy. When physicians asked him for advice he gave it; when a group of anthroposophists who wished

379

to work with maladjusted, retarded or handicapped children asked him for advice as to how to proceed in their work, he gave it. Thus anthroposophical medicine and curative education came into being. When a group of agriculturists asked him for advice as to how to restore to health land that was being slowly destroyed by improper treatment, he gave a series of eight fundamental lectures in June, 1924, from which has arisen the whole biodynamic movement in agriculture. Lastly, we might mention that when a group of Protestant pastors expressed their dissatisfaction with traditional Christianity and its forms of worship he gave them not only many specific lectures but also a new ritual. From this beginning has arisen the Christian Community with its many branches throughout the world, including even Eastern Europe, which is thus far closed to anthroposophy itself.

It goes without saying that none of these people would have asked Steiner for advice on most of these matters if they had not believed that he genuinely possessed developed supersensible faculties that could provide his questioners with new insights of practical relevance in their work. Since he was a gifted educator with wide experience, and since as a young man he had tutored a retarded child so that he was later able to lead a normal life, he might well have been asked for his views on normal and curative education, and it was natural for pastors who were inspired by his insights into Christianity to ask him for his views as to how a new spirit could be breathed into their religion. But doctors and farmers, all specialists in their own fields and rarely given to asking advice from philosophers, evidently believed that Rudolf Steiner could indeed give them advice from his supersensible perception. It is with the results of this work that we shall be concerned in this second part of the book. Some of the ideas we have already touched upon in Part I. In Part II there will be occasion to speak of others not hitherto described, especially in the chapter on biodynamic farming. We do not propose to describe in any detail those institutions that have been founded in so many parts of the world with the purpose of putting some of Steiner's ideas to practical use. We intend rather to continue to speak in somewhat general terms, mentioning a particular institution only insofar as it was a pioneer in the work, as was the case for the Waldorf School in Stuttgart or the anthroposophical medical clinic in Arlesheim founded by Dr. Ita Wegman. It is with Steiner pedagogy in general, with anthroposophical medicine in general that we shall primarily be concerned. Thus Chapter 10 will deal with education for normal children, Chapter 11 with curative education, Chapter 12 with biodynamic agriculture, and Chapter 13 with medicine. We have felt it better to omit the work of the Christian Community, but in the concluding chapter we shall give a brief description of the founding of the General Anthroposophical Society in 1923, and the varied work that is carried on at the Goetheanum, the building in Dornach that is the center of the anthroposophical work in the world. This work includes artistic presentations of certain of the arts mentioned in Chapter 6, and research work in scientific and other fields.

Anthroposophy is perhaps still in the early stages of its childhood, and all that will be spoken of here is only a beginning. But it will at least show that the beginning has been made and that at least some progress may be seen in the fifty years since Steiner's death, small though it may be in comparison with what might, and surely *ought,* to have been accomplished with such riches as he placed at our disposal.

381

CHAPTER X

The New Art of Education
The Waldorf School Movement

It will be remembered from the last chapter that Steiner began to write about the "social question," and stated the fundamental law of social life as early as 1905, but took an active part in working toward a new social order more than a decade later, when the need for such a new order had become so urgent that he could no longer keep silent. It was the same with his work on education. As a young man he had earned his living as a private tutor for some years, and this experience, together with his unique ability to learn something important from every human encounter, however brief, constituted a valuable basis for his later educational work. In 1908, when he gave his fundamental lecture on education, he would scarcely have been known to the public primarily as an educator, nor had he as yet any intention of founding a school. The school had to wait until the urgent need arose, and he was asked for his help. Then he gave it. This is the pattern followed in almost all, if not all, his practical work. He did not personally take the initiative; he was always asked.

It is interesting now to read this fundamental lecture of 1908, which he repeated, as he tells us himself, in several places, "in response to a wish expressed in many quarters," and finally edited for publication as an essay. It contains the germ of almost all that he was to elaborate later in detail when he founded the first Waldorf School and when the movement began to grow in other countries outside Germany. Even now this essay remains by far the best work to use as an introduction to his educational thought and the basic anthroposophical teachings that lie behind it. About this booklet, *The Education of the Child in the Light of Anthroposophy*, Steiner was later to tell a public audience of educators in Oxford, England:

> I was speaking on education there as one who disagrees with much in modern education, who would like to see this or the other treated more fundamentally, and so on. But at the time this little book was written I should not have been able to undertake such a thing as directing the Waldorf School. For it was essential for such a task to have a college of teachers with a knowledge of man originating in a spiritual world.*

This remains true today, and has always been true. A Waldorf or Rudolf Steiner School requires a body of teachers "with a knowledge of man originating in a spiritual world." Perhaps none of the later Steiner schools has ever had such a galaxy of talent available as Steiner had assembled around him when the opportunity was presented to found the first Waldorf School in Stuttgart; all had acquired familiarity with the basic truths of anthroposophy through close contact with Rudolf Steiner himself.

The founding of this school arose directly from the Threefold Social Impulse. Emil Molt, the director of the Waldorf Astoria Factory in Stuttgart, was deeply interested in anthroposophy, and in pursuance of Steiner's suggestion that factory workers ought to be more fully aware of the purpose of their particular work and thus obtain a more human relation to it, arranged early in 1919 for half hour lectures to be given to his employees on social and educational matters. Herbert Hahn (who tells the

---

* *The Spiritual Ground of Education*, p. 40.

383

whole story in the 1958 *Golden Blade*) not only gave the lectures but began to help some of the workers' children with their homework. As a consequence of this contact and the educational lectures, the parents of the children began to wonder aloud whether it might not be possible for the children to be able to have a better schooling more in keeping with the principles of the Threefold Order. Such an idea was also stirring in the mind of Emil Molt, who long ago had read Steiner's brochure *The Education of the Child in the Light of Anthroposophy*. The thought had lodged in him that perhaps he would be the one who, in the words of the brochure, would "call upon the science of spirit to build up an art of education."

When Rudolf Steiner himself came to Stuttgart shortly afterward to give a lecture on the Threefold Commonwealth, he emphasized how important it was for all mankind to have the opportunity to pursue a free cultural life, and more especially industrial workers who from an early age were forced into making a living and could get no education worthy of the name. Hearing words like these, enthusiasm grew in the hearts of the workers and of Emil Molt, in whom it is clear that the idea of a school for his workers was already taking shape, to be run in accordance with the ideas of Rudolf Steiner. A few days later, after another lecture to a different group of industrial workers, Hahn, an experienced teacher and anthroposophist named Karl Stockmeyer, Molt, and Steiner met together. Then and there (April 25, 1919) the decision was taken to open a school. On August 21st Steiner began two parallel series of fourteen lectures each and a seminar, which he gave to the teachers whom he had chosen to open the school. One cycle was, as might have been expected in any such new venture, a *Practical Course for Teachers*, and the other, published under the title, *The Study of Man*, is still used as the groundwork for all courses in Steiner pedagogy given to prospective teachers. It is truly a fundamental course, and not at all easy, dealing as it does with the corporeal, soul and spiritual elements in man. Many other lectures and courses given subsequent to this one, especially those for public

384

audiences who knew little or nothing of anthroposophy, are better used as introductions to the subject for beginners. But these first teachers had already acquired some basic knowledge of anthroposophy itself, and to them this cycle was the culmination of their work of preparation, showing how this spiritual knowledge must be applied in the education of children. For it should be understood, and it will be the main purpose of this chapter to demonstrate the fact, that Steiner pedagogy is based upon *the nature of man.* Therefore everything in the pedagogical methods and curriculum is derived from this, having nothing to do with the demands of governments or employers that children should possess such or such knowledge by the time they leave school, in order that they may be able to fulfill their proper role in society. Steiner pedagogy is thus truly an attempt to *educate,* in the Latin sense of the word, to "draw forth" what lies within the human being so that it may bear fruit in outer life.

The two courses were completed on September 5, 1919, and two days later, on September 7th, the Waldorf School was opened in the presence of Rudolf Steiner in a former restaurant that had been transformed into a school for the purpose.

The Purpose of Schooling. We have just remarked that Steiner pedagogy is based upon the nature of the child, and that it has nothing to do with what government or society demand that a child must "know" when he is ready to take his place in an adult world. In the existing societies of the present day it is obvious that this principle must remain an ideal to be aimed at rather than an actuality anywhere. For nowhere on earth can be found that "free cultural life" that Steiner looked upon as one of the pillars of the Threefold Social Order, and that would find its natural expression in a free education, its content decided upon by educators themselves, and paid for, as of right, by the economy.

Such a notion is quite foreign to present-day thinking, which holds that "he who pays the piper has a right to call the tune." Although it is of course admitted that the costs of education

385

must be borne by the economy, it has come to seem natural that the means by which the money necessary to pay educational costs is extracted from the economy has, and should have, a vital bearing on the kind of education offered. If it is the state government that meets these costs out of taxes, as is overwhelmingly the case in the industrialized world of today, then state bureaucrats will have the task of administering the funds and at the same time lay down the principles for the education given. If parents pay for the schooling themselves, they will almost invariably share some of the assumptions of the state governments, even though they will no doubt have a deeper interest in the welfare of their children. Education, in the minds of almost all legislators, bureaucrats, and parents in our industrial and materialistic age, ought to give young people, above all, the necessary skills to enable them to function effectively in the adult world—the world to which these parents and legislators are already accustomed. In the Western world greater emphasis is laid on the ability of the young person to make a good living for himself and his family; if it is also possible, without prejudice to this first requirement, then he should also acquire a broad cultural background so he can make wise use of his leisure once he has attended to the task of making his living. By contrast, in Eastern Europe more attention will certainly be given to the role that the government will expect the student to play in social or industrial life in exchange for the education provided for him by society. Consciously or unconsciously, those responsible for education place at the center of their preoccupations the fitting of the child into the society into which he has been born. Hence, the strong tendency toward conservatism in education, and the great difficulty in introducing innovations that might have an unsettling effect on society.

Steiner education must also take account of what society and parents demand, or appear to demand. It is always one of the foremost tasks of teachers in Steiner schools to educate *the parents,* so they recognize as fully as possible why the methods

386

and curriculum are as they are. Yet these teachers would certainly regard themselves as failing in their duty if their pupils were not prepared to play their part in the adult world as well as pupils of other schools. But Steiner education takes full account of the soul-spiritual as well as the bodily nature of the child, and it cannot regard education as simply the accumulation of knowledge likely to be useful to him in later life, nor even of skills that he will need. Steiner teachers believe that if a child throughout his period in school has received the education suited for each stage of his development, and in the process nourished his soul-spiritual being, he will at the end be much fresher in mind, more open to impressions from the outside world, more competent in crafts, in a word, in all respects more *alive* and more *ready* for the world, than one who has passed through the regular state-imposed curriculum, however brilliantly he may have performed in it. In almost all Steiner schools compromises have to be made in the upper years of high school because of requirements for higher education imposed by the state or private universities, or, at the very best, a full twelve years of Steiner education will be followed by a thirteenth year in which the various state demands will be met. In short, it is held that a truly "child-centered" education such as that offered by the Steiner schools (and recommended by many modern child psychologists, notably Jean Piaget), in no way handicaps the child who goes through the entire twelve or thirteen years, even though at a given moment he may not have acquired the same standard of "knowledge" as another child of the same age in a state school. At the age of eighteen, after all, it is of no importance whether a child learned to read at four or eight, how large his vocabulary was by the time he was ten, whether he learned to use fractions at ten or fourteen. What matters at eighteen is whether he is mentally alert, alive in his feelings, able to work with his hands, whether he has a basis of general knowledge and wide culture, able *now* to read and write effectively, and to study with interest and concentration. *Now* he

387

can begin to earn his living, or engage in higher education and acquire his professional equipment. But the effects of the kind of education he has received will endure throughout his life. When most people today speak of a child-centered education, they regard it as the kind of education that will give a child the opportunity to develop such talents as he may have inherited, so that he may be able later to choose freely a path of life congenial to him in which he may hope to be both productive and creative. What is good for the individual is likely in the long run to be good also for society, it is usually thought, and the child himself should be given the maximum of free choice under the guidance, as far as necessary, of his teachers. While this approach must surely be better than one that is too authoritarian, it nevertheless begs a number of important questions, especially whether, and if so when, a child ought to make educational choices for himself, and, perhaps the most crucial, what exactly is a child, and wherein does he differ from a small adult?

The point is not a ridiculous or meaningless one. Many cultures, including our own at least until fairly recent times, have treated children as if they were indeed small adults, to be reasoned with, preached to, filled with intellectual knowledge by adults, made to behave in accordance with moral codes evolved by adults, and taught the difference between "right" and "wrong" according to adult norms. Anyone who has studied Chapter 4 of this book will certainly not expect this to be the viewpoint of Steiner education. This education is essentially grounded on the recognition of the child as a *spiritual* being, with a varying number of incarnations behind him, who is returning at birth into the physical world, into a body that will be slowly moulded into a usable instrument by the soul-spiritual forces he brings with him. He has chosen his parents for himself because of what they can provide for him that he needs in order to fulfill his karma, and, conversely, they too need their relationship with him in order to fulfill their own karma. He will inherit a certain kind of body because of what they transmit to him through heredity, and a certain kind of environment.

388

Parents who know these things will naturally have a different relation to their children than those who are ignorant of them. They can never suppose for a moment that their child *belongs* to them and can be treated as their own *possession;* similarly teachers in Steiner schools who have convinced themselves of these facts will *never,* for example, *condescend to* a child, who, as soon as he is asleep and his spirit is no longer clothed in his child body will be in every respect their equal. Teachers too will know that it is their task to help the child to make use of his body, to help his soul-spiritual forces to find expression through it, rather than regarding it as their duty to cram him with information and knowledge that adults consider it necessary for him to have.

The Child of Pre-School Age. Steiner pointed out on numerous occasions and in different contexts how important it is for the very young child to acquire in the right way those three characteristics which distinguish the human being from the animal. They should follow in simple and natural succession—walking upright, speaking, and thinking. In this way the child relates himself to both the cosmos and the earth. Soon after he has learned to speak the power of thought begins to stir in him in embryonic form, and then he will suddenly become aware of himself and cease to call himself by his name as if he were a third person. He will suddenly say "I" and mean himself, though no one has ever taught him to do this. Up to this time, Steiner tells us, the child has been surrounded, bathing himself as it were, in the forces that have been embodied in the earth by the Christ. With self-consciousness and the ability to say "I" he has had, so to speak, his personal "fall," as Adam "fell" when he won for himself the knowledge of good and evil. This is the first great landmark in the life of a child, and as a rule it is only back to this first moment of self-consciousness that he can remember in later life. The moment usually occurs at the age of three.*

---

* It sometimes happens, as Steiner himself was the first to point out, that a child will say "I" much earlier. But careful observation will show that *this* use of the personal pronoun is imitative, and not fully conscious. Very young children do occasionally imitate their elders who use the word "I," but we are speaking here

All children have some difficulty in accustoming themselves to living within their bodies. These bodies, after all, have been the best that were available for them, but are not necessarily ideal. The good, quiet children, according to Steiner, are those whose bodies offer too much resistance to the spirit, whereas the more active noisy children may be clumsy with their bodies, but they are at least learning to make use of them.* It is, in fact, extremely difficult to be a child, but the latter is fortunately not aware of the difficulty since he no longer possesses his spiritual consciousness, and in effect what consciousness he has is still virtually asleep. Now during all the first seven years of life he is gradually becoming accustomed to his body, and the crowning achievement of this epoch is the pushing forth of his own second teeth. The first milk teeth are soft and come to him out of his own hereditary forces, but the second set, by far the hardest part of his whole organism, is expected to last him for life.

Looking at this process, with its culmination, from a somewhat different point of view, we may say that at birth the child has freed his own *physical* body, which was formerly within the body of his mother; during the first seven years of his earthly life his *etheric* body is surrounded by a kind of protective envelope, analogous to the body of his mother in his prenatal state. The child's own forces are working mightily within this protective covering, so that it can be sloughed off at about the age of seven simultaneously with the change of teeth. The body, at seven years of age, is no longer entirely the product of forces of heredity. The child's own soul-spiritual nature has now laid its

---

of the fully conscious use of the word as referring to themselves, and this rarely occurs before the age of three, and may be delayed even until the age of four or later.

* These observations are drawn from the first lecture of the wonderful cycle entitled, *The Kingdom of Childhood*, that Steiner gave in Torquay in August, 1924 in preparation for the opening of the first English school. The really delightful sentence of Steiner that follows, and should be consoling to many overwrought mothers, is worth quoting in full: "We may even regard the wild screams of a child as most enthralling, simply because we thereby experience the martyrdom the spirit has to endure when it descends into a child-body." (p. 21)

stamp upon it, in part as a result of the working of his own personal karma that he has brought with him to earth. Indeed, the more strongly a person's individuality works on his body, the less he will come to resemble his parents and other relatives physically. Some children scarcely resemble their parents at all by the time they reach puberty, nor do they even resemble themselves as they were during the first seven years of life. Such children have brought with them a strong individuality that can be quickly freed from the "group-soul" forces of heredity, even of their nation. From seven to fourteen the *astral body* still has its own protective covering, which is gradually cast off at puberty. When this process is complete the child will have the full use of his now freed astral body, in the same way as at the age of twenty or twenty-one his own *"I"* or ego will take possession of the three sheaths, and he will, as we say so exactly, "come of age."

Now the kind of education that can properly be given is, as may well be imagined, entirely dependent on the development just described. Memory, for example, whose seat is the etheric body, should never be consciously cultivated before the coming of the second teeth. Indeed, the same *forces* that actually thrust forth the teeth are those that now take on the task of thinking and consciously remembering. Of course children can remember *instinctively* before the age of seven, more or less, as already mentioned, from the time they can say "I" to themselves. But memory should not be *cultivated,* nor, as we shall see, should the child be taught to read, before the age of six or seven. The method by which young children learn until this age is, in any event, almost all by *imitation,* not by precept. It is their limb system in particular that is developing now, and they imitate and should imitate what their teachers *do.* Fairy tales and other stories told to children of this age should be full of *happenings;* even an artistic thread, so important in the next seven years, is of little consequence earlier. Children in nursery school and kindergarten are taught to do wonderful things by their teachers in Steiner schools, but always by copying and imitating. There is no serious attempt to make them *learn* anything through the mind, only to acquire certain habits and skills by doing and imitating.

Elementary School: Seven to Fourteen Years. The second seven years of a child's life present a striking contrast with the first seven, a contrast that is naturally reflected in the education he receives. Whereas he lived primarily in his limbs during his first period, it is his *rhythmic* system that now takes command. The center of this system, we may remember from Chapter 7, is the heart and lungs, and children's movements are ordinarily far more graceful and balanced than earlier, or than in the "awkward" period of adolescence that follows. It is no primitive superstition that has always regarded the heart as the center of feeling, but a true perception. All education in the years from seven to fourteen should be artistic, imaginative and poetic, and should above all appeal to the life of feeling. The teacher also should try to maintain a rhythmic balance in everything he does, as for example by being alternately serious and humorous, while calling forth activity at one time from his pupils and at another a more quiet mood of soul.

These years of elementary school are the most crucial of all in Steiner schools. Many such schools throughout the world have not been able, for financial reasons or from a shortage of teachers, to establish high schools of their own. It is certainly a serious deprivation for a child to have to leave his Steiner school at the age of fourteen and go to a state high school, especially in view of the fact that in each of the Steiner high school classes the work done is so often a kind of recapitulation at a different (post-puberty) level of what was given in the earlier years in an artistic imaginative manner appropriate for that period of life. Nevertheless, if a child has been able to pass the crucial seven years between seven and fourteen in a Steiner school, and under the guidance of the same class teacher, he will have acquired a strong foundation on which to build in later years. Much of the benefit will remain with him during the years of high school, enabling him to make better progress there in spite of the intellectual orientation of most modern state education.

The statement in the last paragraph that the child will go through all the eight years of elementary school with the same teacher may at first appear startling to those ignorant of the principles of Steiner education. In any event the reasons for this practice, which may not always be feasible to carry out, should be understood, for it represents the ideal and may be regarded as the most important single feature of the education of these years. Whereas the pre-school child learns by imitating, and therefore *copies* the actions of his parents and teachers, and learns to *do* as they do, a child between seven and fourteen, as the life of feeling unfolds in him, wishes to *be* like his teacher, thereby laying an enormous responsibility on his teacher actually to be or become the kind of person worthy of being loved by his pupils and regarded as their model. This is particularly important in the first years of elementary school when the relationship between teacher and pupil is forming, and before the child has begun truly to experience the outer world as a world separate from and independent of himself—a change that begins to appear about the age of nine. It is natural for a child of seven or eight to believe that his teacher knows everything, and the teacher should in fact answer truthfully all the many questions posed to him by his children, but in a pictorial and imaginative, not a "scientific" manner. In this way the child learns to build up a trust in him.

Once it has been won, this trust gives the teacher the possibility of exercising an entirely natural authority over his pupils that should last for many years—the kind of authority that in earlier cultures used to be exercised by the elders over the younger members of their tribe. In this modern age when the young so soon appear to resent the exercise of any external authority over them, whether by parents or teachers, it is sometimes a great surprise to visitors to see how a class teacher in a Steiner school is usually looked up to and obeyed quite instinctively by his pupils, and wonder how the miracle was accomplished. The main reason is surely the close relationship built between the two over the years, which in turn is based upon the soul-spiritual development of the teacher far more than upon any knowledge he may have acquired. Not all would-be-teachers are actually capable of the necessary development, and can never therefore exercise what we have here called "natural" authority rather than authority based on power and position. Such teachers as a rule soon weed themselves out of the faculties of Steiner schools. But the rule observed in these schools that, except for special and unusual circumstances, the same teacher remains for the full eight years with his class, at least makes it possible for the kind of relationship to be built such as we have described. It is almost impossible for any teacher to learn to know his pupils if he remains behind every year and has to teach a new class the same material that he taught a different class the year before. This is scarcely a *human* relationship at all, and is scarcely much better if he teaches the same subject to several different classes in the same year. In the Steiner school the teacher progresses with his pupils, and if, when he begins to teach he does not know all the material he will be expected to teach in the next seven years, he will have to prepare it as he goes along. But this is precisely what makes a good teacher, that he continues to grow, ever acquiring more experience and more knowledge.

If he remains the full eight years with the same pupils, and if a minimum of children leave the school during these years, then the teacher will also have learned to know very well indeed the parents of his pupils, and every problem of importance will have been discussed with them. No grades are ever given in Steiner schools; the teacher simply evaluates the work of his pupils as he knows it and them, and makes out a careful report for each at the end of the school year. This report will, or should be, helpful to both parents and children, and in practice is almost always greatly valued by both. The children do not thus have to compete with each other but only with the best they themselves have been able to do in the past. If the teacher has been able to develop in himself the kind of living thinking that we have discussed in earlier chapters, especially Chapter 7, he will be able to note almost every change and development in each of his children, and adjust his teaching and his attitude accordingly. To a class teacher in a Steiner school the children can never be simply an undifferentiated group of children. They are *his* children and he will know the temperaments of all of them and how they can be dealt with. Children as a matter of course should be handled differently according to their temperaments, and an imaginative and observant teacher will grasp the sometimes subtle differences as his experience grows. Children of a choleric temperament may well receive different tasks than those given to the phlegmatic or melancholic. But, even more important, the teacher has to learn to deal with each temperament in a different way.* All the temperaments together go to make up his class, and in a certain way his task may reasonably be compared with that of a conductor of an orchestra.

It may be noted that the curriculum of a Steiner school is so organically constructed for these eight years that each year something new is taught that was not taught before, and the content of the same subjects will be different according to the age the children have attained. It goes without saying that all the children in a class will belong to the same general age group because the subject matter is chosen not for its intellectual or knowledge content but because of the particular soul-spiritual qualities that unfold at each age. About the age of nine, for example, Old Testament stories are related to the children as a kind of preparation for history, and this is followed the next year by Norse sagas and myths, which, with their dramatic action, exercise a powerful and salutary influence on children of ten.

---

* A general work by Steiner on the temperaments is his early lecture given in Carlsruhe, January 19, 1909 entitled, *The Four Temperaments* (New York, 1976), but for how to deal with them in a classroom see *The Kingdom of Childhood*, pp. 76-77. The method is far from what an uninstructed person would expect, but it works!

The following year culminates in the teaching of Greek history, still presented imaginatively and pictorially, and not with any emphasis on cause and effect, which is reserved for the following year. At the age of twelve the concept of cause and effect becomes for the first time comprehensible. In earlier years a child may *appear* to have a grasp of it, but a closer examination will invariably reveal that he confused "before and after" with "cause and effect." Even teachers may sometimes be deceived by this appearance. The teaching of Roman and medieval history, taught from the age of twelve, is able at last to take into account this new ability. All these historical subjects, including those given in the seventh and eighth classes, will be taught again in high school, when the adolescent has learned to handle abstractions, and to arrive at judgments of his own.

In the same way that children should not be asked to change their teachers every year while they are in elementary school, they must not change their subjects every hour while school is in session, nor even every day. So the Steiner school, even at the high school level, follows a system under which the day begins with a so-called "main lesson," a block that may last from one and a half to two hours. The same subject is dealt with in a main lesson for usually as much as three weeks at a time. Using the history example again, a child will study perhaps three blocks of history during the same year, and each time he will have the opportunity to enter really deeply into the subject, with no distraction from suddenly having to turn his attention to arithmetic or a science. Since all subjects are taught artistically, the child in almost all subjects makes a main lesson book for himself that he illustrates in color, a task that is always a great joy to him. Foreign languages, however, in contrast to the practice in state schools, are not regarded as *subjects* in themselves. Two languages as a rule are taught from first grade onward, but every day, and whenever possible by teachers, who may be specialists, unlike the class teachers. The language taught should be the mother tongue of these teachers, and the child will therefore never hear the language pronounced incorrectly. These languages are taught rhythmically in the lower grades, and grammar is picked up more or less automatically, up to a certain point, in the same way that we all learn our mother tongue. Eurythmy, instrumental playing, beginning, as a rule, with the recorder, singing, painting, and the other arts and handwork are usually taught in the afternoon, and in any event after the main lesson for the day has been completed.

The class teacher up to class nine is expected to be able to teach all the main lessons, and teach them with imagination and artistry. Even though specialist teachers may take his place for other periods of the day, it is always he who holds the chief responsibility for his class. Since the content of the curriculum changes year by year, not only in order that new subjects may be studied but because some subjects bear a special relationship to the soul-spiritual nature of a child as it unfolds at a particular age,* the class teacher will necessarily find that he himself has to do a great deal of preparation for every class, at least during his first "tour of duty" of eight years. In spite of this load it is a rare school that possesses enough financial resources to enable it to allow a class teacher to give nothing but his main lesson. Most class teachers therefore teach also some art or craft, if only to their own class. When it is considered that all Steiner schools are independent of the state and must therefore meet most, if not all, their expenses from fees and donations, it will be recognized that class teachers must be rare human beings—possessing not only the qualities and capacities enumerated above, but also ready to accept lower salaries than are offered by most public school systems.

It therefore goes without saying that it is impossible to be a good class teacher in a Steiner school unless in effect one wants to be one more than one wants anything else in the world. But if this is what he or she wishes to be, then to teach in this manner, making use of every capacity one has, is a true vocation, a real

---

* For example, at the age of twelve a child can first obtain a valuable relationship to the inorganic world; for this reason he begins mineralogy and geology at that age.

calling, rather than a mere profession, and its intangible rewards are perhaps greater than in almost any other work. But it will readily be understood why it is not possible simply to *organize* a new Steiner school because there are pupils, parents, and funds available, and a "felt need" exists. The teachers, and especially the class teachers, are the heart of the school, and building up a faculty is one of the most onerous and difficult of tasks. But because they are the heart of the school, in almost all Steiner schools they also hold the main working responsibility for the management of the school itself and for the choosing of new teachers, as well as the right to accept or reject new pupils for their own classes. These schools have no headmaster, principal, or chief administrator. The teachers united together in a "college" hold this responsibility, which is usually assumed, for practical purposes by one of their number, for a limited period of time, usually a year. Such a person becomes simply the "chairman" of the faculty—equal in all respects to other members of the college of teachers, but with one added responsibility for as long as he holds the office. Financial tasks may be undertaken in relation to the school by parents and friends, but teaching is a part of what Steiner called "the free cultural life," as we have considered it in the last chapter. Teachers alone can therefore form part of the college of teachers, and bear the responsibility for the free cultural life of the school for they have become teachers in the first place only because as free beings they chose to do so.

The Senior or High School: Ages Fourteen to Eighteen or Later. Although in some peoples, and increasingly in our era among Europeans and Americans, the sexual aspects of puberty itself may present themselves before the age of fourteen, it is always at about this age that the aspect most stressed in anthroposophy, the freeing of the astral body from its sheath, occurs. At this time the young person becomes ready for numerous changes in his teaching to correspond to the changes that are taking place in his physical and soul-spiritual being. At the change of teeth, as was pointed out earlier, those forces that had been hitherto used for creating and thrusting forth the teeth themselves, could be used for building the conscious memory; now they are freed for intellectual thinking, and thinking becomes possible in a way that would have been harmful if it had been systematically trained before. Indeed, a child who has been gently led into deepening his thinking process during the last years of elementary school will now suddenly find himself almost overwhelmed by his thoughts and questions, which are perfectly legitimate and need to be answered in a different way than was possible before. Whereas during elementary school it was the rhythmic system that predominated and teaching had to be imaginative and artistic, the adolescent learns above all through observation and thinking, and by the conscious use of his senses. The whole external world now forces itself upon his attention, and for the first time in his life he really becomes "awake." As all teachers know, however, boys and girls now react to the world differently, a difference that Steiner characterizes clearly in *The Spiritual Ground of Education* (pp. 124–126).

Here he tells us that the boy of fourteen or fifteen finds that the world around him "echoes in his being," and "as a result his inner self becomes a problem to him." By contrast the girl is affected more by what is going on in her own inner being as a consequence of puberty, and she "faces the world in amazement, finding it full of problems; above all she is now a being who seeks in the outer world ideals to live by. Thus many things in the outer world become enigmatic to a girl at this age," as things in his inner world are enigmatic to a boy.*

In a certain sense Greek civilization represents the adolescent period of world history, before the coming of the "I" with the incarnation of the Christ, as was explained in Chapter 2. The attitude of the fully awake adolescent whose development has not been stunted by the premature attempt to train his intellectual faculties should be precisely the attitude of the

* A fine series of comments on this question taken from his own long experience as teacher appear in Harwood's book *The Recovery of Man in Childhood*, pp. 171–174.

Greek toward his world. All knowledge, said Plato, begins in wonder, and what the adolescent should now feel toward *his* world is *wonder* at it, mingled with a kind of reverence and awe at all that there is to be known about it. If he begins his years of puberty and high school with such an attitude, he may never wholly lose it, as so many of us have lost it because we were given too much too early, and too much was asked of us before we were ready. If he retains it into adult life then he may be able more easily to develop a living thinking, such as we have described in Chapter 7, and also adopt that attitude toward the external world that is essential in this age of the consciousness soul, when we must look upon the external world not as raw material to be understood with the intellect and manipulated for our convenience, but as a world created by and peopled by higher beings, with whom it is our task to create a relationship of warmth and love, and thus arrive at true understanding.

After puberty, with his critical faculties awakening, no adolescent would find it entirely natural to do all his studies with the same teacher, nor would he be inclined any longer to regard his teacher as an unquestioned authority. Nor should he do so. He should, as a matter of course, expect his teachers to be able to prove what they say, or at least to give evidence for its truth. But, in view of the changes taking place in the inner lives of their pupils high school teachers should be able and ready to exercise the utmost patience, and should be at least as warm and loving in their attitude toward their pupils as the class teachers are with the children whom they accompany for so many years. High school teachers, however, should gradually become more "comradely," and treat their pupils as equals, showing respect for their qualities of mind and soul as they reveal themselves during adolescence. Many of these older students, faced with the wonder and interest of the new world they are discovering with their minds and senses, tend to undertake too much, and thus even to overwork themselves. The teacher should be on the lookout for this, and more than ever is it necessary for the youngsters to engage in craft work, especially wood carving,

400

which allows the newly found head and will forces to work themselves out in a creative manner; the shaping of hard material by the pupils according to the ideas they have conceived has a wonderfully balancing effect.

The manner of teaching in a Steiner school now becomes quite different in many respects from that of the years from seven to fourteen. The class teacher of the earlier years now yields place to specialists, who have the knowledge and skills to respond to the needs of the youngsters. One teacher in particular may undertake responsibilities for a class similar to those undertaken by the class teacher of earlier years and become the one to whom the pupils turn for personal advice. But he himself will still be one of the specialist teachers, not an "all-rounder" like the class teachers. All these specialists try to imbue their subject with a warmth that can be felt by the young people and only teachers who really *love* the subject they teach can be truly effective at this stage. It can thus be imagined that it may be no easier for Steiner schools to find suitable high school teachers than it was for them to find class teachers, and it may be understood why some schools have never been able to add a high school to their elementary school, even after many years of operation, and even though funds and parental support are available.

The high school curriculum continues to be broad and well-balanced, and the languages that have been taught all through elementary school are now understood well enough for the pupils to be able to acquire a good grounding in the literature of the countries whose languages have been studied. Grammar and composition in the mother tongue are perfected as far as possible. All this would naturally be undertaken in any state school as well as in Steiner schools. But there is one subject that is rarely taught in state schools that is regarded as of the utmost importance in the Steiner high school that begins in the ninth grade and continues until graduation. This is the history of art, beginning with painting and continuing with music, poetry and culminating in architecture in the top grade. Although there are many reasons for the inclusion of this subject, two may be especially mentioned here.

The origin of art is lost in the dimness of prehistory. Indeed, the very first men we know of, long before the invention of writing, seem to have made their tools not only so that they could be put to practical use, but with something added that to us appears to have been an attempt to satisfy an aesthetic sense. Prehistoric men carved in caves far below the surface of the earth, and painted animals in a way we ourselves would find it hard to equal, if we worked with the tools they had and in the dim light that was all that could have been available in the bowels of the earth. So from the very beginning of time man has been an artist, and there has never been a time when there was not something being done by man that we could classify as art, and that has in fact been so regarded by posterity. Thus, this *unpractical* streak in man, if we may so term it, is the cause for the utmost wonder, and allows us, and a young person just becoming aware of and able to grasp with understanding the long history of mankind, the opportunity to *wonder at man* as the Greeks wondered at him, and as the famous chorus in the *Antigone* of Sophocles emphasized, man "as the most wonderful of all wonderful things." Man is not only *homo faber,* as all the world knows, but also *homo artifex.* A child should be able to leave school as a young man or woman with his senses undimmed, with a longing still awake for more knowledge, and also a desire to create through art. What his predecessors have done should be known to him in a living way, and this is one of the aims of the four year course in the history of art.

It scarcely needs saying that anthroposophy, as such, is *never* taught in Steiner schools. But a study of the history of art reveals to an adolescent the fact of the evolution of human consciousness far more clearly than can be done with the study of straight history. What we have attempted in Chapter 2 of this book could not possibly be given to an elementary or high school student in just that form. But the history of art is necessarily taught through slides or reproductions, and thus is presented pictorially to the rapidly awakening intellectual consciousness of the high school years. It thus has a maximum effect, for the students can really feel the gradual incarnation of the human being on the earth, and can grasp how he began to see the external world clearly and tried to reproduce it through his art, and how, with some of the late nineteenth and twentieth century painters he began once more to have glimpses of the etheric world. In the history of music, which in its modern form appeared as recently as the sixteenth century, he can nevertheless experience for himself how the human consciousness evolves with the different composers from Bach to the late nineteenth century. In architecture he can trace the evolution of consciousness in yet another way by observing how, for example, religious architecture has evolved from the Sumerian ziggurat to the medieval cathedral and later. None of these things need be taught explicitly, but the young person, now for the first time made aware of all that men have created in the past, from the earliest times to the present, will come to realize how the men who created in the earliest times could never have conceived the skyscraper, how the men who painted in the prehistoric caves could not have painted character like Rembrandt, how the Egyptian could not yet reach the perfection of form of the Greek statuary because he did not yet see and admire the form of man as the Greeks saw and admired him. If in later years the student ever hears of the evolution of consciousness as the true explanation for historical change, if he passed through a Steiner high school he will have acquired the necessary groundwork for understanding it, and all that he has experienced in this course will then make sense.

It was mentioned earlier that history itself in high school recapitulates in a certain sense what was taught in elementary school, but with more explanation, more discussion of causes and effects than was feasible or desirable earlier when the necessary faculties had not yet emerged. This statement needs some modification and explanation. The order in which history is taught is not at all the same as it was in elementary school. In the ninth grade the adolescent needs to feel himself at home on earth, and the last thing in the world he should have just at this age is a chronological history beginning with the most ancient times, which, for the moment, would be completely alien to him. What he needs is to know above all the forces that have shaped the modern world, both the inventions and the ideas, the Copernican theory and its effects, the steam engine and its effects, the seventeenth century conflicts from which arose new ideas of the dignity of man, and his right to freedom, the notion of democracy, and similar themes, always with an emphasis on the latent idealism that needs to be fostered. Only when the history of the modern age has been completed in several important blocks (the main lesson system is used in high school as it was in elementary school) can the history of ancient times be picked up again, but on a quite different level from that used in fifth and sixth grades. Here also man can be seen coming closer to the earth, with the changes of consciousness from Egypt through Greece, with its birth of conscience, and Rome. As Harwood has pointed out (*op.cit.*, p. 189) "the children are witnessing that birth of thinking which is taking place in them, and which their own thinking is now sufficiently mature to realize."

The next year the history of Christianity and the Middle Ages will bring the students to the point where they picked up history in the ninth grade, leaving the last, twelfth grade as the great opportunity to round off the whole, so that at the end they should possess a comprehensive picture of the whole history of mankind. In addition they can even study some theories of history, so that the problems of interpretation of the past are raised in their minds, and some of the differences among contemporary civilizations can be discerned, as well as some of the essential similarities. Meanwhile all the other classes are going on as always, including the study of the two languages in addition to the mother tongue. There will surely be dramatic performances presented at the end of each term of the upper school years, and particularly by the graduating class, as well as performances of music and eurythmy, an art that will have been taught throughout the school life from the first grade until graduation.

Conclusion—the Steiner Educational Movement: Its Growth and Difficulties. We have tried in this chapter to give a general idea of the kind of education offered in schools run according to the principles elaborated by Rudolf Steiner, and we have attempted, however briefly, to indicate the relationship between these educational principles and his other teachings on man as discussed in earlier chapters. In the limited space of this chapter we have naturally been unable to go into details of the curriculum, but have offered a few examples of the yearly changes, especially in the field of history. Fortunately, all the major lecture cycles on education have been translated into English, and there are books available written by practicing teachers that go into more detail than do most of the lectures on how the principles are put into practice in the real life of the existing schools. The comprehensive list given at the end of the chapter will give the reader a fair idea of what goes to make up this education, and wherein it differs from any other.

It may be emphasized again that this education was not the result of experimental work done by educational specialists on the basis of trial and error and statistical inferences—although many groups of child psychologists, especially in the Gesell Institute in the United States, have discovered that their findings agree in numerous particulars with Steiner's "intuitions." Although, as we have tried to make clear, this kind of education resulted from Rudolf Steiner's view of the world and of man and the relation between them, it should never be supposed for a minute that Steiner himself was without practical experience in this field. From an early age he had tutored young people for a living, including a retarded child whom he educated virtually alone until he was able to enter a school of medicine and become a doctor. This experience, combined with his unequaled powers of observation and the living thinking that he had developed, enabled him at the right time, when he had been

405

asked for it, to give his opinion on the form a truly human art of education should take. The monument to the applicability of his ideas, even in our modern materialistic industrial society, is the more than a hundred schools that have been developed in accordance with his ideas in many countries throughout the world, and which are still functioning and still growing today. If I am not mistaken, this is the largest trans-national educational movement in the world today, with all its component schools everywhere independent of each other, yet using the same methods and principles, usually enjoying freedom from any kind of state control and supported—with the comparatively rare exception of some teachers' salaries paid by the state and occasional state contribution to buildings—entirely by fees and donations. If the education provided were not, from a governmental point of view, effective and efficient as education, few of those present-day states that insist on compulsory education would tolerate it.

Steiner himself on several occasions said that he had no wish to start a Waldorf School movement, with independent Waldorf schools patterned on the original in Stuttgart, such as exists in fact today. He said only that a Waldorf school should be a good school, an example for others to imitate, a "ferment" in the educational life of the world. That this has not happened is due to many causes, certainly not least to the fact that our general social and political life has not evolved as Steiner hoped; governments still think it to be their natural duty to provide the education themselves and pay for it through taxes. The education thus provided is, equally naturally, what the governments think to be in the national interest. Few governments are seriously interested in the "free cultural life" that Steiner thought should form one of the three "members" of the social order of the future. One result of this policy is that those who wish to educate their children along different lines have, as a rule, to support public education through their taxes as well. To make matters more difficult, in a Steiner school, especially a high school, more teachers are needed than in the public schools, including teachers of that unusual specialty, eurythmy, which requires from three to four years' hard work before a diploma is granted permitting the student to teach it. Even if money can be saved on administration, it is quickly spent again on the language teachers and other specialists.

A much more important reason for the necessarily slow growth of the Steiner school movement, however, will surely have become evident in the course of this chapter. The teacher in these schools has to be a rare human being indeed, and it is certainly impossible to turn out a trained teacher in one or two years of a pedagogical course designed for the purpose. Although this training is *also* necessary, enough has been said to show the kind of qualities he must have or be capable of developing, to say nothing of the multifarious nature of the knowledge that it would be good for him to possess. He must also be able to function as a member of a *collegium* of his fellow teachers, without any hope of external advancement or recognition, always ready to take new responsibilities, to put his experience at the disposal of his colleagues, and to play his part in taking collective decisions, including even those involving his own salary and the salaries of his colleagues, always in the light of the funds to be expected during the coming year.

Moreover, almost never will he earn as much as teachers can expect elsewhere, who may be far less qualified and far less experienced than he. But it remains true that any development he achieves, even almost any knowledge or skill he acquires, can be made use of in his work; nothing, almost literally nothing that he does to help himself become more of a human being, hence a better teacher, is wasted. In short, if he wishes and can find the inner strength of soul, he can as a Steiner teacher become a free being—and for all those who remain with the work, eight year cycle after eight year cycle, this is surely the reason why they remain, as it is also the reason why, unhappily, we cannot expect growth in the future to be much more rapid and sustained than in the past.

As may readily be imagined a considerable number of Steiner's lectures on education are available in English, and it is largely a matter of choice or opportunity which of them should be read first. Many teachers in the Waldorf School movement have also made contributions based on their own experience.

Undoubtedly the general reader should start with the famous early lecture revised by Steiner himself for publication, and mentioned in the text. This is called, *The Education of the Child in the Light of Anthroposophy*, and was originally published in 1909 (London, 1975). The cycle that I myself prefer for a fuller introduction is that given at Manchester College, Oxford, to an audience of teachers, August 16–25, 1922, called, *The Spiritual Ground of Education* (London, 1947). By this time the Waldorf School in Stuttgart was already operating and becoming quite famous, resulting in the invitation to Steiner to come to England before there was, as yet, any prospect of opening a school in that country. The lectures are therefore especially suited to a general audience without previous knowledge of anthroposophy. Also of a rather general nature and easily comprehensible by a relative newcomer to anthroposophy are two cycles delivered one after the other, and covering in part the same ground. Both are available in English: *The Essentials of Education*, five lectures given in Stuttgart, April 8–11, 1924 (London, 1968) and *The Roots of Education*, five lectures given in Bern, April 13–17, 1924 (London, 1968). These lectures are exceptionally important for the understanding of the relationship between the soul–spiritual development of the child and how teaching should be carried out.

Two lecture cycles given in England in 1923 and 1924 are a combination of fundamental insights and practical advice, since by this time Steiner knew that a school was to be started in England and he wished to speak in particular of those elements of vital importance for the English speaking peoples. At the same time he almost surely knew he would not be able to pay many more visits to England, and thus the lectures are full of information. They are *A Modern Art of Education* (formerly called *The New Art of Education*), thirteen lectures given in Ilkley, August 5–17, 1923 (London, 1972) and *The Kingdom of Childhood*, seven lectures given in Torquay, August, 1924 (London, 1974). Another cycle of great depth and interest, which presupposes some knowledge of anthroposophy as indeed do all those mentioned in this paragraph, is the vital course that has been called, as an apt description of its subject matter, *Human Values in Education*, ten lectures given in Arnhem, July 17–24, 1924 (London, 1971).

In a different category is the interesting cycle given by Steiner a month before the opening of the first Waldorf School in which he shows the place that has to be taken by education in the Threefold Social Order, *Education as a Social Problem*, six lectures given in Dornach, August 9–17, 1919 (New York, 1969). Seldom does he make as clear as in these lectures why good education for children must be based on a new kind of education for the teachers.

The fundamental cycle referred to in the text called, *The Study of Man*, fourteen lectures given in Stuttgart, August 21–September 5, 1919 (London, 1975), addresses itself to this problem, since this cycle with another one on details of how each subject is taught, *Practical Advice for Teachers* (same number of lectures, same dates, London, 1976) and a *Pedagogical Seminar,* available only privately to teachers, constituted Steiner's instructions and teachings about the nature of the child, as given to the first Waldorf School faculty. It should be recognized that these first teachers had been chosen by Steiner himself, and all had already at their disposal a fundamental grasp of anthroposophy, even if they in some cases lacked as yet teaching experience. The cycle, *The Study of Man*, is therefore, quite naturally, exceedingly difficult for the beginner, and enters into matters far beyond the experience of the ordinary person who knows little or nothing of anthroposophy, however much teaching experience he may have enjoyed. *Practical Advice for Teachers*, by contrast, reads easily enough, but it is wrong to read it by itself since the deeper reasons for this kind of curriculum will be understood only by those who have, at least to some degree, mastered the other works given at this time, as well as having a grasp of the basic ideas of anthoposophy. A useful supplement to the *Practical Advice* is the report by Albert Steffen of another systematic treatment of the teaching itself, thin though such a report must be by comparison with the original. This report of sixteen lectures given at Dornach by Steiner December 24, 1921 to January 7, 1922 is published under the title, *Lectures to Teachers* (London, 1948).

To complete the list of Steiner's own lectures on education, the early lecture, *The Four Temperaments*, given on January 19, 1909, should be noted (New York, 1968), and there is a beautiful single lecture called, *The Three Fundamental Forces in Education*, given in Stuttgart, September 16, 1920 which is also well worth reading (New York, 1944).

The list of books by teachers on the new education in the light of their experience, must start with A. C. Harwood's two most important and helpful works, the smaller *The Way of a Child*, (3rd edit., London, 1979) and the more comprehensive work *The Recovery of Man in Childhood* (London: Hodder and Stoughton, 1958). Harwood was active from the beginning in the first English Steiner school, and was for many years the chairman of its faculty. Another valuable book, based on experience in English schools is John Benians, *The Golden Years* (London, n.d.). L. Francis Edmunds, who was for a long time responsible for the main teacher training center in England, and is now principal of Emerson College in Sussex, a school for adults that includes a teacher training course, wrote a book called, *Rudolf Steiner's Gift to Education: The Waldorf Schools* (4th edit., London, 1979), an excellent brief introduction to the subject. A profoundly illuminating and sympathetic little book was written by one of the first Stuttgart teachers and translated into English: Caroline von Heydebrand, *Childhood: A Study of the Growing Soul* (London, 1942). Dr. von Heydebrand in the last year of her life (1938) helped forward the work of the English Teacher Training course.

Lastly, almost any issue of the two regularly appearing educational periodicals contains one or more articles of interest. These are *Education as an Art*, published by the Rudolf Steiner School in New York, which seems now to appear only at long intervals, and *Child and Man* published by the Rudolf Steiner Educational Association in England.

It may be noted that there are also various shorter specialized works on some feature or subject of Steiner education, including the works on mathematics by Hermann von Baravalle, and by Elizabeth Grunelius on work in the kindergarten. But no attempt will be made to list these here.

CHAPTER XI

Anthroposophy and Curative Education

Although accurate statistics are not available for earlier centuries it appears to be an unquestionable fact that children who are in some way abnormal, either physically or mentally or both, are being born today not only in increasing numbers but as an increasingly large percentage of the population, at least of the Western world. Every institution that tries to care for such children has a long waiting list, but most of them confine their efforts to looking after them, helping them when possible to perform a few practical tasks within the limits of their abilities, but never really understanding them or even trying seriously to educate, still less heal them. Many warm-hearted persons take up this kind of work and they are often selfless and utterly dedicated. But the feeling that predominates in them can scarcely be anything but pity, for lack of the key to understanding the children, both why they are afflicted and what it is that is really required of them if they are truly to help. It is this understanding that Rudolf Steiner was able to impart from his spiritual knowledge to a few of his pupils during the last years of his life. As a consequence of this understanding he was also able to indicate the treatment that would be helpful for the few children who were presented to him for observation. By the time

412

he gave his course on curative education in June and July, 1924 these children were already being cared for in Arlesheim, near Dornach, in Switzerland, and in Lauenstein, near Jena in Germany.

The number of children he could observe and whose cases he could diagnose and for whom he could prescribe was necessarily limited. But the remarks he made on each, as well as his more general lectures, were of such a nature that the more gifted among his auditors, including his chief medical collaborator, Dr. Ita Wegman, were able to use what he had given in such a way as to help develop their own imaginative faculties in accordance with their potentialities. Thus much creative and constructive work has been done with handicapped and retarded children in the fifty years since the course was given. Indeed, this is the work done by anthroposophists that has probably received most recognition from non-anthroposophists, especially in the English-speaking countries. Even those who may remain totally skeptical about Steiner's spiritual knowledge are often willing to admit that the curative education developed by these anthroposophists appears to do more for the children than is done by the practitioners of any other form of therapy. Hence it is quite natural that these institutions should receive more state support than is available for Steiner education, since most governments are only too happy to turn *this* work over to private enterprise.

The Beginnings of Curative Education. It was mentioned in the last chapter how Rudolf Steiner, when still a young man, worked as a tutor in a Viennese family where there was a retarded child who was considered to be ineducable. Steiner eventually cured this boy and he was able to complete his training and practice as a medical doctor. This experience was a vitally important one in Steiner's life, and many aspects of his educational innovations for both normal and abnormal, retarded, or handicapped children stem from it. From the early 1900's his views on medicine were sought by a number of physicians, but it was not until after World War I that the Waldorf School in Stuttgart was founded, as described in the last chapter (1919), and in the next

413

year Steiner delivered his fundamental medical cycle, *Spiritual Science and Medicine*, from which extracts were given in Chapter 7. In 1921 Dr. Ita Wegman, an exceptionally gifted Indonesian-born woman of Dutch parentage, who had many years before been encouraged by Steiner to study medicine, opened the Clinical Therapeutical Institute at Arlesheim, near Dornach, which ever since has remained the main center of anthroposophical medical work (to be discussed later in Chapter 13). Meanwhile, it had been found that among the children who had applied for admission at the Stuttgart Waldorf School several were suffering from various pathological conditions that made it difficult for them to keep up with their classmates of the same age. One of the teachers, Karl Schubert, was especially interested in "remedial" education, as it is now called, and he undertook to teach a special class comprised of children of all ages who needed special attention. He was aided in this by Eugen Kolisko, the school physician, himself also a teacher in the school, who in turn was advised by Steiner as to the particular therapeutical measures necessary.* After the opening of the Arlesheim Clinic in 1921 the demand began to be voiced by many Swiss parents that curative education be also undertaken there. Dr. Wegman therefore opened her first Home (Der Hölle) for these children in 1924, in Arlesheim, close to the clinic, and the work grew rapidly.

Meanwhile three young men well-grounded in anthroposophy but as yet without any formal teaching or medical qualifications had come into touch with a non-anthroposophical home for handicapped and otherwise retarded children in Jena, Germany, and two of them began to work there. The third, who was a student in psychology at the University of Jena, also took a deep interest in the work but for the moment continued his university studies. All the young men felt deeply the need for some kind of anthroposophical guidance in working with the children, and the

---

* For Kolisko's work see especially his pamphlet, *Medical Work in Education* (London, 1929).

psychology student, Albrecht Strohschein, took the initiative and went to Dornach to see if Steiner would allow them to attend some lectures about to be given to a small group of doctors, and afterward give them some advice as to how to proceed. Steiner personally granted them permission to attend the lectures (it was Christmas, 1923) and then gave the three students a personal interview in which he spoke so impressively about handicapped and retarded children that they returned to Jena determined to start a Home of their own and work exclusively along anthroposophical lines. The local anthroposophical doctor in Jena discovered an old house that was available for rent in Lauenstein, near Jena; they borrowed some money, rented the house, made it habitable largely by their own hands, bought some furniture at auction and begged the rest. In May, 1924, they were able, with the aid of some others who had joined them, to move into the house and receive their first children.

When the question arose as to what the Home should be called, Steiner told them that the name should be fully descriptive, and proposed: The Curative and Educational Institute for Children in Need of Care-of-the-Soul (*Seelenpflegebedürftig*). As Albrecht Strohschein, who received the name, comments, "Now I slowly realized for the first time that 'care of the soul' was something belonging to all education, which everyone must be called upon to practice; there was therefore nothing in it to separate our children from others." *

In June, 1924, immediately following the agricultural course given in Koberwitz, to be described in the next chapter, Steiner paid a short visit of a day and a half to the new home in Lauenstein. There he saw all the children, and gave the teachers advice as to how each one of them should be treated. A week later in Dornach he gave his great Curative Education Course, which became the basis for all the later work done in this field

---

* A. Strohschein, "The Birth of Curative Education," *The Golden Blade*, 1958, p. 149.

by so many gifted doctors and teachers. Present at the course were the Arlesheim and Lauenstein workers and physicians, Dr. Kolisko and Karl Schubert from Stuttgart, and a few especially invited guests. It was a most intimate occasion, and many children were brought in to see Rudolf Steiner who spoke on several occasions not only about the children themselves but about their parents (few of whom he had seen) and the links of their karma. This cycle was mentioned in Chapter 7 as one of the most developed and impressive examples of that "living thinking" that Steiner himself possessed in such full measure. Since the cycle became available to the public in English translation in 1972, one should not miss reading it, if only as an example of how during the last few months when Steiner could still lecture, his gifts had reached their maturest and deepest expression.

After Steiner's death in March, 1925, Dr. Ita Wegman took over personal supervision of the "curative institutes" that soon sprang up in many countries, the first English one being founded in 1930. She visited these centers whenever she was able to do so, and there can be little doubt that she herself possessed a remarkable imaginative perception of these children, and was able to give valuable advice wherever she went. Yet the work in the world scarcely owes more to her than it owes to the dynamic Viennese physician Karl König, who joined the Arlesheim Clinic in 1927, and the following year was offered a castle and park close to a Home in Silesia run by Albrecht Strohschein. As a consequence, the two ventures grew together until the Hitler regime in Germany forced Dr. König, because of his Jewish origins, to leave. As a result he returned to Austria and worked there for the next two years. After the Anschlüss in 1938 he again went into exile, finally settling in Scotland where in 1939 he founded the first Camphill Home and the Camphill Movement which rapidly expanded, first into other parts of Scotland, and then to many other parts of the world. At König's death in 1966 the Movement was so well organized that it has continued to expand at a similar rhythm in the two main directions in

416

which it had been guided by Dr. König. These two directions will be discussed in the course of this chapter.

The "Abnormal" Child—General and Karmic Considerations. What distinguishes these Steiner Curative Homes and Schools from all other institutions of the same kind is the type of therapy based on anthroposophical medicine (to be discussed in Chapter 13), the extremely varied nature of the education given, adapted as it is to each individual child, and—perhaps the most important of all—the attitude of the curative educator toward the handicapped child, based on Rudolf Steiner's teachings about reincarnation and karma. Steiner repeatedly stressed that it is a question of destiny if a human being was born with, or later suffered an accident that gave him an imperfect physical instrument with which he must lead his earthly life. Indeed, the karmic reason, as Steiner discovered from his spiritual investigations is often enough a task that such a human being is to carry out *in a later life,* and is not at all necessarily the results of deeds or misdeeds in a former one—still less, of course, of deeds performed by his parents, as some adherents of fundamentalist religions still appear to believe. This fact alone must increase the sense of responsibility felt by the curative teacher for his charge.

It ought to be recognized that there is no such thing as an entirely "normal" development of our physical instrument. As mentioned in the last chapter we "normally" learn to stand upright, to walk, to speak, and to think in a regular succession. If, for example, we speak before we walk, as sometimes happens, we are, to this degree, "abnormal"; and the abnormality may be more or less significant for our lives. We may never learn to walk at all, or we may walk, but neither speak nor think. All these things are due to the imperfection of our physical body, which cannot be used in a normal manner by the incarnating self; this fact must at all times be remembered by the curative educator. The child must be led to make the best possible use of a damaged instrument, and, insofar as medicine and other forms of therapy can help, the attempt must be made to improve the instrument. But at the same time it must also be remembered

417

that when the astral body and "I" leave the physical and etheric bodies, that is, when the child falls asleep, he becomes at once "normal," and his higher being may be far more "perfect" than that of his teacher or parent. It is the improper interaction between the bodies, the abnormal functioning of the totality of a man's being during earthly incarnation, that creates the handicap.

A brain-damaged child, from a physical point of view, may have suffered a prenatal injury, or the imperfection may result from defective or incompatible parental genes. But such a diagnosis, even though it may be true so far as it goes, does not exhaust the matter. The thinking, which is dependent on the brain but is not performed by it, cannot make use of the brain in this earthly life, but at all times the curative teacher will be aware of the spiritual entity behind the apparently backward child, and that this being *is thinking,* even though this thinking cannot find expression through the brain. Indeed, it can happen that the brain-injured child, as an actual result of his injury, can become more aware of *us,* and of *our* inner being, than we are ourselves, as well as more aware of the surrounding world in which we live. Our consciousness is limited by our intellect, whereas his consciousness, unhampered by intellect, may possess a far more acute perception as well as more natural and uninhibited feelings. Furthermore, because his "I" does not function within his body it is impossible for him to *sin;* he can carry no *moral* responsibility for his acts.

Take, for example, a Mongol child, who, looked at from the ordinary point of view, is wholly irresponsible and appears only to follow his instincts—even though it is possible within limits, to train and educate him. If we look at a Mongol child from a spiritual point of view, we may recognize that for the duration of this earth life he is like mankind before the Fall of Man, a being born without those destructive forces that stem from self-consciousness. It is for this reason that the Mongol child is so utterly gay, insouciant and warmly loving. Steiner pointed out that it is a special *grace* for parents to be granted the *gift* of such

418

a child, and that this gift, surprising as it may seem, should truly be appreciated as such. It is true that such a child will never be able to earn his living, nor will he be able to support his parents in their old age, nor will he become what the world thinks of as a "credit" to them. Though he can be trained to do some tasks and will in fact love to do them provided they are in accord with what he feels to be fitting for him and useful, yet he will always remain at heart a child (even though soon after puberty he may often appear to be an old man), incapable of intellectual thought, showing his feelings without inhibition, utterly without malice and supremely forgiving, loving, imaginative, and impulsive—above all a *natural* being, accepting, as Isabel Newitt puts it, "what life has to offer, instinctively knowing its true value and acting accordingly." *

As we have seen Rudolf Steiner himself was able to perceive in exact detail the previous incarnations of the handicapped children presented to him, and could recommend effective therapy from his unerring intuitive knowledge. A curative teacher who does not possess such gifts can nevertheless undertake the task of becoming fully aware, inwardly, livingly, aware of the truths about repeated earth lives that we have been describing so cursorily. For the mere knowledge of the truth must cease to be abstract, and must become profoundly living as we face the children. Then through the most loving, careful, and warmly human observation and study of them we begin to catch a glimpse of the possibilities inherent in the entire life-cycle extending through many earth lives of the entity we now see

---

* I. Newitt, *For the Parents of a Mongol Child*, page 10. The sympathetic reader should also not miss, in particular, the first letter of Karl König's little pamphlet, *The Handicapped Child: Letters to Parents I*, especially the remarks on page 9 regarding the Mongol child as a grace, which are well worth quoting here in full: "Timothy is not a burden but just the opposite. He is a *grace,* which has been bestowed on you and your family, because through him you will learn that the real values of human life do not lie in intellectual capacities only, but in the depths of the human soul. Is he not a better person than most of us? Are his qualities of heart not greater than those of most other children? Why should we not take account of his loving attitude and carefree mind? Is it not a blessing to have children like him among us?"

before us as a child, unable, this time, to make use of his imperfect instrument. Carlo Pietzner, for many years a collaborator with Karl König, and at present head of the Camphill Movement in the United States, suggests that the experience we can have in working with these children may bring home to us forcibly the *actual truth* of reincarnation, that these children with their defective instruments are doing something important *now* that will bear its fruit in later lives.* So many of them have to make enormous efforts to do something that a normal person does without thinking twice about it. On the other hand, others may possess some sense that is especially lively and acute, far more so than in ordinary normal human beings. The experience a child has through such a sense may well be metamorphosed into some other even more valuable capacity in a later life.

But if there were to be no such later life, if there were only the one life and then extinction, as so many in our materialistic age believe, such a single life would be pointless—as, indeed, it would also be if, as some professing Christians imagine, eternal bliss awaits the true believer and doer of good deeds, since these children, to whom moral responsibility can scarcely be imputed, can in truth neither believe nor do good deeds. As a last note on this subject two remarks made by Rudolf Steiner may be cited. The first was made to Albrecht Strohschein in answer to a question on the spiritual meaning of such difficult earth lives for so-called pathological or feeble-minded children. "Rudolf Steiner waited a little while," Strohschein reports, "and then quietly replied, 'When in my investigations I look back, starting from the genius of today, I always find that a genius has gone through at least one such feeble-minded incarnation.' " (*Op. cit.*, p. 147.) The other statement is from the second lecture of Steiner's course on curative education.

It is indeed true, and we must be conscious of the fact that in educating backward children we are intervening in a process which

---

* *Thoughts on the Spiritual Meaning of Mental Retardation*, Lecture 2.

in the normal course of development—if there were no intervention or there were misguided intervention—would find its fulfilment only when the child had passed through the gate of death and come to birth again in the next life. That is to say, we are making a deep intervention in karma. Whenever we give treatment to a backward child, we are *intervening in karma*. And it goes without saying, we must intervene in karma in this way; for there is such a thing as right intervention. . . . But the decision to do this requires courage. This inner courage is the first thing needed if we want to accomplish anything in the domain of Curative Education. And it can be aroused in us if we hold continually before our minds the greatness of what we have undertaken. We must be constantly thinking, "I am doing something which Divine Beings usually do in the life between death and new birth." The fact that you know this is of untold significance. Receive it as a meditation. To be able to *think* it is most important. If we bring it before us every day in meditation—as one says a prayer every day—if we place it before our soul day by day, it will endow our astral body with the character and tone that we need to give it if we are to deal with backward children in the right way.

Medical Treatment. We have now tried to describe the nature of the problem posed by retarded and handicapped children, and how the curative teacher in an anthroposophical curative home learns to look upon his charges. Though little can be accomplished in the absence of the kind of attitude we have described, more is obviously needed if any progress is to be made toward healing or educating them. In Steiner homes the physician's work is of primary importance because, even in the case of children who appear merely to be maladjusted or to have "behavioral" problems there is almost invariably some kind of malfunctioning in the organism. It is only necessary to glance at Steiner's Curative Education Course to see how there is scarcely a single child for whom he did not make some medical recommendation that was then put into effect by the physician in charge. One of the most interesting cases, for example, was that of a kleptomaniac boy (Lectures 8 and 9), in whose case Steiner diagnosed a disturbance in the astral body. Steiner himself, of course, was able to perceive how the etheric and astral bodies, and the ego-organization (as he always calls the ego, the "I," in these lectures) were not able to work in harmony through the physical body, which might, in itself, not be at all seriously damaged. As a result of these perceptions he was able to prescribe the kind of medication and treatment needed. Among those who were present at the lectures or read them afterward, none possessed intuitive faculties developed to the same extent. But, as Steiner had always insisted in the twenty years since he had written *Knowledge of the Higher Worlds and its Attainment*, it is possible to awaken these faculties through one's own efforts and inner attitude. He also made it extremely clear in these lectures how what is needed more than anything else in working with these children is the most careful and meticulous observation along the path Goethe had blazed. As a result it should be possible to train one's thinking so that it will hit upon the *significance* of what to ordinary thinking often appears insignificant. Almost *anything* may be of crucial significance (see especially what Steiner says about this in Lecture 10), but it is for the physician or curative teacher to *notice* this, and then the detail, taken in conjunction with all the other observable phenomena that are customarily noticed, may perhaps provide the key to diagnosis and treatment.

The medical part of this work is therefore essential. There can be no question of simply prescribing a drug or a soporific. The task is to *heal* whenever possible, never simply to make life easier either for the child or for those who care for him. The attempt to help in the education of these children by medical means, however, requires a more subtle kind of treatment than the customary use of standard drugs produced by the pharmaceutical industry. Indeed, allopathic medicine is rarely useful, except in special emergencies. The far wider range of medicaments made available by homeopathic medicine, with its technique of potentizing mentioned briefly in Chapter 7, is better adapted for the type of slow but lasting results looked for with this kind of child. Also available are baths, special massages, and numerous other natural aids that may help to restore the balance between the invisible "bodies" and the physical body, and the physician who works with these children must use all his experience and training to observe how these disharmonies present themselves in them. Lastly, it may be noted that *correct nutrition* is of the utmost importance, and it is therefore desirable for each such Home to make use of the produce of the one or more biodynamic farms, since, as we shall discuss in the next chapter, two carrots may look entirely alike, but may be nutritionally quite different according to the soil in which they have been grown.

Still within the framework of medical therapy rather than education as such, there are other aids that an experienced physician can propose by which the different arts can be employed in therapy. Certain children, whose thinking capacity has not been developed for any reason, not necessarily because of brain-damage, are much more than ordinarily responsive to music, especially the music of stringed instruments, including, above all, the lyre, which is used extensively in these Homes, often being played by the children themselves, who might be unable to use such a complex instrument as, for example, a violin. Especially in recent years curative painting has also been developed, for which teachers were trained for two years by Dr. Margarethe Hauschka in Boll, Germany; a similar training course is available from Vera Taberner, near Gloucester in England.

Steiner's indications in these fields have to be taken into consideration as the basis for all the practical work in curative education, but by far the most important of all was that for which Steiner himself laid the foundation, and already in 1924 was prescribing for almost every child who was presented to him. This is curative eurythmy, a special branch of that eurythmy discussed in Chapter 6 as an art. Under the guidance of a competent and qualified curative eurythmist, some children are helped by the performing of certain movement exercises in eurythmy, others must perhaps do certain prescribed vowels or consonants for therapeutic purposes, while others need to do some exercises in tone eurythmy. Some children are too strongly incarnated within their physical organisms, others are in exactly· the reverse condition. Therefore according to their particular needs the physician will prescribe certain vowels, consonants or exercises, which the curative eurythmist, who is attached to almost all Steiner Curative Homes, will then pass on to the children. It may be noted that Curative Eurythmy is extraordinarily potent, and often has a most immediate and marked effect on the children (or on adults!); it can therefore never be carried out properly except under medical supervision.

Curative Education—the "Care of the Soul." Margaret Farrow, who spent nearly all her adult life as a curative teacher in Sunfield Children's Homes, once wrote a short article in the magazine called, *The Journal of the Three Roses,* published by this Home, which she called, "Homes for Children in Need of Special Care of the Soul"—the title, it will be remembered, chosen by Rudolf Steiner as descriptive of these Homes. This little gem of an article (Autumn, 1951 issue) shows just why Steiner spoke of special care of *the soul* (not simply "children in need of special care," the usual title given to these Homes in England). The physical body, as we know, is usually in some way damaged, and as a result the *spiritual* element of man, manifested through his thinking, that emanates from his "I," cannot function. There is nothing the matter with this spiritual element in itself; it is simply unable to function properly because of the damaged physical body. Thus of the threefold being of man, body, soul, and spirit, it is only to the soul that the teacher has access, and his task becomes above all that of nourishing the *soul* element in the child. This soul element primarily finds expression in the rhythmic system, not in the head and sense-perceptory, nor in the digestive and limb system (see Chapter 7, p. 269ff. for an explanation of the threefold organization of man). The soul element is also the mediator between the thinking and willing, that is to say, it lives in the *feeling* element of man.

In this article Miss Farrow points out that what is necessary

424

first of all for these children is that an atmosphere of feeling, of warmhearted and loving acceptance and tolerance such as should be present in a family, should be created in their new home, something probably lacking in the family into which they were born. Now that they have come to a Curative Home, this family life has to be recreated, so that the persons who look after them will always live closely with them, not be simply teachers or "staff members" who see them for certain hours each day and then go home. Life with the children is really shared.

How this sharing takes place, and how it appeals to the life of feeling in the backward child, are perhaps best illustrated by an extract from this article by Margaret Farrow, which I have the less compunction in offering in that from 1935 to 1936 I myself shared a nursery for a few months with Miss Farrow when we were both working in Sunfield Children's Homes, and Miss Farrow has now been dead for several years.

What will the "Special Care of the Soul" now mean? Here we enter the realm of feeling, where the heart mediates between head and hand. This is the realm of breathing, of rhythm, of colour, music, speech and religion. You will say: "These are what a normal child requires too." Indeed, yes! But with the backward child it is a "Special Care of the Soul" that we must cultivate, particularly as here we have very often no other approach.

What will this mean in practice? Firstly, such daily rhythmical occurrences as Morning Song and Evening Song, in which grown-ups and children take part. The repeating in chorus of the prayer; the singing and the accompanying music; the forming of a circle; the standing in perfect silence, with folded hands, feet firmly together, head held straight. These work almost like magic, and the enthusiasm and joy one can feel when a bent, frightened, clinging child for the first time reverently folds his hands and achieves an independent uprightness, is worth the constant struggle to create the mood, through these often repeated words and deeds, each time quite new.

Then there is the use of colour—for walls and curtains, for bedspreads and pottery. The colours will often be much stronger in tone than perhaps a "normal" grown-up would choose; but for the sake of the experience they bring to the child—the child who longs for and lives in colour—one gladly learns to bear them. The music for the children will also be specially written or selected. Perhaps again the grown-ups might wish for more variety, but, in order that the children may not be harmed by intervals or harmonies which are unsuitable for them, the grown-ups learn tolerance.

The telling of stories and the acting of plays; the celebration with even greater intensity than is usual, of all the festivals, will be an integral part of the life of such a Home; for, through such activities, the children—however backward—come to live in the experience of other human beings and in the life of nature throughout the year. Lastly, the cultivation of feelings of awe and reverence, particularly in connection with the Sunday Services, will be something which permeates the whole life of the Home.

The actual education given to the retarded children follows the general lines described for normal children in the last chapter, but the chronological age of the child will naturally not govern the content of the education as systematically as it does for the normal one. While a backward child may perhaps have to follow a kindergarten curriculum for a longer time, there are nevertheless some milestones that have to be observed, as for the normal child. The backward child should not learn to read and write before the coming of his second teeth. This holds good for the normal child too, because, as we have seen, the forces needed for bringing forth the second teeth are needed for the kind of thinking that accompanies writing and reading. The curriculum of the normal child between the ages of seven and fourteen should be permeated with art and should have a rhythmic quality. This is, if anything, even more true for the backward child at this age.

In the last chapter we did not describe the actual manner of teaching a child in a Steiner school how to write and read. Here we may note that writing should *always* precede reading, as must certainly have been true in the history of mankind itself. First came the picture, then the picture became stylized and turned into a letter, a symbol of the original picture; only after this had been done could men look at the written symbols and attach a meaning to them. In the course of time huge advances were made—intellectual advances—such as the invention of an alphabet, with which the words that had long been spoken could at last be built up out of letters that had each originally been a picture. So the child in all kinds of Steiner schools is first taught to paint the picture from which a particular letter was derived, and gradually the teacher leads him into painting a real word, made up of such pictures. In this way the intellectual part, reading, is left to the end. The chapter in Isabel Newitt's booklet, *Curative Education*, called "Writing and Reading" gives an excellent picture of how this work is done in a Curative Home. But the same system is ordinarily used in all Steiner schools, if with a greater ease and with less expenditure of patience than is needed with the backward children. The next chapter on "teaching ordinary school subjects" in Isabel Newitt's booklet is likewise excellent. The important difference in a Curative Home is that all the children in a class will be in need of special care and in some degree retarded. They will not therefore be forced to try to keep up with normal children in the same age group, and as a consequence will not have to suffer from the psychological difficulties from which retarded children suffer when they are treated in exactly the same way as the other children, having always as a consequence to come out at the bottom of the class in a competitive educational system.

The purpose of education in a Steiner Curative Home is the same as in any other school, to teach the child and educate him in accordance with his potentialities. Some children in these Homes, however, are scarcely educable at all, and more stress has to be laid on therapy than on the subject matter imparted. If in the process a child is healed and can take his place in an ordinary school, this naturally is the goal that is the ideal in our society, but for the majority who cannot reach it at least some education and training is possible, and these Homes do their best to give whatever they can.

The "Family" Atmosphere and Organization of the Homes. We have spoken of the kind of atmosphere that these Curative Homes attempt to create and have noted in particular that the various workers together constitute the substitute family, as it were, of the retarded and handicapped children. In many Homes a special effort is made to build a true community, of which the workers and children form a part. This is made possible because every worker has chosen his or her task from personal dedication to an ideal, whose rewards cannot, even in the slightest degree, be monetary ones. In the Homes and schools for children who are maladjusted and do not fit in with present day society or have behavioral problems, it is possible to employ teachers who simply perform their days' work and then go home to enjoy their private life. But in the Homes for seriously retarded and handicapped children who require all-day care and must be at least under supervision at night, the nurses and curative teachers (usually the same persons fulfill both functions) must live on the premises, and in effect are always on call if not actually working. So it is impossible for them really to have a "private" life of their own except insofar as a married couple can quite easily work in a Home and frequently do. Their work thus truly becomes their life, and their recreation consists of whatever the Co-Workers do together, and with the children. It is entirely natural that the plays and festivals should become the main "recreation"—in the true sense of the word, re-creating themselves.

It will be easily understood therefore why certain Homes, including all the Camphill Schools and their offshoots, function as if all the workers do indeed belong to a single family. No one receives any salary but each Co-Worker's legitimate needs, as he himself sees them, are taken care of by the community. This system can work only when all Co-Workers are made aware of the problems, financial and otherwise, of the community and thus share in the responsibility for them. On the basis of this awareness of the situation of the community, each Co-Worker can perceive whether or not his request is justified. In this way the resident teacher or Co-Worker is freed from having to worry about his personal financial needs, and, indeed, having to think about money at all, and is thus free to devote all his time and energy to the children, while at the same time he will be aware of the economic problems, if there are any, of the community as a whole, and be able to play his own personal part in trying to solve them. There is no administrative bureaucracy; all who take part in the work are consulted and share in all decisions.

The Camphill Villages for Adults. With the beginning of the Camphill Villages for adult handicapped and retarded persons, the system that had already proved successful in the Camphill Schools for Children was modified in an extraordinary and original way. The first of these Villages (in Botton, Yorkshire, England) was founded in 1955 by the Rev. Peter Roth, a leading co-worker with Karl König, and other Villages followed as land and money were made available to the Camphill Village Trust. The first Village in the United States was founded at Copake, New York, in 1961. The truly fertile and original idea for these Villages rests upon the understanding that handicapped adults over the age of eighteen, whether or not they are "graduates" of a Steiner Curative Children's Home, are never likely to become "normal" members of society, but are nevertheless entitled to as normal a family and social life as they can have. The Camphill "Villagers" are therefore given the opportunity of receiving training in some handicraft or other useful work in the Village community, and are given full employment for as long as they wish to remain in it—in principle there is no limit to the time that a "Villager" can remain in the community, while, conversely, he is free to leave if he wishes to do so. If a Villager decides seriously and responsibly, and makes his decision clear in a conversation with those in charge, he is *from that moment* free to leave. He may be helped to find another Village more congenial to him or he can perhaps stay in one of the hostels run by the Camphill Trust. These hostels are intended for those ex-Villagers and others who may not yet be ready for living outside, and may still require the protection and shelter of a home to come back to at night, though they are able to hold down full-time jobs in the daytime.

Each Village is an estate, with workshops of all kinds, and enough land (which is always worked in accordance with biodynamic methods) to meet the greater part of the produce needs of the community. The handicapped persons (Villagers) live together with the Co-Workers in small, self-contained groups within the Village, and as little distinction as possible is made between Villagers and Co-Workers. The quality of the goods manufactured by the Villagers is maintained at a uniformly high standard, and many of the high quality items, such as engraved glass, enamelled copperware, pottery, rugs, cushions, baskets, toys and puppets are sold not only in the local retail shop that exists in most Villages, but in leading London stores. As hand-made items they are sold in competition with other items of similar quality, not simply because they are "made by the handicapped" and sold for that reason.

It is made clear to everyone in the Village that it is one aim of the community to become self-supporting, and this has been found to be a great aid to the morale of the Villagers, who no longer feel that they will always be dependent on some help from outside. In pursuit of their aim of becoming self-sufficient they feel that they are becoming useful and productive members of society, in spite of their handicap, which in some cases is quite a severe one and may indeed limit the economic value of their work. Nevertheless, all the work does in fact contribute to the economic viability of the Village as a whole, and there is no useless work for the sake of keeping the Villager occupied. Since the English Villages accept only those who are certain, or at least likely, to be permanently handicapped, no fees at all are charged. But since most of the handicapped are eligible for government pensions as permanently disabled, the contribution made by the Social Security Services of the government are a valuable source of funds until such time—if it ever should arrive—when the Village becomes fully self-supporting. It may be noted that the certainty of such pensions being available has in the past enabled capital for building construction to be raised more easily than has been true of the regular Steiner schools. Lastly, it goes without saying that the common spiritual work done in the Curative Homes for children also plays a crucial part in the life of the Villages for adults. The great festivals of the year are celebrated here as elsewhere, and the Co-Workers' dedication is as marked here as in the Homes for children, different though the spiritual rewards are in the two different kinds of work.

Conclusion. As in the case of Steiner education for normal children, the work with the handicapped is limited first by the availability of teachers, and only secondarily by financial stringency. Finance is more easily available for the Curative Homes, but teachers are in even shorter supply. Nevertheless both movements are growing and by 1981 well over a hundred of each kind of school were already in operation in more than a dozen countries throughout the world. They are certainly two of the most important of the practical realizations stemming from Rudolf Steiner's work on earth. Their continued vitality attests to the practical nature of his teachings, and to the way in which they appeal to men and women in this materialistic age when "the consumer is king," when most people can think of nothing better to do with their time and energies than to consume what is offered by commercial entertainers and to own as many unnecessary things as commercial advertising can persuade them to buy. Certainly work in Steiner education, whether for the "normal" or the handicapped, offers little material reward worth considering, but it offers non-material rewards of untold value, and is in the highest sense an occupation worthy of human dignity and human potentialities. Or, to put it another way, in the beautiful words of the late Canon A. P. Shepherd:

If the earthly tragedy of the mentally handicapped can be lifted out of the meaningless, accidental, irrevocable, hopeless, futureless

431

explanations of a materialistic outlook, into the spiritual significance of a higher wisdom, in which the last word is not spoken in one earthly life and where the hidden working of a divine love and purpose is a challenge to our earthly love and service, then a new light and understanding falls upon it.*

While scarcely requiring the same love and devotion that must be given to the handicapped, the biodynamic farming that we shall study in the next chapter does offer non-material rewards that surely constitute one of its major claims to the attention of all farmers and would-be farmers. It is, if anything, more vital for the future of mankind than even a new and living form of education. The earth is being ruthlessly destroyed by modern commercial agriculture, with its herbicides, pesticides, chemical fertilizer and monoculture, while at the same time modern farming as a way of life no longer contributes to society the social benefits it once did in a simpler age. Biodynamic farming offers an alternative to this exploitative agriculture, and at the same time offers non-material rewards in the form of an incentive to young men and women to play their part in restoring the earth, making it once again a heritage that we could be proud to pass on to our posterity, instead of the diseased, dying, and Ahrimanized planet we are now in the process of creating.

SUGGESTIONS FOR FURTHER READING
FOR CHAPTER 11.

Rudolf Steiner's twelve lectures on *Curative Education*, given in Dornach from June 25 to July 7, 1924 (London, 1972) are indispensable as the basis for any understanding of the Curative

---

* *Scientist of the Invisible*, pp. 185–186.

Education associated with his name. Other brief indications are given in other lecture cycles by him, but they are relatively few, and no lecture or cycle needs to be mentioned here. The beginning of the work is excellently described in the article quoted in the text, Albrecht Strohschein, "The Birth of Curative Education," *The Golden Blade*, 1958, pp. 146–154.

No works by Dr. Ita Wegman on curative education are available in English, except in periodicals. Karl König has an essay called, "The Mystery of the Mongol Child," in A. C. Harwood, ed. *The Faithful Thinker* (London: Hodder and Stoughton, 1961); a couple of brochures called, *The Handicapped Child: Letters to Parents* I and II (London: New Knowledge Books, 1954), which are little masterpieces of understanding that manage to convey a good deal of knowledge to the uninformed reader, and a reprint of a most valuable article published in the May, 1955 issue of *The British Journal of Physiotherapy* entitled, "Some Aspects on the Treatment of Cerebral Palsy." A helpful book by Dr. König called, *The First Three Years of the Child* (New York, 1969), throws some light on the handicapped child but is, on the whole more concerned with so-called normal children.

Carlo Pietzner, head of the Camphill Movement in the United States has collected a number of articles covering all aspects of this Movement that have been published under the title, *Aspects of Curative Education* (Aberdeen: Aberdeen University Press, 2nd edit. 1973), available in paperback. A physician with a lifetime of working with handicapped children in the Camphill Schools has also published an account of his work, which is now in its second printing. The material is handled in a masterful and highly professional manner. This is Thomas J. Weihs, M.D., *Children in Need of Special Care* (London: Souvenir Press Ltd., 1973).

On the various subjects handled in this chapter there is a valuable little pamphlet written by one of the pioneers of the movement entitled, *Music in Curative Education*, by Julia Bort, M.D. (London, 1929), and a first hand report on some more recent work in the same field: Paul Nordoff and Clive Robbins, *Music Therapy in Special Education* (New York: John Day Co., 1971). Another article in *The Faithful Thinker* is contributed by Joan Rudel, who with her husband runs Peredur Home School for emotionally disturbed children. The article is entitled, "The Challenge of the Handicapped Child," and is a good brief introduction to the subject from an anthroposophical viewpoint. Much more substantial than these smaller works is Isabel Newitt, *Curative Education for Backward and Abnormal Children* (London, 1942), and the informative and sympathetic brochure by the same author, *For the Parents of a Mongol Child* (Clent, Worcs.: Sunfield Children's Homes, 1946). In a different category for its deep spiritual insights is the pair of lectures given by Carlo Pietzner entitled, *Thoughts on the Spiritual Meaning of Mental Retardation*, published in mimeographed form and available from the St. George Book Service P.O. Box 225, Spring Valley, New York. The same book service also published in 1960 two brief introductory essays on the subject of Curative Education by Paul M. Allen and Clive Robbins under the title, *Rudolf Steiner's Curative Education*. On Curative Eurythmy a substantial book and a small booklet are available, both of considerable value. The first is by Dr. Margarete Kirchner-Bockholt, and entitled *Fundamental Principles of Curative Eurythmy* (London, 1977), and the booklet is by Dr. Maria Glas and entitled *Experience in Remedial Eurythmy: Practical Advice for Doctors and Therapists* (available from the author at 57 Cainscross Road, Stroud, Glos).

All these works taken together scarcely amount, with the exception of Steiner's own course, to a really substantial account of the curative education work. A special issue of the quarterly published by the Camphill Movement, called *The Cresset*, however, appeared in Winter, 1972 that contained a view of the work of the whole Camphill Movement seen from many sides, and this issue includes a bibliography that will supplement the above. *The Cresset* is published by the Camphill Village Trust, Delrow House, Aldenham, Watford, Herts., England. Until recently Sunfield Children's Homes published *The Journal of the Three Roses*, which while it lasted was the source of much information on the Curative Movement as a whole. This journal now appears to have suspended publication.

CHAPTER XII

Agriculture in the Light of Anthroposophy
Biodynamic Farming and Gardening

In the course of this book we have several times alluded to the evolution of man's consciousness that from the fifteenth century onward led to a different attitude toward the world of nature. In the age of what we call the consciousness soul, man no longer thinks of himself as having any relationship to the starry worlds nor to higher beings whose existence he usually denies, but regards himself as having a relationship only with the earthly world and its inhabitants. He is a lonely self, differentiated from everything apart from himself, an onlooker, with the consciousness of an onlooker rather than of a true participant. In earlier stages of evolution even his sense perceptions were different; he lacked the ability to distinguish objects in the outer world as sharply as we distinguish them today. This new consciousness enables man to acquire a certain understanding of the inorganic world, especially insofar as it obeys mechanical laws and lends itself to measurement and calculation, but he finds it difficult to understand the living, organic world, which does not so easily yield its secrets to intellectual thinking and sharply focused

436

sense observation. The subatomic world, which he never will see and even in principle can never be perceived by any of man's given senses, is, by contrast, easily to be comprehended by this kind of consciousness since the most certain thing about it is that it is able to be expressed in numbers and equations.

As we pointed out in Chapter 7 it is not impossible to come to an understanding of the living world, but this can be done only by acquiring a new kind of thinking, a thinking that we have called "living." This kind of thinking has to be tinged with the warmth of feeling, and it is a part of the task of the consciousness soul to transcend mere intellectual thinking that is capable only of understanding the inorganic. But it is a task that has to be consciously undertaken. As Rudolf Steiner put it, the thinking of the consciousness soul is in its earlier development essentially cold. Because of this we find ourselves separated from the external world, and can look upon the latter simply as so much organic and inorganic material, which we as men, the most highly evolved of organic beings, are entitled to make use of in accordance with our will. We may be aesthetically moved by various elements in the world, but this is because in the process of evolution we have succeeded, unlike any animals, in evolving an aesthetic sense, a feeling for beauty, which it is reasonable for us to wish to satisfy. But it is thought that this feeling has no significance, and can have no significance for the world, but only for men.

As a contrast to this almost universally held view in the age of the developing consciousness soul, let us consider how anthroposophy views the world. According to Rudolf Steiner, until recently divine-spiritual beings were active in it, constantly creating, and weaving into it cosmic intelligence, which was administered by the Archangel Michael. Man then tended the earth in accordance with the wisdom that was bestowed upon him by spiritual beings, and it would never have occurred to him to defy the will of these beings, nor to consider the earth as a dead conglomeration of material that could be used just as he wished, could be, in fact, exploited for his own use and comfort.

437

But the "onlooker" attitude of the consciousness soul separated man from the external world, causing him to regard it quite differently from earlier times. This new attitude was made possible by the bestowal on man of the cosmic intelligence formerly administered by Michael. At the same time wisdom ceased to rule in the external world, and from the beginning of the age of the consciousness soul the external world has become what Steiner calls the "wrought work" of divine beings.*

So man has become free to do as he wishes with the earth in spite of the fact that cosmic wisdom has been built into it, and he can use it for good or for evil; he can use his responsibilities wisely and lovingly and build it up, or he can use them unwisely and coldly, with indifference, and thus destroy it. Divine beings cannot be expected to prevent this destruction if man should take it upon himself to destroy it, because it was always the divine intention that man should one day assume responsibilities in accordance with the freedom he was to be granted. They will not coerce him into doing good. By contrast, Ahriman and his attendant beings have no compunction in offering their services to man, placing in his path every temptation they can devise. For Ahriman desires to be the lord of the earth, a dead earth in keeping with his own nature, and to wrest man away from his appointed goal by making the earth forever uninhabitable by men possessed of soul and spirit. Today it is scarcely necessary to enlarge upon the brutally effective way these Ahrimanic beings are fulfilling their task, and how they are aided by Luciferic beings who have entered into man's astral body to tempt him in different ways to abandon his goal. Nevertheless, holding the balance between Ahriman and Lucifer is the Christ, who united himself with the earth after his death and resurrection, and who is always available to help man if only man wills it and seeks him.

It has therefore always seemed to me that it is impossible to overestimate the importance of Steiner's teaching in the field of

---

* *The Michael Mystery*, especially Letters VI and XIV.

agriculture and husbandry, because if the earth is destroyed by man's action, the very possibility of man's continuing to pursue the goal laid out for him by divine beings is endangered. Only on earth and during incarnation can man truly make progress, as we have shown in earlier chapters. Thus the lectures given by Steiner in Koberwitz in June, 1924 to an audience of about sixty persons, almost all of whom were actively engaged in farming, constitute a real landmark in man's history. Although Steiner had in earlier years given a few indications in this field and had answered various questions when they had been posed to him, and although as a result the first two of the biodynamic preparations had already been made under his direction, these lectures represent the formal beginning of biodynamic farming. Every suggestion made in these lectures and in answer to the many questions he was asked at the end of the conference has been followed up in the course of the last fifty years, and biodynamic farmers are active in a considerable number of countries. Moreover, it has been possible to set up scientific experiments with acceptable controls that have clearly proved the effectiveness of all the preparations when used according to Steiner's indications, and at the same time to establish a strong case for the importance of hitherto unsuspected planetary influences on plant growth—again in accordance with the "predictions" of Rudolf Steiner. Even occasional apparently offhand remarks were followed up productively by his pupils, and many of these pupils, personally directed by Rudolf Steiner, and their successors have done a considerable amount of independent research within the general framework of the ideas first placed before the world in 1924.

If the actual number of fully biodynamic farms in the world is still relatively small, this can be attributed to the extremely exacting nature of the work involved, its apparent difficulty by comparison with ordinary chemical or even so-called "organic" farming, and to the virtual certainty in present world social and economic conditions that such a farm will not be able to provide what is thought of in the industrial world or the world of commercial agriculture as a "living wage" for all the workers employed on it. As we have shown to be true for teaching in all kinds of Steiner schools, however, there are immense non-material benefits to be gained from this kind of farming, and there is the certain knowledge that one's work is not only aiding in the process of restoring the fertility of the earth itself and in growing food that is truly nourishing, but is playing its part in turning back the tide of destruction that is threatening to put an end to the very possibility, as some ecologists see it, of continued human life on the earth. Lastly, it will be noted at the end of this chapter how perfectly biodynamic farming fits the ideals of so many young people today who long to work together co-operatively for a common end worthy of man, while at the same time the results are qualitatively *and* quantitatively better the more human labor is applied to it—a condition rather difficult to fulfill in the world of today when machines can apparently do some kinds of work much better and more economically than man.

An extensive biodynamic literature exists in many languages today, since biodynamic farmers always try to help each other by disseminating the results of their experiences and their occasional planned experiments. In all countries where there is a sizable number of biodynamic farmers and gardeners there is sure to be an organized association of members and at least one magazine or newsletter. This chapter will therefore make no attempt to digest this kind of easily available information, but will concentrate instead on offering a general presentation of the nature of biodynamic farming, its origins in anthroposophical insights, its aspirations, and the significant differences between it and all other competing systems of working the land.

Ecology and Biodynamic Farming. The biodynamic farmer shares many assumptions with the ecologist, that non-specialized scientist, whose work has attracted so much more attention in recent years than it was able to command before the dangers of modern methods of agriculture were recognized. The ecologist, in general, makes the assumption that man has survived thus far, and the earth has retained enough fertility to be able to nourish the largest population it has ever known, because of the extraordinary ability of "nature" to restore the equilibrium that is constantly being impaired by human beings. He is less likely than other agricultural scientists to minimize the damage man has done and is doing to the earth, and to suppose that man's ingenuity will be able to cope with the problem of feeding our increasing population without further damage.

One of the essential elements in the science of an ecologist is that he recognizes that in what he calls an "ecosystem" every element is related to everything else; if anything is disturbed, the disturbance cannot fail to start a chain reaction. Such chain reactions are almost invariably detrimental to the ecosystem as a whole. In these days ecologists are almost always alarmists because of the arbitrary and willful tendency of modern men to disturb a natural balance, often thinking only of profit, and rarely indeed paying much attention to the long term effects of what they do. As one example, they are, of course, well aware of the tremendously beneficial work that is done within the earth by the common earthworm, without whose aid it is probable that man could not long survive. When an insecticide is sprayed on the land and millions of earthworms are killed in addition to the supposedly noxious insect for whom the spray is intended, it is a curious fact that the bodies of the dead earthworms, in decaying, increase the nitrogen content of the land on which they have died; as a result the next year's crop is likely to give a much higher yield than usual. No doubt the chemical corporation will praise its insecticide not only for having rid the land of a pest, but for having as a side effect increased the crop yield! But the observant and intelligent ecologist will not be fooled. He will be aware that the destruction of the millions of earthworms will alter the composition and fertility of the soil later because the earthworms were killed and did not reproduce themselves. Moreover he will also try to take into account all the other side effects of the use of the insecticide. Birds which ordinarily prey on the insects may well die of hunger if they are not themselves poisoned by eating poisoned insects; in any event they are likely to leave the area, so that a larger dose of insecticide will be needed the next year to kill off those that otherwise would have been eaten by birds. The same birds had perhaps other useful tasks to perform on the farm, none of which they can now perform; and, who knows, perhaps a new species of insect impervious to that particular insecticide will survive and multiply, necessitating further ingenuity on the part of the death-dealing chemists!

Above everything else the ecologist finds it necessary to be an observer. He tries to discover how a reasonable balance of nature was maintained in the past, and to draw deductions from his observations as to how men can now help to restore the disturbed balance. The biodynamic farmer accepts all such data gratefully, but his world is much wider, thanks to the indications given by Rudolf Steiner, full of so many more relationships that can be observed, once the mind and the eye have been attuned to them and the imagination has begun to develop; so many more observable facts become significant once the key has been provided. Some of the facts were mentioned in Chapter 7: the invisible etheric formative forces whose signatures, as it were, can be perceived, even though the forces themselves, like electricity, will be forever invisible; the earth itself as an organism breathing out in the morning and breathing in in the afternoon; the influences of planetary bodies on earthly substances, including plants. Such influences are of course recognized in the case of the sun, though its influence is imperfectly understood, and sometimes in the case of the moon. Other planetary influences do not seem to be worth serious consideration, for lack of the understanding of the *mechanism* by which they work. All these, and many other facts revealed by anthroposophy have to be taken into consideration, and, whenever possible, worked with. The biodynamic farmer must train himself to observe how the invisible forces make themselves indirectly visible in the outer world through their effects.

Another viewpoint of most ecologists is accepted fully by the

442

biodynamic farmer—indeed, any other viewpoint would be unthinkable in the light of his anthroposophical knowledge. It would never occur to him to suppose that crops are *fed, nourished* by fertilizers, whether organic or chemical, as is so often taken for granted in our materialistic age—so much "input" of material, so much "output" of plants. Plants are not mechanisms and do not obey mechanical laws (nor, if it comes to that, are animals and men). Crops will be good, and animals will flourish, if the earth is, as the old farmers used to say, kept in good *heart*. Attention must therefore be given exclusively to maintaining and improving the fertility of the earth. Then, *as a natural result,* the crops, the animals and the farmer will prosper. This is not to say that the specific needs of the various plants will be ignored by the biodynamic farmer. On the contrary, the kind of soil that each species favors, the companion plants that it prefers, the climatic conditions, the time of the year, even the particular planetary configuration best for its sowing—these things will be taken into consideration, but no calculations will be made of its "food" requirements based upon its chemical composition after it has died and been reduced to ash.

It follows that every biodynamic farmer should have an intimate knowledge of his farm, and that he too will regard the parcel of his land that he cultivates as an "ecosystem" in itself, with its quota of animals, higher and lower, its plants of all kinds, cultivated and wild, and its human beings who share the work and are nourished by what is grown on it. It may be that in our present age it is an economic necessity to cultivate certain crops over an extended area, because without them there could never be a surplus of grain to feed the increasing population of the world. It may even be that in order to produce these crops monoculture, with its use of huge and efficient machines and the provisions of ever increasing quantities of chemical fertilizer, cannot be avoided. But if this is at present true, it should never be thought that such practices are ever *good for the land.* It is certain that they lead to ever increasing numbers of noxious insects and weeds, which have to be destroyed by ever increasing quantities of dangerous insecticides and pesticides. Today many ecologists believe that by indulging in such practices we are bringing nearer the time when much of the earth will be a wasteland and will have passed beyond the possibility of restoration. Hence, their ever more urgent advice to take steps to control the increase of world population before famine forces it upon us.

The biodynamic farmer's goal of having a mixed farm with a balanced population of men, animals and plants, can and has been criticized as being not only unrealistic and behind the times, even downright reactionary, and likely in any event to prove forever unprofitable, but also on the grounds that it is not likely to provide a fair proportion of surplus foodstuffs to help feed a hungry world. To this he will reply that he is *caring* for that piece of earth with which he has been entrusted by society, and he is working slowly but surely to increase its fertility, and thus its ability to produce food that is always of good quality and in increasing quantities. He does this by working in harmony with the forces of nature, instead of *forcing* the earth to produce more food of ever poorer quality and at ever increasing cost. He denies that he is a reactionary, wishing to return to a utopian past. He is willing to use certain machines when they do indeed save labor, and damage neither the land nor its inhabitants.

Unlike most farmers who farm in what they speak of as an "organic" manner, the biodynamic farmer recognizes fully that the earth has indeed lost much of its fertility and is losing more every day, and that it is simply not enough in the present age merely to refuse to use herbicides, insecticides and chemical fertilizer, and to manufacture compost from waste farm products in the traditional manner. These things in themselves are good as far as they go, but much more is needed to restore its lost fertility to the earth. The "organic" farmer may well farm "biologically" but he does not have the knowledge of how to work with dynamic forces—a knowledge that was given for the first time by Rudolf Steiner.

444

The biodynamic farmer has at his disposal the knowledge that will enable him to provide what the earth requires. The organic refuse of the farm is treated by means of certain entirely natural substances that ray their forces *dynamically* into the manure and compost that he makes. As a result he will have for use on his farm a material that will increase the fertility of the earth without the addition of factory-made chemical products. The forces that work in and around the earth will be concentrated in his manure and compost; and numerous controlled experiments have been made to show the difference between this manure and compost and the same substances prepared in a traditional manner. The biodynamic farmer also has at his disposal certain sprays that can be made on the farm itself, which both add to the "liveliness" of the earth and aid in the growth of the plants themselves. Other similar sprays help in the control of certain prevalent so-called "plant diseases," as, for example, mildew. Certain kinds of birds, bees, and even some small animals, should be the farmer's natural helpers. But they will not live and thrive except in conditions favorable for them. Hence the need to have a farm large enough to enable him to provide such favorable conditions, while at the same time it should not be so large that he loses control over it and is tempted to forget the interdependence of everything on it. In short, as we have suggested earlier, a biodynamic farm should be a small ecosystem in itself. The biodynamic *methods* can be applied equally to gardens, and are being used with great success. But even a biodynamic garden can never be an ecosystem, though the gardener can do his best to make it as close an approximation as the different circumstances permit.

The "Dynamizing" of the Earth; the Preparations 500 and 501.
For a long time the text of the Koberwitz course given by Rudolf Steiner in June, 1924 was kept within the exclusive circle of biodynamic farmers. Indeed, the present writer himself had access to it only during the few years when he was studying biodynamic farming, and then, to the best of his ability, practicing it under unpromising circumstances. At the end of

445

this time, with the onset of World War II, he returned his numbered mimeographed copy to the Biodynamic Association in England and saw it no more. Since that time the Association has published the course, but I personally have always felt that its content is so deeply esoteric, without perhaps appearing to an outsider to be so, that the original procedure was justified in spite of the fact that Steiner himself authorized the publication of other lectures that he had delivered to members, many of which were surely no less esoteric. Now, several decades later, when I am attempting to write a chapter on biodynamic farming that is intended to be meaningful to a public that may perhaps owe all its knowledge of anthroposophy thus far to this book, I find that everything that can be meaningfully said to such a public was already said by my old teacher, Dr. Carl Alexander Mier, in his article, "What is a Farm?" first published in *The Golden Blade* of 1950, and reprinted in the centenary essays edited by A. C. Harwood under the title, *The Faithful Thinker.* No doubt Cecil Harwood felt the same way about the article, and that any other likely to be written especially for his collection would be inferior to it.

What Mier has done in this article is to crystallize into relatively few words his profound knowledge of biodynamic farming and anthroposophy. In doing this he has made what he says intelligible at the level of a beginner, while hinting at deeper truths that will be recognized only by the more experienced anthroposophist, especially if he is or has been also a farmer. Such a feat I cannot hope to match and can only recommend that his article be read by anyone who is interested and who can obtain it, even while I feel I must also attempt a somewhat similar task within the different context of this present book. Like Dr. Mier, I wish to stress as strongly as I can that biodynamic farming is *not* a method, any more than Steiner education is a *method* that can be applied simply as a kind of technique by those unfamiliar with the science of spirit and who have no wish to work according to the insights of this science. I have purposely chosen to offer some illustrative material and explanations that may help to make clear why the biodynamic farmer should not only know *what* to do (his technique) but *why*. Only if he also knows why will he be able to choose *how* and *when* to make use of what has been placed so lavishly at his disposal.

When therefore I speak of the deeply esoteric nature of Steiner's agricultural course, I mean that every word in it is based upon the picture of the earth, of its mineral elements, its plants, its animals and men that Rudolf Steiner had been giving to his pupils for over two decades, of the unseen etheric formative forces, of the physical, etheric and astral elements that pervade all nature, the influences of planetary bodies on earthly substances, and that this picture was simply taken for granted as the background for all that he said. He himself, to whom the spiritual world was fully open, who had now reached the age of sixty-three, the full maturity of his earthly incarnation, moved confidently in this realm of the unseen and invisible, which to him and to his audience was totally real. To such an audience as he had at Koberwitz he did not have to spell out all the elementary facts of anthroposophy; he was nearing the end of his life task, and he was in effect founding a new science based on a new way of looking at the world and its inhabitants. Therefore, he spoke with the confidence and certainty of his vision, and those who heard him or later read what he had said in so many cases felt inspired to use each one of his indications and engage in research and experiment for themselves. But for anyone unfamiliar with his work and teachings, the course might well have been entirely incomprehensible so far does it move from the ordinary materialistic way of thinking and observing.

As a typical example of the content of this course let us analyze what is said about the two fundamental preparations, the sprays known as 500 and 501, without which biodynamic farming would be scarcely thinkable. In every country in which biodynamic farming is carried on, these preparations are made available through private channels to those wishing to work with them. The raw materials from which the two preparations are made are ordinary cow manure (500) and finely ground quartz (501). By themselves these materials would have no efficacy at all, or only such as inheres in cow manure itself. They become entirely transformed, however, by being subjected to certain processes that endow them with actual *forces*. Mixed with water and made into sprays they have the effect of "dynamizing" the earth, in the case of preparation 500, and what we may perhaps call "sensitizing" the growing plant in the case of preparation 501, leading to an enhancing of its quality, nutritive value, and healthiness.* In order to make preparation 500 the cow manure is packed into a cowhorn, and left in the earth for a winter; then it is dug up and is ready for immediate use. The reasons why the manure is placed in the cowhorn are best explained in Steiner's own words (Lecture 4 of the Agriculture Course).

> By burying the horn with its filling of manure, we preserve in the horn the forces it [that is, the cowhorn] was accustomed to exert within the cow itself, namely, the property of raying back whatever is life-giving and astral. Through the fact that it is outwardly surrounded by the earth, all the radiations that tend to etherialize and astralize are poured into the inner hollow of the horn. And the manure inside the horn is inwardly quickened with these forces, which thus gather up and attract from the surrounding earth all that is ethereal and life-giving. And so, throughout the winter—in the season when the earth is most alive—the entire content of the horn becomes inwardly alive. For the earth is most inwardly alive in winter time. All that is living is stored up in this manure. Thus, in the content of the horn we get a highly concentrated, life-giving, manuring force.

It is perhaps unnecessary to stress the nature of the original

---

* The processes here described are only approximate, not because they are incapable of being described more exactly, but in order not to enter into excessive detail. For those who wish more detailed and precise information as to just what does happen when the preparations are made and used, see C. B. J. Lievegoed, *The Working of the Planets and the Life Processes in Man and Earth.* This essay, described by its author as "study material," makes effective use also of quotations from Rudolf Steiner himself.

raw material, the cow manure. It has always been recognized as a material that in decaying forms humus that restores fertility to the soil. Cow manure, in essence, is plant material that, after having been digested by the cow, still retains cosmic forces within it that were not fully used up by the cow herself. With the manure these forces should now reenter into the fertility cycle of the earth. This already valuable but not much concentrated material, however, can be totally transformed in the process of being converted into preparation 500. The horn of the cow has the property of raying back, as we have seen, "what is life-giving and astral." The manure packed into the horn receives these astral forces into itself; then, by being placed in the earth during the winter season, it receives additional etheric forces. When the winter is over the manure in the horn has become dry and concentrated; it can even be preserved in this condition for quite a long time. Before the substance can release its forces it must be stirred in water for a full hour according to a certain rhythm and in a special way that need not be described here. This process, performed by a human being—tests have shown that the substance does not have the same efficacy if the attempt is made to substitute a machine to do the stirring—releases the etheric and astral forces so that a dynamic spray can now be made of the activated water. This spray is distributed on the earth itself, which can now attract those forces of which the plant is in need. It is these forces that really *nourish* the plant, not the chemical substances that are placed by the ordinary modern farmer in the soil and reappear afterward in the plant, in a much diluted form. The 500 spray helps the soil retain its fertility but it needs composted vegetable matter and animal manure, dynamized likewise by similar processes that we shall describe briefly later, if it is to be able to produce crops of good quality and in sufficient quantity to enable the farmer to make his living.

Preparation 501 is made, as we have already noted, of powdered quartz, which, mixed with water to make a paste, is likewise packed into a cowhorn. But the quartz, or silica, being strongly connected with the forces of light, behaves quite

449

differently when it is placed in the cowhorn. It is to be used for a different purpose, and should contain different forces within it, or rather partly different forces, for the cowhorn in itself has the same activity as for preparation 500. But the silica in the cowhorn spends *the summer,* not the winter, in the earth, because it must be exposed to earth forces permeated by the summer sun. In the autumn it is taken out of the earth, and when it is used the following spring and summer, it must be activated in exactly the same way as preparation 500. But instead of being sprayed on the land, it is sprayed on the various plants at certain stages in their growth, always with a definite aim in mind, sometimes to hold back growth so as to strengthen the plant and sometimes to give it a special stimulus to increase growth, as in the case of the so-called broad-bean or horse bean, which may be inclined to harbor a certain kind of aphis at a particular stage in its growth. If 501 is sprayed on it at just the right moment it may miss this dangerous stage altogether. In general, the use of preparation 501 is intended to increase the nutritive power of the crops, while at the same time they should have a better keeping quality.

It will be clear from the above cursory descriptions that it is never possible to work with these preparations in accordance with a preconceived timetable or according to prescribed rules. The biodynamic farmer therefore has the task of trying to develop his imaginative perception if he is to recognize whether to use a preparation or not. Naturally this perception will be an outgrowth of his experience, but he will be able to learn nothing from experience if he does not train himself to observe in the fullest possible way, noting everything that can possibly be significant, and seeing his farm as a separate living organism in itself. In short, no really successful biodynamic farmer can dispense with the inner preparation that will enable him to perceive in what we have called in Chapter 7 the "Goethean" manner. But this is precisely what we have also spoken of as the characteristic form of thinking (living thinking) that must be developed in the consciousness soul age. It would not be proper for us in this age to look backward to an older form of farming that can be traced back to primeval times when men were taught out of mystery knowledge. Present-day farming must be performed with the aid of all our senses and all our knowledge that has been acquired in the centuries since the beginning of the consciousness soul. But this does not mean that we must farm as if the land were a dead substance, that we must use machines as if farming were an industrial operation, and must use chemicals as if chemicals were all that were needed, in addition to soil, even humus-containing soil, to nourish a plant so that it in turn can nourish men and animals. By observing, thinking and gradually gaining a real and living knowledge and relationship with his farm and everything that lives on it, a biodynamic farmer can gain a love for them that will supply the warmth element missing in the scientific attitude of the present and last few centuries. This warmth, this love, will in turn help him to *perceive* his world in a more all-embracing manner—or, as Steiner once put it, he will learn to unite head and heart in the hand.

Manure and Compost. When we remarked above that without the two fundamental sprays biodynamic farming would be unthinkable, what we had in mind was their uniqueness. No other system of farming has anything at all similar to them, whereas all farming systems have always recognized the value of animal manure because of its ability to form humus, an indispensable element in soil fertility. Organic farmers and most horticulturists are also accustomed to making compost heaps composed of decayed leaves and other plant material that in decaying likewise becomes humus. There can be no doubt, however, that few farmers, even though they may have learned in agricultural school of its importance, pay sufficient attention to their manure, either when it is removed from the barn and heaped up in the farmyard, or later when it has been taken out into the field. As a result of bad handling, nutritive substances that would have been of great value for the land are leached out, thus simply going to waste, while many farmers spread the

451

manure on their land and plough it in before it is fully rotted. The latter practice may actually have a deleterious effect on the next crop, since some of the bacteria that should have been available to aid the new plant will instead complete the process of rotting the old manure—a process that also tends to sour the soil.*

It is, of course, true that all competent farmers and agronomists recognize in theory that manure should be handled properly, but the practice has largely fallen into disuse because of the increasing cost of labor. By contrast, the biodynamic farmer must treat his manure and waste vegetable matter as the treasures they really are, much more important to him than to the ordinary farmer who can always substitute chemical fertilizers. For the biodynamic farmer the proper treatment of these materials is absolutely vital, if only because preparations 502 through 507 have the task of dynamizing the manure and compost heaps, and if the raw material is not in the best possible condition, the preparations will lose much of their efficacy. Indeed, only because these heaps are dynamized by these preparations is the biodynamic farmer able in certain circumstances to make a living at farming in the modern world without the use of chemicals. They enable him to produce highly nutritive foodstuffs, which are sold at premium prices in Germany under the trade name of Demeter, and the quantity thus produced can even compare with the yields of the chemical farmers once the land has been allowed to recover its lost fertility. Such results can eventually be achieved without the use of herbicides, insecticides, added vitamins, hormones, antibiot-

---

* I have tried to keep these technical matters to the minimum required for understanding the difference between biodynamic and ordinary farming. All those interested in further information on the present subject are referred especially to Chapter 5 of E. E. Pfeiffer's, *Biodynamic Farming and Gardening*, still an indispensable handbook for the beginning biodynamic farmer. When scientific tests are referred to, most of them appear in Pfeiffer's book, though modern tests that confirm the same general statements are also available in increasing quantities, and are to be found in the biodynamic periodicals of the different countries.

ics and all the other expensive products of modern scientific genius. Tests have shown that the bacterial content of a manure pile treated with the preparations is ten times that of an untreated pile (Pfeiffer, p. 47), and all of us who have ever worked with treated piles can testify to the huge increase in the numbers of our invertebrate friend already spoken of, the indispensable earthworm!

Chemical fertilizers, manufactured in factories to whatever formula may be desired in accordance with the particular plants to be grown and the soil in which they will be planted, are of course high in potassium, phosphorus and nitrogen, long recognized as the main chemical constituents of all plants, whereas untreated manure and compost will possess less of these elements. This is one of the reasons why so many modern farmers neglect their manure; they believe they are buying a better product than they have already on the farm. In relatively recent years the importance of iron in "plant nutrition" has also been recognized and is now added to the soil either separately or as part of a mixed formula, and the value of the so-called "trace" minerals, substances that are needed in only the most minute quantities, are no longer neglected by the chemists as they used to be. It is interesting to note that Steiner spoke of these trace elements, though of course without naming them, long before the recognition of their importance by the scientific world.* So most farmers rely on the chemists for information on how to "feed" their crops, and do, indeed, at considerable cost, often succeed in producing quite large yields, thus, in their opinion, justifying the expenditure. Even so, there is a considerable waste of fertilizer since far from the entire amount of

---

* The book, *Agriculture of Tomorrow*, by E. and L. Kolisko, discussed in Chapter 7, amply documents the manner in which plants are influenced by certain elements, even though apparently present in only the most minute quantities. In recent times the findings in this pioneer work have been enlarged and confirmed in an impeccably scientific manner by André Faussurier, of the Free University of Lyon. As far as I am aware none of Faussurier's work has yet been translated into English.

mineral substance included in the formula is in fact made "available" to the plants. We shall return to this point later. While agricultural chemical science has been moving in this direction, "organic" farmers, as we have already noted, usually concentrate their energies on improving the handling of manure and compost. They do not use insecticides or herbicides because of their fear that residual poisonous elements will be absorbed into the plant. It is unfortunately not likely that they can avoid having their farms infested by insects and noxious weeds, unless, as sometimes happens, a whole area is engaged in organic farming. Organic farmers thus save the cost of chemical fertilizer, and insect and weed killers, and their produce will be free of residual poisons. There are likely to be more birds on their property, but they will still have many insects and weeds to contend with. Their produce, however, except for the absence of poisons, is not necessarily more *nutritious* than that grown by the chemical farmers because it is unfortunately true that at the present time in almost all parts of the world, manure and compost, however well tended in the orthodox manner, do not provide the soil with enough of those elements that are required for growing fully nutritious crops. So, though it will not be dangerous, since it will contain no poisons, organic produce may contain even fewer of the forces and substances needed for the nourishment of human beings than does the chemically fertilized produce; in any event the yield is virtually certain to be lower. The money saved by not using the fertilizers and poisons will therefore have necessarily to be spent in the greater labor of preparing the manure and compost and in weeding the fields. Thus the prices of organic produce sold in the so-called "health" stores must be higher than regularly fertilized produce to enable organic farming to pay its way—though it certainly deserves well of humanity for its refusal to contribute to the gradual destruction of the earth and of all life, not only on the earth but in the sea, as some ecologists have warned us will happen if we continue using our poisons much longer.

454

Biodynamic farming requires even more labor than plain organic farming, but, as we are hoping to show in this chapter, not only is it a highly satisfying work, demanding the continuing development of our highest faculties of thinking, feeling, and willing, but for reasons that will presently appear, there is a real possibility that it will pay its way because it does not have to forego the high yields of the orthodox farmer, as has already been shown by experiments and in various farms in many countries of the world. The key to this "miracle" is the use of the preparations described above, the "dynamizing" of the manure and compost heap, and the control of insects and weeds by means other than chemical. We cannot deal with all these practices here, and the interested reader will have to be referred to the biodynamic periodical literature. But at least one rather flat statement can be made that has many times been demonstrated by experiment and in regular practice. A truly healthy plant of the kind that is nutritious in the way that biodynamically grown produce has so often been shown to be, is *not attractive* to most pests, which prefer the diseased, weak, and unhealthy plant. The presence of such pests is therefore always the sign that some improvement is needed in the soil. Such an improvement therefore pays a double dividend, in that it reduces the labor needed to destroy or remove such pests as do appear, while at the same time ensuring a more nutritious and healthy crop.

The preparations that are used for dynamizing the compost and manure heaps are numbered from 502 to 507. There is nothing apparently unusual about any of the plants (or, in one case, the bark of the oak) that are used to make the preparations; they are all easy to obtain. But in each case they possess certain inherent powers (as indeed do all plants), and these powers can be intensified when the plants are exposed to certain cosmic and earthly forces, some in summer, others in winter, some in the ground, others in water. Some, but not all, of these plants are given a special relationship with the astral world by being packed in animal organs, as was the case with preparations 500 and 501.* Once these plant substances have been activated in this way they are then placed in the manure or compost heaps in such a manner that the forces from each preparation radiate out from them and stimulate the vital activity of the heap in a remarkable manner. All that will be noticed by the outsider, and can easily be demonstrated by experiment, is that the heaps decay more quickly and form an excellent humus in a much shorter time than would have occurred in similar untreated heaps. This humus is now far more potent than ordinary humus, because the inherent powers of the plants, as, for example, the ability of the stinging nettle to draw iron in a highly diluted form from the wide distances of the earth and from the atmosphere, have been communicated to the entire content of the heap.

Instead of being "enriched" with inert mineral substances manufactured by the chemical industry, the soil, after receiving the "dynamized" humus, is stimulated to new activity of its own and has become capable of making available for the plant in an entirely assimilable form as much as it needs—a need that is in fact far less than is supposed by orthodox agronomists and soil chemists. All that is actually needed to sustain the life of plants is in fact present in almost all soils, but it is not *available* for them. Chemical fertilizing succeeds in its own way in "feeding" the plant by providing it with a massive dose of the various chemical plant "nutrients," from which it takes the relatively small amount that it actually needs for its sustenance. The process, however, weakens its ability to make use of what is naturally in the soil and could become available to it if soil conditions were suitable. This weakening of the plant is the same process as occurs in the human organism when it is given such a mineral as calcium, that it ought to be able to produce for

---

* For information on these preparations, the remarks Steiner himself made about each, how they are activated, the relation of each to a particular planet, and a wealth of other details, the seriously interested reader is again referred to Lievegoed's work already quoted.

itself—especially if it were helped to do so by the use of homeopathic remedies in high dilution.

Biodynamic farming tries to help the soil make available what is needed and to help the plant draw what it needs from the earth and the atmosphere and cosmos. In doing this, it strengthens, not weakens, the plant, and it thus makes available for man the healthy and health-promoting plants that he needs for his own sustenance. Chemical fertilizing, moreover, leaves residues in the soil that are harmful to the life of the earth, and since relatively little of the fertilizer is actually used by the plant, it is extremely wasteful. In many soils ever larger doses of fertilizer are needed each year to grow substantially the same tonnage of crops; the system is also extremely wasteful of water since the chemical fertilizer must be "washed down" with water, whereas, as has often been demonstrated, a healthy, biodynamically grown plant, can survive drought conditions much longer than plants fertilized in an orthodox manner, and can do without irrigation in areas where the orthodox farmer would be unable to bring his crops to fruition.

The Conversion of a Biodynamic Farm. It will be readily understood from all that has been said above that the process of converting an ordinary farm into a biodynamic farm is a long one. Preparations 500 and 501 can certainly be made available at once, and quite possibly the clearing or cleaning up of the land will yield material for many compost heaps, all of which can be dynamized. Such material will usually be available for use within a year and, if cattle and other animals are kept, manure heaps may be constructed fairly rapidly and should also be ready for use by the second year of operation. But the long process of bringing *the land* into good heart will certainly require more than two years, and it will usually take as much as five to seven years before a farm can be considered to have been converted. A soil that has been heavily treated with chemicals may take much longer to convert than a neglected farm that has known neither fertilizer nor insecticides. In any event all the usual good farming practices will have to be adopted from the

457

start, including a suitable rotation of crops, the planting of cover or companion crops, which can later be ploughed in, the use of legumes in the rotation, in addition to the use of the spray preparations and the dynamized manure and compost. The new biodynamic farmer will have to refrain from growing the same crop on his land in successive years, even if such a crop is easily marketable. All these things belong to the technique of biodynamic farming, which can be studied in the available literature and worked out in practice in accordance with the actual situation of the farm at the time of conversion.*

No one should expect to see miraculous results at once, and all new farmers should for some years be prepared for yields inferior to those of chemical farming, and to take temporary and somewhat unorthodox and far from a hundred per cent successful steps against the pests resulting from former practices that are sure to afflict their crops for some time to come. They should be prepared to expend much labor in trying to control weeds and insects, but should have the fortitude never to resort to chemical poisons (though some plant insecticides such as those made from pyrethrum or derris root are acceptable and within limits efficacious). Each year should see some visible progress and after the fifth year a farmer should be able to convince even his skeptical neighbors that he knows what he is doing.

The Organization of a Biodynamic Farm and Garden. Rudolf Steiner often spoke of the ideal biodynamic farm as being a truly mixed one, almost, if not quite, self-sufficient, with by far the greater part of the feed for the farm animals produced on it, as well as a high proportion of the food consumed by the human farm population. Naturally, there should also be a surplus for sale, in order to make the whole enterprise economically self-supporting. Although it must be conceded that few present day biodynamic farms fulfill this ideal completely, it remains true that it is always regrettable—though often for economic reasons at least temporarily necessary—when, for example, there

---

* See especially Chapter 7 of Pfeiffer's book already referred to.

are no cattle on a farm and pigs or chickens are raised for profit, thus creating a shortage of cow manure and a surfeit of pig or chicken manure. The resulting manure heaps are then necessarily unbalanced in their composition. If, however, cow manure can be bought from a local farm or exchanged for some of the pig or chicken manure, the balance may be righted, especially if the next door neighbor is himself a biodynamic farmer—in which case the two farms will complement one another and many things can be worked out together in harmony. If, on the other hand, the neighbor is feeding his cattle on bought concentrated feeds, the manure from his animals will not be of the quality required. Similarly, if a biodynamic farmer has to buy feed for some of his animals, such feed will almost certainly not have been grown according to biodynamic methods, and the quality of the manure will suffer accordingly. It is for such reasons as these that compromises on the biodynamic farms should be as few as possible.

For specialized vegetable farming, and for the ordinary home garden, however, it is obviously impracticable to keep animals in order to have the use of their manure. Here, as a rule, much greater use is made of compost since especially the market gardener or truck farmer has a great deal of material available, and he can prepare his crops for market in such a way that the green material with which they are often sold is detached and kept on the farm. Such gardeners who live in the country will often have access to at least some animal manure that can be added to their compost heaps. Without going into detail here it may be noted that these specialized growers of food for human consumption, often on a small acreage, have other aids at their disposal that are unpracticable on large scale farms. Such aids as planting suitable companion crops and various cultivation practices that need much human hand labor will to some extent compensate for the absence of the balance to be found on the biodynamic mixed farms. Some crops also respond to specially prepared composts that can sometimes be made in the market garden or occasionally in the ordinary home garden. What has

459

been said of the commercial market gardener holds largely true also for the home gardener, though the latter also has other opportunities for improving his crops that might be too prodigal in the use of human labor to be practicable for the former.*

The Values and Rewards of Biodynamic Farming; a Balance Sheet. Let us now, in conclusion, attempt a comparison between biodynamic and orthodox farming, especially the industrial farming of the present day that alone shows consistent profits in the Western world. There can be no doubt that biodynamic farming is expensive in labor. But the biodynamic farmer, in return, does not have to spend so much money on fuel to run his machines, nor does he have any expense for chemical fertilizer, herbicides or insecticides. He has no need to invest the huge quantities of capital required of the industrial farmer, nor will he have to meet an annual interest bill on such capital.

As has already been noted, however, he will have to expend much hard work and exercise much patience before his yields begin to approach those of the ordinary, still less the industrialized farmer. In no circumstances can he expect profits ever to approach those of some industrial farmers, though he will not be suddenly faced with ruin if his government decides to abandon price support for his crops. In this sense he will enjoy the intangible benefit of true independence. But such economic considerations in any event fail to tell the whole story. Even the industrial farmer himself is scarcely likely to claim that he is positively improving the fertility of the soil for posterity, whereas the biodynamic farmer does not pollute the air, he adds no poison to his fields, and he knows that his soil is becoming healthier and the products he grows more nutritious each year that he works his farm. He is not exploiting the land, forcing it to yield crops for his profit, but is working in harmony with it, gently helping it, as it were, to yield a reasonable harvest in accordance with its potential.

---

* See Chapter 9 of Pfeiffer's book already quoted, and other books on gardening to be found in the list at the end of the chapter.

Almost any reader could add to this list of intangible benefits that he derives from his work, and any practicing biodynamic farmer would choose to emphasize other things about his work that satisfy him. But there is one further consideration that needs to be mentioned; it may indeed prove to be of crucial importance in the next decades. Earlier in this chapter we have pointed out how much damage industrial farming is doing to the land, and how air and water pollution are rapidly becoming a threat to human survival. Since late 1973 a new threat has been posed to industrial civilization—the danger that the industrial countries will be forced to curtail their production of manufactured goods because of a shortage of petroleum and its derivatives. Since all the industrial nations are dependent on this fuel to a greater or lesser degree, and will be for at least another decade, some industries may have to cut production drastically, a contingency with which Western capitalist society is not prepared to deal effectively. Most chemical fertilizers are made from petroleum, and large quantities of electricity are used in their manufacture, so shortages and price increases can be expected indefinitely in this industry. If adequate substitutes are not found, in the long run the growth of industrial civilization will be seriously endangered.

Modern farming has taken its present form because of the shortage and high cost of agricultural labor. The industrialized firms could not even make effective use of much more labor than they currently employ, even if wages dropped catastrophically; machines have been designed to do so much of the work, and most agricultural workers are primarily tenders of machines. By contrast, biodynamic farming not only could make effective use of much labor, but must do so; at the same time it needs to use relatively little fuel. The biodynamic farmer, as we have tried to suggest throughout this chapter, is vitally needed for the restoration of the damaged and infested land. It may therefore be that the conjunction of these two conditions, the need to restore the land and the sudden availability of human labor, which even if now unskilled in agriculture could quickly

461

learn (and quite possibly learn to love) the work, will lead to a rapid increase of this kind of farming in the not at all distant future.

The Biodynamic Commune or Community. The movement toward communes or communities that has gained adherents, especially among the young, in so many countries of the modern world in recent years needs to have some important work as its focus and center. The production of handmade goods of all kinds is a natural reaction against industrialized and standardized machine-made goods, and, from the point of view of the artists and craftsmen, it is a wholly admirable and praiseworthy venture. But it is not, *from the consumers' point of view,* filling any vital need; in times of depression such products are likely to be difficult to sell because they are not truly an economic necessity to anyone. But nutritious food products are a truly vital need and are always salable—perhaps even at a slightly premium price. Such communities or communes are a natural form of organization for a biodynamic farm. Examples of this are the Camphill Villages for physically and mentally handicapped adults that have their own biodynamic farms, supplying Co-Workers, Villagers and children with food, as well as providing work for many Villagers.

If the great crises of the years ahead cause upheavals in Western civilization, and if it should happen that a new social order, even one along the lines of the Threefold Social Order discussed in Chapter 8, were to come gradually into being in some parts of the world, the labor-extensive biodynamic farm community would surely find its place in such a post-industrial social order. It can so easily become a self-governing community, with its association of farmers producing its food and selling its surplus to the outside, and its artists and craftsmen likewise making salable goods. This work would represent the economic pole of the Threefold Order, while on the spiritual-cultural side there would be all the never-ending possibilities of study, in particular of the spiritual realities behind the natural world, a school for the children of the community, a theater, and many other cultural activities for which talent is available. In the center would be the democratically chosen body concerned with the maintenance of the rights of everyone.

The Camphill Movement was and is centered around the handicapped children and adults, and its biodynamic farms are naturally subsidiary to its central purpose. But a biodynamic farm could equally well be the center of a similar community with other activities subsidiary to it, though important in themselves. This may well prove to be the pattern for the future in the dangerous and difficult years that lie ahead for all of us.

SUGGESTIONS FOR FURTHER READING
FOR CHAPTER 12.

Rudolf Steiner's *Agricultural Course*, eight lectures given in Koberwitz, June 7 to 16, 1924, is available in a fourth edition, published in 1977, by Biodynamic Agricultural Association, 35 Park Road, London, N.W.1 and the Anthroposophic Press, 258 Hungry Hollow Rd., Spring Valley, N.Y. 10977. This course, and the article by C. A. Mier entitled "What is a Farm?" (*Golden Blade*, 1950, reprinted in *The Faithful Thinker*, ed. A. C. Harwood, London: Hodder and Stoughton, 1961) have been sufficiently described in the chapter to need no further remarks here.

Ehrenfried Pfeiffer was perhaps the leading pioneer in the spreading of the biodynamic movement, and did much of the early research. Whether he was in Europe or in the United States, where he spent the years from the war until his death in 1961, he always retained close contact with the scientific world as well as with biodynamic farmers. All his books, of which a brief list is given here, are of great value, especially for their practical advice, which is difficult to find elsewhere in English. His article in the special issue of the *Golden Blade* for 1958, devoted to recollections of Rudolf Steiner by his pupils, is a good introduction to his work, describing, as it does, the background for Steiner's agricultural course, and following this with a general overview of the biodynamic work and how so many of Steiner's indications came eventually to be accepted by outside scientists and agronomists. His basic work, *Biodynamic Farming and Gardening* (New York, 1940) remains indispensable. His advice to gardeners is to be found in a beautifully practical little book called, *Grow a Garden and be Self-Sufficient* (New York, 1942) and in a work written in conjunction with Erika Riese, *The Fair Garden Plot* (London, 1943). More recently the Biodynamic Farming and Garden Association (Wyoming, R.I., 1967) published a book based on Pfeiffer's work called, *The Pfeiffer Garden Book.* A last book by Pfeiffer, *The Earth's Face and Human Destiny* (Emmaus, Pa.: Rodale Press, 1947) is a wide-ranging general book on the growing destruction of the earth and what is needed to be done about it, written long before conservation and ecology became such popular subjects as they have now become.

Two practical books by John and Helen Philbrick are most helpful: *Gardening for Health* (Blauvelt, N.Y., Rudolf Steiner Publications, 1963) and an unorthodox work on how to dispose of unwanted and noxious insects without the use of poisons, *The Bug Book* (Garden Way Publishing, Charlotte, Vt., 1973).

In Chapter 7 attention was drawn to an important pioneer book by L. and E. Kolisko, called *Agriculture of Tomorrow* (Edge, Glos.: Kolisko Archive, 1946), which is full of information about the preparations, and contains detailed accounts of tests made by the authors of the efficacy of these preparations and "dynamized" compost heaps, using the method of capillary dynamolysis. An excellent contrast to this book is the relatively short essay discussed in the text by Dr. C. B. J. Lievegoed, *The Working of the Planets and the Life Processes in Man and Earth*, (Clent, Worcs.: Experimental Circle of Anthroposophical Farmers and Gardeners, 1951) in which the author makes full use of his knowledge as a medical doctor with experience of working in

464

accordance with Steiner's indications in this field, but, as might be expected, entirely lacking in the experimental material and tests that form such a fascinating part of the Koliskos' book. Lastly, mention should be made of the two major periodicals in English: *Star and Furrow*, a biannual journal published by the Biodynamic Agricultural Association, (Broome Farm, Clent, Stourbridge, England), and *Bio-Dynamics*, a most informative little journal published quarterly by the Biodynamic Farming and Gardening Association, Box 253, Wyoming, R.I. 02898.

CHAPTER XIII

Medicine and Nutrition
in the Light of Anthroposophy

In Chapter 7 on the science of nature in relation to the science of spirit, we were only able to make a few references to anthroposophical medicine. We did refer, however, to Rudolf Steiner's fundamental discovery concerning the threefold nature of man, which he announced in 1917 in his book, *Riddles of the Soul*; we were also able to give a brief description of the "potentizing" of medicaments, a principle that makes practical use of the unseen etheric formative forces. In Chapter 11 we also discussed briefly a few of the healing techniques used by anthroposophists when caring for retarded and handicapped children. In this chapter we shall attempt to deal more systematically with the contributions anthroposophy has been able to make and is still making to medicine, pharmacy, and the knowledge of correct nutrition.

Especially in the last five years of his life, Steiner gave detailed advice to a number of trained medical doctors in connection with the patients they were treating, always unorthodox advice, which nevertheless brought markedly successful results. In addition, although he was not of course himself a medical doctor, he gave several series of lectures to doctors. He always worked in conjunction with one or more trained doctors, and his teachings, and the effective work done by these doctors under his direction, led many students to specialize in medicine who might not otherwise have done so. These students after obtaining their diplomas, naturally moved into anthroposophical medicine, and to this day all anthroposophical doctors and nurses possess the necessary diplomas and have obtained their right to practice from a recognized medical school. Unlike, for example, osteopaths, they do not go to specially organized medical schools of their own. The medicine derived from anthroposophy is an extra discipline that must be learned separately, and most doctors practicing general anthroposophical medicine have a working knowledge of both allopathic and homeopathic medicine, and are thus better qualified than the majority of doctors today who specialize in some more or less narrow discipline.

In addition to all they have learned in their medical training, anthroposophical physicians have to be fully cognizant of general anthroposophy, including an understanding of the etheric and astral bodies, and of the ego organization, how these unseen principles react on each other and how they work within the visible physical body. They have also to take into consideration the threefold nature of man as described in Chapter 7; they have to possess a working knowledge of the properties of a large number of medicaments not used in the ordinary pharmacopoeia, and how these act in the human being; they should be also in a position to prescribe specific color therapy or curative eurythmy where needed. When it is considered that in anthroposophical medical practice it is virtually impossible to use a "book of rules," that, for example, even modern chemical blood analyses are of limited usefulness, and that a developed insight, through which at least the *workings* of unseen forces can be recognized, is absolutely essential, it is perhaps surprising that any doctors at all make use of the knowledge given by Rudolf Steiner and utilize the methods proposed by him!

As if this were not enough in the way of obstacles, in only a few countries of the world are there enough anthroposophical patients to keep such a physician fully employed. It thus becomes necessary for him to care for other patients who are likely to be, at least initially, as skeptical of his methods and medicaments, as are almost all his medical colleagues. In numerous countries governments lay restrictions on the use of some of the medicaments, as well as in some cases holding the doctor liable if he does not prescribe a treatment acceptable to the orthodox medical pundits of the day. To ordinary chemical or spectral analysis the anthroposophical remedies with their high dilutions appear to be nothing but water, leading government officials in some countries to forbid them as "inefficacious," and their use as sheer deception of gullible patients. Therefore, while it does seem that the movement is growing in several countries (not including the United States), and medical congresses, called together for the purpose of discussing anthroposophical medicine, usually attract many outsiders, it is probably true that only in clinics entirely staffed by anthroposophical doctors and nurses can suitable conditions be found for practicing it. Thus the few such clinics in Germany, and above all the pioneer medical center in Arlesheim, Switzerland, are likely to attract believers in anthroposophy and its medicine from all over the world, whereas, except in areas where there are many anthroposophists, the ordinary general practitioner who believes in this kind of medicine and wishes to use it will probably expect to practice it only on relatively few of his patients.

It should, however, be clearly noted that Steiner himself never expected (or even wished) anthroposophical medicine to replace orthodox medicine. His classic statement of his position reads:

I do not mean to say that in recent times medicine has not made immense progress. Anthroposophy recognizes this progress in medicine to the full. Neither have we any wish to exclude what modern medical science has accomplished; on the contrary we honor it. But when we examine what has been brought out in the way of remedies in recent times we find that they have only been arrived at by way of lengthy experimentation. Anthroposophy supplies a penetrating knowledge which by its survey of human nature has fully proved itself in those spheres where medicine has already been so happily successful. But, in addition to this, Anthroposophy offers a whole series of new remedies also, a fact which is made possible by the same insight applied to both Nature and Man.*

On another occasion in response to a question he gave a short dissertation to the workmen engaged in building the second Goetheanum on "healing forces in human nature." Here he explained how in certain cases allopathic medicine is actually to be preferred to homeopathic medicine, according to the area of the body where the illness is to be found. "Anthroposophy," he says, "does not go in for catchwords—allopathic—homeopathic —but it studies the matter and says: the allopath works principally on the stomach, intestines, kidneys; there he is successful. Homeopathy is successful when the source of the illness is in the head, as in influenza." ** Naturally Steiner did not go into detail with these workmen, most of whom had very little knowledge of anthroposophy. But this example is cited here to show how free from fanaticism Steiner was, even or perhaps one should say especially, in an area where fanaticism is so rife.

The beginnings of anthroposophical medicine have been well described by Greta Kirchner-Bockholt, M.D. in a short article entitled, "Widening the Art of Healing" in the *Golden Blade* of 1958. This article enables us to catch the enthusiasm of the first medical work in the Clinical Therapeutical Institute in Arlesheim, opened in 1921 by Ita Wegman, M.D. At this time Steiner took a personal interest in almost every patient in the clinic, and he advised Dr. Wegman and her assistants as to how they should be treated. As yet only the highly gifted Dr. Wegman had been able to develop in herself what Steiner, in speaking of her, called

---

* From a public lecture given in Arnhem, Holland on July 17, 1924, printed in *Spiritual Science and Healing*, p. 27.
** *Cosmic Workings in Earth and Man*, page 34.

her "medical inspiration and intuition." All the other less mature and less experienced physicians were nevertheless able to learn immeasurably from seeing how Steiner and his chosen chief collaborator in this field worked together in practice, and in Dr. Bockholt's account we can see how this observation became for the assistants (of whom she was one) an indelible experience, laying the basis for their own development of the powers necessary for such work. In the last year of his life Steiner crowned his medical work with the book he wrote in collaboration with Dr. Wegman, who by this time had become the head of the Medical Section of the Goetheanum in Dornach (see next chapter). This book, *Fundamentals of Therapy*, epitomized the essential substance of what he had given in so much detail in the course of the years in so many different series of lectures to the doctors and medical students who had asked him for help in their work. It is worthwhile quoting a part of Dr. Wegman's introduction to this book, for it is a first-hand account of what they were trying to do together.

The teaching of anthroposophy is for medical science a veritable mine of inspiration. From my knowledge and experience as a doctor, I was able to confirm it without reserve. I found in it a fount of wisdom from which it was possible untiringly to draw, and which was able to solve and illumine many a problem as yet unsolved in medicine. Thus there arose between Rudolf Steiner and myself a living cooperation in the field of medical discovery. Our cooperation gradually deepened, especially in the last two years, so that the united authorship of a book became a possibility and an achievement. It had always been Rudolf Steiner's endeavour—and in this I could meet him with fullest sympathy of understanding—to renew the life of the ancient Mysteries and cause it to flow once more into the sphere of medicine. From time immemorial the Mysteries were most intimately united with the art of healing, and the attainment of spiritual knowledge was brought into connection with the healing of the sick. We had no thought, after the style of quacks and dilettanti, of underrating the scientific medicine of our time. We recognized it fully. Our aim was to supplement the science already in existence by the illumination that can flow from a true knowledge of the Spirit,

470

towards a living grasp of the processes of illness and of healing. Needless to say, our purpose was to bring into new life, not the instinctive habit of the soul which still existed in the Mysteries of ancient time, but a method of research corresponding to the fully evolved consciousness of modern man, which can be lifted into spiritual regions. Thus the first beginnings of our work were made. In the Clinical and Therapeutical Institute founded by myself at Arlesheim in Switzerland, a basis was given in practice for the theories set forth in this book. And we endeavoured to unfold new ways in the art of healing to those who were seeking, in the sense here indicated, for a widening of their medical knowledge.*

We cannot enter here into much detail concerning the development of anthroposophical medicine in the years since Steiner's death, but must content ourselves, for the most part, with indicating with examples the relevance of his perceptions to medical practice. From our earlier chapters it will be remembered that it is a fundamental perception of Steiner that man is a fourfold being (physical, etheric, and astral bodies and an ego organization) but that man is also to be looked upon as a threefold being, possessed of a nerves and senses system in the upper part of his organism, a rhythmic system in the middle, and a digestive and limb system in the lower part of his organism. This last description may be further refined by pointing out that each of these "systems" is in itself also a triad, as will be clear when we consider the head, which has a "nerves and senses" system in the brain and forehead, a rhythmic system in the nose, used for breathing, and the mouth and jaw, which are part of the limb system, serving to feed the digestive or metabolic system. Lastly, man is a twofold being insofar as he lives between two polarities, the consciousness pole and the life pole. Anthroposophy recognizes consciousness as a death process, whereas our life processes remain in the realm of our unconscious. We can

---

* For Dr. Wegman's own work until her death in 1943 see *Memories of Ita Wegman*, written by a number of those who had worked with her (London, 1948).

scarcely interfere at all with our digestive process, and we move our limbs without the slightest knowledge of how we communicate our wish to move them from the head to the limbs. These are what we call life processes, belonging to the "life pole" of our being.

Now in addition to the ordinary diagnosis of specific illnesses as carried out in orthodox medicine, the anthroposophical physician adds another diagnosis based on spiritual insight. He recognizes in effect that *all* illnesses are the result of an *imbalance*, and that it is this imbalance rather than the specific symptoms of a particular disease that he must try to rectify. The activity of the astral body, which breaks down by contrast with the etheric body, which builds up, may in a certain instance be too powerful for the etheric forces, and the ego organization may be too weak to regulate this balance between the two bodies. Similarly, there may be an undesirable predominance of the neuro-sensorial system over the digestive-limb system, so that the death processes of consciousness predominate over the life processes that work in the unconscious. Or, on the other hand, the exact reverse may be the case. The rhythmic system, which has the task of regulating relations between the neuro-sensorial and the metabolic-limb system, may be unequal to its heavy task, in which case the disease will manifest itself in the rhythmic system itself, in heart or lungs.

For the anthroposophical physician who has access, as explained in Chapter 7, to numerous medicaments that may be prepared in many different potencies, it is essential to know such things as these. He must, for example, know whether a particular medicament in a particular potency stimulates the ego organization, and whether another remedy may be expected to calm down the excessive activity of the head organization. In addition to medicaments he may wish to prescribe curative eurythmy, painting, or music, because he wishes to help his patient in every way possible so that the same causes will not again lead to the same effects. It it his aim to bring balance into the patient's entire organism, including, of course, his soul-spiritual nature.

472

Only if he can do this can he regard his patient as, if not totally cured, at least on the way to a real cure.

The vital importance of a correct diagnosis within anthroposophical terms may be shown by the treatment of diseases of the heart. The rhythmic system, of which the heart is the central organ, cannot *in itself* be ill, but the heart *can* be subjected to strain in its efforts to restore the balance between the neuro-sensorial pole and the metabolic-limb pole. One or the other of these poles will be trying to assert its predominance, and as a result of this effort, it will be the heart that suffers. Which of the two poles predominates will find expression in the particular kind of heart disease and its many differentiated symptoms. When the metabolic pole predominates, the heart disease will ordinarily be characterized by inflammation (endocarditis, myocarditis, pericarditis); when the neuro-sensorial pole predominates there will be a tendency toward thrombosis, various sclerotic features, angina pectoris, and the like. For the anthroposophical doctor the *kind* of treatment to be given differs in each instance, and this includes not only the different medications but also the additional soul-spiritual therapy. His aim will always be to rectify *the imbalance* between the two poles, and thus, as it were incidentally, to heal the heart. Certainly orthodox heart specialists will recognize the nature of the heart disease they are treating and will prescribe medicaments, even surgery, in accordance with their understanding. The picture of the threefold man, the imbalance between the two poles, and the essential function of the heart in maintaining and restoring the balance, however; provide the anthroposophical doctor with a deeper understanding of the nature of the disease and what he must try to do about it.

Few physicians who are not anthroposophists have adopted anything of importance for their own practice from anthroposophical medicine. Nevertheless, there is one great exception to this generalization, to which we shall devote some attention here—cancer therapy. So much has been done and still is being done in this field that it is necessary to go into some detail on the subject. Steiner himself initiated this work some years before his death, when he drew attention to the unique nature of the mistletoe plant, indicating that, when it was prepared and used in accordance with his instructions, it would be found to be a valuable therapy for cancer. It would take us too far to explain how it is that the mistletoe, a plant unique in nature, a parasite that will grow only on certain trees, should have the power to cure such a disease as cancer. But it may be noted that when prepared in accordance with Steiner's indications and administered at the right time and under the right circumstances, it has the property of damping down the etheric formative forces, which are responsible for the unchecked growth of cancer cells in the organism.

The medicament made from the mistletoe, which has been given the trade name of Iscador (*Viscum album*) is used quite widely in Europe and in many other countries of the world by doctors who prescribe it in certain cases of cancer where they think it will have the best chances for success. It is often the case that such doctors use no other anthroposophical remedies, nor do they accept any of Steiner's ideas. In some instances they may have learned about Iscador only through reading about it in reputable medical journals, some of which have published the results of the extensive experimentation that has been carried out under strictly controlled conditions in accordance with recognized scientific methods. Outsiders have been able to check the experiments by duplicating them, but they have never been permitted to manufacture Iscador itself, for reasons that seem compelling.

The manufacture of this remedy is, in the first place, difficult, and requires the use of specially built apparatus; there are also many different varieties of Iscador, which vary according to the tree on which the original mistletoe grew. As with other anthroposophical (and homeopathic) remedies, it is prepared in different potencies. It would therefore be completely impossible to synthesize it, as commercial pharmaceutical houses would at once wish to do, and if the attempt were made, the resulting

474

product would not have the same therapeutical effect as the natural Iscador. Tests have made it abundantly clear that there are vast qualitative differences between even one variety of Iscador and another, and that it can only be the active forces in the preparation that give it its efficacy, rather than the fact that it is an alkaloid of a certain chemical composition and molecular structure. To the perfectly natural question as to why information about Iscador has not been provided to the scientific world the answer must be that the responsible scientists who run the cancer research institute founded in 1949 in Arlesheim (the Hiscia Institute), feel that their duty is to make Iscador available to doctors all over the world who wish to use it, together with the necessary detailed instructions for its use, in preference to revealing to the profession their entire manufacturing procedure, from collecting the mistletoe to the finished product, in face of the virtual certainty that this procedure would never be followed by any commercial pharmaceutical firm. The aim of such a firm would undoubtedly be to create a similar product with similar qualities by different means that would lend themselves to mass production. On the other hand, independent scientists in the field of cancer research use certain recognized methods of procedure in their work—customarily using laboratory animals whom they infect with cancer and then try to cure. Iscador cannot be used to cure laboratory animals artificially infected with cancer; therefore those responsible for its manufacture prefer to make the product itself available at virtually the cost of production to anyone who wishes to use it in human therapy or to make scientific experiments with it.

Although a considerable number of patients suffering from cancer, even with tumors regarded as inoperable and incurable by specialists, have certainly been cured by the Iscador treatment, the possibility of such cures, which are necessarily rare, is not stressed by the responsible doctors at Arlesheim. The latter administer Iscador, as a rule, as do most doctors who use it elsewhere, *before* cancer has actively declared itself and before a tumor is visible, that is, when, in anthroposophical parlance, the

475

disease is still in the etheric body and has not yet reached the physical. Such patients are regarded as being in a "precancerous" state, and they would almost certainly acquire an active cancer if they were not treated. It is at this stage that Iscador is the most effective. Certainly it would be easy to retort that if a "cure" of a non-existent or not-yet-existent disease is claimed, then it is impossible to substantiate the claim that the use of Iscador prevented the patient from getting cancer. After all, who can see the etheric body and any disease that may be latent in it? Is there really any such thing as a "precancerous" condition that can be detected and cured? Obviously, if the patient eventually becomes entirely free from even his "precancerous" condition, if he is pronounced "cured" by an anthroposophical doctor, how can it be proved that in due time he would have acquired a real and visible cancer?

To deal with this objection it is necessary to discuss the methods available for diagnosis. We have referred briefly to both procedures in Chapter 7 in a different context. The sensitive crystallization process invented by Ehrenfried Pfeiffer, following a suggestion made by Rudolf Steiner, is able to make visible the working of the etheric formative forces in human blood. Many diseases can be detected in the slides made from a patient's blood after it has been mixed with copper chloride and precipitated in a particular manner. Much the easiest to detect by this method is cancer, either when it is in an active stage or when it is still latent in the etheric body only. This test has been used for nearly fifty years, but it is quite difficult to read if all the information it can convey is to be obtained. The organ of the body likely to be affected, or actually affected can usually be determined with considerable accuracy. The second such test uses the system of capillary dynamolysis invented by Lily Kolisko, and developed as a blood test for cancer by Werner Kaelin. This test, in use since 1928, makes use of the Iscador preparation as a means for determining whether cancer is present, either in latent or active form. When cancer is present

476

the patient's blood acts differently under the influence of the Iscador; if there is no cancer this reaction does not occur. Neither of the two tests is infallible, and one is often used to check the other. But the rate of success is high, especially in the diagnosis of cancer in its early, but already active and visible stages, when other methods can of course be used to check their accuracy. Both tests, when they show only a "precancerous" condition, will ordinarily be followed by a treatment with the appropriate Iscador therapy. If this therapy is for any reason not instituted, the number of cases of active cancer that follow is much higher than would be the case with a random selection of persons of the same age. The evidence for the existence of a "precancerous" condition must therefore be exclusively statistical, based on those individuals *not* treated after a diagnosis of cancer by one or both of the tests. It is difficult to see how any more precise proof will ever be attained.

By contrast, the post-operative treatment of cancer, which at the present time is the most frequent use of Iscador therapy, can easily be checked by generally accepted scientific procedures— also, of course, statistical in nature but much more definite. In Arlesheim there is another clinic, opened fairly recently for the treatment of cancer patients who have undergone an operation for the excision of a tumor. In the Lukas Clinic, as it is called, careful records have been made that show with a high degree of conclusiveness how valuable the Iscador therapy is at this stage, especially when combined with eurythmy, curative painting, and other artistic and social aids. There is far less recurrence of the disease, and a far greater life expectancy among patients who have undergone this treatment in the Lukas Clinic or elsewhere, than there is among post-operative patients who have had no special therapy, or only such helps as the orthodox medical profession is able to provide. These results have been published, and at the very least, make out a strong prima facie case for the efficacy of Iscador. It is true that orthodox cancer research has been hesitant to recognize any special virtues in the mistletoe plant, and so has done little experimental research with it. But it is unfortunate that orthodox researchers so often simply damn Iscador in advance simply because the process of manufacturing it is secret, and thus in their eyes reprehensible, however many lives it may save.

The anthroposophical treatment of cancer reveals one important feature of all anthroposophical medicine. It regards any human illness as a total one; *the human being is ill,* and he must be helped to overcome his illness *totally.* He is *not* regarded as cured when a particular symptom disappears, a point of view that cancer researchers have been almost forced to recognize. When a tumor is removed, another may appear not long afterward in a different part of the body. Hence the special post-operative treatment given in the Lukas Clinic in Arlesheim, directed toward preventing another tumor from making its appearance. It is recognized that in spite of the excision of his tumor the patient is still ill. What is true of cancer is true of all other diseases in a greater or lesser degree. For this reason anthroposophical remedies are not directed toward "curing" or causing any particular symptom merely to disappear. To use an example mentioned earlier, if the ego organization is too weak to perform its tasks, this will manifest itself in many different symptoms. But the *cause* is the weakness of the ego organization, and this must be helped by the appropriate remedies. The only way a human being can be totally cured of an illness is for him to *conquer it himself* with the aid of the remedies. If his ego organization is strengthened by taking the remedy and by other forms of therapy, including appropriate exercises, then indeed he may become stronger than he would have been had he never suffered from the "illness." Illness is certainly often enough a wretched nuisance, but it also provides an opportunity to make spiritual progress. Those forces, which, with the aid of homeopathic remedies, succeed in overcoming the illness, can be used later for other purposes, as the forces used by a child in his first seven years for building up his organism are then released to be used for thinking (see Chapter 10).

478

Weleda and Wala Products. Remedies Used in Anthroposophical Medicine. We mentioned in the last section that mistletoe is a plant unique in nature and that Steiner himself drew attention to its potentialities as a remedy for cancer because he was able to recognize the potentialities that lay in its uniqueness. It should now be noted that not all the medicinal plants and other remedies used in anthroposophical therapy were specifically referred to by Steiner. But it was he who over several years provided those who worked with him in the medical field with the kind of information they needed in order to be able to recognize whether a plant could be used for therapeutical purposes or not, and if so, how it would work when properly prepared as a remedy to be ingested by the human being. Much of this information was known to country doctors and herbalists in earlier times, either intuitively or through tradition. In the modern age it is necessary to acquire this kind of knowledge consciously. Among the practical realizations of anthroposophy surely one of the most fascinating stories is the progress made in the production and distribution of new medicaments on the basis of the "Goethean" observation of the natural world and its relationship with the human being. The *form* of a plant, how and where it grows, the metamorphoses it undergoes during its growth—these are the elements that must be taken into consideration by the therapist and medical botanist. It is also important to recognize which part of a particular plant will have medical uses, and for which part of the human organism. In general, as was noted in Chapter 7 (footnote, page 299), the root of a plant corresponds to the nerves and senses organization in the human being, and will be used for giving aid to this particular system; the leaf and stalk of a plant will be used for healing disorders in the rhythmic system, and the fruit and blossom the digestive and limb system. Such insights, as we shall see, lie also at the basis of anthroposophical nutrition.

While a great deal of modern medicine is based upon trial and error, and in most countries almost every widely used medicament is synthesized, the Weleda products* are invariably made from natural plant or animal substances, or when necessary from minerals as they appear in nature. When we say that modern medicine is so largely based upon trial and error, we wish to emphasize that it is seldom recognized just why a particular modern medicament should function in the way it does. Its molecular structure is, of course, well known, and indeed the product has probably been manufactured in the first place from various "stable" mineral substances in order that it might have that particular molecular structure. Its properties will certainly have been extensively studied, and before being used on human beings its effects will have been tested on laboratory animals. But *why* it should have the effect it does on the human or animal organism is rarely known, and indeed many researchers regard this *why* as of little or no importance. They are concerned above all with *what* the medicament does and does not do in the organism and they must know if, in addition to its apparent therapeutic powers, it has unwanted toxic "side-effects," since these must also be known before a

* The first steps toward what was to become the world-wide group of Weleda companies were taken in 1921 when Dr. Ita Wegman founded the "International Laboratories" in Arlesheim, Switzerland. In 1924 Rudolf Steiner suggested the name, Weleda, who was the Celtic goddess of health, and whose name was always assumed by the priestess of the cult. The Weleda S.A. in Arlesheim has remained the "mother-house" of the movement, but the factory in Schwäbisch-Gmünd in Württemberg, Germany is the largest center of actual production. There are affiliated Weleda companies or agencies in every country in Western and Northern Europe except Belgium, as well as in the United States and Canada, in Australia and New Zealand, in Argentina and Brazil, and, lastly, in Israel and South Africa. In most of these countries some products are manufactured locally according to specifications laid down in Switzerland, while the more complex medicaments are imported from Switzerland and Germany. The various Weleda cosmetics, soaps, massage oils, hair lotions and similar products as well as tonics, all made from natural products only, enjoy ever increasing sales, in effect making economically possible the production of the much less widely used medicaments that are available only by prescription. The Wala Company, founded by Dr. Rudolf Hauschka in Eckwalden, Germany, also produces a full line of medicaments used in anthroposophical medicine but by different processes than those used by Weleda. These products will receive some attention later in the chapter.

product can be used on human beings (though the distinction between a therapeutic and a "side" effect is, when one comes to think of it, meaningless, for both are equally effects of the medicament). In short, orthodox medicine is almost exclusively empirical, and its theoretic basis is often weak. Hence the constant experimentation with ever new and "improved" products, which, when they have been perceived to work in a "statistically significant" number of experiments, are then permitted to be used in the hope of alleviating human illness. The pharmacopoeia used in anthroposophical medicine rests upon a totally different theoretical basis. The refusal of the Weleda and Wala companies to use synthetic products is not based upon any faddish objection to man-made products as such, but simply upon the anthroposophical insight that man himself has such a close relationship to the natural world that he cannot be fully cured except by substances taken directly from it, whether of animal, plant, or mineral origin. A synthesized medicament, even though resembling the natural one in its molecular structure, and often having a powerful effect within the human organism, is almost invariably, in these modern times, derived from substances of a mineral origin, since only these are regarded as sufficiently "stable." Moreover, as we emphasized in Chapter 7, modern man lacks the capacity to understand fully the realm of the living. Now, according to insights drawn from anthroposophy, substances derived from the mineral kingdom act upon the self, the ego organization of man, whereas it is usually more desirable to act upon the other bodies of man—the etheric body, worked upon by products of animal origin, and the astral body, worked upon by products taken from the plant kingdom. Indeed, for most illnesses it is helpful to have medicaments derived from more than one of these kingdoms. Even when it is desired to act upon the ego organization directly, a real metal or a mineral such as rock crystal, will almost surely be indicated and potentized as necessary, rather than a product of a chemical laboratory.

Although the Weleda and Wala companies, as well as the

Hiscia Institute, engage in a great deal of experimentation and research, it is not necessary to resort to as much trial and error as in orthodox medicine because so many possibilities can be eliminated on the basis of anthroposophical theory. It is, for example, perfectly possible to recognize the probability that a particular plant can be used for medicinal purposes by the *form* the plant assumes. As Steiner pointed out, medicinal plants "have a tendency to develop one part, or part of a process, in excess, making it the outstanding characteristic in their appearance. It is this abnormality that makes the plant a medicinal plant." * Once one has recognized that a particular plant is likely to be of medicinal value, attention can be concentrated on it, to the exclusion of those plants that have "normal" forms and are thus unlikely to be medicinal. All the metals can be used in therapy, and the traditional knowledge that associated the different metals with different organs of the body has been shown to be correct through experimentation. Thus the metals can likewise be used in medicine without unnecessary experimentation.

We have already discussed earlier in this chapter, as well as in Chapter 7, Steiner's fundamental teachings on the tripartite nature of the human being, and we alluded in a footnote to the fact that a plant is, as it were, a human being upside down, with its root system corresponding to the human head, and its fruits and flowers corresponding to the digestive and limb system. This information, as might be surmised, is of the utmost importance when preparing medicinal plants for use as medicaments. It would, for example, never occur to an anthroposophical researcher to try to stimulate the digestive processes by administering the root of the camomile plant, whose flowers, however,

* As paraphrased by Wilhelm Pelikan, a botanist long in the service of the Weleda Company, and author of a work called *Heilpflanzenkunde* (Medical Botany), which has been partly translated into English in the *Journal of Anthroposophy* (New York). The passage quoted here is from the issue of Spring, 1972, p. 47. Pelikan is also the author of an outstanding book on metals, including their therapeutic properites, called, *The Secrets of Metals* (New York, 1973).

are of the utmost value in this respect. The leaf and stalk system of the plant, which corresponds to the rhythmic system in the human being, will naturally be used in connection with circulatory disturbances. Digitalis, the long known remedy used in heart disease, is drawn from the *leaf* of the foxglove, not its flower or root. This kind of information will, of course, not tell us which plants to use as therapeutic agents, but it will certainly eliminate many false trails, thus indirectly aiding in medical research.*

It should be clear from the brief account given above that close observation is needed by the anthroposophical researcher in this field, and that this observation must be fertilized by living imaginative thinking, insofar as this can be developed, so that a picture of the vital processes at work in both human being and plant can be acquired. None of this knowledge is required, by contrast, when a product is simply synthesized from various dead substances. The pharmaceutical chemist has a much more limited field to study. It is his task to try to devise some product that will help in "curing" or alleviating some of the symptoms of a particular disease. For this purpose he must, as a rule, induce the diseases in some laboratory animal, then try out his new compound and see what effect it has. The medical profession is thus becoming increasingly at the mercy of the chemist. A medical doctor simply has to take on trust the results of the experiments and when in difficulties he is likely to try out for himself the latest "wonder drug." In contrast, the anthroposophical doctor must, from his own knowledge, come to recognize what medicament is needed, and in what potency. It is for the anthroposophical pharmaceutical houses to provide it. From the beginning the necessity of the practical working together of the two professions was recognized. They shared the same ideas about disease and health, and the same ideals and the same body of knowledge inspired them both. It would be

---

* The Pelikan article in the Autumn, 1971 issue of the *Journal for Anthroposophy* entitled, "Archetypal Relations Between Plant and Man" deals with this subject in a most enlightening manner.

unthinkable for sales representatives of the Weleda and Wala companies to call upon doctors with samples, urging them to try out their new "drugs," and then perhaps call on them later for testimonials. Innovations that have been made by these companies are at once shared with the doctors, who may in the first place have indicated the need for them.

One example may be given of an innovation made by the Weleda Company in relatively recent times even though it stems from an original suggestion by Rudolf Steiner that was not at once followed up. Instead of the normal potentization of metals, as described earlier, a new technique was tried under which during their growth certain plants were treated with a particular metal. The plants were then made into compost, and used to enrich the soil on which further plants were grown. This second generation of plants would then have the required metal built into them, as it were. Both plant and metal would be needed to treat a particular disease, but when the two are combined in the same plant, the power of the resulting medicament is greatly enhanced. This second generation plant product, which is used in its natural form, and without further potentization, is especially useful in cases where a chronic disease is to be treated. The sudden use of this "plant potentized metal" gives the treatment a better start than could be obtained by using the two medicaments, the plant and the metal, potentized in the ordinary conventional manner. The ten double medicaments currently available have already proved themselves in extensive clinical work as well as in experimentation.

Both the Weleda and Wala companies devote much attention to the skin, and to treatment of disease through the skin—as is, of course, increasingly done in orthodox medicine today. Allied to this work is the production of cosmetics, one of the fastest growing branches, especially of the Weleda Company. It will be recognized from what has been said earlier that only natural products can be used because only they have a natural relationship with the human organism. But in this field also the fundamental insight of anthroposophical medicine and physiol-

484

ogy, that the human organism is tripartite, is used. The skin itself has three parts, the epidermis, which corresponds to the head and senses system of the entire organism, and is actually responsible for the ability to use the sense of touch; the dermis, which contains the capillary system, and is thus a miniature rhythmic system, and the subcutaneous section, which is responsible for the actual nourishment of the skin (in this it is comparable to the human digestive or metabolic system). Each of these three parts of the skin needs its own treatment, and a fundamental medicament such as the marvelous Weleda massage lotion will be made up of elements from all parts of the plant, each directed to the corresponding element in the skin. The rosemary oil and the distillation of the birch leaves that compose the main body of this medicament are directed to the circulatory system of the skin, while the lavender enhances sense perception, and the all-purpose arnica, used in so many medicaments, nourishes the subcutaneous area of the skin. It should be noted that both lavender and rosemary have a considerable fragrance of their own, but neither is used in any sense as a *perfume*. Perfumes, as such, are never used in Weleda or Wala products.

The products manufactured by the Wala Company in Boll, near Eckwalden, Germany, originate from a different process from that used by the Weleda companies, as well as forming a valuable supplement to the line offered by the larger concern. Again the process stems from an indication given by Rudolf Steiner, when he remarked to Dr. Ita Wegman that it would be found to be possible to preserve medicaments in an entirely natural way without the use of alcohol, as had indeed once been true in the remote past. In the years following his death Dr. Wegman had always felt it to be a task laid on her by Steiner that the method of preserving medicaments through the use of cosmic rhythms should be rediscovered, but did not find a collaborator for this work until Dr. Rudolf Hauschka entered the Clinical Therapeutical Institute at Arlesheim in 1929. With her assistance and encouragement and the advice of many

485

anthroposophists Dr. Hauschka was able to solve the problem and a few years later founded his own laboratory and factory at Boll.

It is not possible here to go into detail as to how the Wala preparations are made. It is enough to say that the plant world lives under the influence of rhythms that arise from the relationship of the earth with the universe. The Wala Company submits the medical plants that it intends to use to a rhythmical process as soon as they have been taken out of their natural environment. Under the influence of light and warmth a juice is obtained that is then concentrated and thereafter has a special relationship to the rhythmic system of the human being, and, after being rediluted to the necessary potency, keeps indefinitely. No alcohol is used in this process though glycerine, a natural alcohol that lends itself well to a rhythmic treatment, may also be used for some preparations. The Wala laboratories have engaged tirelessly in research from the beginning, and have created some medicaments not made by Weleda that are used for disorders arising from the spinal column, including all kinds of rheumatism and arthritis. It also offers nine extraordinary elixirs that are imported from Germany into many countries, including Great Britain; these have met with great success. In general the Wala products complement those offered by the Weleda companies, and both, of course, arise from the same impulse.

Nutrition. Rudolf Steiner gave one special lecture on nutrition, but never gave a course on this subject. By explaining exactly how the human being is nourished—a subject on which precise and accurate knowledge is in short supply among ordinary scientists—and through many remarks made incidentally in the course of his lectures on medicine and agriculture he was once again the pioneer of a new science. Today at the center of anthroposophy in Dornach there is an important experimental laboratory where the study of nutrition is pursued, and its director, Gerhard Schmidt, has written numerous papers on the subject, few of which, unfortunately, have been translated into English.

Before dealing with nutrition it should be stressed at the outset with the utmost emphasis that the study of human nutrition in the light of anthroposophy should never lead to any kind of fanaticism. Steiner did not declare himself in favor of certain diets, and indeed on almost every occasion when he touched on the subject, he was careful to comment that he was simply giving the facts as the science of spirit shows them to be, and that he was not *advocating* any particular dietary practice. His hearers were always left to draw their own conclusions for themselves. Individual students of anthroposophy have at times been tempted to pontificate on the subject of diet and nutrition, but usually on the basis either of studies carried out by themselves, not necessarily in the light of Steiner's own teachings, or on the basis of the findings of others who are engaged in this field.

In view of the enormous growth of interest in diet and nutrition—largely an offshoot of our increasing egotism and obsession with our personal selves—and the obvious fact that most of us are extremely ill-nourished, it is always easy to find an audience when our subject is nutrition. But it needs to be stressed that the anthroposophical research in this field is of a strictly objective nature, with personal preferences entirely eliminated, and that it stems only from the quite limited indications given by Steiner. Anthroposophical nutrition has nothing to do with health faddism, nature therapy, macrobiotic diets, nor even with the development of "balanced" diets according to modern notions of scientifically determined food requirements. Any or all of these may in their own realm be justified, even excellent, as far as they go, but they do not stem from anthroposophy. If anthroposophists are inclined to patronize "health stores" it is because these stores are expected to sell food untouched by poisonous sprays and unfortified by noxious chemical additives and preservatives, and because they can

487

usually buy there herbs that are valuable in anthroposophical therapy—not because manufactured "health products" sold by these stores are necessarily valuable for human nutrition as it is conceived of in anthroposophy.

It will be obvious that the matters considered in the last chapter will have particular relevance for questions of nutrition. It is scarcely possible to exaggerate the importance of the *quality* of the foods we consume, and the attainment of quality is, of course, one of the principal objectives of biodynamic farming and gardening. If, for example, we decide that we ought to eat a certain quantity of carrots as a part of our planned diet, it is surely not unimportant whether the carrot has been grown under healthy, natural conditions, in a soil suited for the purpose, or whether it only looks like a handsome carrot but is in effect a chemical product grown in a soil devoid of humus, that has been specially irrigated before harvest to enlarge its size, and has been subjected to poisonous sprays and insecticides. It is not enough, therefore, for the nutritionist to advise us to eat so or so many carrots, so much milk, so much lettuce, and the rest. Ideally, he should prescribe plant products grown in a certain way, and animal products from animals that have been nourished in a certain way. A glass of milk from one cow may be quite different from a glass of milk from another one. Since such a policy is clearly impossible for a nutritionist to follow in view of the fact that few such products are on the market, he simply does not mention the matter at all unless he is in a position to recommend so called "organic" products that may be available. Here we merely draw attention to the matter, and to the connection between correct nutrition and biodynamic farming and gardening, but need go no further into the subject, for in this chapter we are concerned with nutrition as such, and not with the particular quality of the food products available.

According to Steiner, the human being is not nourished directly by the substance of the food that he eats. This food is of course thoroughly broken down by chemical processes. Then the etheric body, which has played its due part under the direction of the ego organization (which is in ultimate control of everything that enters our organism) in the process of breaking down, now proceeds to transform, or better "transsubstantiate" what remains into specifically *human* substance, at the same time regulating the entry of cosmic substance from the cosmos outside. For we are nourished also by the air we breathe, and by all that enters us in the most dilute form from our environment, including even our sense perceptions. All these things together constitute specifically human substance, radically different from what we absorbed in the first place as plant and animal food.

This extremely complex process has been mentioned here—though we can scarcely claim to have explained it—because some general understanding of it is necessary if we are to appreciate the real difference between what we consume from the various kingdoms of nature. Mineral substance does not lend itself to transformation; among those substances that we need, salt alone remains in the organism in much the same state as when it was absorbed. We need a certain amount of salt in our organism as support for our ego organization; synthetic foods taken from the mineral world, chemical additives and the like, remain as alien substances in our organism until they are eliminated. They do not change because the etheric body cannot work upon them.

All food of animal origin originally belonged to the plant world. But through *its* etheric body the animal has already begun to transform it. Thus the human etheric body does not have such a heavy task to perform as when it transforms food taken directly from the plant world. Animal food is thus easier to digest, and it may still be essential for some persons to allow the animal to do a part of the work of digestion for them—although of course most meat eaters are such from choice. The forces that ought to be used to convert plant substance into human are thereby left unused and tend to atrophy, with the consequence that the etheric body is weakened as muscles are weakened when they are not used. The result is that the etheric body can no longer perform all the varied tasks required of it, including spiritual tasks. It is no accident that confirmed meat eaters cannot think as imaginatively nor meditate as profoundly as those who make use of all the forces of their etheric body to digest their food, and thus possess a strong and active etheric body. These are, as Steiner insisted, simply facts, and are not intended to propagandize for vegetarianism. Steiner also willingly admitted that some persons at present, and during various times of their life, cannot do the whole work of transforming the plant into human substance, and must make use of the animal and, it may be added, be grateful to the animal group-soul for the sacrifice it makes so that man can eat animals as meat.*

None of this should be taken to mean that any or all vegetarian diets are good for us, even for those of us who eat no meat at all. Not only should vegetarian diets be balanced, as will be explained later, but a distinction should also be made between raw and cooked foods. We have stated above that food of animal origin is more easily digested than food taken directly from the plant kingdom, because the animal has already performed a part of the task of digestion. The same is true when we cook food instead of eating it raw. The process of cooking brings it nearer to the final stage of becoming human substance, and thus spares our etheric body one of its tasks. So, in principle, it would appear that in order to give our etheric body the maximum amount of exercise we should eat as much as possible of our food in a raw state. This is in fact what many "food faddists" recommend, even if they are unaware of the reason for their recommendation.

Not so Rudolf Steiner. He emphasized that the process of digesting is a warmth process, which in general should be aided by cooking, which is itself, of course, a warmth process. This is

---

* This paragraph has primarily concerned the eating of meat or animal flesh. Other animal products may be of great value because of the forces that the animal has conferred on them through its work. Milk and milk products, and above all honey, belong to this category. For this subject and for the question of raw and cooked foods, see especially Spiritual Science and Medicine, Lecture 10.

especially true of those foods that are most essential for our actual nourishment. Our organisms are unable to bring enough warmth to bear on many foods, especially those that are rich in carbohydrates. The potato, he pointed out, is scarcely digestible at all if it is not cooked. The various cereals, which are the foods above all that nourish the very core of the human being and without which he can never be properly nourished, should ordinarily be cooked, as should plants whose roots are used for nourishment. By contrast, certain foods are already, as it were, precooked (having passed through a warmth process), hence it is ordinarily better to eat these raw—though when the digestion is weak or one has an intestinal illness such as colitis, it is much better—as every doctor knows—to eat even apples and pears in the form of a compote. The leaves of plants usually used in salads have likewise been thoroughly worked upon by the sun and, except in the case of illness, should also be eaten raw. Neither salads nor fruits, however, constitute what Steiner calls the true nourishment for our central organism; they are helpful adjuncts, but we cannot for long live on them alone and be properly nourished. What is to nourish our central organism, such as the cereals, should be already as close as possible to the condition of "humanization" when it is consumed.

While describing the importance of cooking most foods before consuming them, Steiner did give one important indication regarding the use of raw food. It is quite correct, he said, that raw foods do indeed draw forth more forces from the human being than he needs for digesting cooked foods. Raw food, even such roots as carrots, onions, and celeriac, can therefore be used *for remedial reasons* when for any reason it is necessary to stimulate the use of these forces. Such use will ordinarily be only for a limited period; if prolonged it can lead to illness. The use of raw food in particular stimulates the nervous system and increases the flow of blood to the skin. Obviously such stimulation should not be prolonged beyond the time necessary for the remedial effect to take place. Moreover, the nourishment

491

of our central organism will be neglected to some degree for the period that raw food is being used, and the "humanization" of our food will be to this extent impeded.

The last aspect of nutrition to which we shall draw attention here is a further extension of what was explained earlier in this chapter in relation to the choice of medicaments. What was said there about the different parts of the plant apply equally to the choice of foodstuffs. The plant, as we explained, is like a human being upside down, with its "head" in the earth, and its "digestive" system in the air. As a consequence, it is that part of the plant that lies below the surface of the earth, the root, that forms the proper nourishment for the head, nerves and senses system of the human being, and we should always be careful not to omit those plants such as the carrot that are true roots (the potato, of course, is not a root but a tuberous underground stem); otherwise, we shall not have a diet that can nourish us fully. The stalk and leaf of the plant nourish our rhythmic, chest, lung and circulatory system, while the fruit and blossom nourish our digestive and limb system. A diet can be balanced truly only if these essential facts are taken into consideration. We need roots, and we need leaves of plants, and these cannot be substituted even by the most perfect food of all, the grain.

The seed or grain is in a somewhat different situation from the three other parts of the plant. It has already passed over into a new condition of form, with the whole plant concentrated in it; an entire new plant would spring from it if it were planted in the earth. The seed is therefore in a sense the most perfect and concentrated of foods and nourishes the whole organism; hence, according to a correct human instinct, it has always been considered as the most essential element in human nutrition, and bread has often been called, correctly, "the staff of life." There are many differences between the different cereals, however, and the nutritional center at Dornach has devoted much research to the consideration of these differences, including the cosmic and earthly forces that have cooperated in creating them.

With this chapter we bring to an end our discussion of the various practical uses that have been made of Steiner's teachings, and in particular of the flourishing movements in education, normal and curative, and in agriculture. The work in medicine has met many obstacles, and has only become a fairly flourishing movement in a few countries, and it is fair to say that Steiner's ideas on nutrition, which we have just been discussing, have not taken any firm hold except in small circles. Not even all anthroposophists pay much attention to them, in part because the work is not widely known to them, but also in large part because of the apparent difficulty of reconciling it with competing views put forward either by orthodox scientists, or self-styled nutritional experts who often have wide followings. Anthroposophical nutritional science, consisting as it does of some highly suggestive remarks by Rudolf Steiner, and a considerable amount of detailed research by a few of his followers, mostly concerned with the nature of various plants and their activity within the human being, seems often to lack specificity. It recommends little and is slow to forbid. It does not say, eat this, don't eat that, this food is good for you, that food is harmful, count your calories, eat your way to health. Nevertheless, it was thought worthwhile to include nutrition as the last among the practical realizations of anthroposophy at the same time as the study of agriculture and medicine to which it is clearly related. All that remains now is to give a brief description of the founding and organization of the General Anthroposophical Society and to say a few words about the national societies throughout the world. That these societies have persisted, and in almost all cases are increasing their influence and membership, remains a tribute to the fruitfulness of the ideas on which they are based. The subject surely belongs among the realizations to which the second half of this book has been devoted.

This description therefore will form the content of the next chapter, which will bring the book to an end.

Long before Rudolf Steiner spoke to doctors he gave a fascinatingly interesting course on occult physiology to anthroposophists in Prague. Much of what he was to give in practical form later may be found in this cycle, *An Occult Physiology*, eight lectures given in Prague from March 20 to 28, 1911 (revised edition, London, 1951), though as yet there is no mention of the threefold nature of man. Most of the lectures for doctors have already been recommended in Chapter 7. Among these are *Spiritual Science and Medicine*, twenty lectures given in Dornach, March 21 to April 9, 1920, which contain much material on pharmacy and nutrition as well as anthroposophical medicine (London, 1975); *Four Lectures to Doctors* delivered during medical week at Stuttgart, October 25 to 27, 1922 (London, 1928), which include a valuable detailed discussion of what we have called the "ego organization"; *Spiritual Science and the Art of Healing*, three public lectures given at Arnhem between July 17 and 24, 1924, which constitute a most valuable introduction to the subject, insofar as it can be given to a general public (London, 1950). *Fundamentals of Therapy*, a book written by Steiner in collaboration with Dr. Ita Wegman, is in a class by itself, as an introduction for anthroposophists, including those who may hope to become doctors themselves, which was published just after Steiner's death, though he had been able to read the book in proof (London, 1967). Mention may also be made of a useful little brochure that consists of an abridgment of two lectures given in London in 1924, and covering much the same ground as *Spiritual Science and Healing*. This bears the title *An Outline of Anthroposophical Medical Research* (London, 1939).

The article, "Widening the Art of Healing," by Dr. Grete Kirchner-Bockholt in the *Golden Blade*, 1958 was recommended in the text for the attractive account of how the work in medicine started in Arlesheim through the cooperation between Rudolf Steiner and Dr. Ita Wegman, but for a long time there was no comprehensive account of anthroposophical medicine in the English language. This lack has been partly remedied by the translation of a book by the French physician Victor Bott, entitled *Anthroposophical Medicine: An Extension of the Art of Healing* (London, 1978).

Wilhelm Pelikan's *Heilpflanzenkunde* (Medical Botany) and published in translation in several issues of the American *Journal for Anthroposophy* (and also in the *British Homeopathic Journal*) are invaluable; and many sections of the same author's *The Secrets of Metals* (New York, 1973) have a bearing on anthroposophical medicaments. For the most part, however, information must be obtained from Steiner's own lectures mentioned above, especially *Spiritual Science and Medicine*, and from the publications in English of the British Weleda Company, and the German and French publications of the Weleda and Wala companies.

On nutrition, again many references are to be found in *Spiritual Science and Medicine*. In an early and excellent lecture on the subject, given in Munich, January 8, 1909, called *Problems of Nutrition* (New York, 1973), Steiner speaks of nutrition from an anthroposophic point of view and shows the relationship between diet and the inner spiritual activity of each individual. It includes Steiner's most extended statement on the effects of vegetarianism and meat-eating, and remarks on the effects of drinking alcohol, coffee, tea and milk. There is another helpful lecture called, "On Nutrition," given by Steiner to the workmen at the Goetheanum on October 22, 1923, published in the collection of these lectures called, *Cosmic Workings in Earth and Man* (London, 1952). The first two lectures in the cycle given in the Hague in March, 1913 called, *The Effects of Spiri-*

tual Development (Third edition, London 1978) unexpectedly contain much incidental information on the effect of different foods on the human organism. Finally, Dr. Eugen Kolisko gave a series of three excellent lectures on nutrition before World War II, which were published in two brief pamphlets by the Kolisko Archive, now at Edge, Gloucestershire.

CHAPTER XIV

The General Anthroposophical Society
and the Anthroposophical Societies
throughout the World.

In this brief concluding chapter the history of the Anthroposophical Society founded early in 1913 is not of major concern to us, since it was in all respects superseded by the present General Anthroposophical Society founded during a weeklong conference at Dornach attended by some 800 members at Christmas, 1923. It should only be noted that this earlier society evolved out of the original German section of the Theosophical Society when Rudolf Steiner, who had been General Secretary of the latter could no longer acquiesce in the policies of the Theosophical Society and its leader Annie Besant. As leader of this section Steiner had always worked in complete independence, but the formal tie was finally severed in January, 1913, and the following month the section was reconstituted as the Anthroposophical Society. Certain other sections of the worldwide Theosophical Society also preferred to follow the leadership of Rudolf Steiner, and joined the new society. Nevertheless, Steiner did not become the president of this new Anthroposophical Society, and indeed he was not even a member of it. He was its teacher and inspirer, but he would accept no official position in it.

The first Anthroposophical Society, which existed until Christmas, 1923, had many great achievements to its credit. Its members made possible the building of the (first) Goetheanum, designed and inspired by Rudolf Steiner, who also directed its construction. The members who took part in the actual building work were drawn from many nations. Since the greater part of the work was carried out during the 1914–1918 War it was in fact done by nationals of countries that were at war with each other, but who had found a refuge during the war in neutral Switzerland. The building was opened in 1920, but burned down during the night of New Year's Eve 1922–3. Although the old Anthroposophical Society would sooner or later have had to be refounded on a different basis even if this event had not taken place, in effect the burning marked the real end of the old Society. The transition from the old to the new societies should be considered in a little detail here, inadequate though such a brief explanation must be. It is best studied in a series of eight lectures given by Rudolf Steiner in Dornach from 10th to 17th June, 1923 and published under the title of *The Anthroposophical Movement*. Equally indispensable, in my view, are the two lectures given to delegates of the Anthroposophical Society in Stuttgart on February 27 and 28 of the same year, and published under the title, *Community Building*. Of course, to these should be added the lectures and discussions that accompanied the founding of the Society at Christmas, 1923.

Steiner began his first lecture on *Community Building* with a moving description of just what it had meant to every member that the Goetheanum should have been burned to the ground. He emphasized that this was a building unlike all others, that it had been brought into being not only as an earthly home for anthroposophy, for the performance of plays, for the giving of lectures and the like, but that the attempt had been made to

. . . image forth in the direction of every line, in every external architectural and plastic shape, in every colored surface, that which comes from the fountains of anthroposophical conceptions, anthroposophical life, and anthroposophical will. . . . If one stood on the platform and spoke with one's whole heart out of the anthroposophical spirit, then every line as it had been drawn, every moulded form, was something that responded, that spoke together with one. . . . The intimate association of anthroposophical feeling and will with these forms—which were moulded so completely from direct vision and according to this vision, and which never can be replaced by any sort of thought-forms, any sort of interpretations, makes the pain from the loss so very profound. But this must pass over into the memory which can yet be possessed by those who came to love the Goetheanum, who experienced this profound harmony. And we must set it up, in a certain sense, as a memory in our hearts. Since, in a sense, through the very intimacy of feeling I have mentioned we have lost the home that sheltered us, we must all the more intensely seek for a spiritual home in our hearts to take the place of that which we have lost . . .

This "spiritual home" that was to replace the Goetheanum may not yet have taken shape in Steiner's consciousness or imagination as early as February, 1923, but the direction of his thought is clearly shown by the fact that directly afterward he turned to the subject of how to build an anthroposophical community, including his detailed remarks on the nature of such a community, in which "human souls may awake to human souls and spirits to spirits, so that you enter the anthroposophical community with the living consciousness: There for the first time do we become human beings so awake that we then understand anthroposophy for the first time together with one another, and if then, on the basis of this understanding, you receive anthroposophical ideas into an awakened soul . . . then does the real Community Spirituality descend above your place of work" (p. 13).

It is clear from the remainder of these lectures that there were already serious divisions within the Society as it then existed, divisions that were only accentuated by the burning of the Goetheanum, because the experience of a common disaster naturally affected some, especially those who had helped to

499

build it, more deeply than others who had not shared that experience. Many young members felt that they could not work freely with older members, and, as Steiner explains in detail in *The Anthroposophical Movement*, many people had recently come into the Society bringing totally new and valuable, though sometimes disruptive, impulses into it from the outer world, and these found full cooperation difficult with the elders of the Society who had such a different background. The launching of the movement for the Threefold Order, the various economic enterprises started during the immediate postwar years, the big expansion of membership and the great demand by outside bodies for lectures and conferences by Rudolf Steiner—all these things seemed to be diluting anthroposophy itself as well as bursting the seams, as it were, of the Society. So many people wished to work, but relatively few wished either to link on to the past or to acquire a really profound knowledge of anthroposophical teachings. Lastly, the very fact of the burning of the Goetheanum, which was undoubtedly of incendiary origin, showed that the opposition to anthroposophy had become serious, and a united Society was needed to defend it. To quote an excellent brochure by Frans Carlgren published by the School of Spiritual Science at Dornach in 1964 (second edition, p. 42) simply entitled *Rudolf Steiner, 1861–1925*:

Teachers, priests, doctors, biologists, physicists, lawyers, economists, historians,—all the scientists and workers in the practical activities that had sprung up around Rudolf Steiner's work were fired with the zeal of pioneers. They wanted to lay the foundations of a new civilization in the very midst of postwar chaos. The specialists often concentrated their efforts too much on their own special field without enough regard for the whole. Some of the more versatile members moved from one of the practical activities to another in order to partake in as much as possible. They would get one activity going, only to leave it soon afterwards for the sake of another. In the midst of all this the younger generation made its demands. Among them were many who had returned from the war, and felt estranged from the bourgeois way of living and now entered the various branches of the Anthroposophical Movement. They made their first contacts and soon declared that they could get on very well with Rudolf Steiner, but hardly, if at all, with his followers. So things began to fall apart. Some wanted to reach this goal, others that. And much of such striving was in danger of losing depth and intensity. For many overlooked that the need was now, not for an increase in outer activity, of which there was plenty, but a deepening in anthroposophy itself.

The new Goetheanum was already being designed by Rudolf Steiner and the preliminary work was already beginning during this fateful year of 1923. But the certainty that there would be a new and totally different building to replace the old did not solve the problems of the Society. Indeed, in the course of the year Steiner advised the establishment of what was called the Free (or Independent) Anthroposophical Society, created in particular to serve the needs of the younger members—although he was to explain later in his opening address at the Christmas Conference that this advice "contradicted all that is fundamental in the Anthroposophical Society. For what union of human beings on this earth should provide a place where the youth of today can feel itself entirely at home, if not this Society?"

Clearly, the establishment of this Free Anthroposophical Society was a *pis aller;* it was something that Steiner felt could not be avoided at the time, but was not a genuine solution to the real problem, which was, in essence, how could adherents of the Anthroposophical Movement, that is all who felt themselves imbued with a feeling for anthroposophy, accepted its truths and wished to work for it, be brought within the framework of an actual society, with an organization and bylaws, with qualifications for membership, statutory dues, and all that is regarded as necessary if a society, *any* society, is to function in the modern world? The old Society had all these things, and in addition it had acquired, as Steiner himself was only too well aware, what so many societies, especially those of a religious or spiritual nature can scarcely help acquiring—a sectarian nature. In such

501

situations members feel themselves to be "insiders," superior to those not in the society because they have belonged to it for a long time, because they have had access to knowledge not available to non-members, even because they have taken part in esoteric training. Such members are inclined not only to feel superior to others who may be only on the fringe of the movement, engaged, for example, in some practical work for the Threefold Order, or in anthroposophical scientific research according to indications given by Rudolf Steiner, but they may even resent the dilution of the society by the admission of "unqualified" or "semi-qualified" members. In return the young people, in particular, as we have seen, resented what they considered an attitude of superiority on the part of the older members, and in no way wished to become like them. Hence, their preference for a society of their own. In his opening address at the Christmas Conference Steiner spoke of how difficult it would be to get rid of the sectarian tendency in the Society, but, he said, "there must not be a shred of it left in the new, yet-to-be-founded Anthroposophical Society. For this must be a real world-society."

Now the Anthroposophical Movement in 1923 was so much wider than the Society, so many thousands of persons were in sympathy with anthroposophy and its aims who had no wish to belong to any society, still less anything resembling a *sect*, that only something quite new, even revolutionary, in the form of a society could attract them into it. Even a short time before the Christmas Conference Steiner did not, as he himself said, know the details of what he was to propose. And what he did propose, and what was accepted with absolute unanimity by the eight hundred odd members present, was indeed something different from what is to be found in any other society of any kind. Its esoteric basis cannot be dealt with here, but the general form, and the principles that were to be the foundations of the General (or Universal) Anthroposophical Society require a fairly extended discussion, since they remain the same for the present Society more than fifty years later. The General Anthroposophical Society has suffered many tribulations since Rudolf Steiner's death, as might have been expected in the case of a Society founded in the twentieth century with truly spiritual aims. Nevertheless, it has never had to be re-founded, and today the principles or statutes remain those agreed to at the Christmas Foundation Meeting in 1923.

We have thought it best in this concluding chapter of a book intended for those who wish to gain a first insight into the teachings of anthroposophy not to deal with the esoteric nature of the General Anthroposophical Society as it was founded in 1923, and not to emphasize this aspect of Steiner's deed in founding it and becoming its president, thus uniting his own destiny directly with that of the Society—as had not been the case when he remained outside the earlier society as teacher and inspirer. But it is impossible to think of this Foundation Meeting without referring to its central element, the laying of the new Foundation Stone. When the first Goetheanum was founded, Steiner himself laid a real, physically perceptible foundation stone for the edifice. It was, however, a special stone, a double pentagonal dodecahedron shaped "as an emblem of the human soul immersed as a microcosm in the macrocosm." This stone was "formed as the cornerstone of the human being who desires to seek for himself in the spirit, to feel himself in the world's soul, to divine himself in the world's 'I'." *

The Goetheanum that was begun with the laying of this stone in the autumn of 1913 was never quite completed, but it remained nevertheless a unique building that succeeded in arousing the feeling, as Zeylmans expresses it (pp. 27, 29), of "being led further into the world of the spirit through the forms that were made visible there," and could have "led many peoples' powers of thought towards Imagination, if only unconsciously." In 1923 there could never have been any question for Steiner of trying to make a copy of the old Goetheanum. It was

* Quoted by F. W. Zeylmans van Emmichoven in his book *The Foundation Stone*, p. 19, a work of the utmost importance for the understanding of what the old Goetheanum was, and of the new impulse given in 1923.

a totally different building that he now designed and that was gradually completed in the years following his death. But it was not the new Goetheanum *building* that was founded at the Christmas Meeting of 1923, it was the General Anthroposophical Society, and as a gift to this Society Steiner drew down from the spiritual worlds a new Foundation Stone, which he laid *in the hearts* of its members. This unique Foundation Stone in the form of a mantric meditation on the threefold nature of man and his relationship to the divine beings that created him and guide him, and to the Christ, was repeated in a slightly different form, emphasizing the different rhythms in it, each day of the conference. The depths in this meditation can never be fully plumbed, and, in a sense, it is new every day. It was intended to be exactly what Steiner called it, the *Foundation Stone* of the Society, and in meditating it, alone, as individual human beings, the members come together into exactly that kind of community of which he had spoken in his Stuttgart lectures at the end of the previous February. The anthroposophical community is therefore not only a Society with its center at Dornach, as will be explained, but is made up of the many thousand members all over the world who relate themselves personally to the Foundation Stone by meditating it, each giving the best that is in him to the task. Thus the community becomes a spiritual, not an earthly one, and whatever happens in the future or has happened in the past to the Society, through whatever vicissitudes it has passed or may yet pass, the Foundation Stone itself remains untouched and untouchable, and the community of those who meditate it, even though they may be totally unknown to each other, must endure.

Before the Christmas Conference, and in part in preparation for it, Rudolf Steiner had encouraged the formation of autonomous anthroposophical branches in the various countries of Europe by leading members in those countries, and on several occasions he himself was personally present at the actual founding meeting. These branches took the name of the

Anthroposophical Society in Great Britain, or Holland or Norway, as the case might be.* The Anthroposophical Society in America also came into existence at this time (1923), though Steiner himself could not be present. In all the countries where these autonomous societies were formed, working or study groups had already existed for many years. Steiner himself had sometimes been present when a working group was founded; in any event he was always kept informed, and it was, in the main, to these groups of members that he delivered those lectures known as "members' lectures" to which we shall give some attention later. A lecture given on the occasion of the founding of a second working group in the German city of Düsseldorf is of outstanding interest, even now, because of the role that Steiner foresaw for these working groups in the future.** Distinguishable from these so-called "working groups" are the smaller and less formal simple study groups in which members met together to study the anthroposophical literature in common. After the founding of the General Anthroposophical Society Rudolf Steiner wrote a number of letters to the members that were published in the *Goetheanum Weekly*, the official publication of the Society, in which he gave some invaluable advice as to how the group meetings can most fruitfully be conducted.‡

Until 1923 the working and study groups might or might not possess a formal structure of their own, while their members of course belonged to the Anthroposophical Society as it was

---

* According to the Statutes of the General Anthroposophical Society the national societies may choose any structure or organization that they wish provided they are not incompatible with those of the G.A.S. For those interested in the beginnings of anthroposophical work in America including the founding of the Anthroposophical Society in America, an engaging little book is available, Hilda Deighton, *The Earliest Days of Anthroposophy in America* (New York, 1958).

** *Preparing for the Sixth Epoch*, Lecture given in Düsseldorf, June 15, 1915 (New York, 1976).

‡ Later published and available now under the title, *Letters to Members of the Anthroposophical Society*, Vol. 1. *The Life, Nature and Cultivation of Anthroposophy* (London, 1976).

constituted at that time. By contrast, the autonomous national societies could scarcely have come into existence without some formal structure, although there was no standard recognized way of choosing who was to organize them and who were to be their officials, once the structure had been decided upon. Most of the national societies came into existence as a result of the initiative of a few of the more active members who then became the responsible officials of the societies. One thing was common to all the societies, however. Each was headed by an official known as the General Secretary, a name dating from the period of the Theosophical Society, of which Steiner had been the General Secretary for Germany. At the Christmas Foundation Meeting these general secretaries, all of whom were recognized by Rudolf Steiner as the official heads of their Societies, met every day with him in special delegates' meetings, and the results of their deliberations took form in the Statutes of the Society, which were then accepted in plenary session by the entire assembly. This latter, as has already been noted, comprised some eight hundred members, some of whom were delegates from the national societies, as well as their general secretaries. The remainder of the assembly was made up of private members, representing no one, but present as individuals whose destiny had permitted them to be able to be at Dornach at the time. Although the Statutes were amended in minor ways at the meetings of the general secretaries, always with the approval of Rudolf Steiner, it must be emphasized that Steiner himself drew up the original draft, and no changes made subsequently were of any real substance, nor did they in any way change the original structure as he had envisaged it.

What the Statutes did was to provide a number of principles on which the Society from that time has been based; in essence, as Steiner himself put it during the course of the discussions, it was an "aristocratically" rather than democratically organized society, headed by an Executive of six members (incidentally, three men and three women), with Steiner himself as president. Steiner also made it quite clear that the other five members of the Executive Committee, or *Vorstand*, the German name by which it is still almost invariably known even in the English speaking countries, were not in any sense *elected* by the Foundation Meeting, but were his own choice among members who were his closest collaborators in the anthroposophical work. All of them had to be in a position to live at Dornach thereafter and work in cooperation with himself. The meeting merely acclaimed his choice, so that no precedent was really established that could be used as a precedent for the election of future Vorstand members when Steiner himself was no longer on earth. It has likewise never been supposed in later years that the Vorstand should include any particular number of members. In practice what has happened has been that new members have been co-opted by the other members of the Vorstand, and confirmed in office at the Annual Meeting. Steiner also made it clear, however, that when General Secretaries from the national societies happen to be present in Dornach they have the right to sit with the Vorstand as if they were full members of it.

No qualifications for membership were stated in the Statutes except that "anyone can become a member who considers the existence of such an institution as the Goetheanum in Dornach as an independent School for the Science of the Spirit to be justified," and Steiner carefully explained that the use of the words "such an institution" was deliberate in order to prevent any possibility that potential members would refrain from joining the Society because they did not approve of all that was being done at the Goetheanum at that particular time. He also wanted to make it clear that no one had to subscribe to any belief, or to have read any particular books or lectures. No one could therefore pass on the right of anyone to join the Society, nor impose any requirements. Joining the Society, in Steiner's view, was to be an entirely free act of choice on the part of the new member, and this act of choice he expected to be honored by all officials of the Vorstand or any national society. All membership cards, however, had to be signed by the Vorstand member responsible for membership, and Steiner himself insisted on signing the membership cards of all those who applied to join, for as long as he lived.

The Society was to be in no respect secret—and all the material hitherto given only to members in the so-called members' lectures, was now to be made available for publishing. This was an extremely important decision because these lectures, as distinct from his books, were never revised by the author, and sometimes existed only in imperfect stenographic reports or transcripts, having originally been intended to be heard by the particular audience to which they had been given. Many of these lectures were of such an esoteric nature that they could scarcely be understood at all by persons who did not know at least the basic teachings of anthroposophy. It was an undoubted fact, however, that these lectures were already being circulated, if only in imperfect editions; persons with little or no knowledge of anthroposophy were quoting them out of context, and using such quotations in an attempt to discredit anthroposophy as a whole. The decision was therefore made that *all* the lecture material could, in principle, be published, with the exception of lectures given to such specialized private groups as the priests of the Christian Community. But at the same time it was agreed that esoteric members' lectures, when published, should contain a printed statement to the effect that the works were published for Class I of the Independent School of the Science of the Spirit, and that "no one's judgment on these writings is considered competent unless he has acquired the preliminary knowledge either through the School or in a manner recognized by it as equivalent—other judgments will not be taken into consideration in the sense that the authors of the writings in question will not discuss them."

The Independent School of the Science of the Spirit, of which mention has twice been made, was established at the same time as the new Society, and reference was made to it in several of the Statutes of the Society.* In these Statutes it was stated that the

---

* The older translation of the German *Frei Hochschule der Geisteswissenschaft* as The Free High School of Spiritual Science does not seem as descriptive as the

508

School would be composed of three classes, that it was to be a center of anthroposophical work, that it was to be "established by Rudolf Steiner, who is to appoint his collaborators and his possible successor." In connection with this last named provision Steiner stated in his opening lecture at the Foundation Meeting that he would in the future divide the School "into several sections, for the direction of which I shall appoint fitting individuals. These latter who will conduct the several sections in the Independent School of the Science of the Spirit will at the same time be the advisers on the Vorstand which is to be formed." Lastly, it was explained in Statute 9 that "the aim of the Anthroposophical Society will be the *furtherance* of research in the spiritual field; that of the Independent School of the Science of the Spirit, this research itself."

At the end of this first lecture of the Foundation Meeting Steiner named one by one, to the applause of the Assembly, the various members he had chosen as founding members of the Vorstand, and each of these was also given a "section" of the School as his or her special province. Only one section leader was not also a member of the Vorstand, Miss Edith Maryon, who headed a section on the plastic arts. She had worked with Steiner on the sculptured Group in the Goetheanum, but in fact she did not live long enough after the founding of the School to play her intended part in it as head of a section.

Steiner himself did not head one of the specialized "sections" but instead undertook the task of presiding over what he called a General Anthroposophical Section. In this position he regarded it as perhaps the most important of his immediate tasks to establish the three classes of the School, as described in the Statutes. In the course of the early months of 1924 he gave several lectures and wrote various articles in the *Goetheanum Weekly* on the nature and purpose of these classes, and who was

---

Independent School of the Science of the Spirit. Elsewhere in this book the word Geisteswissenschaft has usually been translated as Science of Spirit, but in this chapter, in which we shall be frequently quoting the Statutes in their American version, we shall be using the title exactly as it appears in this version.

to belong to them. He made it clear that only those who wished to accept certain vital responsibilities within the Society should apply to become members of these classes. The decision to apply was to belong entirely to the member, and would carry with it the recognition by the member of the new responsibilities to the Society and to the spiritual worlds that he was thus undertaking. In this respect it was quite a different step to take the decision to join the Society itself, implying, as we have explained, only the recognition that "such an institution" as the Goetheanum in Dornach—the School for Spiritual Activity in Art and Science— "was justified." This recognition thus implied no collateral decision to defend anthroposophy against its enemies, for example, nor even any particular exclusive devotion to anthroposophy. But a member of the School did recognize when he applied for membership in it that he undertook at the same time certain tasks and responsibilities. For this reason acceptance was not automatic, even though the decision to apply was a personal one, and no one ever *invited,* or could invite any member to join. It was for the Vorstand to pass upon all applications—in practice, in Steiner's own lifetime it was he himself who accepted new members and signed their cards of membership both in the Society and the School. Since his death, other procedures have been established that need not be entered into here. Steiner did not live to establish either the second or the third classes. Only for Class I did he provide esoteric material that is read privately to members of the Class by members specially appointed for this task by the Vorstand at the Goetheanum. No further reference to this aspect of the Independent School of the Science of the Spirit is necessary here. The work of the different sections, including new ones established since Steiner's death, constitutes essentially the work now done at the Goetheanum, which is supported by the entire membership of the Society through dues and donations. The work is especially concerned with the arts and sciences, and in principle all anthroposophical research accomplished anywhere

510

in the world is expected to be of interest to the entire membership and is communicated to it through the Vorstand at the Goetheanum.

In establishing the Society and School on the basis we have described, it was Steiner's hope that every member would feel himself united with the center of the Society and School at Dornach, and, conversely, that the leading members whose work lay at Dornach would feel equally united with the "periphery," the members of the national societies, even the most isolated of individual members. Initiatives could, of course, originate either on the periphery or at the center, but the real reason the Vorstand had been constituted as it was, was to enable it to act as a source of anthroposophical initiative. It was in no circumstances to become a bureaucratic body, nor was it ever intended that a bureaucracy should come into being under the direction of the Vorstand—as is inclined to happen in almost all societies, but in fact has never been allowed to occur in the General Anthroposophical Society. Administrative tasks had to be performed by Steiner himself and by other members of the Vorstand, but they were altogether secondary. The Society had been organized as it was simply because Steiner believed that all the members of the Vorstand were capable of taking anthroposophical initiatives and suggesting initiatives to the national societies and to individual members, and that the members would be happy to follow the leadership of such anthroposophically productive individuals as those he had chosen as members of the Vorstand. This was of course preeminently true of Rudolf Steiner himself, without whom there never could have been an anthroposophical movement or anthroposophical society, and it would have been simply unthinkable that a society constituted as was the General Anthroposophical Society could have had anyone else as president, or the School for the Science of the Spirit anyone else as its principal. Although from an institutional point of view all members of the Vorstand were in all respects equal, and Steiner himself was only *primus inter pares,* this could not be said to be the real truth of the matter. Steiner himself could not but be preeminent and in a genuine sense irreplaceable.

During the fifteen months of life that remained to him after the Christmas Conference Steiner, as has already been noted, was more active as teacher and lecturer (as well as administrator) than at any other time in his life, and there can be no doubt that such incessant and concentrated work took a heavy toll on his vital forces. It seems certain that he knew his remaining time on earth was short, but he told members soon after the Christmas Conference that the deed he had performed in uniting his personal destiny with that of the Society had received the approval of the spiritual world, and that as a result his own spiritual forces had been enhanced, and must be used. Hence the tremendous activity of the first nine months of 1924 before he was forced to his sickbed after his last lecture on September 28, 1924. Among all his other activities, however, it must be emphasized that he really did all that was in his power to keep the membership informed about everything that was going on in the Society, as had been promised at the Foundation Meeting. He made detailed reports after every lecture tour; the content of every new course that he gave he outlined to the membership after his return to Dornach. The *Goetheanum Weekly* was filled with information as to what he and other members of the Vorstand were doing, and every effort was made to give full attention to what members on their side were writing and saying to the Vorstand. The early issues of the *Weekly* after the Christmas Foundation were devoted to Steiner's own account of what had been accomplished at the Foundation Meeting for the benefit of those who had been unable to be present. There can be no doubt at all as to the tremendous vitality of the work emanating from the center during this final year of Rudolf Steiner's life, and this work was not that of Steiner alone. All the members of the Vorstand were productive; especially visible perhaps was the work done by Dr. Ita Wegman at her clinic at Arlesheim and that of Frau Marie Steiner in the growing artistic

512

work. But the others all did their part and gave leadership to the sections with which they had been entrusted.

During the six months of his last illness Rudolf Steiner continued to write, even though he could no longer lecture, and without fail every issue of the *Goetheanum Weekly* carried the articles and letters to the members he had written or dictated, some of which form part of his most important legacy to mankind. When he died on March 30, 1925, Albert Steffen, the Swiss poet, head of the literature ("belles-lettres") section of the School and vice-president of the Society, became the Society's new president, and the Vorstand continued to function as a body without for many years adding any further to its own membership. The surviving members continued to occupy themselves with their sections in the School. But obviously the Society could not be the same as it had been in Rudolf Steiner's lifetime; as might have been expected he did indeed prove to be utterly irreplaceable. He it was who had really *presided* over the Vorstand and the Society, and none of the surviving members could hope to wield, nor would have wished to wield such unquestioned and unquestionable authority. It was therefore really impossible for the Society to function in the same fashion as it had done in 1924. Nevertheless, over the years the Goetheanum has been rebuilt, the membership has greatly increased, the national societies on the whole are flourishing in a modest way—even though relatively little progress has been made in the Latin countries and other countries where Roman Catholicism has remained entrenched as a virtually national religion. As might be expected, membership is heavily concentrated in the German speaking world, but societies exist in all the English speaking countries, and membership is on the increase in all of them.

The Goetheanum remains the center of the Movement as well as the headquarters of the General Anthroposophical Society. It is supported, as was originally laid down by the Christmas Conference of 1923, to a large extent by the dues of the individual members, which they pay to their own national societies. These latter contribute a proportion of these dues to the Goetheanum, which is also supported by individual members and special collections made by the national societies. Members are thus encouraged to look to the Goetheanum as a center for which they as individuals are responsible, and in whose activity they can take a personal pride. But this in no way implies that all major anthroposophical activity takes place in Dornach. Active centers are to be found elsewhere in the world, wherever there are members. Special mention might be made of Stuttgart, Germany, where the first Waldorf School was founded in 1919, where there is an important school of eurythmy as well as the oldest and largest training center for Steiner teachers in the world. Close to Stuttgart also is the largest center for anthroposophical pharmaceutical research, as was mentioned in the last chapter.

Nevertheless, it is true that in Dornach and neighboring Arlesheim, an effort is made to have at least some vital work in progress in every field of anthroposophical endeavor. The Goetheanum with its incomparable stage and its lighting system unique in the entire world, is the undoubted center of the public artistic work; Steiner's four Mystery Plays, the many plays of Albert Steffen, and both parts of Goethe's *Faust* are all performed there, while the various clinics at Arlesheim that have stemmed from the original work of Dr. Ita Wegman must still be regarded as the center of anthroposophical medical work, especially its research. Two of the most important eurythmy schools are located at Dornach, there is a center for scientific research, a pedagogical course is given there, various artisanal crafts have been established there, including a school of jewelry, and in 1972 the Goetheanum played host to more than a thousand young people in a great international Youth Conference. The Vorstand is now (in 1981) made up of six members, most of whom have done extensive traveling to the various other anthroposophical centers in the world to give lectures or take part in conferences. Ever since the time of Rudolf Steiner the Vorstand has suggested a general theme for study during the

514

current year by all members and the national societies. But as far as the latter are concerned they remain suggestions that may or may not be followed. They do, however, constitute the themes for the many regular conferences that are held at the Goetheanum throughout the year, more particularly at the time of the great festivals. Especially in recent years news of the activities of the national societies has been provided at the annual meeting of the General Anthroposophical Society, held during the Easter season, and delegates from the national societies have met regularly with the Vorstand to discuss matters of common interest and the future of the Society.

It cannot of course be known how many persons, not members of any anthroposophical society, are sympathetic to what may be thought of as the Anthroposophical Movement, nor is it possible to estimate how many persons throughout the world have become interested in anthroposophy, may still be interested in it, and even accept its teachings as true, without ever having had the urge to join the Society, even if they know of its existence. In France, for example, where this book was written, there is a review entirely devoted to anthroposophical matters (*Triades*) which has always enjoyed a much wider circulation than the entire membership of the French Society, or even all members in French-speaking countries. Presumably the vast majority of the subscribers to *Triades* suppose that they can learn all they wish to without feeling any need to unite with members of the Society. There will perhaps be many who read this book who come to the conclusion that, in the words of Statute 2 of the Society, "there exists at the present time a real science of the spiritual world developed through many years of work, and . . . that the cultivation of such a science is lacking in the civilization of today." The Anthroposophical Society took it as its chief task to cultivate it, and has made it possible for anyone to become a member who "considers the existence of such an institution as the Goetheanum in Dornach as an independent School for the science of the spirit to be justified."

Thus no formal statement of belief is required, no creed has to be adhered to for anthroposophy itself is in no way a dogma. Indeed, those who wish only to study anthroposophy have a perfect right never to become members of the Society, and no one will ever urge them to do so. Perhaps just because it has never tried to make converts, to proselytize, the membership of the Society has remained relatively small by comparison with that of organizations that appeal for members and try to *persuade* them to join. Becoming a member of the Anthroposophical Society was intended to be, and has remained, a free act of a free human being, an act taken by someone who says Yes to what anthroposophy represents. Since it may be, spiritually speaking, the most important act taken by such a person in the course of his entire life, it cannot be taken lightly; the Anthroposophical Society would not be acting in accordance with its true mission if it were to change its policy, make the effort to increase mightily its membership, even try to become a mass organization. It would surely be happy to welcome more members than it now has. But if anthroposophy should ever become a mass movement it would certainly be because its content will have been diluted far beyond any permissible simplification—as will surely be appreciated by anyone who has read through this book with something of the care with which its author has tried to write it.

SUGGESTIONS FOR FURTHER READING
FOR CHAPTER 14.

The best short account of the founding of the General Society and its contrast with the earlier Society is to be found under the year 1923 in Guenther Wachsmuth's monumental, *The Life and Work of Rudolf Steiner* (New York: Whittier Books Inc., 1955), while perhaps the most useful of all the short works on the history of the Society, Rudolf Steiner's work, and background for the Christmas Foundation is the official publication compiled by Frans Carlgren called *Rudolf Steiner, 1861–1925* and published in a second edition in 1964 by The Goetheanum School of Spiritual Science, Dornach. This publication is available in several different languages, including its English translation by Joan and Siegfried Rudel.

Indispensable for background are the two lecture series mentioned in the text: *Community Building*, two lectures given to delegates at Stuttgart February 27–28, 1923, included in the book, *Awakening to Community* (New York, 1975), and *The Anthroposophic Movement*, eight lectures given in Dornach from June 10 to 17, 1923 (London, 1933). The opening address given to the delegates at the Foundation Meeting of the General Anthroposophical Society on December 24, 1923 is also essential reading on this subject (New York, 1943), and the statutes as finally amended and adopted, are available from all English speaking societies to their members. The commentary on the Foundation Stone Mantram by F. W. Zeylmans van Emmichoven called, *The Foundation Stone* (London, 1963), explains the mantram itself insofar as this is possible, and relates this foundation stone to the original one laid in September 1913. A publication with the same title, *The Foundation Stone* (London, 1979) gives the full text of the words spoken by Steiner each day during the Christmas Conference from December 24, 1923 to January 1st, 1924. Several alternative translations are given.

Other works include a transcript of the delegates meetings and material published in the *Goetheanum Weekly* on the Independent School of the Science of Spirit, but these are in mimeographed form only and not generally available.

Index

Abraham, 40, 50, 189
Achilles, 61, 75, 246
Act of Consecration of Man, 176
Adam and Eve, 205
Adolescence, 399–400, 404
Aeschylus, 63–64, 249–250
Agamemnon, 63–64
Agriculture, beginnings of, 32
  See also Biodynamic Agriculture
Ahriman, ascendancy over man's
    physical body, 197
  Christ, opponent of, 177, 193–
    194, 194 *n*, 305–306
  —— in spiritual worlds before
    incarnation, 182, 188
  and economic life, 362, 370
  first influence of, 31, 33
  in Goetheanum Group, 229–230
  intelligence of, 168, 306
  as lord of death, 195
  as lord of earth, 99–100, 156,
    226, 438
  as lord of subnature, 305–306
  Lucifer, contrast and coopera-
    tion with, 99–100, 306
  and modern science, 438
  and nationalism, 328–329, 331
  possible victory of, 212–213
  role in man's freedom of, 25–26,
    55
  and Russian utopianism, 116
  temptation of man by, 56, 86,
    97–101, 98 *n*, 115–116, 192,
    312
Ahrimanic beings, possible ensoul-
    ment by, 168
Aingra Mainu (Old Persian name
    of Ahriman), 33

Akasha Chronicle, information
    from, 29–30, 177, 185, 199,
    202
  nature of, 22, 22 *n*
Akhenaton, 38, 40, 44, 189
Albertus Magnus, 91
Alexander the Great, 44, 49, 75–77
Alexandria, 49, 77–78
Allopathic medicine, when use of
    recommended, 469
Anaxagoras, 72
Anaximander, 72
Andorra, Republic of, 354
Angel, guardian, 155
  See also Hierarchies, Spiritual
Animals, evolution of, 29
  nature and faculties of, 282–285
Anna the Prophetess, 181
Anselm of Canterbury, St., 91
Anthroposophical Movement, lec-
    ture cycle, 498, 500
  relation with Anthroposophical
    Society, 500–502, 515
Anthroposophical Society (1913),
    224, 497–499, 501–502, 505–
    506
  sectarianism in, 501–502
Anthroposophical Society, General
    (1923), aims of, 509, 515–
    516
  branches of (national societies),
    505, 505 *n*, 514
  founding of, 497, 502–504, 506–
    509, 511
  statutes of, 505 *n*, 506–510, 515
  Vorstand of, 506–507, 510–515
  working groups in, 505
Anthroposophy, *passim*
  testing of, 10–11, 13, 263–265

519

Christ (cont.)
Michael, relation with, 328, 362
Moses, revelation to, 51
as Redeemer, 178, 201
Resurrection of, 85, 96, 196–198, 196 *n*, 210
Roman Pantheon, proposal to include in, 84
"Second Coming" of (Etheric Christ), 165, 178, 209–213
as Spirit of the Earth, 55–56, 197, 268, 305, 438
temptations of, 193–194, 194 *n*
transfiguration of, 199
transformation of earth by, 55–56
Christ Impulse, and evolution of consciousness, 85–86
in feeling life of man, 206
permeation of science with, 88
presence of, in very young children, 389
task of, 54–56
and thinking, 135–136, 208–209
in Threefold Order, 362
transformation of earth by, 97
Christian Community, 176–177, 179, 183, 196
in Eastern Europe, 380
Steiner's lectures to, 508
Christian Science, 26
Christianity, early centuries of, 88–90
among Germanic peoples, 90
greater than all religions, 175
and reincarnation, 198–204
Sixth Age, fulfillment in, 116
theology of, 89
in world of today, 214
See also Chapter V, *passim*
Christmas Foundation Meeting (General Anthroposophical Society) in 1923, 498, 501–504, 506, 509, 512–513
Church of England, 108
Cincinnatus, 79
Clairvoyance, in Atlantis, 175
as basis of early civilizations, 158–159

Clairvoyance (cont.)
as basis of early religion, 175, 177
exact nature of, 145–146
mysteries, persistence in, 54
in prehistoric times, 29–30, 188, 203
progressive loss of, after Christianity, 102
in Egypto-Chaldean civilization, 40–41
by Greeks, 54–55
in Middle Ages, 87
as necessary for freedom, 328
Clodia, 82
Clodius, P., 82
Clytemnestra, 64
Color, in children's dreams, 232
in eurythmy, 256
Goethe's theory of, *See* Goethe, color theory of
Luster and Image, 235
Newton's theory of, 233–234
Steiner's teachings on, 231–237
therapy, 467, 472
Communes, rural, 373
Communism, 116
Community, anthroposophical, nature of, 499, 504
Competition, true place of, 334–335
Compost, 444–445, 451–452, 455–458
use of in medicaments, 484
Conscience, beginning of, 64–65
Consciousness, evolution of, definition of, 20
denial by historians of, 20
as shown by art history, 403–404
group soul, 59
source of, 145–146
Consciousness pole, 299–300, 471–473
Consciousness soul, age of, Ahriman's importance in, 206
dates of, 36
education needed in, 400
mission of, 102, 174

Consciousness soul, age of (cont.)
reincarnation, readiness for
idea of, 201
Threefold Order needed in,
321, 324, 330
characteristics of, 36 n, 57–58,
96–101, 147–148, 206, 266
and Christianity, 191, 204
coldness of, 101, 267
and democracy, 327
epoch of, in human life, 38, 96,
148
external world, relation to, 88,
101, 126, 266–268, 436, 438
and freedom, 179
in Goetheanum architecture, 226
and perspective, 232–233, 235
proper task of, 102, 312–313
science created by, 21
skepticism of, 201
and southern Europe, difficulties
in, 89
thinking characteristic of, 201,
304, 450–451
Constance, Council of, 95
Constantine I, Emperor, 82, 88
Constantinople, Council of (869),
91
Copake (N.Y.), 429
Corinthian capitals, 226
Corruptio optimi pessima, 141, 370
Cosmic intelligence, bestowed on
man, 305, 437–438
Courts, role of, in Threefold Order,
341 n
Cow, cosmic forces in, 449
Cuba, 344
Cultural epochs, length of, 31, 31 n
Curative Education, Chapter XI
passim
beginnings of, 413–416
contrast with normal education,
426–427
Steiner's course in (1924), 277–
278, 415–416, 421–422
Curative eurythmy, 423, 467, 472
Curative Homes, community at-
mosphere of, 428–429

Cynics, 54, 77
"Czechoslovakian Spring," 347

Daimonion, 67–68
Damascus, 210
Dante, 23
Danton, Georges, 3
Darwin, theory of evolution of, 281
David, King, 38
Death, human experience after,
149–155
See also Life between death and
rebirth
Deighton, Hilda, 505 n
Democracy, ancient world, 62, 65,
76
as governmental form for con-
sciousness soul, 327
Democritus, 72–73
Denmark, 366
Descartes, René, 93–94, 106–107
Destiny, See Karma
Devachan, 160–161
Lower, as realm of music, 239,
241
Dialectic of Socrates, 66
Diet, animal, 489–490, 490 n
raw versus cooked, 490–492
vegetable, 489–490
Diocletian, Emperor, 88
Dionysius the Areopagite, 23
Dionysus, 63, 245, 250
Disease, attitude of anthroposophi-
cal medicine toward, 478
relation to threefold man of, 473,
485
Dornach, work at, Chapter XIV
passim
See also Goetheanum
Drama, Steiner's teachings on, 247–
251
Drawing, in Steiner schools, 233
Dreams, ancient world, 40–41
See also under Babylonians
Drugs, hallucinatory, 6–7
Dubček, Alexander, 347
Dynameis (Spirits of Motion), 25

Eabani, See Enkidu

523

Earth, breathing of, 287
change of, after Christ, 55–56
Earthworms, 441, 453
Ecclesiastes, 53
Eckhart, Meister, 210
Ecology, 440–444
Ecosystems, 441
biodynamic farms as, 443
Edda, 245
Eden, Garden of, 205
Education, role of in Threefold
Social Order, 356–358
See also Pedagogy
Ego ("I"), after death, 151, 154,
159–160
bestowal of, by Elohim, 204, 206
and brotherhood of future, 330
definition and tasks of, 24, 35 *n*,
36, 144–148
divine nature of, 51, 96–97
equivalent to Spirit, 123–124, 206
experience of, in music, 242–243
in Fichte's philosophy, 109–110
first consciousness of, in childhood, 389, 389 *n*
among Hebrews, 50
incorporation of, in childhood
and adolescence, 301–303
in history, 35, 38, 50–52, 55,
59, 67, 188, 206
through Christ, 189–191, 204–
207
in Indian thought, 159–160
and karma, 155–156, 159
mysteries connected with, 190–
191
outer world, relation to, 126
as reincarnating entity, 198–199
and thinking, 125–126
in three souls, 147–148, 205
Ego-organization and anthroposophical medicine, 476, 481
Egypt, Ahrimanic influences in, 50
Alexander, conquest by, 44
antiquarianism of, 43
astronomy in, 46
decadence of, 34
Hebrew exodus from, 51
holy family in, 180–181

Egypt (cont.)
king-god myth in, 42–43, 46, 84
mysteries of, 34, 50–51
Old Kingdom of, 34, 41–42
speculative thought lacking in, 38
Egyptians, guidance by higher beings of, 61
otherworldly orientation of, 60
Egypto-Chaldean Epoch, 35–38
dates of, 31
Einstein, Albert, 127–128
Electricity, 306
Elemental beings, 240, 280, 284–
285, 291, 309–311
Elijah, 40, 52
Elohim (Spirits of Form), 50, 188,
204, 206
Empedocles, 72
Enkidu, 47–48
Epicureans, 54, 76
Etheric body, before birth, 165
beginning of (Old Sun), 25
building of, in childhood, 148,
293–294
definition of, 24, 27, 30
dissolution of, after death, 149–
150
male-female alternations of, 167
nature and tasks of, 144–147,
472
and nutrition, 488–490
and thinking, 272
and tone, 241
Etheric Christ, *See* Christ, Second
Coming of
Etheric formative forces, 287 *n*,
291–296
in biodynamic agriculture, 447
See also Biodynamic preparations
in blood, 476–477
in medicine, 467
in nutrition, 490
Etheric world (imaginative world),
24, 150, 164–165, 232
See also Christ, Second Coming
of
Ethical individualism, 135–136, 208
Etruscans, 80–81

Gilgamesh, Epic of, 47–48, 48 *n*
Giotto, 105
Gnomes, 284, 286
Goethe, art defined by, 219, 256
  color theory of, 219, 231
  conception of world of, 219,
    267 *n*, 269 *n*
  contrast with Kant, 271
  with Linnaeus, 273–274
  fairy story of, 4–6, 4 *n*
  Faust of, 110, 307, 514
  and plant metamorphosis, 274–
    276
  Schiller, relationship with, 4
  Steiner as authority on, 9
  thinking and observation of, 123,
    265, 269–276, 422, 479–480
  See also Living thinking
Goetheanum (First), 223–227, 234–
    235, 498–499, 503–504
  burning of, 498–500
Goetheanum (Second), 9, 223–224,
    227–228, 247, 249, 252, 256
  Group statuary in, 98, 192, 229–
    230, 258–259, 509
  work at, 470, 510–511, 513–515
Gothic cathedral, 222
Great Britain, early development
    of consciousness soul in,
    107–109
  education in, 358
  Threefold Social Order, ap-
    proaches toward, in, 323–
    324
Great Chain of Being, 282
Great Schism, 95
Greek Chorus, role of, 247–250
Greek Civilization, as adolescent
    period of thinking, 399–400
Greeks, architecture of, 75–76, 222,
    226
  art of, 75–76
  astronomy of, 73, 77–78
  attitude to earthly life of, 75
  ego development of, 38, 53
  geometry of, 74
  gift for generalizing of, 73–74
  inspiration by Muses of, 245–246
  as intellectual soul bearers, 60

Greeks (cont.)
  See also under Intellectual
    soul
  music of, 238, 243
  mysteries of, 62–63
  philosophy of, 65–74, 89
  political life of, 61–62
  science of, 71–74, 77–78
  tragic drama of, 63–65, 249–250
  wonder at man of, 402–403
*Green Snake and the Beautiful
    Lily, The,* 219
Gregory I, Pope, 91
Gregory IX, Pope, 91
Group soul (of animals), 282–283,
    286, 490
Group Soul consciousness (human),
    59, 191
Group Sculpture (Dornach), *See
    under* Goetheanum (Second)

Hahn, Herbert, 383–384
Hamilton, Elsie, 241–243
Hammurabi Code, 47, 80
Hannibal, 79
Harwood, A. C., 399 *n*, 404, 446
Hathor, Goddess, 39
Hauschka, Margarethe, 423
Hauschka, Dr. Rudolf, 480 *n*, 485–
    486
Heart, true nature of, 300
Hebrews, ego development of, 35,
    38, 50–51
  Epistle to, 185
  evil, conception of, 307
  Exodus of, 51
  guidance of, by higher beings, 61
  law of, 51–52
  mission of, 50–51, 177, 188–190
  prophets of, 52–53
  religion of (monotheism), 25,
    39–40, 48–49
Hector, 61
Hegel, G. W. F., 136 *n*
Hellenic Culture, *See* Greeks
Hellenistic culture, 76–78
Hera, Goddess, 81
Heraclitus, 72

535